FILMMAKERS SERIES

edited by
ANTHONY SLIDE

In Preparation:

Alfred Hitchcock and Cary Grant on the set of <u>Notorious</u>.

CINEMA STYLISTS

by John Belton

Filmmakers, No. 2

The Scarecrow Press, Inc.
Metuchen, N.J., & London 1983

Library of Congress Cataloging in Publication Data

Belton, John.
   Cinema stylists.

   (Filmmakers ; no. 2)
   Bibliography: p.
   Includes index.
   1. Moving-picture plays--History and criticism--
Addresses, essays, lectures. 2. Moving-pictures--
United States--Addresses, essays, lectures.
I. Title. II. Series: Filmmakers (Scarecrow Press) ;
no. 2.
PN1995.B344 1983   791.43'75   82-10793
ISBN 0-8108-1585-0

CONTENTS

iv

v

EDITOR'S NOTE

John Belton is an assistant professor of film at Columbia University. Although many contemporary teachers and writers share his interest in classical American cinema, few are, as he is, a genuine classicist, with a Ph.D. in Classical Philology from Harvard University. Once condemned for these credentials by a fellow writer as an "auterist pedant," Belton makes a convincing case in this volume for an auterism that, in its reliance on Wayne Booth's notion of implied author and implied reader, explores the rhetoric of film narration as it is apparent in the style of films made by Hitchcock, Griffith, Borzage, Hawks, and others. Author of The Hollywood Professionals: Hawks, Borzage and Ulmer and of Robert Mitchum and co-editor of the forthcoming Film Sound: Theory and Practice, Belton's critical stature is far from that suggested by his detractors. For example, Belton's "Hawks & Co." essay, reprinted here, has been praised by Robin Wood as "the finest article on Hawks that I have read" and by Joseph McBride as "probably the best critical piece yet written on Hawks."

In The Black Cat, Bela Lugosi responds to a character who labels his ideas "supernatural bologna" with "supernatural, perhaps; bologna, perhaps not." The essays which follow, though auterist, perhaps; are definitely not pedantic. Though serious and devoid of hyperbolic value judgment, they contain an intelligence that all who take more than a fleeting interest in the American cinema will find engagingly innovative.

Anthony Slide

ACKNOWLEDGEMENTS

I would like to thank my first editor, Pauline Dubkin, who got me into print and my most recent editor, Anthony Slide, who kept me in print. Along the way, I received assistance from Andrew Sarris, Joseph McBride, Peter Cowie, Russell Campbell, Jon Landau, and Ted Sennett. I have been nobly defended as a writer by Jeanine Basinger, Robin Wood, Stuart Byron, Melanie Wallace, and the editorial board of Cineaste. My thinking about the cinema has been shaped, in part, by such friends as Tim Hunter, Peter Jazsi, Mike Prokosch, Fred Camper, Dave Grosz, William Paul, Elisabeth Weis, Tom Gunning, and many of my students at Harvard, Brooklyn College, The New School and Columbia. This book is dedicated to my wife Ellen and to my daughters Elizabeth and Jane.

A number of essays reprinted in this book originally appeared elsewhere. "Implied Author and Implied Reader in the Cinematographic Image" was a paper delivered at the Society for Cinema Studies Conference held in New York in April 1981. "Dexterity in a Void" comes from Cineaste, 10, No. 3 (Summer 1980); "Hitchcock in Britain" from The Thousand Eyes, 2, No. 2 (Winter 1979); "Under Capricorn" from Quarterly Review of Film Studies, 6, No. 4 (Spring 1982); "Mechanics of Perception" from The Cambridge Phoenix (October 16, 1969); "The Perversity of Topaz" from Boston After Dark (February 4, 1970); "Frenzy and the Aesthetics of Paralysis" from The Boston Phoenix (August 1972); "Le Boucher" from Cinema (U.S.A.), 7, No. 2 (Spring 1972); "Mulligan: Direction by Indirection" from The Velvet Light Trap, No. 13 (Fall 1974); "The Crucified Lovers" from

Film Quarterly, 25, No. 1 (Fall 1971); "Narrative Distance in Yang Kwei Fei" from The Village Voice (June 29, 1972); "Are You Waving the Flag at Me?" from The Velvet Light Trap, No. 4 (Spring 1972); "Samuel Fuller's Shark!" from Bright Lights, 1, No. 2 (Spring 1975); "Ironic Distance in Douglas Sirk's The First Legion" from Douglas Sirk (The University of Connecticut Film Society, 1974); "Prisoners of Paranoia" from The Velvet Light Trap, No. 5 (Summer 1972); "True Heart Susie" from The Silent Picture, No. 17 (Spring 1973); "The Art of Melodramatic Style: D. W. Griffith and Orphans of the Storm" from The Silent Picture, No. 16 (Fall 1972); "Frank Borzage: Souls Made Great by Love and Adversity" from Monogram, No. 4 (Fall 1972); "Borzage's I've Always Loved You" from Focus! (Spring 1973); "The Broken-field Running of Otto Preminger" from Audio Brandon Film Catalogue (1978); "Hawks & Co." from Cinema (U. K.), No. 9 (Fall 1971); "The Expressive Stylistics of Scarface" from Bright Lights, 1, No. 4 (Summer 1976); "Hawks, Warner Brothers and the War" from UA: Images (1975); "Ball of Fire and A Song Is Born" from Audio Brandon Film Catalogue (1978); "The Narrative Structure of I Was a Male War Bride" from The Velvet Light Trap, No. 3 (Winter 1972); "The Organic Narrative Style of Monkey Business" from Film Heritage, 6, No. 2 (Winter 1970-71); "The Backstage Musical: 42nd Street and French Cancan" from Movie, No. 24 (Spring 1977); "Charles Chaplin" from Audio Brandon Film Catalogue (1978); "Chaplin's A King in New York and the Survival of Classical Style" from The Velvet Light Trap, No. 11 (Winter 1974); "The American Comedy of Harold Lloyd" from Harold Lloyd: The Forgotten Comedian, ed. Adam Reilly (New York: Macmillan, 1977); "Teresa Wright in the Forties" from The Forties in the Eighties (Spring 1980); "James Stewart" from Close-Ups: The Movie Star Book, ed. Danny Peary (New York: Workman, 1978); and "John Wayne: As Sure as the Turnin' of the Earth" from The Velvet Light Trap, No. 7 (Winter 1972-73).

Auteurism is dead! Long live post-auteurism! To paraphrase André Bazin, the existence of auteurism as a phenomenon precedes its essence. In other words, as long as there are works, critics will search for an author whose existence in some way explains those works' creation. Even Pauline "Circles and Squares" Kael, who blasted Andrew Sarris' auteurist stance over eighteen years ago, now writes about "De Palma" and "Peckinpah" films.

Auteurism has even survived the onslaught of the cultural revolution of May 1968, regenerated in the guise of structural auteurism via Peter Wollen's critical Noah's Ark Signs and Meaning in the Cinema. Thus the 'seventies, the era of "post-ism" in which modernism becomes postmodernism and structuralism becomes post-structuralism, finds auteurism firmly entrenched as post-auteurism. As with other "post-isms," post-auteurism is defined more in terms of where it has come from than in terms of what it is.

What it is becomes, in part, determined by its response to structuralist critiques of auteurism and it is therefore necessary to consider those arguments before attempting to define the notions of authorship put forth in this collection of more or less post-auteurist essays. Roland Barthes, in an essay written in 1968 and prophetically titled "The Death of the Author," views the author as a conduit through which language and culture speak, not the author. The author's only power lies in his ability "to mix writings" which are taken, as it were, from a dictionary of pre-existent

writings. [1] Thus in Hitchcock, the images of the Statue of
Liberty in Saboteur (1942) and of Mt. Rushmore in North by
Northwest (1959) derive their meaning from their identities
as landmarks of American culture, possessing, like words
in a dictionary, a definition or value which pre-exists Hitchcock's usage of them.

   For Michel Foucault, in a 1969 paper exploring the
question "What Is an Author?" the author emerges as less a
source of discourse than a function of it. The author becomes an entity or identity assigned to a work to fill the
space left empty by the disappearance of the traditional notion of author. The author does not create the work; he or
she merely signs it. "The function of the author," says
Foucault, "is to characterize the existence, circulation, and
operation of certain discourses within society."[2]

   Peter Wollen, attacking traditional beliefs that the
author "expresses himself" in a work, similarly associates
the author with processes outside the work itself, in this
case identifying the author as a structure which can be
extrapolated from a group of works. Wollen's author becomes a product of critical analysis, a figure who comes
into being after the work itself. [3] Wollen's "Hawks," as a
structure, does not even exist a posteriori in any one of his
films because the structural antinomies which define Hawks
consist of the adventure films and the crazy comedies.
(Wollen unfortunately ignores films like Rio Bravo and El
Dorado which combine these two "oppositions.") Wollen's
"Ford," unlike his "Hawks," is a structure permitted to
underly individual films, but it, too, exists only after the
fact. A complex of shifting antinomies--of "garden versus
wilderness, ploughshare versus sabre, settler versus nomad,
European versus Indian, civilised versus savage, book versus gun, married versus unmarried, East versus West,"
"Ford" becomes nothing more nor less than the genre of the
western itself, whose borders these oppositions define. [4]
Wollen's auteur, for the most part, functions as a common
denominator linking together a body of works and providing
the neo-Proppian critic with a finite number of texts from
which a structure can be scientifically derived. The structural auteur remains an author in name only.

   Given pre-structuralist, traditional notions of authorship, it is no wonder that Barthes, Foucault, and Wollen
have reduced the author to an empty space, a function and
a name. Bourgeois notions of art as "self-expression" have
led, in the past, to the vulgarest sorts of auteurism, i. e. ,

biographical auteurism, wherein the work finds its meaning
or is explained by an incident in the author's life. A critic
discovers that, in his youth, Sam Fuller once lost his ability to speak and uses this to explain the hero's muteness
in the final asylum scenes in Shock Corridor (1963). Even
a critic as sophisticated as Gavin Lambert indulges in vulgar
auteurism, reducing art to an adjunct of biography. In an
essay provocatively entitled "The Benefits of Shock," Lambert recounts the often-told anecdote of Hitchcock's experience as a child: "Wishing to punish his son for an offence
... Mr. Hitchcock sent him with a note to a family friend,
the local police inspector. 'This is what we do to naughty
boys,' the inspector explained as he locked the child in a
prison cell. Release came after only fifteen minutes, but
it came too late to release an incurable fear of the police."[5]
The anecdote figures in innumerable discussions of the
"wrong-man" motif, parent-child relationships or the paranoid world view in Hitchcock's work, and it serves to explain certain films, much as Hitchcock's Jesuit upbringing
and English Catholicism are marshalled forth to explain the
presence of confessions and exchanges of guilt in his films.
But this biographical data really serves to mask meaning,
to provide an apparent source of meaning which then closes
off further examination of the works in question. Ignoring
the artistic context within which such "biographical" events
occur, the critic turns criticism into biography. This process is no more than a modern, Freudian reworking of the
questionable critical practices of the ancient scholiasts,
whose readings and emendations of certain passages in classical texts were used to reconstruct biographies of authors
about whom little was known.

The collection of essays on individual directors which
follows eschews, for the most part (nobody's perfect!), vulgar, biographical auteurism, in favor of the more complex
notions of authorial voice set forth by Wayne Booth in The
Rhetoric of Fiction (see my essay "Implied Author and Implied Reader in the Cinematographic Image" for a more detailed discussion of this approach). For Boothian auteurists
like myself, the author does not exist outside of the work.
The author's existence is neither a priori nor a posteriori.
He is neither a flesh-and-blood entity who gives birth to the
work nor a ghostly structure arising from its ashes. Rather, the author exists in the work itself--in the ongoing process of its narration. The author can be found in the film's
narrative voice, in the selection of the events which enter
the narration and in the presentation of those events to the
viewer. The author resides in the rhetoric of the work; in

other words, in its style.　It is not the body but the voice of the author that I seek:　death to the author--long live the narrator!

　　　Hitchcock and Hawks represent different narrative voices, producing different narrative styles.　The subsequent essays have been organized stylistically, that is, in terms of the narrative and visual styles of the narrators under discussion.　Though a greater range of styles admittedly exists than is present in this volume, Hitchcock and Hawks do provide the boundaries for a certain limited stylistic spectrum, notably that of classical American cinema. If Hitchcock's total articulation of the elements within his frames represents one extreme of stylization, then Hawks's and Renoir's more modest articulation represents another. For Bazin, there are "those directors who," like Hitchcock, "put their faith in the image and those who," like Renoir, "put their faith in reality."[6]　Between Hitchcock, whose manipulation of the plastics of the image forces pre-existent reality (even the Statue of Liberty and Mt. Rushmore) to speak in his voice, and Hawks and Renoir, whose respect for the integrity of events and characters enables those elements to speak in large part for themselves, lie a number of other styles and stylists.　The intrusive narrative presences of Chabrol, Mulligan, Mizoguchi, Fuller, Sirk, and Ulmer represent the infusion of varying degrees of self-consciousness into classical style.　More restrained, less self-assertive voices such as those of Griffith and Borzage stand at the head of a narrative tradition which leads, in part, to the less emotional, hard-boiled stylistics of Lewis, Preminger and Siegel.

　　　The last section of the book, devoted to actors as directors and to actors as directed, attempts to deal with other kinds of voices.　Chaplin, Lloyd, Wright, Stewart, and Wayne represent another limited spectrum of styles-- acting styles.　And these voices are seen not as secondary noises interfering with the narrator's more dominant signals, but rather as voices harmonized with that of the narrator.

　　　In his critique of the politique des auteurs, Bazin seeks to redress the imbalance that auteurists at Cahiers introduced into the relationship between works and authors. Circumscribing the autonomy of the auteur, Bazin gives back to that figure "the preposition without which the noun auteur remains but a halting concept.　Auteur, yes, but what of?"[7]　This collection of essays seeks, in part, to

xii

reinvestigate the work-author equation. For me, the author, as narrator, is in the work and the work is the process of the narration.

NOTES

1. Image/Music/Text, trans. Stephen Heath (New York: Hill and Wang, 1977), p. 146.
2. Screen 20, No. 1 (Spring 1979), p. 19.
3. Signs and Meaning in the Cinema (Bloomington: Indiana University Press, 1972), p. 168.
4. Ibid., p. 94.
5. The Dangerous Edge (New York: Grossman, 1976), p. 235.
6. What Is Cinema? volume one, trans. Hugh Gray (Berkeley: University of California Press, 1967), p. 24.
7. "La politique des auteurs," in The New Wave, ed. Peter Graham (New York: Doubleday, 1968), p. 155.

IMPLIED AUTHOR AND IMPLIED READER
IN THE CINEMATOGRAPHIC IMAGE

In The Rhetoric of Fiction, Wayne Booth questions the notion of objective narration in the novel and argues that the author, speaking in a variety of different voices, always betrays his presence. Booth maintains that although "the author can to some extent choose his disguises, he can never choose to disappear."[1]

In the act of writing, the actual author creates a "second self" which functions as a narrator of the fiction. The second self can adopt a variety of voices: that of omniscient, third-person or limited first-person narrator, privileged or distant narrator, reliable or unreliable narrator, an objective observer or a character within the story, etc. In creating a second self, Booth's implied author employs rhetoric, shaping the narrative for an implied reader. As Booth explains it, "the author creates ... an image of himself and another image of his reader; he makes his reader, as he makes himself."[2] Implied author and implied reader complete a circuit of discourse which exists within the rhetoric of the work itself and which exists independently of any actual author or actual reader. What Booth does is to situate the personae of author and reader within the work. And he does not merely identify among a narrative's characters author and reader figures. This is essentially what S. S. Van Dine does with detective fiction wherein the detective functions as a surrogate reader of a mystery authored by a criminal or what Tzvetan Todorov does with the literature of the fantastic wherein the reader necessarily shares the limited perspective of a character who hesitates between natural and supernatural explanations of

1

fantastic events. Booth's system of discourse between implied author and implied reader remains independent of characters and, for that matter, of story. It exists within the work's style, tone, or technique--or within whatever it is that constitutes the process by which narrative content is given articulation.

Though Booth's acknowledgement of the role of the reader is particularly modernist, prefiguring, to some extent, structuralist approaches by Barthes, Foucault, and others to texts in terms of their destination--the reader--rather than their origin, his attempt to preserve the notion of author in the age of the death of the author raises certain problems. For Barthes, "it is language which speaks, not the author."[3] The author is not a source of discourse but rather a function of it: the author becomes an entity or identity assigned to a work to fill the space left empty by the disappearance or death of the traditional notion of author. But if the traditional conception of the author has given way to language, culture, literature, and ideology which become the source of discourse-- which "speak"--the notion of author has not so much been destroyed as redefined. As long as discourse has a source, it has an author.

If Booth's notion of implied author is redefined to incorporate the voices of language and culture, his discussion of discourse as rhetoric becomes less problematical. In fact, it actually becomes a valuable model in that it provides a necessary corrective to the structuralist approach which emphasizes the importance of langue and de-emphasizes that of parole. Though a plurality of voices pre-exist the work, supplying it with material which enables it to come into being, those voices become focussed upon the reader through the articulating agency of style, that is, through the rhetoric of the fiction. If a work's underlying structures derive from language and culture, its realization as discourse derives from parole, from the specific articulation given to these structures.

It is this mediation of Booth's understanding of narrative as an author/reader discourse--rooted in the process of its representation--which prompts me to apply his notion of implied author and implied reader to a different mode of representation--to the cinematographic image. For it strikes me that representation in the cinema involves a similar discourse. But, at the same time, the precise nature of that representation--that is, the ontological bond that exists between an object and its representation--introduces a complexity to the kind of discourse which occurs in the cinema.

We might begin by distinguishing between the photographic and the cinematographic image. The photographic image lacks temporality and, for that reason, lacks a dimension necessary for the creation of a narrative. A still photograph--say of a car about to hit a man--excludes "the before" and "the after" which the viewer must supply in order to construct a narrative. In other words, the narrative process exists outside of the photograph and within the mind of the viewer. Thomas' photographs of the couple in the park in Blow-Up (1966) function as a narrative only when placed alongside one another and only when Antonioni's panning camera forces a successive relationship upon the individual stills. Attempts in painting to represent the temporality of a narrative --such as Goya's "The Third of May, 1808," which shows, within a single frame, an execution by firing squad that contains the bodies of those who have been shot, those who are being shot, and those who are about to be shot--depend upon the creation of a narrative outside of the work itself, in the process of its viewing. Even the projected image of a photographic slide and a film of the same static image will, as Columbia philosopher Arthur Danto argues, differ in terms of the psychology of their respective images.[4] The film image will have a beginning and an end, giving it a narrative dimension absent in the slide, which has neither.

The cinematographic image consists of a succession of still photographs, creating through their combination a narrative sequence. Though it may be argued that the locus of narration exists in the viewer's mind, which assembles these still images and projects motion upon them, the source of successivity ultimately lies in the filmstrip itself and in its projection upon a screen. At any rate, what interests me here is the source rather than the destination of the narrative, the narration which occurs within the film itself not in its perception. Though Barthes sees the focus of the text to be within the space of the reader, the source of the text projected upon the reader lies within the work itself.

The rhetoric of the cinematographic image functions similarly to that which Booth identified in fiction. The author creates a second self through a shaping of the plastics of the image and the soundtrack. The plastics of the image include, as Bazin observes, "the style of the sets, of the make-up, and, up to a point, even the performance, to which we naturally add the lighting (and/or color) and, finally the framing (i.e., camera angle and distance) of the shot which gives us its composition."[5] The plastics of the soundtrack, to borrow terms from David Bordwell and Kristin Thompson, include its

loudness, pitch, timbre, spatial qualities, rhythm and fidelity. [6] Implicating him or herself into the image or soundtrack through this rhetoric, the author or narrator also
postulates a viewer or listener who can see or hear only
that which the implied author presents. Thus Dreyer's facial close-ups in The Passion of Joan of Arc (1928) force
us to detach the characters from the world in which they
exist. In addition to inscribing him or herself into the
"static" plastics of the image, the implied author declares
him or herself through camera movement and other devices
of temporal narration such as zooms, the length of takes,
editing and so forth. As Danto points out, the moving camera announces its own presence, inscribing itself upon certain events. It makes "the mode of recording part of the
record." [7] Thus the camera, as it "reads" the profilmic
event, integrates that reading into the narration itself. The
camera assumes the roles of both author and reader. The
famous crane-down-and-in to the key clutched in Alicia's
hand in Notorious (1946) simultaneously narrates and reads
the action, combining the functions of author and spectator.
The process of narration and the act of reading or viewing
become embedded in the record of the event itself. Even
the less didactic, reflexive tracking shots in Otto Preminger's Daisy Kenyon (1947) or Advise and Consent (1962),
which respond to the movements of characters within the
frame, register actions and reactions to those actions in a
way which describes the Newtonian nature of Preminger's
rhetoric: for every action, there is an equal and opposite
reaction.

     The zoom provides an even better example of author-
ial voice, as can be seen in Hitchcock's Strangers on a
Train (1951). During a tennis match between two unidenti-
fied characters, the camera registers the hero's sudden
consciousness of the villain's presence through a zoom-in
onto the latter as he sits in the stands, his eyes riveted to
the hero, while the heads in the crowd around him turn
metronomically back and forth, following the movement of
the tennis ball. Here character and viewer-author share a
single consciousness. The zooms and rack focuses in Chabrol's Champagne Murders (1967) and in Blake Edwards' Darling Lili (1970) similarly reflect intrusions of consciousness
upon the narrative, but in both instances those conscious-
nesses exist outside of the characters. For both Chabrol
and Edwards, the zooms function as readings of the mask-
like surface of the image, attempting to penetrate the veil
of appearances that obscure the latent content of the shots.

At the same time, the ontological nature of the cinematographic image calls into question traditional notions of representation in general and Booth's theory of subjective narration in particular. As Bazin argues, cinematic representation, unlike that in the plastic arts, "shares, by virtue of the very process of its becoming, the being of the model of which it is the reproduction."[8] For Bazin, the image is, in part, an articulation of its contents and an inarticulated reproduction of its subject. It contains meanings which Barthes calls "obtuse." The cinematographic image narrates, but so do the objects which it contains, subverting Booth's notion of implied author with another, more objective voice.

In other words, the cinematographic image is both a perception of an object and that object's representation of itself. Thus the cinematic image is a representation unlike all others. It exists both as an image and as an image of something. Take, for example, the image of the street light which opens Howard Hawks's Scarface (1932). As an image, it exists in a system of other images; in particular, it is related to the neon sign advertising Cook's Tours with the slogan "The World Is Yours." As an image, it is a representation produced by the director or cameraman. Its meaning derives from its relation to other images and to what it represents. When it goes off, it signifies the coming of dawn, when street lights around the city are normally turned off. It also foreshadows the gangland murder which is to follow: Louis Costillo will be snuffed out like a light. And it also represents--on a more abstract plane--the cyclical impermanence which is the subject of the film: lights blink on and off endlessly, like the repetitive rise and fall of gangsters in the underworld. But most importantly, the light which goes off retains its objectivity--its thingness. It remains a light which merely goes off. Hawks's symbolism, unlike that of more abstract directors like Hitchcock and Lang, is rooted in the physical reality of objects and things. His symbols, like the neon sign and the bowling pin which falls as a gangster is gunned down, function primarily as the things themselves, not as symbols. It is only secondarily that they stand for other objects or things. The implied author "Hawks" establishes a dialogue with the otherness of objects and things in his films, reintroducing the notion banished by Booth from literature that objects and actions can speak for themselves. Thus the image of the Pompeiian lovers who are unearthed near the end of Roberto Rossellini's Voyage in Italy (1953) is even more problematical in terms of implied authorship and readership. For the film's central characters, the image signifies the complex state of their relationship which, though dead, is about to be reborn through their responses to these dead lovers, to their environment, and to one another. Yet, as ontological imprint, the petrified lovers embody a mysteriousness which defies their apparent symbolism in terms of the narrative. The scene represents an encounter between consciousness and the other.

Images in the cinema are both perceptions of an object or action and those objects or actions themselves. In other words, cinematographic images owe their meaning to processes of signification but owe their existence to the objects in whose place they stand. These objects, in effect, deposit tracings of themselves upon the film's emulsion. In producing images of themselves, they usurp the presumably human activity of sign production. Because the image is both a perception of an object and that object's representation of itself, it combines two identities. It is both an image of something, produced by culture or by the rhetoric of the implied author and it is the essence of that thing, its being transferred to film. Or, in terms of Bazinian aesthetics, the image depicts reality--for Bazin, reality is the author of the image--as it is filtered through the consciousness of the director--for Bazin, the director is the reader of reality.

The ontological nature of the cinematographic image calls into question any wholesale rejection of objective narration. Certain elements of the image remain resistant to "rhetorization" and to meaning. Though directors like Ford and Hitchcock saturate their images with the voice of rhetoric, giving articulation to everything--or almost everything --within the frame, directors like Rossellini, who inhabit the other end of the rhetorical spectrum, refuse to dissolve away, through the processes of signification, the essences of the objects of their representations.

In the cinema, especially in American narrative cinema, the image reflects both the presence of an implied author and that author's absence. Within it is staged a confrontation between the author's second self and the world's second self--i. e. , the other. The cinematographic image presents us with things which remain outside of understanding, which remain "other. "

In non-cinematic representation, perception of other-ness is problematical. At the moment of perception, the other becomes the self. It is drawn, through the process of its perception, into the realm of human understanding. Representation becomes pure rhetoric, even in the most mimetic works.

Within the cinematic image, however, are visible both the process of the perception of the other--that is, a record of the recording of it--and the other itself. The self--by which I mean the consciousness inherent in the rhetoric of the image and in the camera's presence at an event--and the other--by which I mean the thing being filmed--exist in a state of perpetual engagement and disen-gagement, like cogs in two wheels which intermesh, then separate, as the wheels rotate.

A painting, on the other hand, offers us only a per-ception of the other. The object of its representation--i. e., the other--exists outside of the painting not within it. But a cinematic image contains within it not only a perception of the other--an assimilation of it into a consciousness, a shaping of it into a rhetoric--but also its undigested essence which eludes our consciousness of it. As Bazin argues, "no matter how fuzzy, distorted, or discolored, no matter how lacking in documentary value the image may be, it shares, by virtue of the very process of its becoming, the being of the model of which it is the reproduction; it is the model."9 The cinema puts us in the presence of things and events whose meaning we can only intuit; the cinema forces, as no other art form does, the self to maintain discourse with the other.

NOTES

1. Wayne C. Booth, The Rhetoric of Fiction, (Chicago: University of Chicago Press, 1961), p. 20.
2. Ibid., p. 138.
3. "The Death of the Author," Image/Music/Text, trans. Stephen Heath, (New York: Hill and Wang, 1977), p. 143.
4. Arthur Danto, "Moving Pictures," Quarterly Review of Film Studies 4(1):1-21, Winter 1979.
5. André Bazin, What Is Cinema?, volume one, trans. Hugh Gray, (Berkeley: University of California Press, 1967), p. 24.

6. Film Art: An Introduction (Reading, Mass.: Addison-
    Wesley, 1980), pp. 192-200.
7. Danto, p. 19.
8. Bazin, p. 14.
9. Bazin, p. 14.

PART ONE: THOSE WHO PUT THEIR FAITH IN THE IMAGE

1. IN DEFENSE OF PURE CINEMA: ALFRED HITCHCOCK

"Pure cinema," as Hitchcock uses the term, refers specifically to Kuleshov's famous editing experiment with the actor Mosjoukine. But on a more general level, Hitchcock's cinema achieves a purity that goes beyond montage. Hitchcock's total manipulation of the plastics of the image gives him a control over his narrative material that is rare in the cinema. His stylization of content reflects a self-consciousness on the part of the narrator which distances him from the subject of his narration. In fact, it is more accurate to say that Hitchcock's cinema takes itself as its subject. Depicting processes of narration and perception within his films, Hitchcock's self-reflexive cinema represents an obsessive fascination with pure form that sets him apart from the other directors discussed in this book.

a. Dexterity in a Void: The Formalist Aesthetics of Alfred Hitchcock

Marxist critical methodology hinges upon the interrelatedness of aesthetics and ideology. Hitchcock, whose cinema synthesizes Expressionist and Constructivist aesthetics, poses something of a problem in that the ideology of each of these aesthetics is opposed to that of the other. Expressionist aesthetics are essentially decadent, the product of bourgeois idealists in perpetual flight from reality whose chief concern lay in spiritual salvation. Constructivist aesthetics are essentially progressive, the product of a materialist vision whose goal is to foster not spiritual regeneration but political, social, and economic change. Expressionist directors like F. W. Murnau construct idealist images, manipulating the plastic elements of lighting, set design, camera movement, and composition: Marxist directors like Sergei Eisenstein and Dziga Vertov deconstruct images through montage by drawing attention to the means of their production.

If Hitchcock, as Andrew Sarris points out in The American Cinema, "unites the divergent classical traditions of Murnau (camera movement) and Eisenstein (montage)," then what kind of ideological significance does Hitchcock's hybrid aesthetic have? The answer is perhaps less intriguing than the process by which it is derived. Hitchcock is a decadent progressive whose interest in the cinema is purely formal and non-ideological. [1] This is not to deny the ideological nature of Hitchcock's subject matter, his anti-Fascist tracts (Foreign Correspondent, Lifeboat, Rope), his cold-war spy thrillers (North by Northwest, Torn Curtain) and his aborted anti-Communist projects of the Fifties (Flamingo Feather) display, on the level of content, a cynical, but decidedly capitalistic bias. John M. Smith has written a very interesting study of Hitchcock's English films which touches on this entitled "Conservation Individualism" (Screen, Autumn 1972). It is on the level of form, however,

13

that Hitchcock's aesthetics obscure their ideological identity
and declare themselves to be "about the cinema."

Both Expressionism and Constructivism are formalist
aesthetics. By that I mean quite simply that they explore
the means of artistic representation. Expressionism, for
example, is in large part a reaction against the observation-
al nature of Realism, Naturalism, and Impressionism. In
rejecting the world as its model and replacing that with man,
the Expressionists abandon traditional mimetic representational forms in favor of non-representational forms such as
music. For how can man's inner spirit be depicted repre-
sentationally? Murnau's titles for Nosferatu ("A Symphony
of Horror") and Sunrise ("A Song of Two Humans") and the
films themselves reflect this attempt to find a form for pure
feeling. Sunrise, in particular, employs a musical structure, shifting from broodingly tragic to farcically comic
moods in its theme-and-variation study of the couple.

Constructivist interest in form is rooted in a rebel-
lion against bourgeois content and in an analysis of the ma-
terials of art. In Constructivist and Formalist criticism,
for example, thematics give way to stylistics, meaning to
morphology, literature to language, semantics to semiotics.
In film, Kuleshov can claim that content is nothing and that
what is important is montage.[2] Though montage theories
differ considerably within the Constructivist movement in
film, its essential nature, which fragments then reassembles
the world, remains consistent with larger, Marxist goals.

In terms of their shared interest in form, the differences between Expressionist and Marxist aesthetics can
best be illustrated by contrasting their notions of the shot.
For Eisenstein, the shot is representational; it is a photo-
fragment of reality whose meaning derives from its sequential combination with other shots. For Murnau, the shot
becomes a unit of expression within which reality is transformed. Eisenstein's narration occurs between shots; Murnau's within them. Eisenstein analyzes by juxtaposing shots;
Murnau, working within the frame, "edits" by superimposing
shots, thus interiorizing his narrative. Double exposure in
Nosferatu (1922), hallucinatory revels in The Last Laugh
(1924) and split-screen fantasies in Sunrise (1927) reflect
Murnau's attempts to build up a subjective reality, evoking
its mystic spirit. Montage objectively breaks reality down,
demystifying it.

Hitchcock's point-of-view editing combines the subjectivity of Murnau and the analytical objectivity of Eisenstein and Kuleshov. It is interesting to note how Hitchcock transforms Kuleshov's Mosjoukine experiment in telling Truffaut about it in their book-length interview. For Kuleshov, the sequence of shots has nothing to do with point of view. There is no suggestion that Mosjoukine sees what is intercut with shots of his face. The shots are not seen; they are rather signs which the viewer assembles. In fact, because it is subjective by nature, point-of-view editing (and identification, for that matter) is antithetical to the detached, analytical perspective of Constructivist aesthetics. But Hitchcock, in his Rear Window (1954) for example, subjectifies the whole process by having Jeffries (James Stewart) look and react to what he sees. The shots in which Hitchcock's characters look and react are objective: the audience sees the character and remains outside him or her. The insert shot of what the character sees, however, is subjective: the viewer sees as if through the character's eyes. Thus Hitchcock transforms a Constructivist editing experiment into an Expressionist tool by sandwiching an Expressionist shot within a non-Expressionist frame. In hallucinatory point-of-view sequences in Blackmail (1929) and Sabotage (1937), Hitchcock's indebtedness to both Kuleshov and Murnau is made even clearer: Alice White looks, sees a cocktail shaker which dissolves into a knife, and then we see her reaction. Mrs. Verloc, coming out of a swoon after learning of her younger brother's death, looks, hallucinates him, and then reacts.

Hitchcock's use of point of view calls attention to the processes of identification between the spectator and the characters on the screen. The insert shot forces identification; the reaction shot forces opposition. The spectator is torn between the two, entering a state of ambivalency, which is reinforced by the moral ambiguity of Hitchcock's own attitude toward his characters. When his voyeuristic heroes and heroines look and react, they function as audience surrogates, as spectators within the text. The film which best illustrates the point-of-view identification process--Rear Window--is also Hitchcock's most self-reflexive work. Its hero, L. B. Jeffries, is both spectator and director. He not only watches his neighbors but also manipulates them, writing a blackmail letter ("What have you done with her?") which keeps the suspected killer from leaving town and later luring him out of his apartment with a phone call so that it can be searched. Jeff's phone call "directs" the killer in a way similar to Hitchcock's own direction of the neighbors, who have been outfitted with flesh-colored receivers and whose actions he controls by short wave radio from a vantage point behind Robert Burks' camera.

As William Paul observes, Jeffries--as director--gives the characters across the way names ("Miss Torso," "Miss Lonelyhearts") and makes up stories about them. In order to get a closer view of the killer's apartment, Jeff uses first binoculars, then a telephoto lens from one of his cameras, the increasing image size reflecting his increased involvement in the mystery and also mirroring Hitchcock's own lens changes as director.

With characteristic perversity, Hitchcock dresses and makes up the killer, played by a curly-haired, overweight Raymond Burr, to resemble David O. Selznick, a producer known for his meddling with his directors' work and for whom Hitchcock made Rebecca, Spellbound and The Paradine Case. Hitchcock reportedly rehearsed Burr in Selznick's gestures and mannerisms, coaching him on how to hold a telephone or smoke a cigarette. The Selznick reference only confirms the notion that Rear Window is "about the cinema."

As Bazin notes, the identification/opposition process works differently in the cinema and in the theater. Because the space of the cinema is separate from that of the audience, identification is made easier. There is no need, as there is in the theater, for a viewer to deny, through an act of will, the actual physical presence of the actor. In the cinema, the actor is both present and absent, his image standing in for him. The spectator in the cinema need not deny his physical presence before accepting him as a fictional character; the cinema has already done this by reproducing not him, but his image. Rear Window plays with the segregation of spaces essential to the cinema. Jeff, like the spectator in the cinema, remains secure in his apartment until the very end of the film when the killer, crossing the footlights, so to speak, enters Jeff's space. A figure of identification becomes one of opposition. The film's dominant point-of-view editing style suddenly yields to Eisensteinian montage as Jeff and the killer struggle, the editing cathartically resolving Jeff's and the spectator's passive complicity with the killer by violently dramatizing their opposition.

Hitchcock's montage sequences are stripped of Marxist ideological significance. One only need compare the "Odessa Steps Sequence" with Hitchcock's tongue-in-cheek parody of it, when the birds attack the children outside the Bodega Bay school in The Birds (1963), to see that montage has become pure form. Where Eisenstein's editing uses the collisions between shots to deconstruct and reconstruct the violent history of the Russian Revolution, to trace a chain of cause and effect through an escalation of violent action and reaction, Hitchcock's montage sequences detach violence from history, and from cause-and-effect logic, emphasizing its irrationality.

The violent subject matter of Eisenstein's films--strikes, mutinies, revolutions--suits the formal properties of montage. By contrast, non-violent intellectual montage, such as the shots of Kerensky and Napolean in October (1927), seems less effective. It does not function as a machine designed to convey the spirit of "revolutionary brotherhood" and to stir viewers' emotions. Hitchcock's montage sequences reveal an intuitive understanding of its basic properties. The shower murder in Psycho (1960), and the downhill ride in a runaway car in Family Plot (1976) exploit the violent nature of montage. In a way, they are montage sequences which are about the nature of montage. That the survival of montage in the sound cinema of Hitchcock and others occurs almost exclusively in scenes of violence is, in terms of Bazinian notions of the evolution of the language of cinema, existential proof of its essence.

The precise nature of Hitchcock's formalist approach to editing can best be seen in his use of suspense. Suspense, though considered by literary handbooks as merely a tool to be used in the construction of a narrative and in the manipulation of an audience, becomes, in Hitchcock's hands, a self-reflexive form, a means of exploring the nature of the cinema. As in all temporal arts (e.g., music, drama), film exists in a perpetual present tense. Though filmed at an earlier date, whatever is seen on the screen suggests presence. Though we know the action happened then, before a camera, it is also happening now, before an audience. The camera's presence captures a moment which is reduplicated in projection. Narration is a temporal, sequential phenomenon: it consists in the movement from one moment to the next, from one action to the next, as Aristotle's analysis of plot in terms of beginning, middle and end illustrates. In this sense, suspense, which accentuates the

tension between one moment and the next by prolonging
transitional movement, is a form of manipulation which
calls attention to the narrative process.   Intuitively aware
of the sequential nature of suspense, Hitchcock regularly
breaks his suspense sequences down into a series of inter-
rupted actions, either by cutting back and forth sequentially
between simultaneous actions as in the tennis match/sewer
sequence in Strangers on a Train (1951), by drawing out a
single action through cutaways as with the falling bottle in
the wine cellar in Notorious (1946) or by means of a simple,
Griffithesque race against the clock as with the time bombs
in Sabotage and 4 O'Clock which are animated into the status
of "characters" involved in a parallel action with the hero.

      Hitchcock's manipulation of suspense is similar to
his own cameo appearances in his films: each cutaway announces Hitchcock's intrusive presence as a narrator. [3]   By
that I mean that the cuts are not so much determined by the
action as imposed upon it.   Like his walk-ons, Hitchcock's
suspense editing makes the audience conscious of the process of narration.   Significantly, his signature appearance
in Notorious as a champagne-guzzling guest sets in motion
a suspenseful race between the hero-and-heroine and the
clock.   Here time is measured in the consumption of champagne.

      The intrusiveness of Hitchcock's suspense technique
contrasts with the "invisibility" of Griffith's.   Though both
establish parallel sequences of events, Griffith's respect for
the integrity of each individual event prevents him from
cutting away in mid-event, as Hitchcock does repeatedly in
Strangers when Bruno reaches for Guy's lighter in the sew-
er.   Nor does Griffith ever create temporal ellipses in his
suspense sequences, as Hitchcock does at the end of the
chase across the moors in The 39 Steps (1935)--Hannay,
last seen waiting outside the Professor's door, has vanished
when Hitchcock cuts back to the door as the police arrive.
Griffith's respect for an action's temporal integrity is
matched in Harold Lloyd's suspense comedies by a respect
for spatial integrity: suspense arises not through cutting,
but through the action itself.   Lloyd scales buildings and
clings to the faces of skyscraper clocks (Safety Last); his
precariousness in space produces suspenseful anxiety in the
audience.   Suspense within the shot is, in a Bazinian sense,
non-manipulative.   The action set before the camera speaks
directly to the viewer without the intervention of a narrator.
Hitchcock, even when his suspense sequences are potentially

spatial, heightens the suspense through cutting.   As his
characters hang from the Statue of Liberty in Saboteur (1942)
or from the face of Mt. Rushmore in North by Northwest
(1959), Hitchcock abstracts the action by cutting.   I cannot
think of a suspense sequence in all of Hitchcock which does
not involve an intrusive breakdown of the action into separate shots.   Even Rope (1948) and Under Capricorn (1949),
which some may argue are not very suspenseful pictures and
thus exceptions which prove the rule, develop suspense primarily through reframing and through a manipulation of off-
screen space rather than staging suspense action within the
frame.

At the other end of the spectrum from Griffith and
Lloyd stands Eisenstein, whose suspense sequences are so
self-reflexive that they often do not work.   In Potemkin
(1925), the meeting with the squadron contains so many cutaways that the focus of the scene--will the fleet fire on the
Potemkin or not?--is lost.   Even the famous teetering baby
carriage first advances toward, then retreats from the edge
of a step, revealing the Russian's hand as it stirs up the
film's suspense action.   As Annette Michelson observes,
the raising of the bridge sequence in October calls attention
to the "materiality" of the editing, performing a Marxist
deconstruction of the action (Artforum, January 1973).   Midway between Griffith and Eisenstein, Hitchcock emerges as
an invisibly visible presence: he tests the limits of suspense narration but refuses to break them.

Like Kuleshov and Eisenstein who were denounced by
Stalinist critics in the Thirties as "formalists," Hitchcock,
as "Master of Suspense" and "Master of Directing Technique," has been dismissed as a mere craftsman.   Typical
of this view of Hitchcock is Bosley Crowther, who titles his
1951 New York Times review of Strangers on a Train, "Dexterity in a Void."   Crowther deftly pats Hitchcock on the
back with one hand and stabs him in it with the other.
Hitchcock's experiments with montage, suspense, sound
(Blackmail, Secret Agent), color (Vertigo, Marnie), location
shooting (Shadow of a Doubt, I Confess), long takes (Rope,
Under Capricorn), 3-D (Dial M for Murder), restricted
spaces (Lifeboat, Rope, Rear Window), flashback narration
(Stage Fright), identification (Vertigo, Psycho) and point-of-
view editing (Rear Window, et al.) reveal an obsession with
form for its own sake.   That he could abandon montage
completely for long takes in Rope and Under Capricorn illustrates the purity of his formalism.   The traditionally

opposed aesthetics of montage and mise-en-scène are, for Hitchcock, equally viable as forms, whose cinematic potential is to be explored for its own sake. In a sense, Crowther is right. Hitchcock's formalism is "dexterity in a void." But that "void" is cinema and that "dexterity" is no futile exercise but a meditation on the formal properties of cinematic expression.

NOTES

1. If ideology is defined, as Richard Dyer does in Stars (BFI, 1979), as "the set of ideas and representations in which people collectively make sense of the world and the society in which they live," then every character, plot, narration, and element of style in a film is ideological, embedded in the ideology(ies) of the culture which produces it. But to the extent that a film refers more to itself than to the world or to society, as Hitchcock's films often do, it makes itself less available to ideological analysis. The degree to which Hitchcock's aesthetics are ideological depends upon the extent of their self-reflexivity. Since Hitchcock is, as I will argue, invisibly visible in his films, the extent of his self-reflexivity is problematical. I tend to see his presence everywhere and have thus stressed the non-ideological nature of his visual/aural style.

2. Similarly, Russian Formalist Victor Shklovsky, in attacking symbolist notions of artistic creativity, writes that "poets are much more concerned with arranging images than with creating them." See "Art as Technique," in Russian Formalist Criticism: Four Essays, Lee T. Lemon and Marion J. Reis, eds., (Lincoln: University of Nebraska Press, 1965), p. 7.

3. Shklovsky's famous discussion of Sterne's Tristram Shandy focusses on a similar manipulation of narrative elements, through digressions, temporal displacements and other devices, which signal the intrusive presence of the narrator and which serve to defamiliarize the narrative. Shklovsky's essay is reprinted in Russian Formalist Criticism, cited above, pp. 25-57.

b. Hitchcock in Britain

Only a handful of Alfred Hitchcock's British pictures have ever been commercially revived in this country, undoubtedly because of the unavailability of the films themselves but also because of the contemporary critical backlash, led by writers like Robin Wood, that has sought to redeem Hitchcock's American films at the expense of the once-heralded British films. The time has come for an objective reevaluation of this period of Hitchcock's career. By this stage of film history, Hitchcock, whether British or American, is nonetheless Hitchcock. His name has come to mean a certain kind of cinema that has little to do with nationality.

Hitchcock's English films are most "English" in terms of plot and character and least "English" in terms of style. His adaptations of popular novels and plays give his films of the Twenties and Thirties topicality and reflect British character, while his synthesis of Soviet and German aesthetics--constructivist editing and expressionistic set design and lighting--reveal a formalist approach to cinema that is less British than European. The antithetical tendencies of expressionism and constructivism seem oddly resolved within the context of the English thriller, which blends psychological approaches to characterization with abstract editing patterns. Thus Hitchcock's collaborations with screenwriter Charles Bennett, who wrote the scripts for The Man Who Knew Too Much, The 39 Steps, The Secret Agent, Sabotage, Young and Innocent and the original play on which Blackmail is based, reconcile British plot and character with an international, almost avant-garde, stylistic experimentation.

Robin Wood's reevaluation in the third edition of his Hitchcock's Films begins with an acknowledgement of the influence on the director's work of German Expressionism and Soviet montage. 1 Soviet montage reflects a materialist (rather than spiritualist) aesthetic, an outgrowth of the Constructivist movement in the arts and, as such, is at loggerheads with Expressionism. Eisenstein, as a theorist of socialist

21

realism, abhors Expressionism, viewing it as mystic and decadent, the product of a declining (bourgeois) rather than ascending (proletarian) class. For him, The Cabinet of Dr. Caligari is "this barbaric carnival of the destruction of the healthy, human infancy of our art, this common grave for normal cinema origins, this combination of silent hysteria, particolored canvasses, daubed flats, painted faces, and the unnatural, broken gestures and actions of monstrous chimeras."[2] Reacting against Expressionism, Soviet cinema deals not with man's spiritual salvation but with his economic and social welfare--with his consciousness of the material nature of the world. As Walter Sokel points out in The Writer in Extremis,

> The Expressionist is an ethical idealist. This
> distinguishes him radically from the Marxist. His
> goal is spiritual, not material. It is the rule of
> the spirit on earth. The Marxist bows to history
> and the iron laws of necessity.... Thus Marx-
> ism ... does not include ... inner spiritual re-
> generation. [3]

Constructivist editing functions as a machine designed to produce material change and, as such, draws attention to the means of its own production (e. g. , the shots of the editing process in Vertov's Man With a Movie Camera, 1928).

From the vantage point of England in the Twenties, Hitchcock, as a spectator of world cinema, observes and absorbs both Expressionism and Constructivism. In the Truffaut book, Hitchcock pays homage to Murnau, whose "titleless" Last Laugh (1924) advances the cause of totally visual expression, and to Kuleshov (via Pudovkin's book on editing, translated into English by Hitchcock's associate, Ivor Montagu), whose editing experiments influenced Hitchcock's own notions of point-of-view cutting and "pure cinema." Though he here acknowledges the twin poles of his own aesthetic, Hitchcock's visual style remains more Germanic than Russian. He is less materialist than the Russians in his approach to editing and, like the Germans, fascinated by the psychological nature of experience. The fairground milieu of The Ring (1927) echoes that in Variety (1925) in that both are less evocative of real places than of moral states; the amusement park sequences in Strangers on a Train convey the expressive qualities of those in Caligari (1919) and Sunrise (1927). Corridors and staircases, which serve as a locus of psychodrama dominating the action in

Hintertreppe (1921), Genuine (1920), Destiny (1921), and
Pandora's Box (1928), play an expressive role in virtually
every Hitchcock film from The Lodger (1926) to Frenzy
(1972) and Family Plot (1976)--except, of course, single-set
films like Lifeboat and Rope--but figure most spectacularly
in the penultimate sequences of Notorious (1946) and Vertigo
(1958).

The common bond between Hitchcock and the Expressionists can be seen thematically as well as stylistically.
The Jack-the-Ripper story which underlies The Lodger (1926)
and Frenzy (1972) surfaces as Expressionist material in the
final, fairground sequence in Paul Leni's pre-Hitchcock Wax-
works (1924) and again in the London sequence of Pabst's
Pandora's Box (1928). The doppelgänger which haunts the
pre-Expressionist novels of E. T. A. Hoffman, Robert Louis
Stevenson, Edgar Allan Poe, and Franz Werfel, the Expres-
sionist plays of Kleist and Kaiser, and the films of Weine,
Wegener, Murnau, Lang, and others structures not only
Hitchcock's "exchange of guilt" films (Shadow of a Doubt,
I Confess, and Strangers on a Train) but also his "wrong
man" pictures (Young and Innocent, The Wrong Man, and
Frenzy). Doubles structure not only spy pictures (North by
Northwest) but suspense comedies (Family Plot).

The Hitchcockian spy thriller also has its roots in
German soil: Lang's Spione (1928) and his Mabuse series
predate Hitchcock's own entry into the genre with The Man
Who Knew Too Much (1934) and The 39 Steps (1935). His
indebtedness to Lang is apparent, in part, in his incorporation of Mabusan mesmerism in the former and his dramatic
unmasking of a stage performer as a spy, as Lang does in
Spione, in the latter. Hitchcock's interest in the spy film,
however, only flirts with Langian thematics of predestination,
paranoia, and ironic social commentary. His concern lies
more in the exploration of the spy film as a metaphor for
the cinema, wherein the voyeuristic secret agent, like the
viewer, sees but is not seen (Elsa and Ashendon in Secret
Agent) or, like a character on the screen, is seen but does
not see (Thornhill in North by Northwest). In probing the
voyeur and what the voyeur sees, Hitchcock explores the notion of responsibility, involvement, and identification--ques-
tions and issues crucial to contemporary film theory.

Like Eisenstein, Hitchcock has been repeatedly attacked as a "formalist," though in Hitchcock's case it was
less "that old devil montage" that became the focus of attacks

on him than it was his overall emphasis on style and crafts-
manship.   His problem, as his British films show, lies in
the absence in England of a larger cultural aesthetic within
which he could work and with which he could identify.   The
fact that he was a Jesuit-trained Catholic in an Anglican
country only serves to complicate matters.   Hitchcock's
Chestertonian vision of a paradoxical world may help reconcile the existence of the traditionally conflicting poles of
montage and mise-en-scène in his work, but it is still not
exactly what one would call "British."   British Hitchcock
emerges as a fascinating mixture of plots, characters, and
styles which remain in constant flux.   It is a body of work
marked by the same sort of restless experimentation that
characterizes the director's American period.   It reveals a
Hitchcock who is constantly searching for new forms of expression and for new methods of perfecting his art.

The Pleasure Garden (1925)

The Pleasure Garden is a curious amalgam of heavy German
expressionism and light British wit.   The structure of the
film grows out of two sets of doubles: showgirls Patsy and
Jill constitute one pair; their admirers--Levet and Hugh
Fielding--the other.   Parallel action develops the contrasts
between characters: Hitchcock cross-cuts from the vampish
Jill in the act of betraying her fiancé, Hugh, for a wealthy
prince to Patsy being seduced by the bounder Levet.   Hitchcock has often been labelled "misogynistic" and his portrayal
of Jill does little to discredit that tag, yet his equation of
Jill and Levet reveals a larger, misanthropic vision: if the
devil is a woman, he can also be a man.

      The theme of the doppelgänger falls short of its pro-
per resolution: the doubles do not confront and kill one
another, though the missionary doctor does act on behalf of
the fever-ridden Hugh when he shoots Levet, whose murder
of his native mistress has driven the latter insane with guilt.

      Hitchcock's comic wit derives less from plot than
from character: the theater manager smokes in front of a
"NO SMOKING" sign; a lecherous admirer asks Patsy for a
lock of her golden hair, so she removes her blonde wig and
gives him a curl from it; a dog licks the bottom of Jill's
feet as she prays before going to bed.   Though the film's
script announces its theme to be the suffering of victims
Patsy and Hugh, its comedy, culminating in the final image

of the dog chewing contentedly on the cord of the landlord's wireless, lends a disconcerting note to this would-be passion play.

The Lodger (1926)

If it were possible to rewrite film history, ignoring the films Hitchcock made before The Lodger, we could very nicely observe that Hitchcock began his career with a woman screaming, the image which opens The Lodger. Nonetheless, the image does announce the expressionist style and content of the film, shrieks (and staircases) being an integral part of expressionist visual iconography (as can be seen in the work of Edvard Munch).

Strangely enough, Hitchcock blends expressionism (low-key lighting, distorted mirror reflections) with realism, documenting the gathering, reporting, and dissemination to the hysterical populace of news of the Avenger's latest murder. Here, as later with his incorporation of montage and mise-en-scène into a single visual aesthetic, Hitchcock reveals an interest in synthesizing disparate styles.

He stacks the decks against the lodger of the title from his first appearance as a shadow cast on Daisy's door, to his curious black medical bag, his neurotic reaction to portraits of blonde women, his pacing in his room, his reaching for a fire poker while playing chess with Daisy, to his threatening gestures as he embraces her later. Here, as Truffaut observes, Hitchcock films his love scenes like murder scenes and murder scenes like love scenes.

Also of interest is Daisy's jealous boyfriend, Joe, a policeman investigating the case. Linking love and duty, Joe promises Daisy that first he'll put the rope around the Avenger's neck, then the ring around her finger. When Joe begins to suspect the lodger, his suspicions are as much inspired by jealousy as by methodical deduction. Love and duty become confused, a confusion solved only by the accidental capture of the real Avenger and Joe's last-minute rescue of the lodger from a mob of angry Londoners.

Easy Virtue (1927)

It is hard to imagine a silent film version of a Noel Coward play. Coward's verbal wit and timed dialogue constitute a

significant part of his skill as a dramatist.   Hitchcock's
silent adaptation of Coward's Easy Virtue may thus be an
unimaginable film but, paradoxically, it is in no way hampered by its silence: Hitchcock's witty visuals reveal an
articulateness the equal of Coward's verbals.   His focal
shifts, dolly shots, match cuts, and cuts from the present
testimony to the action in the past in an artist's studio on
which the testimony is based given an ironic character to
the divorce trial which opens the film and which introduces
the notorious Larita Filton.

The film displays considerable Lubitschean subtlety:
when Larita's new conquest, John Whittaker, hears her answer to his marriage proposal on the telephone, Hitchcock
shoots the scene from the point of view of the eavesdropping
hotel switchboard operator.   A close-up of a tag on her lug-
gage then reveals to us the outcome: there is now a Mrs.
John Whittaker.   And a match dissolve from a French poodle
sitting on their baggage to an English bulldog in the same
position informs us of the couple's return from the Riviera
to England.

The past, which always haunts Hitchcock's characters,
catches up with Larita when the Whittaker family learns of
her scandalous divorce.   The film concludes with her uncon-
tested divorce from John and with Larita's absurdly melodramatic last words to the photographers who have contributed to her notoriety: "Shoot!   There's nothing left to
kill!"

The Ring (1927)

The title of Hitchcock's The Ring identifies it as a boxing
picture, which it is: the film traces the rise of "One-
Round" Jack Sanders from fairground attraction to heavy-
weight champion.   But "the ring" also serves as the film's
dominant graphic and structural element, from the circular
bass drum, revolving merry-go-round and roll of tickets in
the amusement park where the film begins to the circular
gong, overhead lights, stop watch and water bucket which
Hitchcock emphasizes at the championship fight which ends
the film.

What is intriguing about The Ring, however, is its
foray into expressionism, a factor which undoubtedly accounts for its resemblance in story line to Variety (1925),

Dupont's film about a trapeze artist whose wife leaves him
for a more famous performer.   Hitchcock's expressionism
conveys the vertiginousness of his characters' passions.
From Jack's jealous point-of-view we see a hallucinated
shot of his wife and rival, Bob Corby, kissing, then distorted and elongated superimpositions of dancing girls, piano
keys, guitar strings and spinning records.   Yet Hitchcock
places his character's subjective vision within an ironic
context: his own narrative presence, felt most strongly in
the film's circular structure, stands apart from his characters' more immediate feelings.   Hitchcock remains more
intrigued by overall design than by individual desire.

The Farmer's Wife (1928)

On her deathbed, Mrs. Sweetland extracts a promise from
her maid, Minta, to look after her husband, reminding her
not to forget "to air your master's pants."   Pathos gives
way to comedy in The Farmer's Wife as Sweetland sets
about to find himself another wife.   Her empty chair, to
which Hitchcock poignantly cuts throughout the party celebrating the marriage of Sweetland's daughter, becomes a
haunting, recurrent image throughout the film.   Sweetland
even imagines each of the area's most eligible spinsters
sitting in the chair, but all seem absurdly out of place
there.   Only Minta, to whom Mrs. Sweetland entrusted the
care of her husband (and his pants), does not violate the
spirit of the space.

Sweetland's first prospect neatly puts him down when
he proposes and asks her to say "yes": "'Yes' be a very
short word."   She snaps back with: "But there's a shorter."
Another of his choices becomes hysterical when he pops the
question, causing a delightfully comic scene at a local garden party.   Hitchcock's social satire has a nasty edge to it
and one feels that the emotional center of his film lies
somewhere near the Dickensian figure of Ash, played by
Gordon Harker, who cynically comments on his master's
activities: "Beer drinkin' don't do half the harm of love-
makin.'"

Champagne (1928)

Champagne is worthy of note for three reasons.   One is its
almost obsessive fascination, like Downhill before it, with

sadistic aspects of the parent-child relationship. Here, a
father interferes with the marriage plans of his rather reck-
less daughter, leads her to believe that the family fortune
has been lost, and hires a detective to follow her and report back on her activities, voyeuristically following through
on his sadism.   Another is its use of Betty Balfour, England's top box office attraction at the time, in the central
role.   In fact, Champagne is largely a vehicle for Balfour,
whose portrayal of the spunky, lower-class Squibs character
in a series of popular comedies for other directors made
her a star.   Champagne enables her to display her comic
range.   Finally, Champagne abounds in perverse camera
positions, from point-of-view shots through the bottoms of
champagne glasses to tilted shots which reflect the perspective of a first healthy, then seasick passenger on a rocking
ocean liner.   Champagne is a playful little film that, unlike
Downhill, refuses to take its serious themes seriously.

The Manxman (1929)

Like the image of the Catherine wheel which opens the film,
The Manxman takes the shape of a three-spoked wheel.   The
points of Hitchcock's love triangle--Pete, a poor fisherman;
Phil, his best friend; and Kate, an innkeeper's daughter who,
like Alice White in Blackmail, is an archetypal Hitchcockian
bitch who is made to pay for her teasing and sexual flirta-
tions--are inscribed within an ironically circular plot pattern which, in a gradually descending spiral, culminates in
sexual betrayal, attempted suicide, and public humiliation.
It is characteristic of Hitchcock, shooting his last silent
film on location on the Isle of Man, to incorporate the island's official insignia into the fabric of his picture: the
Catherine wheel is to the Isle of Man as the Statue of Liberty is to New York and as windmills are to Holland.   Even
the isle's local mill figures as cinematic grist, serving as
a rendezvous for Phil and Kate and as a reception hall for
the celebration of their marriage.   As Kate's father, slowly
turning the mill wheel and speaking for Hitchcock, observes
at the reception, "The mills of God grind slowly."   Hitchcock's plot crushes his characters under the weight of its
inevitability; they are nothing more than spokes in a wheel.

Blackmail (1929)

Blackmail, Hitchcock's first sound feature, is often referred
to as the first British talkie.   It is not: that honor goes to

The Clue of the New Pin. What Blackmail does offer, however, is a new approach to the relation between sound and
image. Blackmail begins as a silent film, its montage and
camera movements revealing the grandeur of the silent film's
expressiveness. Then, after the first reel, the film bursts
into sound. What is amazing is that Hitchcock's camera
does not lose its tongue, that he displays an expressiveness
in the sound medium which rivals that in the silent sequence.

It may be argued that the film's best scenes are those
nightmarishly expressionistic "silent" sequences during and
immediately following Alice White's murder of the artist who
attempts to seduce her. But what is fascinating about Blackmail is its mixture of silent and sound aesthetics, foreshadowing Hitchcock's subsequent use of pure cinema, "silent"
sequences (for example, his montage sequences in North by
Northwest, Psycho and The Birds) in his sound films.

Hitchcock's visuals never efface themselves before
sound: even in the oft-cited "knife" sequence, the short
pans connecting the gossipy neighbor and Alice or the bread
knife and Alice are as important as the manipulation of the
volume on the sound track. The paralysis of the central
character lies as much in the claustrophobic pans which
catch her in the center of a battle between one blackmailer,
Tracy (who symbolically holds one of gloves which she lost
at the scene of the crime), and another, Frank, her Scotland Yard beau, who holds the other, as in the sounds which
haunt her.

Murder (1930)

Murder, an atypical Hitchcock, is the director's only whodunit, though the film is arguably more about performance
and the theater than detection. Hitchcock is generally less
interested in mystery--a high-mimetic mode in which the
audience is slightly inferior to the plot and characters--than
in suspense--an ironic mode in which the audience knows
more than, and is thus superior to, the plot and characters.
The unsuitability of the genre for Hitchcock is reflected in
the way his direction struggles against its restrictions, employing a logic that is more ironic than deductive. Thus,
once Hitchcock's amateur sleuth, the famous actor Sir John
Menier (Herbert Marshall), discovers the identity of the real
killer, he writes a Hamletesque play in which the murder is
re-enacted and invites the killer to an audition to read for

the part.   Like Hitchcock, Sir John is something of a voyeuristic sadist: he enjoys watching the killer betray his
guilt.   And Sir John's presence during the killer's dangerous
high-wire, acrobatic performance at the circus serves, in
part, as a catalyst, prompting the killer's fall and subsequent death.   Hitchcock's only whodunit is no genuine whodunit; it is a murder mystery with his own brand of English
on it.

The Skin Game (1931)

The class conflict which forms the crux of the John Gals-
worthy play on which The Skin Game is based is ultimately
less a concern to Hitchcock than the universality of corruption and guilt.   The auction which dominates the middle of
the film combines these various thematic strands, superficially serving as a forum for the battle between the aristocratic Squire Hillcrist and the self-made industrialist Hornblower over a section of unspoiled land known as Centry
Meadows.   But while the men bid openly for the land, the
women, Lady Amy Hillcrist and Chloe, Hornblower's daugh-
ter-in-law, engage in a silent conflict of wills: Lady Hillcrist arranges for an old acquaintance of Chloe's to attend
the auction, revealing her intent to blackmail Chloe by
threatening to expose her as a former corespondent in a
number of divorce cases.

The fluid tracks, pans, and whip-pans which begin the
auction gradually break down into subjective point-of-view
shots as Chloe spies her would-be accusor, much as the
roving pans which scan the audience as the auction starts
break into a rapid montage of faces as Hillcrist bids against
Hornblower.   Later, Hitchcock again links the two plots as
Chloe, who has drowned herself in shame of her past, is
carried in the foreground toward the Hillcrist house while
the two families struggle in the background for possession
of the deed to Centry Meadows.   The felling of a statuesque-
ly magnificent old tree in the film's last shot is symbolic
not only of Hornblower's ultimate triumph over the landed
gentry but also of a more universal tragedy--a post-edenic
loss of innocence.

Rich and Strange (1932)

Truffaut, Rohmer and Chabrol single out Rich and Strange
as an unacknowledged masterpiece.   Though the film does

have a thematic richness more characteristic of Hitchcock's
American melodramas than of his English thrillers, the film
is hardly a Shadow of a Doubt, a Vertigo or a Psycho.
Though it does reveal an amazing maturity of vision, it
bears little resemblance to the sort of picture audiences
identify with Hitchcock and it thus invariably leaves these
viewers a bit unsatisfied.

Travel in Hitchcock is more than movement through
space: it is psychological as well as physical. The journey
which constitutes the bulk of Rich and Strange is seen as
escape. Initially it is an escape from the dull, middle class
routine of nine-to-five office work, and then it is an escape
from the confinement of bourgeois marriage. Fred and
Emily Hill, Hitchcock's voyagers, grow rich, when a relative leaves them some money, and then estranged, as they
travel around the world on that money. When Fred becomes
chronically seasick, Emily sightsees with Commander Gordon, a lonely but attractive and romantic bachelor. Later,
a naïve Fred is seduced and fleeced by a fake "princess,"
who quickly drops him once she has his money.

Hitchcock's visual metaphors for the marriage consist of the vehicles on which the couple travel: the claustrophobic London commuter subway becomes a spacious boat
train; later, the Hills sight-see in separate rickshaws that
crash into one another; their luxury liner gives way to a
tramp steamer, which sinks and is replaced, in turn, by a
Chinese junk. Yet at precisely the point at which the marriage (represented by the steamer) sinks, it is reborn: the
couple's squabbling with one another becomes externalized
into a conflict between them and nature: they briefly run
the risk of drowning. Fred and Emily enjoy a second honeymoon of short duration, terminated by their return to London
and their resumption of bourgeois routine.

Number Seventeen (1932)

Number Seventeen is a tongue-in-cheek thriller. It opens
with all the familiar icons of mystery: a dark, windy night;
a tree casting eerie shadows on the sidewalk; leaves flutter-
ing in the wind; a haunted house (No. 17) whose front door
springs open at the approach of our hero. Within the house
are mysterious lights moving along darkened corridors,
threatening shadows on the walls, candles that inexplicably
blow out, a corpse which later disappears, and a group of
odd characters struggling over possession of a stolen necklace.

Hitchcock's screenwriter, Rodney Ackland, explains:

> As the heroines of thrillers were invariably dumb,
> the leading lady of No. 17, Hitch decided, must
> literally be dumb--must never utter (a word) from
> beginning to end of picture.   As the climax of a
> thriller was invariably a chase (generally between
> a car and a train at this period), No. 17's climax
> must be a chase-to-end-all-chases--its details so
> preposterous that excitement would give way to
> gales of laughter.

Later, just before the commencement of the chase,
the dumb heroine excuses herself and announces, "I'm not
going.   I'm not so dumb after all."   As Ackland points out,
"There was no conceivable reason in the story why this
character should pretend dumbness but, as Hitch had pre-
dicted, her explanation was never questioned and to this
day, its satiric intention having been completely missed,
Number Seventeen is accepted as simply a minor Hitchcock
--a slightly better than average thriller."

The Man Who Knew Too Much (1934)

In recent years, Hitchcock's first version of The Man Who
Knew Too Much has become the target of polemical attack,
largely because his 1956 remake provides critics with a con-
venient yardstick by which to measure not only the earlier
film but also the difference between the director's English
and American work.   It is true that both films are based on
the same situation.   Blackmailed into silence by spies who
kidnap their child, the couples in both films are torn between patriotic duty and personal feeling.   The fact that the
situations in both films result in the moral and emotional
paralysis of the couple complicates any attempt to distinguish the films thematically.   All of Hitchcock's films concern themselves with paralysis of one kind or another.

If we are to see the original on its own terms, however, we must look for differences, not similarities, and
we must consider those differences, as Northrup Frye argues, in terms not of comparative but of positive value.
Godard, in an article on the remake, isolates a paradoxical
conflict in that film between predestination and free will--a
conflict symbolized by the lyrics of "Que Sera Sera."   This
observation articulates one of the differences between the two

films: the remake tends to abstract the plot situation while
the original remains closer to a literal reading of the story.
Hitchcock's use of pans, instead of the remake's cuts, in
the original's Albert Hall sequence reveals an interest in the
literalization, rather than abstraction of space that further
distinguishes the two works. The bullet hole in the glass
window and the snapping of the thread upon the death of the
secret agent are additional literalizations of action that the
more psychologically oriented Hitchcock of the Fifties would
tend to avoid. Hitchcock's original focuses on the mechanics
of paralysis; the remake focuses on their metaphysics.

The 39 Steps (1935)

In adapting John Buchan's spy novel, The 39 Steps, Charles
Bennett and Alma Reville changed practically everything but
the name of the hero, Richard Hannay. Hitchcock does re-
tain Buchan's theme which presents survival as dependent on
strength of will and on the ability to role-play faultlessly,
but employs it only as a sub-theme.

Rohmer and Chabrol have already isolated the transference of guilt as a consistent Hitchcockian motif, but the
transfer that takes place in The 39 Steps is not that of guilt
but that of paranoia. The belief that there are invisible
forces out there waiting to destroy you is passed, like state
secrets, from agent Annabel Smith to Hannay who, in turn,
conveys it to the girl who shares his Scottish adventures,
Pamela. This transfer can be seen quite clearly in the
visual strategies Hitchcock uses. Tight, claustrophobic
close-ups break up the integrity of space, as in the introduction to the Music Hall, and unseen forces, symbolized
by the disembodied hand firing a revolver, turn order into
chaos.

Transfer of paranoia occurs at the moment when dis-
belief turns to belief: the phone rings after Annabel's death
and when Hannay looks out the window, he sees two sinister
men in the phone booth below. Later, Pamela comes to believe Hannay's fantastic tale when she sees two men phoning
the Professor who heads "the 39 Steps." It is no accident
that point-of-view, long shots mark this transfer for now the
characters suddenly see the world in a different light. The
fragmentary pieces suddenly fit together. Ironically, it is
only when the source of terror is perceived that the terror
becomes real. Only then can characters begin to fight it.

Secret Agent (1936)

The alternating antinomies of the spy genre consist of love
and duty. This basic dramatic conflict torments secret
agents from Garbo in The Mysterious Lady and Mata Hari,
to Dietrich in Dishonored and to Julie Andrews in Darling
Lili. But it is Hitchcock, especially in Secret Agent, Notorious, and Topaz, who most rigorously explores the predicament of characters caught between their personal feelings toward one another and their professional roles as
spies.

In Secret Agent, Hitchcock's hero, Ashendon, and
heroine, Elsa, are rather poor spies, misled by their Axis
counterpart into killing an innocent man instead of their real
target. Even at the end of the film, Ashendon and Elsa
bungle their mission: it is only British bombs which kill
the much-sought-after spy and prevent valuable information
from being transported to the enemy.

The central characters' paralysis--their inability to
take decisive steps as agents--is a direct result of the con-
tradiction between the roles they must play to preserve
their cover and their feelings. Elsa is haunted by feelings
of guilt: a coin spinning in a bowl recalls the button in a
roulette wheel which "identified" the wrong man and she
faints. The film begins with the hero's "funeral," engineered by the Secret Service, and the remainder of the film
depicts his struggle to return to life, to renounce his impersonal identity as a secret agent and to yield to his feelings.

On the other hand, of course, spy films, as Hitchcock reveals here, are really metaphors for the cinema itself, whose concern for voyeurism and acting they share.

Sabotage (1936)

The definition of "sabotage" which provides the background
to the titles of Sabotage appears fairly conventional until it
gets into secondary meanings. If "sabotage" can be con-
strued as an act "which induces public uncomfortability,"
then the word describes not only the acts of secret agent
Verloc in the opening moments of the film, but also Hitchcock's cinema itself. The sequences depicting Stevie unwittingly transporting a time bomb concealed in a film can
across the crowded city of London and being delayed by

street peddlers and parades are excellent examples of cinematic sabotage for, if they do nothing else, they make the
audience extremely uncomfortable.

The explosive ending of the film, like the ending of
Blackmail (here screenwriter Charles Bennett emerges as
potential auteur), sabotages justice: the real killer, aided
by her policeman/lover, gets away with a justifiable murder
and a man, innocent of the crime but guilty of other crimes,
dies in her place. The inadequacies of civil law, however,
are compensated for by a higher morality: Hitchcock's innocent killers pay not with their lives but with their souls.
Guilt will make them and the men who come to share their
guilt forever uncomfortable.

Young and Innocent (1937)

Based on Josephine Tey's A Shilling for Candles, which it
only vaguely resembles, Young and Innocent is, according
to London Observer critic C. A. Lejeune, Hitchcock's apol-
ogy to critics and audiences horrified at his blowing up of
the young and innocent boy in his previous film, Sabotage.
Whether or not Lejeune senses a contriteness in the master's
tone, Young and Innocent does refrain from launching bird
attacks on children's birthday parties or kidnapping the young
offspring of tourists and, thus, is something of a departure
for Hitchcock.

This is not to say that the film imposes no hardships
on its youth: Robert Tisdall's innocence is subject to elaborate trial, as is the faith of Erica, the chief constable's
teenage daughter, in Tisdall. Erica is even sent to her
room for helping Tisdall, a suspected murderer, escape the
police!

Actually, Young and Innocent is one of Hitchcock's
most stunning films, sustaining visual and dramatic interest
from its close-up, melodramatic opening, to the discovery
of a dead woman's body on the beach, intercut with slow-
motion shots of screeching seagulls, to the second most
spectacular crane shot in all of Occidental cinema (the most
spectacular, of course, is the crane in to the key in Ingrid
Bergman's hand in Notorious).

A corrective to the bleakness of films like Sabotage,
Young and Innocent looks forward to the cross-country come-

dy of North by Northwest and serves as a milestone in the
evolution of the uniquely Hitchcockian genre of the comedy
thriller.

The Lady Vanishes (1938)

The Lady Vanishes is arguably the most famous English
Hitchcock and, even though it is not set in England, it is,
as a result of its isolation and analysis of English national
characteristics, the director's most British British picture.
Popularity and critical esteem, like elements in a Newtonian
physics equation, have an inverse relationship: the more
popular the film, the less seriously it is regarded. Consequently, The Lady Vanishes suffers from an unwarranted
critical disrepute.

If the film is to be taken seriously, it needs to be
seen not only as a political metaphor for Britain's relationship with a pre-war Europe threatened by fascist forces but
also as the personal, psychological odyssey of Hitchcock's
central character, Iris (Margaret Lockwood), from neurosis
(she suppresses her reluctance to return to England to marry the coldly aristocratic Sir Charles), through apparent
psychosis (she insists, against all evidence to the contrary,
that Miss Froy exists), to a kind of stable mental health
(she and Gilbert, a musicologist, uncover the conspiracy,
rescue Miss Froy, and elude Sir Charles, the source of
Iris' initial anxiety, on their arrival in London).

Miss Froy's disappearance and the subsequent substi-
tution of a double for her by the conspirators (strangely prefiguring Invasion of the Body Snatchers) clearly represent
Iris' conception of marriage to Sir Charles, to whom she is
journeying, as a loss of her own individuality (the missing
Miss Froy serving as a displacement of her own fear of
losing her identity). Hitchcock thus links the political and
the personal: Iris' initial hesitation about marriage is transformed into a larger hesitation centered on the uncanny disappearance of Miss Froy. Our heroine's sanity and the
stability of Europe both rest upon the strength of individual
will (read bulldog-like British character) in the face of an
anonymous conformity which offers a reassuring security
but which destroys the individual's will in the process.

Jamaica Inn (1939)

Hitchcock's last British picture before his departure for
Hollywood and David O. Selznick, Jamaica Inn is, like many
overly-packaged pictures, a hodge-podge of talent. Based
on a best-selling Daphne Du Maurier novel, produced by
Erich Pommer and Charles Laughton for their own Mayflow-
er Productions, and starring a theatrical, undirectable
Laughton, the film is only nominally Hitchcock's. As New
York Times reviewer Frank Nugent observes, Laughton here
"wears costume and a putty nose. No director can spot Mr.
Laughton a putty nose and still hope to lead him by it."

When Mary Yellen, the film's heroine, visits her
Aunt Patience who runs an inn on the Cornish coast, she
finds herself in a den of shipwreckers and murderers, led
by her uncle who, in turn, takes orders from Laughton's
Squire Pengallan. But it is Laughton who dominates the
film from his introduction amidst his sleepy, aristocratic
dinner guests whom he amuses by parading his latest horse
around the room to his final bow when, characteristically
referring to himself in the third person, he plunges from
the top of a ship's mast to death below, shouting, "Make
way for Pengallan!" He even gets a few words in after his
death, twice calling out for his faithful servant Chadwick,
thus adding a new dimension to the aesthetics of subjective
sound.

Stage Fright (1950)

Stage Fright reveals Hitchcock's experimentation with the
limits of point-of-view narration, taking the melodramatically distorted perspective of a character like Lina in Suspicion several steps further. While Lina merely mistakes
the intentions of her husband, believing he wishes to kill,
the narrator of the flashback with which Stage Fright begins
knowingly lies. In a novel, the truth of a third person narration is incontestable; only a character within the fiction can
lie. For this reason, all first person narratives, where the
"I" is both a narrator and a character, can be viewed as
suspect. Films like Stage Fright complicate this process
further: Jonathan Cooper, the narrator of the flashback, is
also a character within it, thus his tale should be looked at
skeptically. But the camera, which mechanically reproduces
reality, transferring reality from the things itself to its re-

production (as Bazin observes), affects our psychology of the image.   Thus we believe that the image cannot lie.   The flashback in Stage Fright gives us two narrators, Cooper and Hitchcock's camera, and both of them lie, though Hitchcock never shows Charlotte killing her husband and lies largely by omission.   But sins of omission are as deadly as those actually committed.

But if Hitchcock is occasionally a rogue, he is nonetheless an engaging one.   Besides, he was, as usual, just a bit ahead of his time in exploring the limits of narrative. Since Rashomon and Robbe-Grillet, the untrustworthy narrator in film has become a commonplace.

NOTES

1.   Robin Wood, Hitchcock's Films, Third Edition, (New
         York: A. S. Barnes, 1977), pp. 11-12.
2.   S. M. Eisenstein, Film Form, (New York: Harcourt,
         Brace & World, 1949), p. 203.
3.   Walter Sokel, The Writer in Extremis, (Stanford, 1959),
         pp. 146-147.

c. Under Capricorn: Montage Entranced by Mise-en-scène

In 1938, Alfred Hitchcock celebrated the virtues of montage in a brief polemic directed, in part, against the long take. In what is tantamount to a critical credo, Hitchcock wrote that

> if I have to shoot a long scene continuously I always feel I am losing grip on it, from a cinematic point of view. The camera, I feel, is simply standing there, hoping to catch something with a visual point to it.... The screen ought to speak its own language, freshly coined, and it can't do that unless it treats an acted scene as a piece of raw material which must be broken up, taken to bits, before it can be woven into an expressive visual pattern. [1]

Ten years later, Hitchcock becomes an equally eloquent advocate of the long take. Discussing Rope (1948), he now writes that "there's nothing like continuous action to sustain the mood of actors, particularly in a suspense story."[2] What accounts for this apparent Jekyll and Hyde transformation? Are there two--or more--Hitchcocks, one nested within the other, like Chinese boxes? In what way does this change reflect an evolution in Hitchcock's art and what are its consequences in terms of the aesthetics which inform his subsequent films?

During the first decade of his American career, Hitchcock was under contract to David O. Selznick for whom he made three pictures. Though Selznick's influence on Hitchcock has yet to be fully appreciated, it is no secret that their collaboration was less than ideal. The producer left Hitchcock alone on the set but repeatedly interfered with his script preparation, casting and post-production work. As documented in Rudy Behlmer's Memo From: David O. Selznick, Selznick vetoed Hitchcock's improvisatory initial treatment for Daphne du Maurier's Rebecca and ordered a

39

rewrite that was more faithful to the novel. [3]   The producer
himself rewrote The Paradine Case, receiving sole credit
for the screenplay, and closely supervised the production.

In retrospect, Hitchcock's project/assignments for
Selznick--Rebecca (1940), Spellbound (1945) and The Paradine
Case (1947)--stand out as more conservative in subject matter and style than not only his post-Selznick work but even
several of his other films from this period.   Hitchcock's
foray into the world of screwball comedy with Mr. and Mrs.
Smith (1941), on loan-out from Selznick to RKO, represents
an attempt to break with his popular image as "Master of
Suspense," and emerges as an iconoclastic venture which
arch-typecaster Selznick would undoubtedly never have under-
written.   Shot entirely in the enclosed space of a small
dinghy, Lifeboat (1943), made on loan-out to Fox, is an experiment that defies the conventions of commercial Hollywood
filmmaking by unnecessarily imposing technical limitations on
the production.   Yet Hitchcock's interest in problems involved
in shooting in restricted space here and later in Rope, Dial
M for Murder (1953) and Rear Window (1954) reveal an obsessive fascination with his craft that is as integral to his
art as are any of the director's thematic concerns.   Selznick's cinema and Hitchcock's meet only briefly in the melodramatics of romantic obsession; Selznick never shared
Hitchcock's fascination with the formal aspects of filmmaking.

Selznick's interference as producer, in addition to the
fact that he loaned Hitchcock out for seven pictures and made
a considerable profit in selling the director's services to others, annoyed Hitchcock, according to his friend and screenwriter Charles Bennett. [4]   As a result, when his tenure with
Selznick was over, Hitchcock turned to independent production, teaming up with an old friend from the London Film
Society days, Sidney Bernstein, who conveniently owned a
large chain of movie theaters in England.   Together they
founded Transatlantic Pictures and announced their intention
to produce three films--Under Capricorn, Rope and I Con-
fess--which were to be shot in this order and to be distri-
buted by Warner Bros. [5]   After battling for years with Selznick over scripts, casting and budgets, Hitchcock, for the
first time, exercised complete control over his own productions.   His independence during this period lends credence
to arguments that Rope and Under Capricorn (I Confess was
subsequently made for Warners after Transatlantic folded)
represent projects freely chosen and personally endorsed by
Hitchcock, that his involvement with them was more personal
than that with his Selznick pictures.

The issue is complicated by the fact that those critics
who take his work most seriously (Eric Rohmer, Claude
Chabrol, Jacques Rivette, and Jean Domarchi) consider a
film like Under Capricorn to be more "Hitchcockian" than
his previous American films while other critics, like John
Russell Taylor, whose image of him is that of a popular
entertainer, find these films less "Hitchcockian."[6]   Though
the absurdity of Hitchcock being "more" or "less" himself
in certain films is obvious--Hitchcock can never be anything
but "Hitchcockian"--the relation of Rope and Under Capricorn
to his career remains problematical. Under Capricorn, in
particular, reveals a Hitchcock with whom the general public
and the majority of critics are unfamiliar. Moreover, the
visual style of both films forces us to reevaluate our notion
of what is "Hitchcockian" and what is not.[7]

The stairway montage sequence at the end of Notorious (1946), in which Devlin (Cary Grant) rescues Alicia (Ingrid Bergman) from a den of neo-Nazis, lasts slightly more
than ninety seconds and contains, in the movement from bedroom door to front door, fifty-nine shots. Rope, shot in
continuous thousand-foot rolls, consists of nine shots, though
its intended effect is that of a single, 81-minute take. Released the year after Rope, Under Capricorn (1949) runs almost two hours yet has fewer than 170 shots. In the period
of less than three years Hitchcock seems to have completely
transformed his visual style. Yet this stylistic change is
largely superficial. There is, in essence, no change.

As early as The Lodger (1926) and Downhill (1927),
Hitchcock had synthesized the disparate stylistics of Soviet
montage and Expressionistic mise-en-scène into a finely-
balanced formula which welded suspense to character development. The nearly-total effacement of montage in Rope
and Under Capricorn lops this old balance to one side; it
calls for a reevaluation of our notion of the aesthetics within
which Hitchcock works before, during, and after these two
films. The following essay, intended as a reading of the
visual style of Under Capricorn, views these films both as
challenges to and re-affirmations of Hitchcock's other work.
They are films which synthesize montage and camera movement in an entirely new way. Instead of alternating between
montage and camera movement in separate scenes or shot
sequences (e.g., the shower murder in Psycho followed by
camera movement out from Marion's eye which re-estab-
lishes space), these films fuse them together in single shot-
sequences. Both films reveal, in their avoidance of mon-

tage, its survival/transformation within a mise-en-scène
aesthetic. ⟩

André Bazin, in a very elliptical passage in What Is
Cinema?, observes that "Rope could just as well have been
cut in the classic way whatever artistic importance may be
correctly attached to the way [Hitchcock] actually handled
it."[8] Bazin's remarks on the reel-length takes in Rope are
somewhat less enigmatic in his short career-survey of Hitchcock, reprinted in Le Cinéma de la Cruauté.[9] Here Bazin
argues that Rope, unlike Citizen Kane, only seems revolutionary in its mise-en-scène.   Whereas the use of deep focus
and long takes by Welles and Wyler contribute to the evolution of the language of cinema, Hitchcock's long takes are,
in effect, the equivalent of the classic shot breakdown of the
Thirties.   As Bazin explains, "le découpage continu de
Hitchcock reconstitue en fait le découpage classique."[10] In
other words, Hitchcock's long takes consist of a succession
of reframings and each reframing becomes a new shot.
Though each "new shot" is connected temporally and spatially to that which precedes and follows it, the continual reframing "breaks down" the action of the entire shot into a
series of successive actions which results, for Bazin, in a
camouflaged analytic découpage.   Welles and Wyler, on the
other hand, stage their actions in depth within a static
frame.   Their camera does nothing to break down the action.   As opposed to traditional analytical découpage or to
Hitchcock's continuous découpage, the "découpage in depth"
of Welles and Wyler involves a breakdown of the action not
by the filmmaker but by the viewer.   Découpage in depth,
argues Bazin, is "more realistic and at the same time more
intellectual" than analytical découpage "for it forces the
spectator to participate in the meaning of the film by distinguishing the implicit relations which the découpage no
longer displays on the screen like the pieces of a dismantled
engine."[11] Thus the shot in Rope which dolly-pans from a
close-up of one of the young killers' faces to a tight shot of
the rope used to strangle their victim and then dolly-pans
back to a reaction shot of his face is, in fact, a disguised
angle-reverse angle cut which predetermines the way the
viewer reads the scene.

Rohmer and Chabrol expand upon Bazin's contention
that Rope "is only a camouflaged classic shot breakdown,"
observing that "Hitchcock is expressing himself in the same
manner he had previously used, and would continue to use
in the future."[12] Rohmer and Chabrol, however, take issue

with Bazin when he distinguishes between Hitchcock's "perpetual succession of reframings" in Rope and the use of depth of field by Wyler and Welles. They rightly argue that the deep focus of Wyler and Welles is, in effect, "a montage spread over a surface." By this they mean that depth is illusory and that deep focus compositions actually juxtapose foreground and background on a single dimensionless surface (i. e. , the flat screen). Thus deep focus itself involves a kind of internal shot breakdown.

Bazin's concept of découpage in depth is itself problematical--especially when used as a tool for comparison of Hitchcock and Welles--in that it ignores the selectivity of the viewer's perceptual processes. In other words, deep focus is not read by the eye as deep focus but as a matrix of depth cues arranged on a flat plane. A viewer's eye will focus selectively on the foreground or on the background of a deep focus shot but cannot focus on both grounds at the same time. As Julian Hochberg points out, images are perceived not in toto but sequentially and selectively, according to certain saccadic patterns: "If an object of any size is to be seen in its entirety, the eye must move, scanning it in a succession of glances, like a flashlight probing the dark."[13] Thus Hitchcock's continuously reframing camera mimics the perceptual process. It is the static deep focus shots of Welles and Wyler which camouflage the essential subjectivity of perception, not Hitchcock's. The underlying issue involved is not so much static deep focus versus continuous reframing as the psychology of the deep focus and reframed images. And it is here that Bazin's comparison of Hitchcock and Welles is germane. The viewer senses the continuous field of a deep focus shot, even if his eye shifts from foreground to background. The viewer perceives that different objects and grounds exist simultaneously, although they can only be read successively.

Because of the limitations of the human eye which can only focus selectively, deep focus and mise-en-scène have a certain affinity with montage. Traditionally, montage and mise-en-scène are viewed as opposing aesthetics: montage fragments space; mise-en-scène preserves the integrity of space in time. (Brian Henderson's "Two Types of Film Theory" to the contrary, Bazin never opposes montage and mise-en-scène.[14] His concern is with spatial integrity. Threats to spatial integrity come less from montage per se than from close-ups and selective focus which are elements of the montage style. As Kuleshov observes, close-ups and

shallow focus make the shot more readable for the viewer
by eliminating surrounding space.) Where montage tends to
establish abstract, i. e., metaphorical, relationships between
different spaces, mise-en-scène explores continuous space.
Yet it does so by digressing, through camera movement,
from detail to detail.   In its own sequential way, it is as
analytical a device as montage.   Whether revealed through
camera movement, reframing or deep focus, relationships
remain successive.   The major difference between montage
and mise-en-scène, then, lies in the way in which space,
time, and relationships are digested: montage breaks down
the space for the viewer a priori; mise-en-scène normally
requires an a posteriori reading of relationships within a
continuous space.   I say "normally" because a shot-reading
can be predetermined by a number of factors--by composition, lighting, set design, blocking of action, actors' performances, etc.   What makes Under Capricorn a remarkable
challenge to Bazinian aesthetics is the way in which Hitchcock predigests his long takes and camera movements.
Where Wellesian mise-en-scène reflects, for Bazin, democratic antivaluation (in which no single element in the frame
has more dramatic value than another), Hitchcock's rests on
an heirarchic valuation.   Hitchcock's mise-en-scène style
predetermines, through close-ups and selective focus, the
meaning of each shot.

       But there is another, larger issue which the film ad-
dresses, and that is the nature of the relationship between
style and content.   Bazin views Hitchcock's shift to mise-
en-scène in Rope (and, presumably, in Under Capricorn) not
as a break with the director's pre-Rope aesthetic but as
"only a change of style" which "in no essential way alters
the subject matter."[15]   Bazin's comment clearly contradicts
traditional critical logic: changes in style create changes
in content.   But his statement functions as a provocative
paradox, though he hedges with the qualifying phrase "in no
essential way."   But, in point of fact, Hitchcock's changes
of style do alter what Bazin calls "the subject matter," i. e.,
the content.   It alters the way in which the dramatic content
of the shot is read by the viewer: the viewer unconsciously
senses the absence of montage and, mesmerized by the long
takes and camera movement, perceives the story through
the barrier of the stylized suppression of traditional editing
techniques which tend to naturalize the action.   The lack of
montage functions as a structuring absence which distinguishes
Under Capricorn from Hitchcock's earlier work.   The absence of montage limits the audience's involvement with the

action and characters by eliminating suspense and point-of-
view editing.   On the other hand, the long takes and camera
movement become an intrusive presence which distances the
viewer from the film's story.

Nonetheless, it is possible to argue, with Bazin, that
there is no essential change in the subject matter because,
contrary to Bazin's contention, there is no essential change
of style.   Hitchcock's use of long takes and camera movement is less a break with his pre-Rope aesthetic than an
extension of it.   His earlier use of montage and mise-en-
scène in separate sequences becomes here fully synthesized
in single shot sequences which employ montage techniques.
Hitchcock's mise-en-scène reveals that categories of style
are not absolute.   The fact is that aesthetics like montage
and mise-en-scène are contextual: they derive their meaning from the way they are used.   A long-take tracking shot
in an Ophuls film is different in look, feeling, and meaning
from one in a Mizoguchi film.   By the same token, Welles
and Murnau use similar means (expressive camera movement, set design, and spatial distortion) to achieve different
thematic goals.   In Under Capricorn, Hitchcock so transforms his long takes and camera movements that they bear
little relation to elements in a Bazinian aesthetic.   The relationship between style and content in Under Capricorn
emerges as essentially paradoxical: the more Hitchcock
changes, the more he remains the same.

                     *   *   *

The publicity surrounding the releases of Rope and Under
Capricorn emphasizes Hitchcock's innovative, long-take format, presenting it, like the use of 3-D in Dial M for Murder, as a kind of gimmick.   Under Capricorn's pressbook
features a publicity story with the following headline: "$9\frac{1}{2}$-
minute Scene, Record Take, In Warners' Technicolor Film."
With a fascination characteristic of all pressbooks for sta-
tistics and production detail, the press release explains that

> The longest individual scene ever taken by a movie
> camera in any country of the world was played by
> Ingrid Bergman and Michael Wilding in ... Under
> Capricorn. ...   The scene played $9\frac{1}{2}$ minutes, beat-
> ing by a few seconds Hitchcock's previous longest
> in Rope and was not only the longest but among
> the most difficult and moving ever filmed.   In the
> middle of it, Miss Bergman had one recital of

560 words, which is 104 words more than the
longest soliloquy in Hamlet.

(The scene referred to is Lady Henrietta's confession to
Charles Adare after their return from the Irish Society Ball
at Government House in Sydney.)

But in spite of what the publicists suggest, the use
of long takes in Under Capricorn is no gimmick. Rope
could possibly be called a "stunt" in that it is an attempt
to do something that had not been done before on the screen:
it presents the story without a break. But the long takes
find historical justification in Patrick Hamilton's play, Rope,
on which the film is based. The play rigorously observes
the dramatic unities of time and place; it is designed to be
performed on a single set without scene or act divisions.
Even if one views the 9-minute takes in Rope as somewhat
akin to durational stunts like flagpole sitting, it is nonetheless clear that his long takes in Under Capricorn are less
novelty items than they are the groundwork for a new aesthetic. Ironically, these long takes achieve that status
largely because they exist within the context of editing. Because a cut would destroy the effect of a film like Rope, it
remains a stunt. What makes Under Capricorn a truly innovative film is that Hitchcock is free to cut at any time in
the film and that, for the most part, he doesn't. There can
be no question in Under Capricorn, as there is in Rope, of
Hitchcock being manipulated by an idée fixe, of his being
forced to shoot the film in a certain way because of an obsession with the inviolability of the extended take. In this
light, the differences between the two films are instructive.
Under Capricorn does not maintain unity of time and space:
it takes place over a period of weeks, not hours, and plays
out in a variety of locations--downtown Sydney, Government
House, and Minyago Yugilla (the Flusky mansion). And unlike Rope, it is rather intricately plotted: Charles Adare,
the governor's nephew, falls in love with Henrietta, the wife
of a former convict (who is also her family's former stable
boy). Encouraged by her husband, Sam Flusky, to help cure
Henrietta of alcoholism, Adare alienates Flusky's housekeep-
er, Milly, who plots to kill Henrietta and hopes to marry
Sam. Milly's plot is exposed; Adare is accidentally shot by
Sam but clears him of any wrongdoing before himself returning to Ireland.

Similarly, Rope and Under Capricorn differ in their
handling of suspense. Deprived of suspense editing, Hitch-

cock finds a way of creating suspense in Rope by "juxtaposing" on-screen action with off-screen action; the omniscient camera reveals details, like a tell-tale rope hanging over the edge of a chest containing a body, to us before the characters themselves, entertaining guests off-screen, see them. But this sort of on-screen/off-screen suspense is virtually non-existent in Under Capricorn: it is used only in the introduction of Lady Henrietta (also referred to as "Hattie"), an off-screen event which is seen entirely in the reactions of others within the frame to her. In point of fact, Lady Henrietta's introduction is more surprise than suspense: Hitchcock's traditional suspense technique involves the fragmentation of parallel actions, not the sort of slow disclosure that occurs here. In addition to abandoning suspense, Hitchcock is forced to modify his use of point of view. Normally, he establishes point of view through a montage consisting of three shots--one of a character looking, one of what the character sees, and one of that character reacting to what he sees. In Under Capricorn's long take system, the character looking, what he or she sees, and his or her reaction exist within a single shot. Instead of seeing through the character's eyes (thus identifying with him), the viewer in Under Capricorn sees the character looking and what the character sees through another perspective, which combines voyeur and spectacle within a single shot.

By the same token, there is a certain sterility to Hitchcock's camera movements; they have beginnings and middles but no ends. With only one or two exceptions, the camera movements in Under Capricorn have no goal. Unlike the elaborate cranes in Young and Innocent and Notorious which voyeuristically search for and descend upon crucial objects (the drummer's twitching eye, the key), the camera movements in Under Capricorn do not explore space or reveal secrets within it. Yet the lack of "destination" to these camera movements functions as another structuring absence and their role is suddenly clarified when the exceptions I spoke about above are considered. There are two camera movements in the film which, like the cranes cited earlier, have goals and thus satisfy the desire of the viewer to see or discover something at the end of the shot. Both are point of view dolly-ins on shrunken heads, one occurring when a peddler tries to sell Sam Flusky a shrunken head on the streets of Sydney, another when Lady Henrietta sees a head on the edge of her bed. Both shots involve violations of the aesthetic I've been discussing; they employ a character's point of view, are preceded or followed by cuts and convey a sense of reaching a destination.

The absence of montage, of clearly-established point
of view editing and of revelatory camera movements reflects
the narrative's lack of causality, which is the film's subject.
Montage, by its very nature, forces a relationship upon shots
which, in part, determines their meaning. Whether analytical or descriptive, montage successively assembles information, often functioning, especially for analytical directors
like Hitchcock or Eisenstein, as a means of establishing
causality. Eisenstein's editing, for example, reveals the
process which underlies events and which shapes history.
One action causes another--thus the cossacks shoot--cut--a
mother falls--cut--and her fall sets in motion a baby carriage. It is a chain of events which unmasks the source of
czarist tyranny.

Under Capricorn contains no such logic. The causes
which produce what we see remain invisible. Lady Henrietta's self-destructive alcoholism and the fears which have
driven her and her husband into estrangement are suddenly--
through the dolly-in on the head--given a concrete source.
In other films, Hitchcock gives tangible form to the forces
which determine character behavior--the ring in Shadow of a
Doubt, the key in Notorious, the lighter in Strangers on a
Train, Mrs. Paradine's bedroom in The Paradine Case,
Mrs. Bates' room in Psycho. The absence of a source of
evil in Under Capricorn--or rather its suppression until the
second shot of the shrunken head--places the characters in
a kind of psychological, moral, and emotional limbo. The
fact that there is no visible source for us of evil or of Hattie's fears forces us to perceive her as hopelessly neurotic
and frustrates our expectation that she might be cured:
there is no apparent trauma to work through, no tangible
forces to fight. However, once the source of evil is identified and made public, it becomes real. The discovery of
the source of her fears enables Hattie to exorcise them.

It is worth pausing for a moment in our discussion
of long takes to consider Hitchcock's use of shrunken heads
in the film. The heads appear twice and their meaning is
partly a product of context. When Sam is offered a head by
a peddler, he pushes the man away in disgust and the peddler lashes back, calling Sam a "murderer." (Sam was
sentenced for the murder of Dermot, shielding Hattie, the
real killer). The imagery and the accusation analogically
connect the head and Sam's killing of Dermot. When Hattie
sees the head at the foot of her bed, she screams and begs
Adare to shoot it. What distinguishes the two appearances

of the heads are the different reactions to them by Sam and
Hattie. Sam violently rejects it; later when Hattie sees it,
she cannot refrain from staring at it. She is strangely
drawn to this horrible object much as she nurses the sickness within herself.

Hattie's fascination for the head is illustrated near
the film's conclusion in the slow pan from her looking at it
to the object itself. Milly appears and removes the head.
With the same fixed gaze, Hattie watches Milly prepare an
overdose of medicine for her. The connection of Milly with
the head reveals to Hattie an agency for her fears; Hitchcock suddenly abandons long takes and camera movements;
he begins cutting. The point of view cutting has the effect
of externalizing Hattie's self-hatred and locating its source
in the person of Milly. Sam's subsequent discovery of
Milly's villainy and his expulsion of her from the house become, then, important steps in Hattie's recovery process,
a process which is begun by Adare and, ironically, con-
cluded by his expulsion from Australia.

If the film's long takes and camera movements can
be said to have a paralytic quality, the cutting which occurs
in the "exorcism" sequence has a cathartic quality: the
meaning of the long takes becomes clear only in the context
of editing and of the film's overall formal pattern. Through
its limited use of editing, Under Capricorn avoids the claustrophobic irresolution of Rope and explores the vital interdependence of mise-en-scène and montage.

Before discussing the relationship between the film's
long take style and its themes, I'd like to look in detail at
its long takes and camera movements. The first long take
occurs in the office of Mr. Potter, the banker, on the
morning after Charles Adare's arrival in New South Wales.
The entire sequence is shot in one take and, though staged
in depth with bank customers in view through a window in
the background, the scene is shot with a lens of limited
focal length which blurs the background. The selective focus
throughout the film fragments one level of depth from another. At the same time, the viewer senses the unfocussed
level. Where Gregg Toland's deep focus in his Welles and
Wyler films "democratically" permits the eye to wander
within the shot (since all objects are in focus), Jack Cardiff's shallow depth of field here frustrates a reading of the
shot in depth.

Hitchcock plays with selective focus later in a most elaborately choreographed long take when Adare arrives at the Flusky mansion for dinner.   Midway through the shot, other guests begin to arrive and Adare, conversing with Mr. Rigg in the foreground, watches Flusky greet them in the background.   Instead of cutting to point of view shots of each new guest on his entry, Hitchcock uses pull focus from Adare to the new arrival and back, fusing the three separate elements of his customary point of view shot sequence into a single shot.   In this way, Hitchcock not only "suggests" Adare's point of view but directs the viewer's attention in a predetermined way, much as he would in a montage sequence.   The focus pulls, like selective focus, reveal layers of depth.   Something happens at one level of the shot and a reaction occurs, later, at another.   Though Hitchcock puts the subject and the object of perception into the same shot, they do not share the same space but rather are fragmented into different grounds.

The extended take in which these focus pulls occur has thematic significance in that it introduces us, with Adare, to the Flusky house.   The action, in which Adare eavesdrops on his host before announcing himself, identifies Adare as a voyeuristic intruder into the Flusky household, an identity which subsequent action reaffirms.   The camera, which watches Adare watching others, underscores his intrusiveness and by making the viewer conscious of the voyeuristic process, dampens our identification with him.

Adare's movements from exterior to interior, from public to private spaces in the Flusky house (culminating in his visit to Hattie's bedroom), while they convey a sense of violation, reveal the set to be unified and continuous.   But the shooting of the sequence tends to fragment that unity. Welles' camera direction, in the somewhat similar ball sequence in The Magnificent Ambersons, explores space, gradually disclosing elements within it.   The camera movements in this scene (and throughout Under Capricorn) do not so much explore the continuity of space as cut one space off from another.   The camera does not disclose; it conceals. Part of this is due, no doubt, to the claustrophobic camera distance used.   (Rope is even tighter in its framing than Under Capricorn.)   Whereas Welles tracks in medium and long shot, Hitchcock tracks in medium shot and close-up, cutting off the surrounding space from our view.   The track along the dinner table at the end of this long take is shot entirely in close-up and studies the reactions of the seated guests to Lady Henrietta's unexpected, off-screen entry. The shot ends with a tight close-up of Sam and is followed by a cut to a close-up of Lady Hattie's bare feet; it dollies back to a close-up of Sam as she moves into the dining room and puts her hands on his shoulders. Then the camera pans up to reveal her face. The tight framing in both shots denies Hattie's presence in real space; she does not relate to the objects and character around her in a physical way nor is she spatially connected to them. A being who inhabits an unseen, non-physical space, she exists in the film's space only in the reactions of others to her entry and in close-up, fragmentary glimpses of parts of her body (her feet, hands, etc.).

A similar revelation of the separate spaces which exist within the "unified" Minyago Yugilla set occurs after dinner as Flusky and Adare walk on the porch outside the house. The camera tracks with them. As they discuss Lady Hattie and walk beneath her room, the camera cranes up to reveal Hattie, totally oblivious to what is being said below, standing on her balcony directly above the men. From the image of her standing in a posture of romantic torment, the wind blowing through her hair, Hitchcock cuts back to Flusky and Adare, unaware of Hattie's presence; they continue to walk and talk. The cut (rather than another crane) underscores the tableau-like nature of her pose: the shot ends emphatically with her rather than continuing to search out the more fluid composition of the two men below. The next shot, because of the cut, gains a rhetorical force, rhyming with the previous shot. The camera tracks with the two men as they walk to the end of the porch, talk, and begin to walk back. As they continue their discussion of her problems and Flusky tells Adare that he may be able to get Hattie interested in riding again, Hitchcock cranes back up to Hattie's balcony, which is now empty. Through Hattie's bedroom window, Milly can be seen pouring her a glass of wine and Hattie's voice can be heard off-screen imploring Milly to hurry up. Though the two spaces remain separate throughout the sequence, the crane shots connecting them establish a relationship between the past, which Flusky and Adare discuss, and Hattie's present state. The second crane shot follows Flusky's request that Adare try to help Hattie with a movement which links Adare, Hattie's potential savior, with Milly, Hattie's accomplice in her attempts to destroy herself. Though both cranes connect one space with another, they also reveal the gap which separates Adare and Flusky from Hattie. The second crane functions ironically:

it reveals Milly working at cross-purposes to Adare and
Flusky.   The action in one space undercuts that in another.

This sort of fragmentation within a unified space
looks forward to the backyard set in Rear Window, which
similarly separates characters spatially in individual apartments and relates them to one another through the third
person narration of the camera movements. In Under Capricorn, the omniscient camera traces the invisible lines
which connect one space with another, functioning as a narrative presence which points out the inter-relatedness of the
film's conflicting thematic antinomies--past and present,
self-destructiveness and self-therapy, victimization and vic-
timizing, guilt and innocence, and love and hate--at the same
time that it explores the endlessly fascinating configurations
of the film's triangular conflicts among characters--those
among Adare, Flusky, and Hattie or among Adare, Flusky,
and Milly.   And implicit in the two triangles actually seen
here are two more that are not seen--that of Adare, Hattie,
and Milly and that of Flusky, Hattie, and Milly.

The film's extended takes have a static quality; they
tend to lock characters in time and space.   Nowhere is this
more in evidence than in the famous $9\frac{1}{2}$-minute take after
the governor's ball when Hattie tells Adare about her marriage to Sam and reveals the secret which binds her and Sam.
In response to Adare's plea that she leave Sam, Hattie tells
him of her romance with Sam years ago in Ireland.   As
Hattie begins to act out the past, she looks off-screen as
if at an unseen character in her tale.   As she walks past
Adare and talks of how Sam used to follow her, keeping five
respectful paces behind her, she motions with her hand for
Adare to rise and follow her, which he does.   Then, she
reenacts her elopement with Sam and her murder of her
brother, Dermot, forcing Adare, hypnotized by her story,
to act out the parts, first of Sam, then of Dermot.   The
monologue has a mesmerizing effect--the endless flow of
words, Bergman's trance-like performance and Cardiff's
fluid camera complement one another, creating and sustaining a dream-like atmosphere.   Hitchcock's style--uninter-
rupted takes--mirrors his content--uninterrupted monologue.
Sam's sudden entry, as Adare and Hattie embrace, motivates
a cut-away (to Sam) and appears to break the spell of the
past over the characters.   Yet the power of the past overrides this cut--the past uncannily begins to repeat itself.
As before, two men struggle over Hattie.   A gun goes off;
Adare, like the aristocratic Dermot, is shot by the lower

class, emancipist Sam; and Sam's accidental action leads
crown prosecutor Corrigan and the governor to arrest him
and to return him to prison.

    The circular camera and character movements during
the confession sequence trap the characters in a cyclical,
repetitive, no-exit pattern, undermining the therapeutic nature of the confession itself, much as the absence of cutting
frustrates any sense of dynamic progression toward cathar-
sis.   Hattie's confession does not absolve her guilt nor does
it erase the horror and disgust of when she lived in the
slums of New South Wales waiting for Sam's release from
prison.   Nor does her confession serve its stated purpose
of convincing Adare that she and Sam are bound by an un-
breakable bond--Sam's assumption of her guilt.   Adare
merely repeats his request that she run away with him.
The ineffectuality of Hattie's confession is reaffirmed by its
repetition; as in a nightmare, she confesses again but no one
listens.   Her attempt to save Sam from prison by publicly
confessing to the murder of Dermot results only in charges
being brought against her; Sam remains in jail for shooting
Adare.   He is saved not by Hattie's confession but by Adare's
when the latter lies about the shooting and convinces his
uncle that it was an accident.   Negating her gesture by refusing to testify, Sam tells her that they have both sacrificed
themselves for one another enough.

    For Jacques Rivette, confession operates as a form
of ritualized exchange of guilt in Hitchcock. [16]   The act of
confession transfers part of the burden of guilt to the person
who receives the confession.   Rivette explains that confession is "the liberation from a secret," which frees the mind
from memory and the soul from sin. [17]   But Rivette's analysis ignores the quality of the confessions in Under Capricorn.
Neither the characters' transferences of guilt nor their confessions are cathartic.   Flusky's assumption of Hattie's guilt
has not liberated her; in fact, it has driven her into a state
of guilt-ridden alcoholism.   Nor has the presence of Adare,
Corrigan, and the governor at her confession eased the burden of her guilt; it is clear that they in no way share her
guilt.   If a transfer of guilt takes place at all, it occurs
largely on a schematic level.   Adare and Milly become
scapegoats; their banishment functions as a displaced purga-
tion whereby Sam and Hattie divorce themselves from all
guilt.   The departure of Adare and Milly serves to restore
the couple to one another and, presumably, to their former
innocence.   The film's last scene relegates the regenerated

Hattie and Sam to figures in a flat tableau depicting happily-
ever-after marital bliss, erasing their multi-layered problems as a couple in a climax which foregrounds the complexity of Adare's feelings as he takes his leave of them.

As Fred Camper has noted, the subject of Under
Capricorn is paralysis--the moral, psychological, and sexual paralysis from which Hattie suffers. This paralysis
finds its equivalent in the static nature of the film's images. [18]
Though the same thematic concern appears in Hitchcock's
other works, its development here, because of the film's
unique visual style, is different. Under Capricorn's long
takes, which sweep the characters along in a fluid field of
objects, events, and other characters, deny them their individual wills and strip them of power, much as his montage
is stripped of its cathartic energy by its integration into extended shot sequences. In denying himself and his audience
the easy pleasure of suspense and point-of-view identification, Hitchcock's narrative style itself undergoes a kind of
expressive paralysis within which, paradoxically, it discovers a new means of articulating the film's concern with the
powerlessness engendered by guilt, fear, and despair, revealing a unique and profound enthrallment on the director's
part with his own thematic.

In terms of Hitchcock's development as an artist, the
long take experimentation of Rope and Under Capricorn signals a significant shift in the director's concerns. Hitchcock's staging of action within claustrophobic, single set
spaces results in changes in his sense of graphic design,
set decoration, and space. As Rohmer and Chabrol observe, Rope (and Under Capricorn) "contributed in no small
way to freeing the film-maker from his obsession with painting and making of him what he had been in the time of
Griffith and the pioneers--an architect. It put the set back
into a position of honor and revived the importance of the
actor's performance."[19] Settings are fragmentarily introduced in his English films through establishing shots, like
those of the Swiss Alps in The Man Who Knew Too Much or
Secret Agent, which have no geographical connection to the
subsequent action which supposedly occurs within them. But
the Sebastian house in Notorious, the killers' apartment in
Rope and Minagua Yugilla in Under Capricorn become fully
realized, dramatic spaces which the camera relentlessly
explores and which play important narrative roles in these
films. Hitchcock's increasing concern for unified dramatic
space culminates in Dial M for Murder and Rear Window, a

concern which survives these single-set films in fully articulated settings like the Bates house in Psycho.   A side-effect
of Hitchcock's long-take style was a new, revolutionary dependence upon actors, whose performances he could no longer recreate in the cutting room.   Relating to their spaces in
a way denied to them in earlier films, Hitchcock's actors
become fused with their settings.   This integration of character and setting appears most dramatically in Rebecca,
where Joan Fontaine is understood only in terms of her relation to Manderlay, and assumes major importance in the
"neo-realist" location films, Shadow of a Doubt and I Confess.   Not only are characters understood more and more
in terms of their settings, but Hitchcock also comes to rely
on certain performers--James Stewart and Cary Grant--
more than he has on other actors in the past.   During the
Fifties, Hitchcock becomes an actor's director and this shift
of interest, perhaps prompted by his new role as producer
of his own films, is most pointedly documented in his relationship with Vera Miles and "Tippi" Hedren, whom he
"discovered" and put under personal contract to him.   Though
Hitchcock still continues to manufacture performances
through editing in the Fifties, he never violates the performance that occurs within the shot.   At the same time,
he takes a greater interest in drama within the shot (rather
than in the relation of shot to shot):   the search focus shot
from Miriam's point of view as she looks for Bruno in the
amusement park in Strangers on a Train would probably
have been broken down into point-of-view and reaction shots
in a film made before Rope.

     The advent of widescreen processes in the early Fif-
ties and Hitchcock's shift to the VistaVision format enables
him to continue the exploration of space, even after abandoning the long take.   His increased interest in set design in
the Fifties, marked in part by his move from the more
modest art work of Warners to the more lavish art direction of Hal Pereira and Henry Bumstead at Paramount, coincides with the new demands for space-filling detail produced by CinemaScope and widescreen.   The fact that Vista-
Vision's wider angle-of-view results in an image which takes
longer to read, thus requiring longer takes to give the viewer time to read them, makes this obsession with space, set
design, camera movement, and long takes a logical outgrowth
of the period's technological innovations.

     Hitchcock's experimentation with the long take format
was not unusual for the era, though it was--in its ten-minute

take manifestations--characteristically compulsive.   Orson
Welles had shot a reel of Macbeth (1948) in a single take.
Even earlier films like The Life of Emile Zola (1937) and
The Letter (1940) contained four-minute takes and, as Barry
Salt points out in "Film Style and Technology in the Forties,"
average shot lengths increase "from about 8 or 9 seconds
in the late thirties ... to around 12-13 seconds in the period
1946-50."[20] The opening, extended-take shots of films like
Since You Went Away (1944) and The Big Clock (1948) are
indicative of the movement toward a long take style which
dominates mise-en-scène in the Forties.

    But the most important by-product of Rope and Under
Capricorn was their relation to the growth of lyricism in
Hitchcock's work, epitomized in films like Rear Window,
The Man Who Knew Too Much and Vertigo.   By "lyricism,"
I mean sustaining a mood, tone, or emotion in a work over
a period of time.   The most lyrical sequence in Under Capricorn, of course, is Hattie's confession, in which Hitchcock
and Bergman prolong a mood of hypnotic reverie for an entire reel of film.   Even though Hitchcock abandons the long
take format with Stage Fright (1950), he manages to sustain
moods and emotions by other means.   In Vertigo, Scottie's
voyeuristic pursuit of Madeleine around San Francisco and
its environs--a twenty-minute sequence containing little or
no dialogue and accompanied only by Bernard Herrmann's
haunting score--is filmed largely in point of view, forward
tracking shots and reverse tracking, reaction shots.   The
cutting and the staging of the action erase logical constraints:
we don't know whether Scottie is following Madeleine or
whether she is leading him. [21]   Actually, it is both.   But in
the process, logic gives way to feeling; a detective's methodical investigation gives way to confused emotional involvement, which Hitchcock sustains, through fluid camera moves
and shot transitions, throughout the first movement of the
film, which ends with Madeleine's "suicide."   In a larger
sense, the feeling of vertigo, introduced in the film's first
point of view shot, is sustained throughout this pursuit sequence.   Hitchcock inscribes the vertiginous pattern of near-
simultaneous attraction and repulsion, i.e., vertigo, into the
staging of his action and into the design of his editing,
achieving a lyricism absent from his earlier work.

    Rope and Under Capricorn, often dismissed by critics
and by Hitchcock himself as failures, are crucial to an understanding of Hitchcock's oeuvre.   Whatever we mean by
the term "Hitchcockian," it must include the "Hitchcock" of

these films, for without them it is impossible to chart his evolution as an artist.

NOTES

1. Alfred Hitchcock, "Direction," in Film: A Montage of Theories, ed. Richard Dyer MacCann, (New York: Dutton, 1966), p. 56.
2. Alfred Hitchcock, "My Most Exciting Picture," Popular Photography November 1948, p. 48.
3. Rudy Behlmer, Memo From: David O. Selznick, (New York: Avon, 1973), pp. 306-312.
4. Charles Bennett, interview with the author, Los Angeles, March 21, 1978.
5. "Under Capricorn" clippings file, n. d., Film Study Center, Museum of Modern Art.
6. John Russell Taylor, Hitch: The Life & Times of Alfred Hitchcock, (New York: Berkley Books, 1980), pp. 209-210.
7. The terms "Hitchcock" and "Hitchcockian" refer, except when used in a biographical context, to the implied author of the narratives directed by Alfred Hitchcock. Hitchcock, as Peter Wollen might argue, is a structure derived from a critical examination of certain works which a particular individual--Alfred Hitchcock --has signed.
8. André Bazin, What Is Cinema?, vol. 1, trans. Hugh Gray, (Berkeley: University of California Press, 1967), p. 50.
9. André Bazin, Le Cinéma de la Cruauté, (Paris: Flammarion, 1975), pp. 131-134.
10. Ibid., p. 134. For a discussion of the meaning of the term "découpage," i. e., "shot breakdown," see Noël Burch, Theory of Film Practice, (New York: Praeger, 1973), pp. 3-4.
11. André Bazin, Orson Welles: A Critical View, trans. Jonathan Rosenbaum, (New York: Harper & Row, 1978), p. 80.
12. Eric Rohmer and Claude Chabrol, Hitchcock: The First Forty-Four Films, trans. Stanley Hochman, (New York: Ungar, 1979), p. 95.
13. Julian E. Hochberg, Perception, (Englewood Cliffs, N. J.: Prentice-Hall, 1964), p. 25.
14. Brian Henderson, "Two Types of Film Theory," Film Quarterly 24(3):33-42, Spring 1971.
15. Bazin, What Is Cinema?, vol. 1, p. 50.

16. Rohmer and Chabrol, Hitchcock, pp. 115-116.
17. Ibid. , pp. 98-99.
18. Fred Camper, "Under Capricorn," MIT Film Society,
       March 3, 1969.
19. Rohmer and Chabrol, Hitchcock, pp. 96-97.
20. Barry Salt, "Film Style and Technology in the Forties,"
       Film Quarterly 31(1):47, Fall 1977.
21. Tim Hunter, "Alfred Hitchcock: The Mechanics of
       Clarity," The Harvard Crimson, June 12, 1968.

d. The Mechanics of Perception

In one discussion of Rear Window (1954), Alfred Hitchcock described his unique approach to cinematic narration:

> The story is told only in visual terms.... It's composed largely of Mr. Stewart as a character in one position in one room looking out onto his courtyard. So what he sees is a mental process blown up in his mind from the purely visual. It represents for me the purest form of cinema which is called montage: that is, pieces of film put together to make up an idea.

In other words, when Hitchcock cuts from a shot of L. B. Jeffries (James Stewart) looking out of the window to an insert shot (i. e., a closer shot of what he sees) of Miss Torso, the director thus represents visually the state of his protagonist's mind.

Hitchcock's use of montage and his theory of "pure cinema"--by that I mean his attempt to record, through cutting, the emotional effect of an action on a character and to transmit it to the audience by means of point-of-view identification--reflects the director's perceptual approach to cinema. In terms of "pure cinema," the core of Hitchcock's film technique consists of a stylized use of point of view and insert shots directed towards an examination of perception, i. e., the way characters see, feel and experience their surroundings. For example, in the prairie stop sequence of North by Northwest (1959), he first sets up the scene with a high-angle shot (omnisciently objective) of the bus as it drops Roger Thornhill (Cary Grant) off at the desolate crossroads. The next few cuts establish Thornhill's relationship to his surroundings (i. e., his verticality as opposed to the horizontality of the landscape is established in a series of objectively descriptive cuts). Then Hitchcock intercuts point-of-view shots (i. e., subjective shots of what Thornhill sees) with shots of Thornhill looking, knitting the point-of-

view and "looking" shots together with eye-line matches.
The dramatic impact of this scene depends largely upon his
subjective manipulation of audience identification by a suspenseful use of point of view and insert shots.   Hitchcock
presents the world as his character perceives it.

     As Hitchcock's cinema becomes "purer" and "purer,"
his treatment of point of view and perception become more
and more abstract.   In his later films, especially in The
Birds (1963) and Marnie (1964), Hitchcock's use of point of
view and insert shots becomes so abstract that the whole
film serves, as it were, as an insert shot of the world as
his characters perceive it.

     In his first few American films, Hitchcock's treat-
ment of point of view and perception functions, for the most
part, on the simple plot level.   Rebecca (1940) announces
his perceptual approach to cinematic narrative in its opening shot: a long-take, point of view tracking shot of the
mysterious Manderley is subjectively accompanied by Joan
Fontaine's voice-over narration.   More significantly, at the
first perceptual climax of the film, Hitchcock dramatically
alters the film's point of view, which has hitherto been
bound to Fontaine's perceptions, providing us with another
perspective, that of Max (Laurence Olivier):   during the
scene at the beach cottage, Hitchcock's reverse-angle cutting suddenly shifts the point of view as Max "confesses" to
Fontaine; Fontaine, formerly a dramatized narrator, now
becomes a dramatized "audience figure."   Hitchcock's development of point of view narration in Rebecca and his alteration of perception provide most of the psychological suspense upon which the action of the film is based.   In Suspicion (1941), a film that serves as a paradigm of perceptual processes for Hitchcock, Lina's (Joan Fontaine) conception of her husband--initially, as in Rebecca, an adolescent
and romantic one--deteriorates as she accumulates more
and more suspicious information about him.   The lighting
parallels this change, becoming more and more shadowy.
One might argue that the famous "glass of warm milk scene,"
in which we see her husband ascend the dimly-lit staircase
to her bedroom bringing her a potentially poisonous glass
of warm milk, represents her suspicious point of view of
him; even though the shot is not strictly a point of view
shot, her perceptions so dominate the narration of the film
that they "spill over" into shots she could not possibly see.
Lina's misperception results, as did that of the Fontaine-
character in Rebecca, in a disintegration in her relationship

with her husband and culminates in her nervous breakdown.
Here, as in The Paradine Case, Dial M for Murder, The
Wrong Man, Under Capricorn, Vertigo, and Marnie, Hitchcock, through a considered use of point of view and insert
shots, develops a disparity of perception (i. e. , the central
character perceives things differently than do the surrounding characters) which culminates in a psychological breakdown of sorts on the part of his protagonist.

The disparity of perception most obvious in Rebecca
and Suspicion finds more subtle treatment in Hitchcock's
acknowledged masterpiece of the early Forties, Shadow of a
Doubt (1943). The initial structure of the film, i. e. , the
parallel introductory shots of the two Charlies, establishes
a strong identity between the two characters which Hitchcock's treatment of perception gradually undermines. As
Charlie's perception of her uncle changes, so does her relationship with him. Their spiritual wedlock (symbolized by
the ring which he gives her and through which she shares,
both figuratively and literally, his guilt), like the marriages
in Rebecca and Suspicion, disintegrates into a spiritual and
physical estrangement. This very ring, a totemic object
much like Guy's cigarette lighter in Strangers on a Train
(1951), brings about their separation: Charlie (Teresa
Wright), threatening to use it as evidence against him,
wears it in public, thus forcing her uncle out of town.
Hitchcock, through the manipulation of objects, alters the
perceptions of his characters and traces, through an elaborate love-relationship metaphor, the "divorce" of Charlie's
perceptions from those of her uncle. His use of objects to
illustrate changes in perception marks an important addition
to the director's narrative technique and prepares the way
for his abstract treatment of objects as reflections of perceptions, which finds its culmination in the menacing machinery of North by Northwest.

In almost every Forties film, Hitchcock plays with
point of view. The Salvador Dali dream sequence in Spellbound (1945) is nothing more than an elaborately extended
point of view shot, a projection of the hero's unconscious
and its perception of an action. Together with the hero's
(Gregory Peck) traumatic, point of view flashback of his
brother's death, it provides the key to his own self-percep-
tion and to his true identity. In fact, Hitchcock often associates misperception with change in or loss of identity.
In Shadow of a Doubt, he confuses the identities of the two
Charlies; the Cary Grant characters in To Catch a Thief

(1955) and North by Northwest attempt to hide their real
identities, as do many of Hitchcock's "wrong-men-in-flight"
protagonists (e. g. , the heroes of The 39 Steps and Young
and Innocent).   Marnie intentionally changes her identity to
avoid both apprehension and confrontation with her self.
Finally, of course, there is Psycho (1960) in which one
identity becomes totally absorbed in another.

Hitchcock's own discussion of the function of montage
in Rear Window reveals an extremely complex approach to
perception and point of view in the film.   Just as the objects
(the smashed camera and the photo of a racing accident) in
Jeffries' (James Stewart) room account for his physical condition, explaining the events which led to his broken leg, so
the characters and events which he sees through his window
reflect his psychological condition; they account for the state
of his mind.   What Jeffries observes through his window reflects different aspects of his own life--most particularly,
aspects of his relationship with Lisa (Grace Kelly).   The
fact that the camera rarely leaves Jeffries' room (except at
the end when he does) reinforces this notion that the action,
seen from one, unique point of view, is a reflection of the
way Jeffries perceives his environment.   The conclusion of
the film, when Jeffries faces his perceptions dramatized in
the person of Thorwald (Raymond Burr) and struggles with
them, represents, in the abstract, a conflict of perception,
a disparity between appearances and reality.   Jeffries'
means of defense from Thorwald--the flash attachment of a
camera--illustrates his distance from reality and the artificial quality of his perception.

The narration of The Birds begins with the introduction of Melanie ('Tippi' Hedren), who then functions as an
identification figure for the audience for the remainder of
the film.   Though the film employs other points of view,
such as Mrs. Brenner's (Jessica Tandy) when she surveys
the damage done by the birds at Dan Fawcett's place, one
possible reading of the film would be that The Birds presents us with Melanie's mental projections.   The whole
world of the film, like that of the neighbors across the way
in Rear Window, can be seen as a reflection of Melanie's
state of mind and as her unconscious commentary on her
relationship with Mitch (Rod Taylor).   The world of The
Birds is the world as she sees it.   The menace and threat
of the birds, like Lina's compulsive suspicions in Suspicion,
correspond to the depth of Melanie's involvement with Mitch:
the attacks come more frequently, furiously and irrationally

(wreaking havoc on innocent neighbors and school children) as she becomes more involved with and dependent upon Mitch. The first scene in the pet store and the subsequent scenes with the caged love-birds both associate birds with her relationship with Mitch and suggest her subconscious conception of a love relationship: it is a cage, a trap. The attacks of the birds in Bodega Bay are clearly associated with Melanie (an hysterical woman in the diner even blames Melanie for the bird attacks). The first attack comes immediately after she sees Mitch waiting for her on the dock; in fact, the gull swipes her right after we see her point of view shot of Mitch. If one views the birds in terms of Melanie's perception, the suspenseful scene in which the birds attack the Brenner house, while Melanie and the Brenners huddle in corners inside, functions, like the demons in Forbidden Planet (1956) and Curse of the Demon (1958), as a projection of her psychological state upon external events. This view of the birds as furies born in Melanie's mind is supported by the way in which much of the scene is shot: the birds are heard but, for the most part, are not seen. They thus owe their existence to certain mental processes, i. e., we, like Melanie and the Brenners, construe their existence from the abstract noises on the soundtrack.

The climax of the film--Melanie's ascent to the upstairs bedroom and her fight with the birds--works as a visual representation of her mental breakdown and marks a complete disintegration, on her part at least, in her relationship with Mitch: rescued and regaining consciousness, Melanie fights Mitch off as if he were a bird. Melanie's emotional and physical collapse strangely coincides with the quiet roosting of the birds who, for the moment, cease hostilities. This subsiding of the birds enables Melanie and the Brenners to escape.

The Birds is one of Hitchcock's most abstract works. The extreme technical artificiality of the film, e. g., the use of back projection and process shots which give the birds themselves an eerie, unreal quality, situates the action in a quasi-make-believe context. This artificiality reinforces a perceptual interpretation of the action, suggesting that the film represents mental rather than natural processes.

Marnie, though perhaps less total in its restriction to one character's point of view, treats thematic material

similar to that in The Birds.   The stylized use of back projection, miniatures, settings, and color suggest that the
world of the film is a reflection of the world as Marnie
perceives it.   The red suffusions, for example, which color
the image at moments of crisis for Marnie reflect, like the
process shots in The Birds, the inward state of the protagonist's mind, projecting that state upon the surface of reality.   The painted backdrop of the ship which looms threaten-
ingly at the far end of Marnie's mother's street and the
back projection which accompanies, as Robin Wood has
shown, almost all her movements symbolize the superficiality of her world and her imprisonment in that world: her
world is deprived of depth nor is there any possibility of
real movement through it.   Through a nightmarish reper-
ception of the traumatic event which crippled Marnie's perceptions, Hitchcock adds more depth to her world.   She
finally comes to understand her mother's point of view and
gains a new perspective on herself.   But the shock that accompanies this new perception paralyzes Marnie.   And, although the last scene, in which Marnie and Mark (Sean
Connery) leave the grip of the past, dramatically expands
the depth of Marnie's world, the high-angle shot which observes their departure suggests that her ultimate escape
from her perceptual prison seems unlikely.

e.   The Perversity of Topaz

Unlike the complicated spy syndrome of Leon Uris' bestsell-
ing potboiler on which the film is based, Alfred Hitchcock's
Topaz presents a mechanized world of plastic precision and
coldly geometric composition in which characters sacrifice
individual emotion to patriotic devotion and personal sentiment to political sentimentality.   The perverse pessimism
of Hitchcock's unconventional vision consists primarily in
the profoundly disturbing ambiguity which threatens to plunge
the superficial order of almost every character and every
scene in Topaz into utter chaos.

    The basis of Hitchcock's perversity lies in his satan-
ically manipulative treatment of audience-identification.   In
Topaz, as in Rear Window, Vertigo, Psycho, and Torn Curtain, he forces his audience, by means of point-of-view and
insert shots, to identify with morally ambiguous characters.
In Topaz, for example, the direct and indirect consequences
of the espionage of Hitchcock's hero, André Devereaux
(Frederick Stafford), are disastrous--the political assassina-
tions of two sympathetic characters, the suicide of one, the
torture of another man and his wife, the estrangement of
Devereaux's own wife who is driven into adultery, and the
involvement of his son-in-law in an escapade that nearly
costs the young man his life.

    The moral scheme of this international spy saga
(which concerns the Cuban missile crisis and a group of
high-level Russian secret agents who have infiltrated the
French government) is so complex that it becomes impossible to tell the good spies from the bad spies without a
scorecard.   Even the alignment of specific characters behind specific flags doesn't always untangle the film's complex moral patterns.   For instance, the parallel opening
shots of the Russian and American embassies--in which a
sinister face reflected in a mirror of the bad guys' em-
bassy is visually equated to that of good-guy, CIA agent
Mike Nordstrom (John Forsythe) in the American embassy--

blur moral distinctions between the two flags, embassies,
and agents. Similarly, when Nordstrom tells the daughter
of the Russian defector that he and his men "will be waiting
outside" to assist them, Hitchcock immediately cuts to a
shot of the Russian security guard waiting outside the door
to the room in which the girl is making the call.

The perceptual ambiguity of Hitchcock's treatment of
characterization carries over into his equivocal approach to
objects. For example, gifts which seemingly represent
friendship and love are revealed as, in reality, tools for
destruction and espionage. The defector Kusenov (Per-Axel
Arosenius) tells the CIA that the Russian technicians in
Cuba "came bearing gifts"--gifts which prove to be nuclear
missiles. Mike Nordstrom's offer of flowers to Devereaux
and his wife on their arrival in New York becomes an ex-
cuse for enlisting Devereaux's assistance in another spy
mission. That very mission, which leads to a Harlem flower shop in which a funeral wreath is being prepared, further
qualifies the apparent innocence of the original gift of flowers. Devereaux's gift to his Cuban mistress and agent,
Juanita (Karin Dor), contains, in addition to a genuine love
gift, electronic surveillance equipment. Similarly, her
farewell present to him--a book inscribed "from Juanita
with love"--contains vital photographs of secret missile in-
stallations in Cuba.

Hitchcock's characters consistently sacrifice affection
for political necessity. In the suspense-filled opening de-
fection sequence, when Kusenov's daughter eludes a Russian
agent in a Danish china shop, her actions are ambiguously
destructive. When she picks up and looks at a set of porce-
lain lovers, she hesitates briefly; but the necessity of her
situation (duty) overcomes sentiment (the love represented
in the figurine); she deliberately smashes the piece of porce-
lain, using the action to facilitate her escape.

The same sort of momentary hesitation, reminiscent
of this earlier scene but colored by a deeper romantic re-
morse, occurs when Devereaux, having just read Juanita's
inscription in the book she gave him and having just learned
of her death, sadly turns his head to look out of the window
of the plane on which he is fleeing Cuba. He momentarily
seems to regret the disastrous consequences of his role in
the emotionless world of espionage. But he, like the Russian girl, puts aside romantic consideration and returns to
the necessity of his occupation, discovering the film which
Juanita had concealed in the book.

Although Hitchcock uses audience identification techniques in Topaz, the episodic nature of the story, the multiplicity of major characters and the moral-emotional ambiguity of his protagonists distinguishes this film from his more linear, character-centered narratives of the early Sixties, such as Psycho, The Birds and Marnie. However, the emotional distancing, alienation, or, to phrase it more positively, the audience's semi-identification with Michael Armstrong (Paul Newman) in the last half of Torn Curtain (1966)--in which the audience remains painfully aware of Armstrong's amateurish clumsiness (e.g., the grotesque murder of Gromek who is stabbed, strangled, and gassed) and egocentric destructiveness--operates throughout Topaz. Hitchcock's undermining of moral distinctions frustrates the audience's identification with the film's characters. As the film progresses, it becomes more and more difficult to distinguish between heroes and villains. For example, John Vernon's Rico Parra, like Claude Rains's Alex Sebastian in Notorious (1946), becomes, as a lover used by the heroine then jilted, a highly sympathetic figure, as do the nominally villainous Frenchmen Jarré (Philippe Noiret) and Granville (Michel Piccoli), by the end of the picture. As the villains become more and more attractive, the heroes become more and more sinister. The world of Hitchcock's film blurs all distinction between good and evil, between black and white; grey becomes the dominant moral color.

In spite of its seeming lack of structure, Topaz emerges as a highly-crafted work. Its basic pattern, like Torn Curtain, but unlike linearly climactic films such as North by Northwest, is circular. The credit sequence, shown against a Moscow May Day parade of men and machines, establishes both the thematic and stylistic concerns of the entire film: a parade of characters, events, places, problems, and situations which comes full circle--both visually and narratively--in the "Hollywood" montage which reprises and links, through fluid dissolves, the film's characters and events which are, in turn, superimposed over a newspaper headline announcing the end of the missile crisis at the end of the film.

If the film begins and ends with a parade, it, at the same time, centers upon the tragedy of individuals who try to escape that parade. Kusenov, who opens the film with a dramatic escape from the parade (the titles during the credit sequence describe him as a man who disagrees with his country's show of force and what it threatens, making his

escape implicitly an escape from the May Day parade we
are witnessing) ultimately joins another, almost indistinguish-
able parade through his complicity with the CIA to whom he
gives information in exchange for asylum.   Kusenov's sensitivity, which Hitchcock carefully develops both directly
through insert shots showing the defector's interest in porce-
lain and indirectly through his daughter's charm and talent
as a classical pianist coupled with Kusenov's initial refusal
to give information to the CIA, makes him a highly sympathetic figure.   But Kusenov's tragi-comic adaptability,
which surfaces in the coffee-pouring sequence near the end
of the picture, casts an uncertain shadow on his earlier
heroic, individualistic stance, and reduces his sensitivity to
handling coffee cups and admiring sunsets.   Significantly, what
he has to say to Devereaux at this point carries no weight.

At the literal and figurative center of this circular
film stand Rico Parra and Juanita.   They live, like the
earlier Kusenov, by a code of individuality and emotionality
that poses a threat to impersonal international intrigue,
politics, and the parade psychology in general.   They are
romantics.   The freedom implied in the disorder of Parra's
room in the Hotel Theresa marks out his personality in particular and that of the revolutionaries in general as a visual
contrast to the neatness and order of espionage (compare
the immaculate setting of Devereaux's home).

Even Hitchcock's shooting style during the central
Cuban sequence reflects a romantic mood: long takes,
sweeping camera movements and a noticeable lack of dynamic montage dominate the style.   Moreover, the lighting
and the colors suddenly become warmly romantic--the hot
colors (red and purple) of Juanita's dresses mark a departure
from the drab colors worn by females in other scenes.

The precision of the editing, which gives Topaz a
fast pace; the framing, which carefully balances opposing
figures in a complex moral scheme; and the striking perpendicular compositions, which dramatically set off groups
of twos and threes at ninety degree angles to one another,
reinforce the mechanization of action and affection which
ultimately dominate the film.   A work whose content and
structure suggest the inevitable frustration of both physical
action and emotional involvement, Topaz explores an inferno
of espionage which cripples the emotions of those who inhabit
it and which perversely undercuts the mythically heroic stature of its heroes, who lose their emotions in the machinery
of politics.

f.   Frenzy and the Aesthetics of Paralysis

Hitchcock's films have rarely been praised upon their initial
appearance.   In fact, American critical opinion, excepting
Andrew Sarris, is vituperatively anti-Hitchcockian.   When
Psycho, now an undisputed classic, first came out over
twenty years ago, Bosley Crowther, New York Times critic,
panned it.   But the film's tremendous commercial success
forced Crowther to look at it again, and Psycho ended up on
that critic's ten-best list at the end of the year.   Similarly,
Marnie (1964), a film which disappointed even a Hitchcock
enthusiast like Sarris who labelled it a "failure" on its release, has proven itself, on repeated viewings over the
years, to be one of Hitchcock's greatest films and is even
considered by some to be the director's best work.

It is not only important but it is also pleasurable to
look at Hitchcock's films again and again.   In attempting to
come to terms with Hitchcock, it is crucial for us to laugh
at the ironic wit of Psycho's screenplay on viewing it for
the second time and to experience, from a different point
of view, the strange fascination that Scottie Ferguson (James
Stewart) has for the Madeleine/Carlotta/Judy character (Kim
Novak) in Vertigo.   Similarly, it is a rich and strange experience to look back over Hitchcock's career from the vantage point of one of his last films.   It is possible not only
to see new ideas and themes emerge and grow but also to
appreciate the variety of his work and the ultimate uniqueness of each of his films.

All of the critical attention focused on Hitchcock in
the Sixties--especially the enormously popular Truffaut in-
terview--forced the director to confront and acknowledge,
quite publicly, a number of his themes.   After the Eric
Rohmer and Claude Chabrol book in the late Fifties, the
"exchange of guilt" theme became a critical cliché which
even Hitchcock saw as such and avoided in his subsequent
films.   After Robin Wood's book extolling the stylized use
of back projection in Marnie (a stylization which many other

critics, including Hitchcock himself, deemed sloppy crafts-
manship on the part of Universal's technicians), the director's reliance upon back projection and special effects gave
way to the more naturalistic location backgrounds and effects
of (most of) Torn Curtain, Topaz, Frenzy and Family Plot.
At the same time, Hitchcock's work became less subjective.
Where formerly he involved his audiences in the subjective
perceptions of a central character (as in Rebecca, Suspicion,
Rear Window, Vertigo, and other films) through a use of
point of view and insert shots, since the Sixties (as in the
second half of Torn Curtain and in all of Topaz, Frenzy,
and Family Plot) Hitchcock approached his characters more
objectively. Though still sympathetic towards them, he now
regarded them from a distance and rarely established identification with them; the effect is to frustrate his audience's
sympathy with these de-romanticized central characters.

Though a film like Frenzy (1972), with its unique
blend of horror and humor, preserves the traditional image
of Hitchcock as an ironic and macabre storyteller (an image
that looks back to the narrative voice of Psycho), Frenzy
differs from Psycho in its self-conscious reflectiveness. In
Frenzy, Hitchcock carefully calculates his effects and then,
as in the potato-truck sequence, brilliantly pushes them beyond traditional aesthetic limits. As a result, Frenzy's
horror is more grotesque than that in any other Hitchcock
film; its humor blacker and more perverse.

At the same time, the film retrospectively comments
on practically every one of the director's fifty-one previous
features, reworking old themes and situations in entirely
new ways. In contrast to the warm romanticism and rich,
major characterization of Hitchcock's Forties, Fifties, and
early Sixties films, the absence of a central romantic relationship in Frenzy and the cold precision of its shooting
suggest an objective reexamination of the director's earlier,
romantic involvement with his material. Where Hitchcock's
earlier films dealt with interiors, with the moral complex-
ities of certain relationships, psychological motivation and
the subjectivity of perception, Frenzy, in its observation of
behavior, is a film of exteriors and surfaces. Yet its concern for detail and its abundant assortment of engaging
minor characters give the film's stylistically detached surface a highly articulated background. In effect, the film
resembles a translucent sheet of ice exquisitely flawed with
swirls, air bubbles, and crystalline flecks.

In spite of Hitchcock's critical self-consciousness in
the Seventies, certain themes and situations recur in his
work from the first, The Pleasure Garden (1925) to the last,
Family Plot (1976). The thematic situation that most frequently shapes these narratives is an interest in the psychological, moral and emotional paralysis of his central characters. Images of powerlessness, passivity, and paralysis
fill Hitchcock's films; the most literal examples appearing
in Rear Window (1954) and The Wrong Man (1957). Recuperating from an accident in which his leg was broken, photographer L. B. Jeffries (James Stewart) thinks that a murder
has been committed by one of his neighbors and, with the
help of some friends, tries to solve it. Jeffries' confinement in the room, which limits his experiences to a voyeuristic level, culminates in a moment of total helplessness
when Jeffries sees the suspected murderer return to his
apartment and find Lisa (Grace Kelly), his girl friend, there
looking for clues. Throughout the scene and later when the
murderer confronts Jeffries in his own apartment, Hitchcock
concentrates on Jeffries' physical powerlessness: both
scenes symbolize the larger, more universal sort of paralysis that Hitchcock finds in the personalities of almost all
his characters.

Often the inability of Hitchcock's characters to function normally has its roots in some past event. Marnie's
traumatic experience as a child, re-invoked by encounters
with certain colors and things in her adult environment,
haunt her and make her powerless. In Psycho (1960), the
past, symbolized by the looming, Victorian, Bates house
in which time has stopped, overwhelms the present, seen
in the modern, ranch-style motel.

Or paralysis can have no source. In The Birds,
Melanie becomes trapped in a telephone booth when a flock
of birds attack Bodega Bay. Later, at the Brenner house,
she gets caught in a roomful of savage birds where her unconscious body, propped against the door, hinders her rescue. Yet none of the terrifying scenes of entrapment in
The Birds can equal the traumatic arrest and imprisonment
of the innocent Manny Balestrero (Henry Fonda) in The
Wrong Man. The film opens with shots of the routine of
Manny's life--leaving work as a musician at the Stork Club,
his ride home to Queens on the subway, his regular snack
at an all-night cafeteria. At home, Manny takes in the
milk, looks in on his two boys who are asleep and enters
his own room to find his wife awake because of a toothache.

The next day, when Manny is mistaken for a robber, the
ritualistic, pseudo-documentary quality of the film's opening
(i. e. the return home from work) is transformed into the
nightmarish routine of police pick-up, interrogation, and
identification which takes him further and further away from
home. Manny becomes a powerless prisoner of this coldly
methodical process as he is driven around Queens from
liquor store to delicatessen, paraded before robbery victims, escorted from one anonymous room to another in the
police station, requestioned, booked, and fingerprinted. An
overall pattern of progressively impersonal, progressively
confining routines emerges, beginning with the shots of him
leaving the Stork Club framed briefly between two policemen,
leading to the shots of Manny (seen through tellers' bars) at
the insurance company and climaxed by his actual imprisonment in a jail cell.

Another sort of entrapment that appears in Hitchcock
films takes place on a more psychological, more moral
level. In Strangers on a Train and I Confess, murderers
force innocent men into silent complicity with their crimes.
In Strangers, the innocent man's (Guy's) indirect responsibility for the crime and his relationship with the murderer
prevent him, even though he is actually innocent of the
crime, from going to the police. The moral premise of
the film, as screenwriter Raymond Chandler notes, is that
"if you shake hands with a maniac, you may have sold your
soul to the devil." This "exchange-of-guilt" paralysis operates with even greater complexity in I Confess in which a
priest hears the confession of a murderer, is then suspected
of the crime himself and is unable to clear himself. Ironically, since the murdered man was blackmailing the priest,
the priest has a motive for killing him. The added complexity of I Confess hinges on a point of religious law--the in-
violable secrecy of what is heard in confession. The
priest's sense of personal guilt, like that of the innocent
man in Strangers, implicates him indirectly in the crime
and, at the same time, the seal of confession prevents him
from proving his innocence. For the greater part of the
picture, the priest is seen as a passive figure, made powerless by his religion and his guilt. The source of paralysis
in both films lies in the paradoxical logic of Hitchcock's
Catholic equation of real and venial sin--an equation which
grows out of a belief in the universality of human guilt
(Original Sin). Hitchcock's vision of a post-lapsarian universe inhabited by flawed, fallen characters makes their
paralysis--no matter what form it takes--a metaphor for

man's powerlessness and hopeless imperfectibility in the
face of a larger, more perfect order.

Frenzy is a more difficult film to understand. Its
characters, though as powerless and helpless as those in
any other Hitchcock film, are less obviously "paralyzed" in
the traditional sense, i. e. , by passive voyeurism, moral
dilemmas, the past. For example, Hitchcock's introduction
of Blaney (Jon Finch)--a cut from the discovery of a neck-
tie murder to a shot of Blaney reflected in a mirror, tying
his tie--links him less to the murders or to actual guilt for
them than to a scheme of events and a pattern of logic that
coincides with that of the real murderer (the presence of
the mirror and reflected image make this clear on second
viewing). What makes Blaney seem like a murderer, first
to us, then to the police, is his behavior. His early-morn-
ing brandies, his uncontrollable temper, his anger, his
cynically bleak wit--in short, the general abnormality of his
behavior work to convict him of murder.

Not only Blaney but Rusk (Barry Foster), the sexual
psychopath, seems a victim of his own character, paralyzed
by invisible, inarticulated flaws in his personality. Unlike
Hitchcock's earlier killers (Keller in I Confess, Bruno in
Strangers on a Train, Bates in Psycho), "Uncle Bob" Rusk
remains a mystery; he neither exercises any control over
nor seems to understand his actions. Though we meet his
mother and enter his room twice, nothing we see adequately
explains his craziness. Unlike the early, more psychological Hitchcock, Frenzy doesn't specify the source of its
characters' paralysis. Because Frenzy eliminates this notion of psychological causality it is one of Hitchcock's bleakest, most enigmatic, most chaotically irrational films.

In his earlier work, Hitchcock views his characters
both objectively and subjectively, simultaneously looking at
them from the outside and the inside. (Stylistically, this
roughly corresponds to Hitchcock's idea of pure cinema:
reaction shots which surround insert or point of view shots).
In other words, he suggests the source of paralysis by
means of details in the psychological make-up of his characters (subjective), but the paralysis itself surfaces in the
characters' inability to function in their environment (objective). Hitchcock's narrative style in Frenzy, ironically detached from but also sympathetic towards his characters,
concentrates less on interior motivation than external behavior. The complexity of the film comes from his juxta-

position of three, distinct behavioral patterns--that of Blaney, Rusk and Inspector Oxford--each with its own logic and
mood.   The last scene in the film, a resolution of sorts,
locks these three separate threads together in the same
frame.   Yet the frozenness of each character in space undercuts the feeling of resolution with a disjointedness.   We
remain outside the triangle of characters, unaware of what
they are thinking and unable to fully understand what forces
have brought them together.

2. From Distant Observers: Chabrol, Mulligan, and Mizoguchi

Chabrol, Mulligan and Mizoguchi represent three quite different cultures yet share a common concern for stylization and for narrative distance. Chabrol's work reflects the fascination of the French auteurists at Cahiers in the Fifties for style and for the American cinema's greatest stylists. Mulligan constructs a narrative consciousness through which his characters and stories are filtered. Like Chabrol, Mulligan takes more interest in the telling of the tale than in the tale itself. Mizoguchi's visual style, though more Occidental than Ozu's, is nonetheless alien. Mizoguchi establishes a distance between subject matter and narrator that allies him more closely to the ironic stances of Ford and Ophuls than to the naïve world views of Griffith and Borzage.

a. Le Boucher

Until recently, Claude Chabrol was one of the least understood, least appreciated, most underrated of the French New Wave directors. His best early films, Les Bonnes Femmes, L'Oeil du Malin (released here as The Third Lover), and Le Scandale (The Champagne Murders), were brutal, ugly, and relentlessly perverse; and, because of this, the weird, often cruel beauty of Chabrol's vision went unnoticed.

The present revival of interest in Chabrol--marked by the appearance of the director and his films at international film festivals and the more or less regular, though slow, distribution of his recent work in this country--dates from the appearance of Les Biches in 1968 and of its equally successful successors: La Femme Infidèle (1968), Que La Bête Meure (This Man Must Die, 1969), and Le Boucher (1969). Chabrol's new-found popularity stems partly from the rise to stardom of Stephane Audran, the director's leading lady and wife, partly from a happy collaboration with his new producer, André Génovès, and from an apparent softening of Chabrol's bleak view of the world, making his unusually perverse aesthetic more palatable to the general public.

Chabrol's latest films, especially Le Boucher, though less total in their perversity and less coldly satiric than his earlier work, attain, because of the warmth and humanity, a greater complexity than ever before.

The plot of Le Boucher, abandoning the Langian narrative structure of Que La Bête Meure for a more traditional suspense melodrama, takes the form of a double action: 1) a charmingly innocent love relationship grows between a country schoolteacher, Mlle. Hélène (Stephane Audran), and the village butcher, Popaul (Jean Yanne), drawn to each other by virtue of their mutual estrangement from the rest of the village; and, independent of this, 2) a mysterious series of unsolved, brutal, irrational murders of young women occurs in the neighborhood.

77

Chabrol's approach to his plot and his characters is
tremendously ambivalent.   The love relationship--Mlle.
Hélène's reaction to it, in particular--revels in melodrama.
At the same time, it is pure amour fou.   The murder mystery, a grotesque counterpoint to the love story, becomes a
device, for Chabrol, that both ties his characters together
and holds them apart.   When a cigarette lighter, originally
a sort of love gift from Mlle. Hélène to Popaul, is found by
Mlle. Hélène at the scene of a murder implicating Popaul
and she conceals her discovery from the police, the two
narrative threads intersect, providing the film's central
moral/emotional dilemma.   Hélène becomes bound more
closely to Popaul by what she knows or suspects and, at
the same time, her fear and horror of what Popaul seems
to have done separates her from him.

The same sort of ambiguous, love-hate relationship
that arises between the characters also underlies Chabrol's
treatment of them.   By drawing attention to each character's
limitations--e. g. , Mlle. Hélène's fear of emotional involvement, Popaul's voyeuristic attachment to and child-like dependence upon her, Chabrol thwarts his audience's attempts
at total identification with them.   Yet, by also drawing attention to their essential humanity and to their real, almost
edenic innocence, Chabrol partially involves our emotions
with them.   In effect, Chabrol is coldly critical of his characters, yet also strangely sympathetic towards them.   It is
the double-edged vision of brutality and compassion that
makes Chabrol one of the most complex and most modern
of artists.

The Film's Compositions

Chabrol's visual style also reflects this ambivalent, double
vision.   His sparce, simply constructed, two-dimensional
compositions arouse, through their simplicity, intensely
complex emotions.   Each object in his frames fights with
each other for control of the frame.   Objects, for instance,
frequently obscure one another.   In one shot of the bride
and groom, flowers blot out the bride's face.   Or in the
slow tracking shot in the woods that partially circles around
Mlle. Hélène and Popaul, a tree in the foreground briefly
obscures first one, then the other.   Yet one object, character, or part of the frame never completely overpowers
another.   What interests Chabrol is not the physical supremacy of one object over the other, but rather the psycho-

logical aspects of their interaction.   For example, when
Mlle. Hélène gives Popaul the lighter, Chabrol cuts to a
close-up of the lighter as Popaul first lights it, with Mlle.
Hélène's out-of-focus face filling the background.   Chabrol
creates a conflict between the two objects for our attention.
Do we look at her only? or at it?   Clearly Chabrol wants
us to look at them both singly and in their interaction.
What affects us is not one or the other, but the combination.   As a result, our feelings about them become a synthesis of two distinct, often contradictory feelings.   The
result is total ambiguity.   Everything in Chabrol's frames
becomes ambiguous, unascertainable, and impenetrable.
The objects and elements of Chabrol's frames become reflections of things, surfaces of reality upon which we project our own perceptions.   Consequently, each action has
more than one meaning; each event becomes ambiguous.
Faced with this ambiguity of objects and actions, we try
to distinguish between objects and to judge actions.   As a
result, Chabrol elicits our moral involvement and engages
our moral point of view.

Chabrol's images are, essentially, self-critical.
They call into question the elements and the nature of the
composition itself.   For Chabrol, the existence of two or
more objects, of two or more ways of perceiving things,
makes real knowledge impossible, makes truth relative and
ultimately incomprehensible.

Chabrol's images--even the pastoral ones of the
countryside--are really masks which obscure the possibility
of understanding anything.   They are elaborate, beautifully
designed surfaces that conceal real feelings.   Though the
images themselves mask feeling, the director's emotional
involvement with his images, seen in his selection of them,
the way he chooses to shoot and edit them, betrays the fact
that feelings do lie beneath these surfaces and masks, that
feelings do exist in his world.

Chabrol works with a number of dialectics in his
films in order to evoke these emotions in his viewers.   The
image of the police (background) and the school children
(foreground) thrusts guilt (the presence of police) and innocence (children) into the same frame.   On a larger scale,
this is similar to the overall shape of the film which sets
the two unusual and, at times, abnormal lovers against a
normal, uncomplicated background of village ritual, small
talk, and routine.   Often, the frame's ambiguity is concen-

trated into a single object or shot. For example, Chabrol's
treatment of the lovers towards the end unites the film's
ambiguities into a single image. When we see them, we
perceive them in two ways: Popaul is both lover and killer,
Mlle. Hélène is both lover and potential victim. (And ironically, she is also his killer.) Both perceptions of each
character exist in our minds simultaneously; each is equally
valid and true; one does not overwhelm the other.

The compositional balance of the images changes as
the film progresses. At the start, they are light and orderly. The presence of the village, the villagers, and the
children gives stability to the frames; they give us a sense
that order, sanity, normality, and the forces of control are
in command, or, if not actually in command, at least present as a mitigating force. During the film, this background of normality gradually disappears, leaving the two
central characters alone in a chaotic world of their own.
In the film's most terrifying sequence in the dark, empty
schoolroom, the darkness of the images now reveals that
the original balance of power has been inverted. Irrational
forces, as in the sequence at the end of Rear Window in
Jeffries' dark apartment, are in control.

What Chabrol is working towards here is a climactic
explosion of the film's ambiguities: Popaul's double confession of crime and of love, and his self-destruction. After
a brief, almost cathartic moment of irrationality and chaos,
order returns. Mlle. Hélène, previously frozen with fear,
regains control. Switching on the lights, she restores order
somewhat to the frames. She extracts the knife, helps
Popaul to her car, and drives him through the night to the
hospital.

But this return to order is an ambiguous one. After
Popaul's death, Mlle. Hélène does not go back to the school
house, but instead stands alone at the edge of the river,
looking blankly into space and apparently paralyzed by her
experiences. Chabrol first cuts in to her to reveal the ambiguous emptiness of her mask-like expression. Then he
cuts away from her, in three shots of increasing distance,
to a long shot which obscures her in the river's mist. We
are left with a sense of her loss, complicated by her inability to express it. She and her feelings remain locked within
the impenetrable surface of the larger, foggy countryside.

The Limits of Chabrol's Universe

Claude Chabrol's Le Boucher explores the possibility/impossibility of love in a morally fatalistic universe. Working within the conventional context of a suspense thriller, the director creates a world limited by its characters' own perceptions and a love relationship restricted by the imperfect nature of that world.

Nevertheless, Chabrol's sympathetic direction of the story permits his characters a range of emotional expression--although not articulated and tragically unrealized--that makes their frustrated love affair strangely beautiful. The director develops this love relationship on two levels: first, through the use of genre and genre material to define the ambivalent nature of their love and, second, through an infusion of uniquely Chabrolian, moral elements to investigate the impossibility of his characters' redemption through love.

Le Boucher's use of a suppressed thriller format and its repeated references to Hitchcock continue a New Wave tradition of filmic film criticism. But Chabrol's formalism is never forced; he uses Hitchcockian elements because they belong, naturally, to the genre. And he uses a thriller structure because it best describes the relationship between his two central characters. In this respect, Le Boucher is more than a film about film, for Chabrol's characters have a real life of their own; they have a relationship outside of the superficial one given them by the conventional aspects of the story.

Chabrol's characters transcend convention in their attempts to escape the very patterns of expectation it thrusts upon their lives. When Mlle. Hélène for example, goes into a yogic trance after discovering the murdered girl, her action seems to reflect her desire to disengage herself from the consequences of the plot (the police ringing the doorbell downstairs). Similarly, the "liberating" LSD sequence at the end of La Rupture--especially when Stephane Audran stands in a tableaux with three old ladies over the body of her dead husband--allows her to avoid coming to terms with the consequences of the film's plot.

If Chabrol's films have had any flaw in the past, it has been their overly schematic formalism--like the use of the Hamlet motif in Ophelia which is ultimately too powerful an analogy for Chabrol's own melodrama to overcome. But

in Le Boucher, the formalistic aspects of the plot (thriller
convention) actually serve the thematic interests of the film's
love story.   What's most important in Le Boucher, as with
Yvan in Ophelia and Jacqueline in Les Bonnes Femmes, is
that the central character imposes a romanticized thriller
perception upon her relationship and, by willing it so, forces
her affair (and the film) to its tragic conclusion--for instance, Hélène's overelaborate frenzy to bolt all the doors
when Popaul comes to her house seems to force their final
confrontation as the natural consequence of a melodramatic
thriller.

Not only Chabrol's use of the thriller genre but also
his references to Hitchcock have more than a schematic
function; they help define the complexity of the central love
relationship.   The painting scene in Le Boucher, for example, invokes a similar scene in I Confess in which Logan
and Keller paint a room in the rectory.   The scene in Le
Boucher has the same visual and thematic effect as that in
I Confess: a fresh layer of paint covers over the past, and
the action becomes symbolic of a sort of moral purification
or attempt at moral purification.   Specifically, it represents
an attempt by Hélène and Popaul to return their relationship
to the comparative calm and innocence it had had after the
scene in the woods, despite all that has come in between.
On a visual level, the painting over of the past clearly reflects the redemptive potential of the Popaul-Hélène relationship.

Yet, when Popaul spills white paint on Hélène's rug,
the image immediately recalls an earlier scene where drops
of bright red blood fell on a little girl's sandwich, and undercuts the redemptive aspects of the white paint.   By drawing this parallel between the two scenes, Chabrol re-invokes
the traumatic mood of the earlier scene.   As a result, when
Popaul finds his lighter in Hélène's drawer, we sense that
he is just as horrified by his discovery as she was by hers.
(The use of point-of-view shot here strengthens the dramatic
weight of his perception and reinforces the parallel to the
scene in which Hélène sees the lighter next to the body.)
Moreover, the similarity of the two scenes underlines the
similarity of the moral/emotional dilemma that faces Hélène
and Popaul: each is bound to the other by what he knows,
but each also fears the other, and this fear isolates them.
In short, the dilemma paralyzes them morally and emotionally.

The exploration of the limits of love within a limited universe has been one of the chief concerns of Chabrol's cinematic career. Le Boucher is the most subtle, most concise, most gentle, and perhaps most beautiful realization of this uniquely Chabrolian motif. The central characters, Popaul and Hélène, have, as we are shown in the opening wedding scene, an intangible bond between them; the two-shot framing and the cutting from the bride and groom to them reinforces their spiritual union. But they also lack something; Chabrol's anonymous introduction of them and their apparent uneasiness together (e. g. , Popaul's awkward entrance into her classroom with a leg of lamb instead of flowers, like a lover, or an apple, like a student) make their relationship seem somewhat limited. There is a mysterious gulf between them, and it is this lack, this absence, which dooms their relationship.

Their Perceptual Gap

The cigarette lighter that represents their love relationship paradoxically ties them together and tears them apart. As an object, it symbolizes the divergent forces within each one which limit their ability to love one another. When Hélène first presents the lighter to Popaul, right after she has turned down his awkward sexual proposal, it represents a surrogate relationship, but a relationship nevertheless. Later, when she finds the lighter by the murdered girl's body and hides it from the police, the lighter, originally a symbol of her love for him, becomes a symbol of the new state of their relationship, of her tacit complicity with him and his guilt. It not only implicates her literally and psychologically (her rebuff of his advances?) in the murder through a Hitchcockian transference of guilt, but also widens the invisible gap that holds them apart.

As Chabrol's brilliant treatment of the subsequent scenes suggests, it is not really important whether the lighter belongs to Popaul or not. What is important is that Hélène believes that it does. In a sense, then, it is the limitations of each character's perceptions that circumscribe their relationship. As Hamlet says, in lines as characteristic of Chabrol as Shakespeare, "there is nothing good or bad but thinking makes it so." By refusing to turn the lighter over to the police, Hélène surrenders to her private fears about Popaul. Her thoughts destroy the innocence of her relationship with him. Like Lina (Joan Fontaine) in

Suspicion, she concedes to her own lack of faith, to her own
human weaknesses.

   The major difference between Suspicion and Le Boucher, of course, is that Lina thinks her husband (Cary Grant)
is guilty, and he is not, whereas Hélène thinks Popaul is
guilty, and he is.   Le Boucher, then, is like Les Bonnes
Femmes minus the illusion.   Nevertheless, Chabrol draws
as great a distinction between Hélène's perception and the
objective truth as he does with Jacqueline in Les Bonnes
Femmes or as Hitchcock does with Lina in Suspicion.   Two
examples:

   1)   Hélène discovers a murdered girl and, next to
the body, a lighter just like the one she had given Popaul.
Assuming Popaul guilty, she hides the lighter and is dis-
traught with suspicion.   But the next time she sees Popaul,
he lights her cigarette with what is apparently the original
lighter.   Hysterical with relief, she breaks into tears.
This scene, rather than acting as a mere red herring, en-
forces an incongruity between Hélène's interpretations and
the facts by pointing out how limited her perceptions were
before, even though correct (we learn later that Popaul
bought a substitute lighter).   In other words, Chabrol is
making us see that Helene suspects him not because he is
guilty, even though he is guilty, but because she thinks he
is guilty.

   2)   After Popaul discovers the hidden lighter, he
confronts Hélène in the schoolroom at night and stabs himself.   He kills himself not because he is guilty, even though
he is guilty, but because she thinks he is guilty.   As he
tells her, "I know that I horrify you, and I can't stand that."
In fact, the objective truth may be no more of a motivation
here than it is in Ophelia, where Adrien kills himself because his stepson Yvan thinks he is guilty, even though he
is innocent.

   Why should Chabrol point out a disharmony between
perceived guilt and real guilt when both of them ultimately
point to the same truth?   Because he sees a fundamental
imperfection in the universe which allows no possibility of
the absolute truth and the perceived truth coming together,
even when they are the same.   Like Sirk, he sees a whole
universe and a universe limited by the characters' perceptions, which, although superimposed on each other, are at
the same time as separate as binary stars.   Thus, it is

not Popaul's real guilt that keeps the two apart, but an imperfection in perception, an imperfection in the world, a
state of Original Sin.   In this light, then, Chabrol's distinction between absolute truth and perceived truth is analogous to the relationship between real sin and venial sin,
which Catholic dogma paradoxically distinguishes between
and equates.

     In Le Boucher, Chabrol creates a universe in which
there is no possibility of redemption or salvation for his
characters.   He represents evil, for the most part, as an
absence, as something unseen but, nevertheless, deeply felt.
It might be useful to recall that Chabrol once prefaced an
article on Hitchcock ("Hitchcock Confronts Evil") with the
following quote from Saint Basile:

          Do not think of Evil as a material substance;
          perversity does not subsist as if it were some
          living thing; it will never appear before your eyes
          as if it really existed, for Evil is simply the
          denial of Good.

     Even the film's first sequence casts a sinister, al-
most fatalistic mood over the subsequent action--a mood
which tends to limit the possibilities of the central love relationship.   When the baker's boy stumbles and falls, the
incident, although humorous, gives rise to a certain ominous-
ness which, like the priest's fallen bicycle in I Confess, integrates an ironic sense of humor into a mysterious but
characteristically Chabrolian metaphysic of evil.   This fore-
boding action, despite the film's initially optimistic atmosphere, shrouds Chabrol's characters, their actions, and
their relationships in the fatalistic shadow of Original Sin.
They can not escape the consequences of the existence of
evil in their universe.

                         Absence and Evil

Just as the presence of children in the first half of the film
lends the Popaul-Hélène relationship an aura of innocence
(grown-ups seemed transformed in their presence), their
absence in the second half (according to Saint Basile) becomes tantamount to an aura of evil (the dark, empty schoolhouse at the end).   Here, again, evil need not be more than
the absence of good.   Absence also tends to change the nature
of the environment during the course of the film, to make it

turn in upon itself.   The school, for example, which was
originally a symbol of innocence, a sanctuary for Mlle.
Hélène, a protective insulation against the evils of the world,
suddenly becomes a trap, a prison, a theater for the expia-
tion of guilt.

Similarly, as Hélène and Popaul's relationship grows
tenser and tenser, their environment, undergoing a similar
transformation, becomes more and more restricted.   Initially, Chabrol shows the pair in extremely public situations--
in the wedding scene which the whole town attends at the
beginning of the film, in Hélène's classroom after a Balzac
lesson, in the woods with two children in the background,
and at the school rehearsal of an 18th-century, courtly
dance.   The repeated presence of children, as mentioned
above, lends their relationship an idyllic atmosphere of in-
nocence--an innocence which the bright red drops of blood
on a little girl's piece of bread devastatingly shatter.   Later, there are fewer children in the background, more intimate scenes (e.g., when they eat cherries in her room),
more cutting, higher contrast lighting, more indoor scenes,
more night sequences, and more close-ups.

In other words, Le Boucher moves from public to
private.   The film begins with long sweeping pans, sugges-
tive of a visual openness.   In the first part of the film,
moreover, Chabrol's shots have a sense of leading from
one into the other, like the form cut from the wedding cake
to the real bride and groom.   Chabrol goes to great lengths
at the beginning of the film to preserve the continuity of
characters in their setting--note his use of a long, back-
ward-tracking shot which follows the pair home from the
wedding or the lateral track as they sit and talk in the
mushroom-picking sequence.   All these shots present the
characters in a smooth temporal and spatial continuum and
help to define their seemingly impenetrable surfaces as their
sole reality.   But the second half of the film is quite different.   Chabrol begins to cut intensively during the last
schoolhouse scene and the editing seems to destroy this initial continuity of surface.   During the car drive to the hospital, the cutting gets faster and faster; the images themselves become more and more abstract or expressionistic.
In short, Chabrol's cutting gives this section of the film a
sense of conflict and of personal emotional turmoil which
the long takes and public tracking shots in the first half
lacked.

The last scene of the film, in terms of editing, is a
sort of enigmatic compromise.   Chabrol's cuts in and out
on the same axis (from medium to long to longer shot),
which give an illusive sense of a syncopated tracking shot
(like the end of Lola Montes), break the continuity of time
and space that a single track or zoom would create.   As a
result, the editing adds a highly-charged emotional element
to the scene in that it both traps Hélène in a sadly melancholic setting (long shots) and suggests, in its discontinuity,
her emotional isolation in that setting.

In many ways, this last scene represents the purification of the absence that has haunted the film from its first
scene.   Spatially, it leaves Hélène with no architectural
stability to cling to, no protective environment.   Where, at
first, the solid presence of the village seems to give Hélène
moral strength, to make her almost invulnerable, now its
absence leaves her defenseless and alone.   The absence of
emotion in her face, a purification of her difficulty in articulating emotion throughout the film, transforms it into a
mysteriously inscrutable mask, concealing the depth of her
emotion.   The camera movement which draws away from
her at the end becomes a cosmic statement on a character
unable to transcend her limitations, and leaves us with a
sense that we have been seeing, through Chabrol's vision,
not a limited view of the universe, but a view of a limited
universe.

b.   Robert Mulligan, Direction by Indirection

If it is possible to isolate any trends at all in contemporary
cinema, one of the most outstanding ones must be the film-
maker's distance from his material, the elevation of style
over content, a greater concern with self-expression than
with telling a story, more interest in ideas than in characters.   Directors Rocha, Bertolucci, and Straub, aesthetic
descendents of Resnais, Rossellini, Godard, and others,
lead the vanguard of a cinema that rejects traditional narrative forms.   Directors like Preminger, Edwards, Siegel,
Karlson, Schaffner, Johnson, Wendkos, Hellman, and others
remain within this tradition but their critical reputation--at
least in non-auteurist, intellectual circles--suffers for it.
The modern emphasis on self-analysis, whether it be Freudian or Marxist, reduces experience to fragmented bits and
pieces of ideas and feelings and leaves it that way, without
re-assembling it.   Disjointed plot and disparate chunks of
emotion produce anarchic films that more often stimulate
the mind than the heart.

One of the few directors who combines modern distance with an archaic sense of emotion, examining experience yet not destroying it, is Robert Mulligan.   In the next
few pages, I'd like to re-examine some of Mulligan's films
and to explore those qualities in them which make him both
modern and classic, which make him both a Godard and a
Griffith.

Robert Mulligan's To Kill a Mockingbird (1963) begins
with large, caressing close-ups of a child's treasurehouse of
objects: crayons, marbles, a cigar box containing a broken
watch, pen knife, spelling medal, and soap dolls, a whistle
and a ticking, gold watch.   Dissolves and tracking shots,
interspersed with shots of a child's hand drawing and sounds
of a child singing to itself, lead from one object or group
of objects to the other.

This scene is emblematic of Mulligan's narrative

technique.   Like the beginnings of many other Mulligan
films, it works as an initiation into a very private world
of childhood thoughts, secrets and memories.   The close-
up introduction transforms microcosm into macrocosm.   It
blows up the film's world, making each object intensely felt,
each detail tremendously vivid.   Our imagination, aroused
by the camera's enlargement of things which, in turn,
evokes in us a childlike sense of wonder, draws us into the
objects and into the subjective emotional reality their presence creates.

The simplicity of form, the detailed clarity of definition, the pure, geometrical shape of the objects, and the
uncluttered sparseness of the open spaces between them are
offset by the intricate pattern these objects make in the total
composition of the image.   Though the world of Mockingbird
is a child's world, one of mood and feeling more than one
of ideas or action, it is also a complex world, full of imagination and mystery.   Its complexity grows out of the emotional tension Mulligan's compositions create between simplicity of shape and intricacy of overall design.   Each object has its own mood or tone and also shares another:
that is, the combined tone of the other elements in the composition.   As a result, each shot goes beyond the specific
objects as real things in themselves and creates a sense of
their unknown (to us), nostalgic significance as visual tokens
of inarticulated feelings and vividly remembered experiences.

What makes this credit sequence of Mockingbird so
characteristic of Mulligan's narrative style as a whole is
that its images work simultaneously on a literal and a figurative level.   By looking at the world through his character's
feelings towards it, Mulligan filters objective reality through
subjective experience.

Mulligan's narrative style is characterized by its indirectness.   Unlike Hawks or Griffith, Mulligan never faces
action head-on.   Instead, sacrificing action for tone, he
tilts his camera, obscures action with reflections or shadows, or shows its effect in a reaction shot.   Mulligan does
this partly because of his sensitivity to and respect for the
privacy of his characters' emotions and partly because he
knows that obliqueness can suggest more than directness can
actually show, that it can modulate and sustain an intensity
of emotion over a longer period of time.   By engaging the
imagination of his audience, Mulligan magnifies feelings and
events into larger-than-life proportions.

The opening of Summer of '42 (1971) is one of the
clearest examples of this.   After a credit montage of stills,
the film begins with a close-up of a yellow flower.   A focal
change in the zoom lens shifts our attention to the background of the shot: we see the image of the rising sun reflected on a wet beach.   The camera pans up to a shot of
the surf, the horizon and the sun itself.   There is a cut to
a close-up of a clump of flowers on the edge of a hill over-
looking the sea.   In the middleground, out of focus, three
figures are seen running up the hill.   The next shot, taken
on top of the hill, slowly focuses in on these figures.

The whole scene, built on stasis, has the audience
looking for real movement (as opposed to focal movement).
The absence of movement leads gradually into the motion of
the three boys and into the reality of their world.   The use
of close-ups, zooms, and out-of-focus shots introduces us
to the subjective reality of their world; these devices--like
the shot of the sun reflected on the wet beach--identify it
as a world of memory, feelings, and experience that can
only be felt indirectly through a stylized view of the landscape and its inhabitants.   The style of the film makes us
aware of vividly real experience gradually emerging through
the haze of a tremendously subjective visual technique.

The most private, most intimate sequence in Summer
of '42, Hermie's evening visit to Dorothy's house, works as
the film's most moving sequence primarily because of the
beauty of its indirectness.   The camera follows Hermie into
Dorothy's living room, leaves him, looks around the room
with him and, after circling the room, returns to him.
Carefully selected details--a photograph of Dorothy's husband, the scratching of a phonograph needle at the end of a
record--construct an atmosphere haunted with frustrated
romantic feeling.   The long take, growing in emotional
weight with each successive detail and each successive moment, gradually arrives at Hermie, transferring to him our
feelings toward what we have seen in the shot.   By concluding with him, the shot inferentially draws Hermie into the
room's mood.   The room becomes a part of him and he a
part of it.   The experience that follows remains inseparable
from the environment in which it occurs.

Later, as Hermie and Dorothy dance, Mulligan tracks
in to their shadows projected on the wall.   He cuts to close-
ups of their faces and, as the music ends, to a close-up of
her hand taking Hermie's.   Mulligan conveys the characters'

emotions more through editing and a stylized use of environment than through the actors themselves.   Even the absence
of dialogue--verbal indirection--contributes to the effectiveness of the scene by suggesting an unspoken, mutual understanding between the two.   The sexual encounter that follows
is one of the most beautifully understated sequences in all of
Mulligan.   As they lie together in bed, the camera tracks
around the room, looking at objects in the dark and stops at
an open window seemingly fascinated by the image of the
moonlight shining on the lace pattern of a translucent curtain.

The sense of mystery that Mulligan achieves in this
scene grows directly out of the distance he imposes on the
action.   In Herman Raucher's book, the narrator takes us
into Hermie's mind.   He describes what happens and Hermie's thoughts color our perception of the event.   Hermie
thinks of comforting Dorothy, of offering her marriage, of
saying something to her.   In contrast, Hermie's silence in
the film and the impenetrability of his thoughts are more
eloquently expressive than words or thoughts could ever be.
By remaining outside of the character and viewing his experience as it is reflected in select details and objects in
the room, Mulligan suggests Hermie's mood of bewilderment
and makes the whole experience movingly enigmatic.

Mulligan shoots Hermie's silent departure through
windows, from outside the house.   In one take, the camera
tracks alongside the house, following Hermie from window
to window out to the porch.   Then Mulligan slowly zooms
in on him, barely discernible through the porch screen and
the night.   The framing of Hermie through windows and behind walls as he leaves puts a barrier between us and his
emotions at a traumatically crucial moment in his life.   The
long take creates a continuous surface in time between us
and him that both magnifies and obscures his feelings.   The
indirectness with which the whole sequence at Dorothy's is
handled makes Hermie's experience both confusing and mysterious.

The next day, on his way to Dorothy's, Hermie meets
his friend Oscy.   One almost unbearable long take holds
them both together in the same frame yet worlds of experience apart.   Oscy talks and asks questions, totally unaware
of what has happened to Hermie.   Hermie remains silent,
unable to understand fully what has happened to him.   When
he gets to Dorothy's house, Hermie finds her gone.   Framed

in the doorway window of the porch, he finds a letter she left for him and reads it. In it, she tells him, "I will not try to explain what happened last night because I know that, in time, you will find a proper way in which to remember it." As Hermie finishes the letter, his face falls out of focus. The camera re-focuses on a shot of some flowers and the film concludes with a reprise of several shots with which it began.

Earlier in the film, Oscy and Hermie, talking about their favorite subject, girls, walk on the beach and wade out into the surf. Oscy tells Hermie that he's been waking up in the middle of the night and that he's been dreaming about one girl in particular. "I hope that doesn't mean I'm in love with her," Oscy remarks, "because I hate her."

Like Oscy, Hermie never really understands his own ambiguous emotions nor fully comprehends what mysterious thing has happened to him. Clearly, he never will find a "proper" way in which to remember his night with Dorothy. Like the focus changes from his face to the flowers, his experiences, memories, and associations with the place have become part of him. The film ends as it began with voice-over narration (spoken by Mulligan): "Life is full of small comings and goings. And for everything we take with us, there is something we leave behind."

An ambivalent sense of attainment and loss pervades much of Mulligan's work. In Summer of '42 and To Kill a Mockingbird, his two memory-nostalgia films, the act of growing up is seen in the interaction between a child's and an adult's world and in the emergence of a brief moment of mutual awareness between characters living in separate worlds. Hermie, for a moment, becomes part of Dorothy's life and she an unforgettable part of his. Scout reaches out and takes Boo Radley's hand, losing her fear of him and gaining an understanding of other people. The films' characters gain an understanding of the world around them and, at the same time, lose a part of their own innocence.

Growing up is not the only way Mulligan conveys loss-in-gain. His editing technique also tends to view reality and action ambiguously. Characteristically, Mulligan will often cut from one event to another, from one emotional reality to an almost antithetical one. His editing achieves a complexly muted synthesis of two distinct moods in a single scene. One of the best examples of this occurs

in the Tale of Two Cities sequence in Up the Down Staircase
(1967).

The scene, literally illustrative of the script's concern for "antithesis," begins with a reading of the first sentence of Dickens' novel: "It was the best of times, it was
the worst of times...." Throughout the sequence, Mulligan
switches from Miss Barrett, teaching her best class of the
year, to one of her students, Alice Blake, working up enough
courage to jump out the window of an adjoining classroom.
(Mr. Barringer, one of contemporary cinema's oiliest villains, had just torn Alice's heart out by correcting for
spelling and punctuation a love letter she had sent him.)
The antitheses are starkly moving: Mulligan cuts from
Miss Barrett's crowded classroom to Alice's empty one,
from noise to silence, from lively confusion to deadly determination, from a "recall to life" on the part of many students to the attempted suicide of one, from the successful
attempt of a teacher to communicate with her students to
her failure to do so.

Yet, what is important about the sequence is not
Miss Barrett's success or her failure but rather their simultaneous coexistence in the same moment. Because Mulligan views every action in terms of the action around it,
all action and all emotion seem to flow together into one,
intricately woven fabric. Paradoxically, the emotion generated by one action is both magnified and undercut by that
generated by its opposite.

Mulligan's treatment of José Rodriguez and Joe Ferone
reveals a similar sort of antithesis: her success with one is
both increased and diminished by her failure with the other.
In her attempt to reach Joe, Miss Barrett passes over José.
Several times in the film, the camera, registering her effort
to communicate, tracks in on Joe, sitting in the back of the
room. Ironically, the track-in goes right past José, the one
student she is reaching (he's the "me" who leaves her notes
in the suggestion box).

When Joe comes to see her after school, he misun-
derstands her attempts to recall him to life intellectually for
sexual come-ons. As Joe approaches her, Mulligan cuts in
to close-ups of her hand on Joe's cheek, emphasizing their
closeness. Physical contact occurs but not an emotional or
intellectual one. The close-ups seem claustrophobic and
tense, almost compelling the two to spring apart. When

Joe sees that Miss Barrett does not want him, he draws
away, leaving her hand alone in the shot, and leaves.

Unlike the scene with Joe, the final sequence with
José Rodriguez is shot in long shot.   The great cavernous
spaces of the high school auditorium separate him from
Miss Barrett.   Though there is no physical contact, there
is an emotional one.   When José tells her that he's "me,"
the two, small figures at either end of the frame, seem
magnetically drawn toward one another.   At the same time,
the distance between them makes their awareness of one
another tremendously moving.

Structurally, the scene with José answers that with
Joe.   The stability of the long shots are a visual reply to
the earlier, more volatile close-ups.   More importantly,
the shooting here sums up the impetus of the film as a
whole towards its antithetical-paradoxical goals: contact
without touching, communication in silence, closeness in
distance.

Much of the effectiveness of Up the Down Staircase
comes from the film's strong sense of place.   Mulligan
constructs a private, self-contained world out of the high
school which, in its vitality and vividness, excludes the
existence of any world outside the school.   All the film's
action is confined to the school and to the streets immediately around it.   When Alice Blake jumps out the window,
she literally leaves the film's world: the character disappears and is not mentioned again.   The same thing happens
when Joe Ferone leaves.   And we never see Miss Barrett
outside of the environment of the school.   In a way, the
film is more directly about place than people.   The bustle,
confusion and noise at the beginning of the film introduce
us to an atmosphere and mood more than to characters.

More exactly, Mulligan views people in terms of
place.   In Summer of '42, Hermie's experiences with Dorothy are felt in terms of place--the island, the sound of the
sea, her house and the things in it are as much the experience as the actual encounters between the two characters.
In Up the Down Staircase, the events that occur and the
emotions that the characters feel are understood more by
the way Mulligan chooses to shoot them in the environment
than by the characters themselves or by the script.   What
emerges in the film, and in much of Mulligan's other work,
is a tremendous sense of the character's emotional integra-

tion with their setting: their feelings are part of it and it
is part of them.

The opening of The Stalking Moon (1969), which sil-
houettes Sam Varner on a rocky hill against the early morning sky, visually illustrates the way Mulligan integrates
character and setting.   Varner is clearly a man at home
in nature.   Later in the film, Varner and Salvaje, an Indian
savagely trying to regain his half-breed child, stalk one
another in the New Mexico woods.   Mulligan creates suspense and arouses our fear by the way he shoots the scene,
obscuring the action with the environment, more than by any
direct conflict between man and his setting.

When Varner leaves his house to track down Salvaje,
there is, as in a Joseph H. Lewis pursuit film like Cry of
the Hunted (1953), a great sense of spatial disorientation.
Mulligan begins the stalk by cutting to close-ups of feet
running through the woods; he rarely shows us Varner and
Salvaje in the same frame so that we never know where one
is in relation to the other.   Moreover, Mulligan fills the
foreground of his close-ups and medium shots (he rarely
uses a long shot in the stalking sequences) with ferns and
trees, obstructing our view of the characters.   What Mulligan strives for in this sequence is the feeling created by
characters in the place not the action of one man attempting
to master another or an environment.

The way Mulligan uses environment in his films has,
I think, been greatly misunderstood.   It is a simplification
to imply that the world around Mulligan's characters is directly hostile to them.   It is less evil than alien, less a
threat than a terrifying unknown.   It is its otherness that
makes it fearsome.   When the outside world threatens his
characters, that threat is always shown as an indirect force
that is filtered through the perceptions of characters.   In
Mockingbird, it takes the form of a menacing shadow on the
Radley's back porch.   Or, in the film's most beautifully
terrifying sequence when Jem leads Scout, dressed as a
ham, home through the dark woods on Halloween, the menace
becomes all the more frightening because of its obliqueness.
In tight close-ups, a hand reaches out for the children,
knocks Jem down and grabs Scout.   Still in close-up, another hand, seemingly coming out of nowhere, enters the frame
to rescue the children.   As in Stalking Moon, the conflict is
suggested stylistically through indirectness and is not the result of any direct hostility on the part of the setting.   Shown

in terms of characters' reactions to it, conflict becomes in-
ternalized rather than externalized.

Mulligan's characters inhabit a very private world of
their own.   Around that private world revolves another,
more public one peopled by minor characters that tangentially intersects with it.   Mrs. Dubose, the old lady with the
"confederate pistol in her lap" in Mockingbird, the passengers waiting for the stage to Silverton in The Stalking Moon,
the obtuse druggist in Summer of '42 represent, for Mulligan's central characters, an alien, outside world and are
seen through the subjective experience of an enclosed, private one.   The vivid encounters between these two worlds
provide a sense more of estrangement than of conflict.
What we and the central characters feel is the presence of
an "otherness," the result of the interaction between two
distinct worlds not quite in tune with one another.

In Summer of '42 Dorothy's world is, for Hermie,
one of sexual mystery, romanticism, and wonder.   When
he and his friends spy on Dorothy and her husband at the
opening of the film, Mulligan makes the disjointedness of
the two worlds clear stylistically, much as he does in the
Tale of Two Cities sequence in Up the Down Staircase.   As
Hermie watches Dorothy, Mulligan slowly zooms in to a
close-up of his face.   Then the director cuts to lyrical slow
motion shots of Dorothy, suggesting the strange wonder with
which Hermie views her.   By cutting back and forth from
close-ups of Hermie looking to slow motion shots of what
he sees, Mulligan captures Hermie's paradoxical attraction
to yet distance from Dorothy's world.   Mulligan mixes a
sense of fascination with one of estrangement and achieves,
through this mixture, tremendously complex emotions.

Mulligan uses "otherness" in almost all his films,
but nowhere is its use as beautiful as in The Other.   In
The Other twelve-year-old Niles Perry feels both attraction
to and revulsion for his charmingly demonic twin brother,
Holland.   The emotional intensity that the film creates
arises from the tension between these two contradictory impulses; the film's mystery lies in the magic of their simultaneous coexistence.

What Mulligan's visual style creates throughout the
film is a sense of involvement and distance.   The film begins with a breathtakingly slow tracking shot that moves
down from the branches of a tree, through a green wood,

past a brook, and that eventually comes to rest on the figure
of a small boy (in long shot), kneeling--seemingly praying--
in a brightly-lit clearing.   The camera slowly zooms in on
the boy, collapsing our sense of the space between him and
the camera.   A close-up of the boy's hands, apparently
clasped in prayer, and one of his face, with his eyes shut
in thought, draw us closer to the boy.   This introduction
functions as an initiation into the very private world of the
film's central character, into its strangely religious mood
and into the Great Game with which the film is preoccupied.

As Mulligan himself has said about this scene: "I
want to get the audience looking with this opening shot.   I
want them to take time to get into the film and the character.   I want to put them into the body of the boy and to
make the experience of the film, from beginning to end, a
totally subjective one."

Though we are drawn into the boy's world, we are
drawn into it indirectly.   What we feel in the first sequence
is determined partly by the beauty of the natural environment in which it is set and partly by the artificial mechanics
of the zoom shot and the editing.

Later, when Niles plays the Great Game with his
grandmother, Ada, and enters into the body of a crow, a
similar sort of simultaneous involvement and distance is at
work.   By intercutting static shots of Niles' face with fluid
aerial shots from the bird's point of view, Mulligan breaks
up the scene into shots of total involvement, e. g. , aerial
shots, and distance, e. g. , the static close-ups.   In effect,
we are torn between objective and subjective reality, between Niles and his imagined flight.   Intercutting one world
with another, Mulligan attains both fusion and fission.

The Other ends with a tracking shot from the burnt
ruins of a barn to the second story window of an adjoining
farmhouse from behind which Niles looks out.   As in the
first shot, Mulligan again zooms in--this time to a closer
shot of the boy's face.   The boy blinks once.   The frame
freezes, and the film ends.   Again Mulligan's camerawork
leads us into the child, into the reality of his world.

But this time, because of what has occurred during
the course of the film--the deaths of a boy, a neighbor and
a baby, we draw back.   The intervention of the window which
now separates us from the child becomes a visual emblem

of the distance that exists between his private world of horror, magic, and imagination and the world around him.
Like the opening shot of Georgette behind the bus window in
Baby, The Rain Must Fall with the passing countryside reflected on the surface of glass in front of her, this last shot
in The Other affirms the ultimate impenetrability of a private world of personal feelings.

What makes The Other one of Mulligan's best works
is this sense of direct involvement of the audience with the
characters.   Mulligan's treatment of the Niles/Holland world
--especially his faithfulness to period detail--makes it vividly real for us and, through visual stylization, makes it unreal as well.   Though Niles' world, as Ada says, is very
real for him, for us it is one of indirection--of stylized
composition, zooms, freeze frames.   Mulligan, at his best,
creates a level of experience in his films that is simultaneously very real and very stylized.   As a result, he cuts the
immediacy of his films' emotions with a sort of distance
that mysteriously sustains and enriches these emotions.

c. The Narrative Distance of Robert Mulligan

Over the past fifteen years, Robert Mulligan has, with little
or no critical acclaim, directed a series of films as aston-
ishing for their stylistic subtlety as for their emotional power. The Sixties, due in large part to Andrew Sarris' auteur
polemics, marked the emergence of the director as super-
star, each director emerging with his name, like Frank
Capra's, displayed prominently above the title. In spite of
his success, Mulligan has kept a low profile, rarely giving
interviews or publicizing his films. Even though the British
Film Institute singled him out for a retrospective in 1971,
Mulligan has remained a director without recognition in his
own country.

Mulligan's self-effacing denial of directorial authorship and his relative anonymity in the industry are part and
parcel of the very vision which makes him an auteur. Mulligan is clearly not the author of his films in the way that
Ingmar Bergman is: he does not create his own stories or
write all the dialogue in his films. Mulligan is, however,
a storyteller, interpreting the stories of others. As Mulligan describes it, "Things have to sift through me. That's
me up there on the screen. The shooting, the editing, the
use of music--all that represents my attitude toward the
material."* In his role as storyteller, Mulligan interposes
his personality between the tale and the audience: he makes
the story his own by supplying attitude. It is this attitude
or tone which becomes the true subject of a Mulligan film,
not character or plot. Thus in a Mulligan film, no single
individual--director, screenwriter, producer, or actor--
stamps the film with his personality; the feelings generated
by Mulligan's view of specific characters in specific situations and settings are what count most.

---

*This and all subsequent quotations come from an interview
with Mulligan conducted by the author and William Paul in
May 1972.

Mulligan, as interpreter, chooses pre-existant plots
and characters for the stories of his films. His best films
have been based on best-selling novels that have in common
strong subjective narrations and settings which are inseparable from character and plot. To Kill a Mockingbird was
based on the Pulitzer Prize winning novel by Harper Lee;
Baby, the Rain Must Fall had as its source screenwriter
Horton Foote's play, The Traveling Lady; Inside Daisy Clover was based on Gavin Lambert's novel about Hollywood
studios and stars; Up the Down Staircase on schoolteacher
Bel Kaufman's popular book on her experiences in a New
York City high school; The Stalking Moon on Theodore V.
Olson's novel; Summer of '42 on Herman Raucher's nostalgic
best-seller; and The Other on former actor Tom Tryon's
immensely successful, Thirties gothic novel. Mulligan's
flops during this period, on the other hand, were based
either on original screenplays (Love with the Proper Stranger, though not a disaster, does not equal Baby, the Rain
Must Fall) or on unspectacular novels (The Pursuit of Happiness and Nickel Ride). Even in his period as contract director at Paramount and Universal, Mulligan relied heavily
on best-sellers (Jimmy Piersall's Fear Strikes Out and Gar-
son Kanin's The Rat Race), autobiographies (Fernando Waldo
Demera's life was the basis for The Great Imposter) and
novels (Jan de Hartog's The Spiral Road, a story of an agnostic doctor's discovery of God told in Lloyd C. Douglas
fashion.)

The number of Mulligan films based on pre-sold properties tells us less about Mulligan, however, than about
industry practices in the Sixties and Seventies, though Mulligan's television work in the Fifties consists largely of
adaptations (e. g. David Copperfield, The Bridge of San Luis
Rey, The Moon and Sixpence, The Member of the Wedding
and The Catered Affair). Original screenplays became less
and less marketable; best-sellers whose popularity had been
proven guaranteed film financiers a return on their money.
Mulligan's films with producer Alan J. Pakula, though the
director's best, do reflect the packaging psychology pre-
dominant in the industry during the Sixties: a pre-sold
novel or play and a pre-sold star (Gregory Peck, Steve
McQueen, Natalie Wood, Christopher Plummer, Sandy Dennis, Eva Marie Saint) insure a profit at the box-office.
The Pakula-Mulligan team produced a string of distinctive
films: Fear Strikes Out (1957) with Tony Perkins and Karl
Malden, To Kill a Mockingbird (1963) with Gregory Peck
(which won Academy Awards for Best Actor, Best Screen-

play, and Best Art Direction), Love with the Proper Stranger
(1963) with Steve McQueen and Natalie Wood, Baby, the Rain
Must Fall (1965) with McQueen and Lee Remick, Inside Daisy
Clover (1966) with Natalie Wood, Christopher Plummer, and
Robert Redford, Up the Down Staircase (1967) with Sandy
Dennis, and The Stalking Moon (1969) with Peck and Eva
Marie Saint.

After Stalking Moon, Pakula and Mulligan dissolved
their partnership, Pakula choosing to produce and direct his
own productions. His first film, The Sterile Cuckoo (1969),
was an adolescent love story reminiscent of the films he and
Mulligan had made but with Klute (1971) Pakula established
his own identity as a filmmaker. Klute, The Parallax View
(1974) and All the President's Men (1976) deal, as no Mulligan film does, with the struggle between the individual and
the invisible machinery of a corrupt corporate power, striking a decidedly more moral attitude and a more political
note than any Mulligan film, even the seemingly committed
and political The Pursuit of Happiness (1970). Pakula has
shored up his contemporaneous and controversial projects
with the solidity of star presence--Donald Sutherland, Jane
Fonda, Warren Beatty, Robert Redford, and Dustin Hoffman
--and relied on the proven box-office potential of the Wood-
ward-Bernstein book, All the President's Men.

Mulligan, on the other hand, has turned inward,
toward a more personal, intimate drama (Mulligan himself
delivers the voice-over narration of Summer of '42 (1971)
with whose adolescent experiences Mulligan, 17 years old
in 1942, perhaps identifies). His recent films are clearly
extensions of the sensitive Pakula-Mulligan best-seller projects of the Sixties but without the star packaging on which
Pakula seems to rely. Mulligan's films, retreating from
the real world to which Pakula anchors his suspense melodramas, have become more and more subjective, beginning
with Summer of '42 which concerns the real but nostalgically
magnified memories of one character, culminating in The
Other (1972) which explores one child's fanciful recreation
of his dead twin and continuing into Nickel Ride (1974) which
contains a quite disturbing fantasy sequence in which the
hero imagines a bloody battle with the men sent to kill him.

Mulligan's choice of subject matter lacks the topicality of Pakula's. His choice of period setting--the Thirties
in The Other and the Forties in Summer of '42--fortunately
coincided with a revival of popular interest in these periods

and Summer of '42 became the biggest box-office success of
his career, grossing over $20.5 million domestically (on its
rerelease it was double-billed with another Warners picture,
Klute, reuniting briefly the Pakula-Mulligan team).

Mulligan's interest in the reality of feelings, imagination, and memory is apparent even in his very first film,
Fear Strikes Out, which deals with the nervous breakdown
of centerfielder Jimmy Piersall, played by a pre-Psycho
Tony Perkins whose adolescence and latent emotional instability Mulligan exploits to advantage. Fear Strikes Out also
reveals Mulligan's interest in the dramatic potential of the
parent-child relationship. Piersall's father, played by Karl
Malden, is a frustrated sandlot ballplayer who pressures his
son to become a major-leaguer. Mulligan suggests the
paralytic nature of this pressure early in the film with a
high-angle shot of father and son playing ball together in a
small, enclosed backyard. Later, when Jimmy starts to
play pro ball, Mulligan repeatedly separates the two on
either side of wire fences, hinting at the repressed and potentially explosive nature of the feelings within each.

The Rat Race (1960) is the first of Mulligan's New
York films. Of all the graduates of the New York television
industry in the Fifties--Arthur Penn, John Frankenheimer,
Sidney Lumet, Sidney Pollack, Martin Ritt--Mulligan is the
only member of the American New York Wave who continued
to project in his films a New York sensibility and a concern
for the cynicism and callousness of big city life. In addition to The Rat Race, Love with the Proper Stranger, Up
the Down Staircase, and The Pursuit of Happiness are situated in New York--and Summer of '42 is set in a summer
vacation spot for New Yorkers.

The environment of Mulligan's films plays a major
role in establishing tone. The impersonal setting of New
York provides an atmosphere of isolation and loneliness
against which his characters' attempts to reach out and
make contact with one another are played out. Musician
Tony Curtis and dancer Debbie Reynolds in The Rat Race
platonically share an apartment, each so intent on making
it in the big city that they literally ignore one another and
their feelings for each other for two-thirds of the film.
Love with the Proper Stranger, shot almost entirely on location in New York, deals, as its title suggests, with the
anonymous nature of life in a city of crowds. Mulligan
repeatedly stages intimate conversations between Rocky

(Steve McQueen), a musician, and Angie (Natalie Wood), a
Macy's salesgirl whom Rocky has gotten into trouble, in
extremely public settings.   The title sequence establishes
the mood of the film: an empty musicians' union hall slowly fills with musicians looking for work.   The chaotic movements and activities of the surrounding people, all heading
in different directions and concerned with their own affairs,
make meaningful communication between Rocky and Angie impossible.   Rocky does not even remember his one night stand
with Angie, who angrily walks out.   The union hall and the
fifth floor of Macy's (where their second encounter is set)
become decors which frustrate contact, preventing any growth
of romantic feeling between the two.   Indeed, romance seems
impossible in an urban setting.   Rocky, in love with himself
as much as his showgirl mistress, Barbie, is in love with
herself, is unwilling to take on the responsibility of a deep
commitment to another: he is even estranged from his own
parents whom he seldom sees (as illustrated in a remarkable
playground reunion with them as he attempts to raise more
money for Angie's abortion) and he views married men as
"prisoners of Zenda."   But Rocky's cynicism yields to Angie's romanticism.   Angie, dreaming of a lover as a knight
on a white horse, says she will know that she is in love
when she hears "bells and banjoes."   At the end of the film,
Rocky, playing bells and a banjo and carrying a sign that
reads "Better Wed Than Dead," chases Angie through the
crowded city streets outside Macy's.   The high-angle long
shot of these two "lovers" lost in a crowd recalls the opening sequence in the union hall, but here Rocky has rejected
the deadness of his previous lifestyle, having taken a first
step when he prevented Angie from going through with an
abortion in a cold, desolate-looking abandoned apartment
building.   Rocky's actions here and at the end of the film
reflect a triumph of feeling over environment, which is also
the subject of Mulligan's subsequent New York films, Up the
Down Staircase and The Pursuit of Happiness.

Actually, New York City is, like the Indian Salvaje
in The Stalking Moon, rarely seen in Up the Down Staircase,
but its off-screen presence is felt throughout the film.   Mulligan's camera remains focused on Calvin Coolidge High
School and the streets surrounding the school and refuses
to explore the lives of characters outside of this setting.
The school, with its banging lockers, grim halls and stair-
ways, and bustling crowds of students and teachers, is the
subject of the film, revealing quite clearly the primary role
places play in the director's films.   The immediacy of Mul-

ligan's environment in this film excludes the existence of
all others--there is no world outside of the school. Sandy
Dennis' novice schoolteacher, Sylvia Barrett, is less in
conflict with this environment than in awe of it, initially
unable to understand it or to discover what it takes to survive in it.

The bustle and apparent confusion in the school's
halls during class changes captures the directionless vitality of the place; an energy is there which teachers, in the
semi-order of the classroom, attempt to channel. Miss
Barrett's after-school encounter with Joe Ferone marks a
change in the sense of place: when Joe turns off the lights
and approaches Miss Barrett and Mulligan shoots the encounter in dramatic close-ups, the "schoolness" of the room
vanishes; the order and stability of the setting has been
transformed. Even within a single environment, a variety
of moods can co-exist, reflecting the complex inter-relationship between specific people and specific settings.

The Pursuit of Happiness is less a New York film
than an "Estrangement of Youth" film, though the city and
the central character's experiences in it (e.g., the auto-
mobile manslaughter, the car's breakdown in traffic) contribute to his judgment that, "There's a nervous breakdown
going on out there, and I don't want to be part of it." En-
vironment--the city--becomes the focus of William's (Michael
Sarrazin's) rejection of the values of his parents and of the
society around him. Unable to understand it or come to
terms with it, as Miss Barrett does at the end of Staircase
when she makes contact, though separated in space, with
José Rodriguez, William can only dissociate himself from
his environment. As Tom Ryan writes in Movie 21:

> The film's final sequence provides an exhilarating
> if precarious feeling of liberation, as the tiny
> plane carrying William and Jane soars away from
> the urban landscape filled with skyscrapers, endless
> rows of cars and a veil of smog. The only pos-
> sibility for escape in the film has seemed to rest
> with individuals' ability to move away from the
> places with which their roles are linked ... and
> to move towards the discovery of an independent
> identity.

Mulligan's central characters frequently view the
world around them as a hostile body which, after they es-

tablish brief contact with it, they ultimately flee, either literally as in Pursuit or figuratively, by withdrawing into
themselves or into a world of memory or imagination.   The
"real" world in To Kill a Mockingbird is incomprehensible
to Scout, who narrates the film.   It is an adult world, represented by the courtroom sequence, which deals with adult
problems: race and sex.   The presence of Scout, Jem, and
Dill in the courtroom, as Atticus (Peck) defends a Black ac-
cused of rape, marks a confrontation between innocence and
worldliness, much as Scout's taking of Boo Radley's (Robert
Duval) hand at the end of the film represents her confrontation with and victory over the childish fears which Boo earlier represented.   Yet the narration of the film, told from
the point of view of a child, views the adult world with a
distance and incomprehensibility.   The world of grown-ups
has an alienating otherness.

Mulligan has suggested the separateness of parent and
child earlier in his career by isolating them in the frame or
by separating them with fences (Fear Strikes Out) or with
screen doors (Baby, the Rain Must Fall).   In Summer of '42,
Hermie spies on adult experience, Dorothy and her husband,
from a distance, a distance which Mulligan underscores by
filming Dorothy from Hermie's point of view and in an idealized slow motion.   Though Dorothy later initiates Hermie
into this world, it remains a mystery to him: he returns
to her house to find it locked and a note for him left on the
closed door.   The distance between parent and child, between
the world of adult and of childhood experience is realized
structurally in Mockingbird and in Summer via the narration
which accompanies childhood memories.   In both, narrators
look back upon experiences of their youth and attempt to understand them, both as they really were then and as they
seem now.   We sense simultaneously the immediacy of these
memories as they appear on the screen and the narrator's
distance from them.

The "otherness" of one's own experiences, seen in
the aesthetic distance of Mockingbird and of Summer, becomes the literal subject of The Other (1972), a film about
a boy who, through imagination, restores to life his dead
twin.   Niles (Chris Udvarnoky) has a close relationship with
his grandmother, Ada, who has encouraged his imaginative
powers.   (His mother has withdrawn into her own private
world after the death of her other son.)   As Mulligan explained Ada's character, "She was the heart of the house.
She has a primitive sense of imagination and drama, which

is the greatest thing an adult can give a child. ... Her only
failing is that she has a maternal love so strong that it
blinds her to what is happening. Though she enriches and
turns on the child's imagination, her gift is used in a destructive way by the child. " Indeed, Niles becomes responsible for at least three deaths (four, if we count the Niles-
induced heart attack of a neighbor).

The film's first shot, a slow, descending crane and
zoom shot like that which opens Mockingbird, initiates the
audience into a very private world of imagination, inhabited
only by Niles, his recreated brother Holland (Martin Udvarnoky) and their grandmother, Ada (Uta Hagen). The private-
ness of this world is so total that, as Mulligan pointed out,
"If Niles could have life just the way he wanted it, his world
would contain only Ada, Holland and himself--preferably only
Holland and himself'--which is the way the film ends. It is
a child's world of imagination, drama and magic (which Niles
performs and which facilitates his escape from the burning
barn at the end). It remains emotionally distanced and separate in tone from the world of those characters around
him.

Though Mulligan never cheats in the film--Niles and
Holland are never in the same frame at the same time but
are always separated by a cut or a pan across space, the
audience believes in the existence of Holland, so totally are
we immersed in the subjectivity of Niles' point of view, until Ada shatters that subjectivity for us. Late one night,
Niles sneaks downstairs and talks to Holland in the living
room. Mulligan pans from one twin to the other--always
from Niles to Holland as he has done previously, affirming
Niles' point of view. But when Ada comes downstairs, the
camera suddenly shifts to her point of view and we see that
Holland is not there. The next day, Ada shows Niles Holland's grave but fails to undo the harm her imaginative powers have caused.

One of the major subjects of the film is the power of
imagination both to liberate and to imprison. This subjective
reality--as Ada tells Niles, "your world is very real ... for
you"--lies at the core of all of Mulligan's work. Similarly,
The Great Imposter features a childlike character whose fantasies give him moments of escape, yet ultimately, imprison
him: he never comes to terms with himself or with those
around him who care for him.

Mulligan's treatment of the Niles-Holland world makes it vividly real for us and, through visual stylization makes it unreal as well. Yet Mulligan is not a mere stylist. He holds his audience better than any other American director, except for Alfred Hitchcock. Less interested in plot mechanics than in mood, Mulligan creates a mood that produces its own sense of reality. For example, the director carefully tries to reconstruct a Thirties atmosphere through period detail. Yet as Mulligan points out, "Objects don't have specific meanings in my films; they are only part of the mood I'm trying to create." Similarly, his controlled suspense techniques heighten the spectator's involvement in action by pulling back from violent or climactic events. Like Fritz Lang, Mulligan lets his audience imagine rather than see the violence and, as a result, magnifies it in their minds.

Mulligan's editing creates a rhythm that entrances his audience. "I cut a lot in The Other from long, open shots to tight, constricting close-ups," he explains, referring in particular to the bird in flight sequence. At the same time, Mulligan alternates long, fluid camera movements with short static shots, making, like a composer of music, a variation on the rhythmic pattern of long shot and close-up. Towards the end of the film, he breaks even spatial continuity (in the barn burning) to intercut shots of Ada's face with the face of the "Angel of a Brighter Day" (a stained-glass window angel in a nearby church) and suggests Ada's transformation as it appears in Niles' mind. Mulligan's rhythmic editing reflects the film's narrative dialectic between imagined and real experience.

The alternation between subjective and objective reality in The Other's narrative and the incorporation of the alternation into the film's visual style make it one of Mulligan's most complex works. At the same time, The Other appears to be Mulligan's most controlled work, every camera movement, every cut contributing to the film's suspense and plunging the audience into the labyrinthine subjectivity of a very private world.

d. Kenji Mizoguchi: The Crucified Lovers

"In the beginning, man is nothing."--one of Mizoguchi's favorite sayings from Zen.

In a long, fascinating, anecdotal but perceptive letter to Cahiers du Cinema, [1] Yoshikata Yoda, a screenwriter who knew Mizoguchi for over twenty years, describes the demanding experience of working with the great Japanese director:

> I remember as if it were yesterday, that to finish my scenarios, I would help my weak body by thinking, almost desperately, of all the obstacles I had to overcome, and which were set in front of me by Mizo-san (Mizoguchi). "Be stronger, dig more deeply. You have to seize man, not in some of his superficial aspects, but in his totality. We have to know that we lack, we Japanese, all ideological visions: the vision of life, the vision of the universe...." Completely discouraged by these words from Mizo-san, and making myself sorrier by thinking of the weakness of my brain, I tried to write, without ever being sure of myself....

What Yoda's story tells us that is so necessary to Mizoguchi's directorial method is that he establishes obstacles for himself, his assistants, and his characters only to transcend them. If, as Mizoguchi claims, the Japanese lack a vision of life, a vision of the universe, what he and his cinema do is to create that vision, to push not only his cameraman, his scriptwriter and his actors but also his visual style, his story and his characters beyond their superficial limitations to a deeper, more coherent, more total, more transcendent vision of the universe.

What is so great about Mizoguchi's Chikamatsu Monogatari (1954) is its ability to create a vision of the world which allows his characters to transcend the original limitations of that world and to find redemption from their own weaknesses through love and one another. The narrative of Chikamatsu (the film is known as The Crucified Lovers in England and France) is, then, primarily a redemption-through-love story. Even though it presents a broad spectrum of 17th-century Japanese society, what defines its characters is their degree of detachment from the formal aspects of that society: their ability to overcome its obstacles to love. There is no possibility of redemption for Doki (Osan's dissolute brother), for example, because he has no love for anyone but himself. Like Osan's husband, Ishun, Doki remains within his limitations and those of the world around him. In a sense, it is the failure of the film's minor characters to escape their isolation that makes Mohei and Osan's (the lovers) final transcendence so powerful. Otama, whose attempted sacrifice fails to get her Mohei, becomes a tragic figure through her failure and magnifies the triumphant achievement of the film's central characters. The limitations within Mizoguchi's universe are real (the tragic pathos of Otama) and overwhelming but ultimately surmountable (Mohei and Osan).

The Central Obstacle: Confinement

An intensely confining and confined film, Chikamatsu has, like several of the director's other late films, both a circular and a linear structure. Although it lacks the flashbacks which give a cyclical framework to Life of Oharu and Yang Kwei Fei, Chikamatsu does have a circular narrative-- the first crucifixion procession works, in the context of the film, as a sort of fatalistic flash-forward to the second. Though the repetition is artificial, it is only through artifice that there is ever any real feeling or emotion in Mizoguchi. Mizoguchi's decision to end the film tragically, in contrast to the happy ending of Chikamatsu Monzaemon's (1653-1724) original Bunraku[2] play on which the film is based, not only remains consistent with the film's overall, claustrophobic thematic tone but also reaffirms its basic circularity with a sense of frustrated confinement. As a result, although the film's first crucifixion has no more than symbolic force, the second, towards which the whole film slowly builds, invests symbolic ritual with a deeply personalized emotional intensity. Mizoguchi vitalizes this final procession; he gives the lovers a sense of purpose, of mission, which the first, anonymous set of lovers seemed to lack. He creates, through his art, a way of seeing an action that transforms

that action. Though this final crucifixion questions our perception of the first and changes our perception of other
events in the film, at the same time it enriches these
events by making our involvement with them more personal.

Mizoguchi's treatment of the final procession complements the linear quality of the lovers' relationship. Throughout the film, the nature of their relationship changes, becoming more open, free, and honest from scene to scene,
until it culminates in the final transcendence, as a pair, of
their original restrictions. In the last scene, they attain a
freedom in confinement that is both circular and linear:
though bound, they are bound together. Though about to
die, through death they will escape the social mores which
confine them. Mizoguchi transforms the event--his characters transcend their imprisonment and, for the first time
in the film, are really free.

In a sense, this paradox defines the nature of Mizoguchi's unique, personal vision and distinguishes it from
that of other Japanese directors such as Toyoda, Ichikawa
and Kurosawa. Even though the subjects of Mizoguchi's
best films, Shin Heike Monogatari, Street of Shame, Sansho
the Bailiff, for example, concern the question of social and
political freedom, as does the central narrative thread in
Chikamatsu, the freedom that his characters find comes
from within themselves, from the way that they look at the
world rather than from their actual ability to change that
world. 3 For this reason, memory and the use of flashbacks
are essential to the realization of Mizoguchi's characters'
inner freedom. It is his characters' ability to personalize
their environment--e. g., the use of form cuts and dissolves
on gestures or objects in Sansho and Oharu to introduce
flashbacks--and to shape their perception of it (e. g., Mizoguchi uses the subjective flashback as the central narrative
device) that liberates them from the objective reality of
their situation. The freedom which Mizoguchi's characters
enjoy, then, is very much like the freedom of the artist,
of Mizoguchi himself perhaps, who creates his own universe
within himself and his art.

Decor as Obstacle

Mizoguchi achieves a sense of oppressive confinement early
in Chikamatsu. Unlike the long introductory takes which set
up a sort of initial spatial geography in Sisters of Gion, Shin

Heike and Yang Kwei Fei, Chikamatsu begins abruptly with
a brief, high-angle, exterior, establishing shot, then cuts
quickly indoors, and thereby disrupts any continuity of time
and space. Mizoguchi then introduces each central character in a different part or level of the same house, but he
never ties the various parts of the house together spatially.
This initial fragmentation of setting separates the characters
from one another--it's as if the confining interiors of the
scrollmaker's establishment hold them apart. The first
shot of the apprentice Mohei--a long shot through the internal
frame of a stairway--seems to trap him alone, to isolate
him in a dark, intricately detailed background. The confinement of Mizoguchi's set becomes, then, a metaphor for
the confinement of 17th-century Japan's rigid social mores.

   Yet Mizoguchi's use of set and detail--his rigid but
subjective ordering of objects in the frame--is more than
just a social or political metaphor. Mizoguchi's use of the
internal frame, like Ford's, is a consistent compositional
device which isolates characters, objects, and textures
artifically: one is always aware that the frame is created,
like a painting. In other words, his set is not a social or
a political but an artistic metaphor.

The Confining Camera

In order to intensify the film's sense of oppressive confinement, Mizoguchi's camera remains glued to his characters
and their movements. It never strays from them to consider inanimate objects, as it does with the ancestral heads
in the temple scene of Oharu, or the natural environment,
as it does during the song sequence of Sansho. The camera's claustrophobia is very much a part of everything else
in the film: because the characters and their mores are
rigid, so is the camera and their environment (just as the
lyrical, relaxed camera movements in Yang Kwei Fei reflect
the world of its characters). In Chikamatsu when Osan's
brother asks her for money, the camera holds both characters together in the frame and follows them with short camera movements as they move about. At the same time,
Mizoguchi rarely cuts away from his action to long shot
(with the notable exception of the film's last shot); his tight
framing excludes any sense of space around his characters
and holds them in medium shot and medium close-up throughout most of the film. Mizoguchi gives no sense of a world
outside of his characters, except for that of their immediate

setting and background.   Even when the lovers run away
from the confinement of the scrollmaker's shop, Mizoguchi
alternates backgrounds of open countryside with backgrounds
of tight, prison-like urban surroundings.   In Osaka, for
example, the lovers are chased through a tight maze of
thick, barrel-shaped, wooden pillars and when they spend
the night with Mohei's father, they sleep in a small hut with
bars on the door.   Even the forest which surrounds them
when they are separated in the morning is constricting.

While Mizoguchi's tight, unimpassioned camera movements increase the claustrophobic nature of Chikamatsu, his
unusually jolting editing serves to further fragment his characters and their actions by destroying the continuity of their
environment (i. e. , by changing the backgrounds).   Although
Mizoguchi's traditional one scene-one take method tends to
preserve the integrity of his characters' actions and movements (e. g. , he cuts, like Ford, before an action is begun
or after it is completed), his cuts violently change the emotional intensity of each complete action in juxtaposition to
each other complete action.   When Ishun tries to seduce
Otama and she tells him that Mohei is her fiancé, Mizoguchi suddenly cuts to a different camera set up for a reaction shot, altering the background and, as a result, the
tone of the scene.   Again, when Otama tells Osan of Ishun's
proposition, an abrupt reverse-angle cut jars the stability
implicit in a constant, unchanging background and immediately heightens the emotional level of Osan's reaction.

Redemptive Nature of Love

The linear aspects of Chikamatsu's narrative tend to work
against this sort of fragmentation.   The linear quality of
Mohei and Osan's love arises from its redemptive nature
and its sense of purpose--in short, our emotional involvement with the lovers at the end.   The film's initial fragmentation and compartmentalization of its central characters
gives way to more open settings and fluid shots--e. g. , the
slow crane shot as Osan chases Mohei down a steep hill:
both characters are contained within the same frame; the
background and the edges of the frame no longer impinge
upon them.   The characters seem to have moved linearly
from one point to another, to have escaped the confining
interiors of the first half of the film.

On a more simple, narrative level: Mohei's earlier
sickness (he is introduced lying down and sick in the internal

frame shot discussed above) seems to vanish almost at the
moment of his commitment to his mistress, Osan. His
miraculous restoration to health represents on the physical
level the curative power of his relationship with Osan. The
spiritually redemptive nature of this relationship is best expressed visually with a remarkably beautiful four-minute
take during Mohei and Osan's mutual confession of love in
the boat sequence. Partly because of the length of the take,
the slightest movement of characters or camera acquires
tremendous emotional weight. Their mutual declaration of
love redeems them and gives meaning to their lives. Osan's
decision not to take her life, for instance, immediately follows Mohei's confession of love in the boat. The water and
grey fog which surround the lovers' boat, unlike the intricately lit interiors with their tense, detailed, constricting
backgrounds, contribute not only to the pure, lyrical beauty
of the scene but also to the thematically important sense of
liberation which that lyricism creates. At the end of this
long take, when Osan throws herself on Mohei, her action
causes the boat to move; her action changes the position of
the boat in the frame from parallel to perpendicular to the
surface of the frame and the slow, clockwise movement of
the boat--the direct, physical result of her emotion, of her
love for Mohei--becomes a metaphysical statement of sorts,
defining wordlessly the transcendent quality of the lovers'
relationship.

Though Chikamatsu is a hard film to enjoy, because
of its concern with confinement and obstacles, it is nonetheless great because it treats this concern so beautifully. Its
characters' attempts, both successful and unsuccessful, to
break out of their isolation, to break away from the forces
which separate them is nothing more than the artist's attempt to create a universe for himself. What makes the
film essential to Mizoguchi is its explicitness: it transforms
reality. What was originally a real object or character becomes a form, an abstract figure, a subjective creation
through which we can escape reality.

Ultimately Chikamatsu works because of its careful
control then powerful release of tensions. By working with
and against its own expectations, i.e., the circular deter-
minism of the plot, the film's final moment of liberation is
triumphantly cathartic.

NOTES

1. Yoda's letter is presently being translated from French
   by Mike Prokosch.   The translation I use is his.
   Yoda's letter, titled "Remembrances of Mizoguchi,"
   appears in Cahiers du Cinema, 1965-6.   I don't have
   the exact issue numbers.
2. The Bunraku is a popular form of drama, similar to
   Kabuki, which grew out of street theater.
3. Andrew Sarris, in Confessions of a Cultist, makes a
   similar point which I discovered only after I had
   written the body of my article.   Sarris writes, "From
   the first frame of Oharu to the last, one is aware of
   sublime directional purpose.   To understand the full
   meaning of a Mizoguchi film is to understand the art
   of direction as a manner of looking at the world
   rather than as a means of changing it.   There is
   not much that even the greatest director can do with
   a face or a tree or a river or a sunset beyond deter-
   mining his personal angle and distance, rhythm and
   duration.   With Mizoguchi's first tracking of Oharu
   weaving and bobbing across a licentious world to a
   religious temple, we are in the presence of an awe-
   some parable of womankind."   I trust that my argu-
   ment is dissimilar enough to be unique.   The Sarris
   quote comes from his review of Oharu, Confessions
   of a Cultist, (New York: Simon and Schuster, 1970),
   p. 138.

e. Narrative Distance in Mizoguchi's Yang Kwei Fei

The recent revival of critical and commercial interest in
Japanese film, though it has brought us a number of good,
generally unavailable films, has almost totally overlooked
the work of Kenji Mizoguchi, Japan's and possibly the world's
greatest director. His films remain the hardest to see and,
judging from their repeated commercial failure when screened,
the most difficult for audiences to appreciate.

Mizoguchi's films, though supposedly less meditative-
ly Oriental, less static, more fluid, and more Western than
Yasujiro Ozu's, have, paradoxically, less commercial appeal
in the West. What apparently bothers Occidental audiences
about Mizoguchi, especially in contrast to an immediate,
simplistically sentimental artist like Ozu, is his narrative
distance, his stylized dislocation from his material. Yet
it is in this distance that his greatness and emotional power
lie.

Mizoguchi's use of narrative distance--memory flashbacks, distant period settings, and fairy tale plots that blend
history and legend--make him most resemble John Ford.
But where Ford's more or less static shooting style, especially as felt in the last shots of The Searchers, Cheyenne
Autumn, and Seven Women, uses distance to evoke a profound sense of loss and homelessness, Mizoguchi's transcendent camera movements and cranes create a sense of
triumphal attainment (gain) and of unity, suggested most
beautifully in the last shots of Chikamatsu Monogatari and
Sansho The Bailiff.

Yang Kwei Fei (1955) is, in many respects, Mizoguchi's most distant film. It is his only Chinese film: shot
outside of Japan (on Formosa) for Hong Kong's Shaw brothers, its story concerns a fabled Chinese empress. Also,
since it is almost completely a studio picture, its sets,
lighting, and dramatic use of color appear--in contrast to
Mizoguchi's more naturalistic, almost neo-realistic lighting

and decor in Ugetsu--more artificial, more idealized, and,
as a result, more consistent with an abstract emotional
reality.

The story documents Kwei Fei's rise from scullery
maid to empress and her eventual sacrifice of herself to
save her emperor. Using a love story format as counterpoint to politics, the film sets up the familiar Mizoguchian
situation: conflict between personal freedom and political
necessity.

The film opens with a statement of this dilemma:
the ex-emperor, sitting in an abandoned wing of his former
palace, wants merely to be alone with his memories and
to listen to the noise of the city outside which reminds him
of a rare moment of real freedom he once had with Kwei
Fei at a village celebration. Two servants, sent by the
present emperor (his son), interrupt him and ask him to
move to a newer wing of the palace.

Again and again, the affairs of state and those who
represent them force Mizoguchi's central character to bend
his will to that of a larger political need. When the flashback begins as the ex-emperor thinks of Kwei Fei, Mizoguchi reintroduces the emperor by means of his music,
which his ministers consider a purely personal indulgence.
Two beautiful tracking shots show him, through a sheer
silk curtain, playing; their lateral movement seems sympathetic with the delicacy of the moment.

When his ministers intrude with their pressing affairs
of state, Mizoguchi shoots them head-on, as they push their
way through the silk curtain: their interruption works thematically as a visual metaphor for the secondary characters'
systematic and brutal violation of the momentary beauty created by the central character.

Surrounding his two lovers with scheming ministers
and power-hungry governors, Mizoguchi accentuates their
powerless but graceful fragility. He regularly frames them
within internal frames of statuary or pillars and associates
them with music or sculpture. For example, we first see
Kwei Fei, in an abrupt cut to a high-angle shot, as a statue
in that deserted wing of the palace which the ex-emperor
haunts. Within the flashback, her first encounter with the
emperor occurs in an idyllic cherry orchard where she listens to his music. He first notices her, in a later scene,

because of her resemblance to a portrait of his dead wife;
and he first falls in love with her when she plays his
cherry-orchard composition for him.   Mizoguchi turns her
every gesture and movement into graceful ritual.

At the same time, Mizoguchi dresses the lovers in
soft blues and pale yellows, surrounding them with harsher
blues and reds, to isolate them and their emotions, on a
more abstract, more artistically sensitive level, from the
other characters in the film.   In short, his direction, endistancing his two central characters from those around
them, subtly transforms Kwei Fei and the emperor into
beautifully unreal characters whose love, by virtue of this
unreality, reflects a freedom unattainable in the mundane
world.

This process of transcendence through love works
most clearly in the film's closing sequence.   Yang Kwei
Fei's opening scene, which consists of just two shots, begins with a long take.   When the ex-emperor addresses
Kwei Fei, we cut to a high-angle shot in which her statue
dominates him, an image which brilliantly reflects their
relationship.   In the last scene, after the flashback concludes, Mizoguchi's camera follows the ex-emperor as he
moves toward her statue and falls dead at its base.   Then
the camera cranes up, linking him, now dead at her statue's
feet, to her, as it did in the first scene; but here it does
it in one continuous movement without an intervening cut.
His death, in other words, erases what separated them in
the first sequence, i.e., his life, and frees him to be with
her at last.

At his death, the ex-emperor speaks to her statue
and she answers him; the sound track mirrors the fusion
that takes place on the visual level.   As the camera moves
away from them to look down a long corridor, their voices
turn to laughter.   For the first time in the film, the lovers, breaking away from all outside restraints, duties, and
pressures, are able to articulate the liberty that their love
has given them.   It is this sublime laughter which conveys,
for Mizoguchi, the purity of their hard-won, but final, freedom.

3. The Shock Troops of Style: Fuller, Sirk, and Ulmer

If the Jesuit fathers in The First Legion can be referred to as the shock troops of Christ, then Fuller,
Sirk and, to some extent, Ulmer emerge, in the context of the more passive ecumenicalism of classical
cinema, as the shock troops of style. Fuller's aggressive, muscularly dynamic camera style characterizes his narrative voice as third person and singular.
Sirk's active distancing distinguishes him from the
more passive narrative distance found in Chabrol,
Mulligan, and Mizoguchi. Ulmer, more meditative
and more psychologically-inclined than Fuller or Sirk,
nevertheless shares their outrageousness. Only in an
Ulmer film could a character (Tom Neal in Detour)
stare at a five dollar tip and refer contemptuously to
it as a "piece of paper crawling with germs." Yet
behind this outrageousness lies a narrative control
that overrides all improbabilities of story and character development. Ulmer's faith in the image makes
him a high priest of the mysteries of the cinematic
medium.

a.   Are <u>You</u> Waving the Flag at <u>Me</u>?

"Politics bore me, but the politicians do not bore me, because they're characters. "--Samuel Fuller

Of all the criticism that has been written about Samuel Fuller's films, perhaps the least valuable is that which insists on viewing them as political tracts rather than as narratives.   A <u>Cinema</u> (UK) review of the Will and Wollen Edinborough monograph on Fuller faults Fuller critics (like Wollen) with a "failure to face the fact of Fuller's anti-communism. "   The reviewer continues,

> Presumably most of the contributors [to the book] are left-wingers, and they cannot believe that Fuller really means it when he makes Nat King Cole, the sympathetic second lead in <u>China Gate</u> and the singer of the theme song, say that he is continuing to fight because "there are still some commies left," or words to that effect. [1]

To confuse the political/social/racial attitudes of Fuller's characters with those of the director himself betrays a simplistic understanding of how narration works in the cinema (or in any narrative form, for that matter).   Fuller's characters are the <u>creations</u> of the director and, as such, enjoy an existence <u>independent</u> of him.   Fuller, as narrator, establishes, through his camera work, editing, decor, lighting, and soundtrack, a voice which, more often than not, questions the moral, religious, racial, and ideological positions of his character.

The political beliefs of Fuller, the man, survive in only a highly-mediated form in his films, making any one-for-one correlation between Fuller the person and Fuller-as-narrator highly suspect.   Moreover, when critics identify certain elements as "political" in the works of directors like Fuller (or Griffith or Ford), they automatically and irre-trievably violate the integrity of these directors' films.

They isolate "political" elements from their context in the
film; they analyze, classify, and transform these elements
into a political superstructure independent of the films themselves.   Instead of seeing the director's film, they see
their film.   Instead of writing real film criticism, they
write sociological pseudo-criticism.

Admittedly, these ideas about the purity and integrity
of art are conservative, unfashionable, and reflect a highly
debatable system of values.   Indeed, if someone were to
force me to classify my artistic tastes politically, I would
have to confess that I love "reactionary" art; that I am
drawn to art that looks backward, that reaffirms traditional
values and beliefs in conventional forms.   Though it makes
no sense critically, I prefer Griffith's nineteenth-century,
melodramatic vision to Eisenstein's twentieth-century, didactic one; Ford's collapse of events into the timeless order
of memory to Capra's forward-looking, visionary utopianism; Hitchcock's profound, romantic fascination with the
past to Kubrick's empty, futuristic cynicism.   Yet an essentially irrelevant fondness for reactionary art on my part
is not criticism but bias.   It obscures the distinction that
must be made and preserved between politics and cinema;
as such, it threatens this article's first assumption that art
is, finally, apolitical and that politics is not art.

Griffith, Ford, and Hitchcock are great not because
of their affirmation of traditional values and beliefs but because of the way in which they make this affirmation.   This
is also true of Fuller.   Although the content of his films
is often political, his style transforms the politics into art.
What stands out in his films is the explosive interaction of
style and content.   This interaction creates a distance between Fuller and his characters.   It is this distance which
makes a purely political interpretation of Fuller's films ab-
surd and meaningless.

*   *   *

Fuller's first film, I Shot Jessie James (1949), begins with
razor-edge, close-up cutting between Jessie and a bank
teller.   The first scene ends with a short track-in to a
close-up of money (dropped by the robbers when the alarm
foils the stick-up) strewn on the ground outside the bank.
The oppressiveness of this opening sequence, conveyed
visually through the use of tight close-ups and tense editing
and narratively through the frustration of the action (the

aborted hold-up) brilliantly epitomized in the scene's final
image of money scattered in the dirt, haunts the remainder
of the film.

Fuller structures each successive scene in the film
in similar terms of conflict--often moving into close-up at
the pitch of tension, as in the famous face-off in the saloon
between Ford and the ballad singer. But Fuller repeatedly
refuses to resolve this conflict. The ritualistic reenactment
of the James killing on stage seems to hypnotize Ford: he
fails, in one performance, to "shoot" Jessie in the back
and, thereby, find release from the tense guilt that haunts
him. In the final shoot-out with Kelley, Ford tries to confront him, to face the man whom he thinks has stolen his
girl. But Kelley, turning his back on Ford, refuses to
face him. The effect of the repetition of such aborted conflicts is the creation of a nightmare world which frustrates
Fuller's central character, imprisoning him in a dream
world of ineffectuality and irresolution.

*   *   *

"I'm not interested in who's a red or an anti-commie.
If I feel that the hero should be a fascist, then I'll
make him one.   I'm just interested in characters."
                                        --Samuel Fuller

Steel Helmet (1950), Fuller's first war picture, contains a
tighter, more dramatic narrative than that in Jessie James
and also reveals a remarkable refinement and subtlety of
visual style. The characters' racial and political biases,
which embarrass those critics who mistakenly confuse them
with Fuller's own, set up rigid systems of belief which
serve to isolate characters from one another. Fuller's
characters operate on a set of principles that is so inflexible that change results in insanity or death rather than
flexibility.

Fuller's treatment of character and subject matter
establishes a distance between the director and his characters that draws attention to the limited perspective of his
characters' world. At the same time, the unattractiveness
of Fuller's characters, together with their outrageous anti-
communism, calls into question not only their politics but
also the validity of their actions. Fuller achieves this distance most strikingly in his use of the temple Buddha. The
presence of this statue dominates the action in the temple

during the second half of the film--especially in the battle
sequence when Sgt. Zack, cradled in its arms, uses the
statue for cover as he fires at the attacking enemy.
Throughout all this chaotic action, the statue's serenity,
emotionless detachment and sublime transcendency heighten
the brutality, stupidity, and insanity of the characters beneath it. The bleakness of the film's conclusion rests
largely on its characters' inability to see, as the third-
person presence of the religious statue seems to, the futility and pointlessness of their actions or to escape the
closedness of their universe.

                          *   *   *

Pickup on South Street (1953), one of Fuller's most visually
exciting films, opens with a scene on a crowded subway
car. Fuller's use of densely-packed space and his tightly-
framed, close-up editing create a sense of enclosure and
emphasize the claustrophobic nature of his characters' environment. The tense, subway pocket-picking sequence that
follows brilliantly illustrates the total self-containedness of
each of Fuller's characters within this closed universe.
The initial cutting and tracking opposes characters--Skip,
Candy, the government men--and detaches them from one
another. Skip, standing next to Candy in the train, without
actually touching her and without her knowledge, steals her
wallet. Fuller's facial close-ups, together with a lack of
eye contact between the two, have the effect of insulating
the one character from the other.

        This initial isolation of characters within a cramped,
claustrophobic set becomes a metaphor for the remainder
of the film. Skip's cynical self-sufficiency, like Candy's,
becomes his only means of self-preservation in a restrictive
and imprisoning world. His greatest strength--his self-
centered independence--is also, in Fuller's hands, his
greatest weakness. Fuller's introductory, high-angle shot
of Skip's shack on South St. and the set itself suggest the
character's self-imposed isolation from the rest of society
and his confinement in that isolation: only a narrow wooden
bridge connects Skip with the rest of the world.

        The thrust of the film, implied in Fuller's thematic
use of cross-cutting to pair independent and separate characters and actions, is toward a realization of each character's
need for other people, toward greater interdependence. In
the hospital sequence at the end, when Skip, looking at Can-

dy's badly bruised face, finally realizes the sincerity of her
love for him, the camera slowly tracks in on him, framing
him between the bars of Candy's bed.

When Skip breaks his emotional isolationism, accepting Candy's selfless sacrifice for him and resolving to
avenge Joey's assault on her, Fuller cuts to a more loosely-
framed shot of Skip's face that no longer implies his incar-
cerating insulation.

Often misunderstood as a McCarthyite, anti-communist tract, Pickup really explores, using contemporary politics as its base, the question of freedom and strength
through commitment--but commitment on a personal and
emotional, not political, level.

*   *   *

The visual style of Run of the Arrow (1957), with its open-
ended frames, uncluttered images, and more moderate use
of close-ups, differs markedly from that of Pickup. 2 Yet,
though Fuller's camera does not imprison in Arrow as it
does in Pickup, it does isolate characters by means of visual contrast. The total effect is similar to the constricting
style of Pickup: it sets Fuller's characters within the context of a larger order which both comments on and defines
their actions.

Near the beginning of Arrow, after Sgt. O'Meara
shoots Lt. Driscoll and brings him to the field hospital at
Appomattox, he sees General Lee, in long shot, immediately after his surrender to Grant. As Grant prepares to
leave, O'Meara draws a bead on him and is about to shoot
him when a medic's words, warning of Lee's disgrace if
Grant were to be killed by one of his men, stops him. In
a tightly-composed frame Fuller contrasts O'Meara's blind
hatred and determined inflexibility, suggested by the sharp
angle of O'Meara's rifle and the distorted expression on his
face, with the calm but resigned logic of the medic.

O'Meara's intenseness here and in the subsequent
scene with his mother and his neighbors on the village
bridge seems out of place; he looks a misfit and ill at ease.
In comparison with the stasis, visual stability, and strength
around him, he appears distinctly neurotic.

O'Meara's journey west, shown mostly in long shot,
seems, at first, to ease the visual tensions of the earlier

sequences and to provide him with both a means of escape
and an outlet for the tense uneasiness he projects when he
shares the frame with other characters.   Yet Fuller's long
shots of O'Meara, taken in the larger context of the whole
film, work, in effect, to isolate him as an outcast against
the beauty of the landscape.

Later, when O'Meara finds Walking Coyote, an Indian
who, like himself, left his own people to live with another
people and is now in search of his home, Fuller's use of
the journey to drive home O'Meara's total alienation from
society becomes clear.

Fuller's selection and use of the landscape in Run of
the Arrow works, like the indifferent presence of the Buddha in Steel Helmet, to override the violent emotions and
idiosyncratic neuroses of his characters.   Cuts from long
shot to close-up and back again to long shot--especially
during the actual run of the arrow where its immediate effect is to slow down the characters' motion, as if they were
in a dream--freezes the characters in the sheer, dead
beauty of the landscape, like insects in amber.

Again and again, Fuller's visual style in Arrow overwhelms his characters and transforms his script, which
superficially concerns O'Meara's acceptance of and re-inte-
gration into an American identity, into a story about a man,
ultimately unable to escape his limited perspective, who
continues to wander without destination.   The final, high-
angle crane shot of O'Meara and the wounded soldiers only
restates the claustrophobic entrapment that dominates Fuller's
vision of the world.

*   *   *

The Crimson Kimono (1959), one of Fuller's best and least
appreciated works, presents a bleakness in human relationships that far exceeds that in any Fuller film before his
greatest masterpieces, Shock Corridor and The Naked Kiss.
The grotesque, close-up introduction of Sugar Torch and the
high-angle crane shots that follow her as she is chased down
the street outside the burlesque house, unlike Fuller's almost romantic high-angle cranes and close-ups in Park Row,
create a mood of oppressive vulgarity and pessimistic frustration that regulates the tone of the entire film.   These
high-angle crane shots seem to pin characters helplessly
against the ground and to give a sense both of their vulnerability and their isolation.

At the same time, the circular structure of the movie, with opening and closing sequences of similar content shot in similar ways (high-angle), creates a closedness that mirrors the film's world. Within the body of the film itself, every shot seems to cramp characters; the cluttered, tightly-composed frames press in upon those who inhabit them.

Yet Fuller's frames and narrative structure are also highly chaotic. As in Arrow, characters wander almost aimlessly with no awareness of their destination. Blindly pushed along in the flow of events, they become prisoners of the irrationality of their own emotions. Fuller's crazy parallel editing between Mac and Charlie or Charlie and Joe, though structurally imposing order on separate, unrelated events, actually reaffirms the chaotic state of the film's relationships and that of its characters' feelings.

The final shot of the film, an aerial view of Los Angeles at night, brilliantly returns the narrative to the beginning, undercutting Joe's simplistic realization that "you only see what you want to see in other people's faces": cutting away from his ant-like characters and their petty, melodramatic emotional drama in the street, Fuller expands their separateness and frustration into that of distinct, lonely lights. In their resemblance to a constellation of stars, these small lights suggest a larger, more cosmic order of isolation of which the film's characters are only a part.

*   *   *

All of Fuller's characters exist in a closed universe of their own from which escape is impossible. What is fascinating about Fuller is the powerful, visual way in which he conveys this closedness. His use of intense, long takes that transform real time into dream time; of short, tight, muscular tracking shots that seem to lead his characters helplessly along; of limited two- or three-foot crane shots that call attention to the dynamics of his compositions; of claustrophobic close-ups and high-angle shots that make his frames bristle with a compositional tension imposed from without. The design of the frames themselves becomes a dominant force in each film, shaping the way we see characters and their actions. In other words, Fuller's third-person visual style, distancing us from his characters, becomes a measuring rod by which we evaluate them and their actions. An understanding of how this visual style works and the larger concerns implicit in it will, I hope, make the confusion of

Fuller with his characters impossible and show how absurdly limited one's view of him as a director is if his films
are seen as political polemics rather than as the stylized
narratives of an intrusively critical storyteller.

NOTES

1. Cinema, No. 5:9, February, 1970.
2. After writing this, I realized that I had seen Run of the
   Arrow in 16mm, without proper masking in projection.   Projected correctly in a 1.85 format, the film
   becomes more claustrophobic and what were formerly
   medium shots become medium close-ups.   Thus the
   film does not violate the style of Fuller's earlier
   works.

b.   Shark!

Samuel Fuller's Shark! was released on the bottom half of
an action double bill in 1970.   It played for about three days
in one or two theaters and then disappeared, resurfacing
years later on late-night television.   Though, for a variety
of reasons, the film has none of the artistic integrity of
Fuller's most recent work, Dead Pigeon on Beethoven Street
(1972) or The Big Red One (1980), it is somewhat more ac-
cessible than Dead Pigeon and is certainly worthy of more
critical consideration than it has so far received.

   Shark! is a magnificent mess and it is almost impossible to say why the film doesn't work--or, more exactly,
to assign blame, to put the finger on who did what.   The
film contains a few sparks of genius, but much of its glit-
ter is not genuine; it flashes in the pan, but there is still
much more mud than gold.   Furthermore, Fuller's dispute
with his producers over its final version makes the film
particularly difficult to discuss--it puts all criticism of the
controversial work (for director-oriented analysts, that is)
into a swamp of speculation and conjecture.   Just as a
Hawks admirer, for example, claims that what is good
about the Hawks-Conway Viva Villa (1934) is the Hawks half
(exteriors and the Mexico City sequence) and what is bad is
Conway's contribution (interiors), so a Fuller fan credits
the best parts of Shark! to Fuller and the worst to those
who tampered with Fuller's original cut.   But whatever
claims and criticisms are made about Fuller or Shark!,
ultimately the film's failure must stand as one of the best
arguments in defense of the much-misunderstood auteur
theory: Shark! lacks the single, coherent, unifying narrative intelligence that underlies Fuller's earlier work, from
the bleak iconoclasm of I Shot Jesse James (1949), to the
offbeat, Forty-Second Street Freud of Shock Corridor (1963)
and the stark cynicism of The Naked Kiss (1964).   Fuller's
characteristically hard-fisted, uncompromising, tight direction has been softened, compromised and loosened up somewhere along the line in Shark! and the film's final version
simply makes no sense.

At any rate, Fuller disowned Shark! and requested
the producers to remove his name from the work. And although Fuller's control over the film is apparent in the
script, in the direction of actors and in the shooting of
many scenes, the sloppy editing of the film and the poor
post-synchronization of the sound track reveal the disastrous
consequences of Fuller's absence and of the alteration of
his original conception of the film.   It is hardly necessary
to explain the director's disavowal of the "finished" product:
the producers' final cut leaves almost nothing of Fuller in
the film but his name on the credits.

If you look closely at the textual emendations of Mil-
ton's Paradise Lost or at Tottel's metrical/textual emendations of Wyatt and compare the corrections with the original,
you often discover that what seemed wrong to these critics
made the most sense in terms of the works they edited.
In fact, their misreadings frequently become the most useful tools for understanding the poet's original meaning.
Similarly, the errors and stupidity of myopic film producers
often damage the most essential aspect of scene in a film.
Although we do not have the original version of Shark!, it
is possible to get some idea from the film itself and from
the remarks that Fuller makes about it of what Fuller is
trying to do with the film.   In an interview with Eric Sherman and Martin Rubin in The Director's Event, Fuller talks
about Shark! and describes his original ending:

> I like the idea of a love affair where the man
> (Caine: Burt Reynolds) finds out the girl (Anna:
> Silvia Pinal) has used him. I gave her a great
> line of dialogue. In the last line of the picture--
> now I find that the producers have put it in ahead,
> and it's no longer the last line--she says to him,
> "We're both a couple of bastards--only I'm a rich
> one." That's the whole flavor I wanted. I shot
> some great stuff. For instance, when the boat is
> sinking at the end, he takes a lighted cigarette
> and throws it into the sea. I just stay on that
> cigarette. A fish sees it (the fish being a sym-
> bol of the shark), thinks it's something, and
> grabs it--pssshht! (Sound of a cigarette being
> extinguished). That's the end of the picture.
> Now I think they've cut it out. A lot of things
> like that were cut out. [1]

In the final version, this last shot of the cigarette
ended up on the cutting room floor--replaced by a shot of

the girl's boat sailing off into the sunset. Although the two endings may not, at first, seem that disparate, the difference between them is essential to the film and an awareness of that difference argues for the superiority of Fuller's ending. Even though the final shot shows Anna sailing off in a slowly sinking boat, the shot itself is a cliché and, as such, detracts from the uniqueness and uncompromising integrity of the original story. Fuller's final shot, which avoids any suggestion of cliché, is not only fresh and exciting, but also remains consistent with the narrative approach to his characters that he employed in Shark! and in his other films. In Shock Corridor and The Naked Kiss, for example, Fuller's characters exist in a closed universe of their own (the asylum, Kelly's prostitution) from which it is impossible to escape. His favorite last shot--e.g., see Crimson Kimono, Forty Guns, The Naked Kiss--is often a paralytic high-angle long shot or a claustrophobic close-up--e.g., see I Shot Jesse James. Whereas Fuller's final shot in Shark! reaffirms the closed nature of the universe within which his characters operate, the last shot in the producers' version --the long shot of the boat sailing away--opens up the film: it leaves the girl's fate and the action unresolved. By understating the girl's eventual destruction, the bastardized version of Shark!, unlike Fuller's version which makes the film's outcome quite dramatically clear, places Fuller's story and characters in a slightly ambiguous or uncertain framework and compromises the corrosive cynicism of the director's final statement.

The editor's attempt to open up the film reveals itself less clearly but just as damagingly in the insertion (on unmatched stock) of impersonal, irrelevant, "atmospheric" establishing shots of anonymous crowds in a Sudanese marketplace. This spatially disorienting library footage works against the thematic thrust of the film as a whole: it suggests a world outside of that in the film, a world foreign to Fuller's characters and a world of which his characters remain ignorant. The insertion of such shots creates a sort of open-endedness in the visual narrative and places Fuller's characters in an alien context of everyday normality.

At times, the editing betrays Fuller's characters, tries to make sense out of them and seeks to impose an order or rationale upon their actions and words. For example, when Caine meets Anna, there is a lot of cross-cutting between the two which sets up each as trying to out-

wit the other. But the shots themselves are flat and ac-
tionless; the backgrounds of each are almost indistinguish-
able from the other; the composition of the shots tells us
nothing about the characters (unlike, for example, the classic cross-cutting sequence in Hitchcock's Strangers on a
Train [1951], which puts each character in a distinctive and
psychologically revealing environment). When Fuller cross-
cuts close-ups of two separate actions in The Crimson Kimono (1959), he revitalizes the nature of the device--he
works against its conventional function as a means of ordering the narrative; the actions he parallels are dissimilar.
But in Shark!, the parallel editing and the parallel dialogue
on the sound track are much too schematic: they establish
a structural clarity of intention and motivation that undercuts the complexity of the characters' actual encounter with
one another a few scenes later.

Nevertheless, Shark! contains some magnificent moments, some brilliantly shot and edited purple passages.
Whether these scenes were shot and edited by Fuller himself or by someone else is of less significance than the
actual shots themselves. The pre-credit, underwater sequence which opens the released version of the film works
remarkably well in establishing the moral context within
which the relationships within the film operate. The picture
begins with long and medium shots of a skin diver as he
descends through the blue-green water to explore the ocean
floor. Fluid, point-of-view tracking shots bring him to a
wreck. The camera tracks along the deck of the ship and
we cut to an interior shot as the diver goes down a hatch.
He discovers an aqua lung inside and signs of recent salvage
activity. As the diver swims away from the wreck, Fuller
cuts to a shark approaching the camera in long shot. The
shark attacks the diver and kills him. In the next scene,
Anna reimburses the diver's mother for the loss of her son.
The Arab woman takes the money and counts it--first mois-
tening her thumb like a cashier in a bank. Throughout the
film, all the relationships between the four central characters are predatory and mercenary. The shark which guards
the wreck and attacks divers is not so much a symbol as an
extension of the desires and wills of Fuller's characters.
In Shark!, people act like sharks towards each other. The
sharks themselves are not separate entities that stand for
something else (symbols) or which inhabit an alien, hostile
universe or adhere to a separate system of morality as they
do, for example, in Hawks's Tiger Shark (1932), but rather,
they exist co-extensively in a single temporal and spatial

universe with Fuller's characters. Whereas for Hawks, the
surface of the water, the line which divides the sea from
the sky, visually represents both a physical and moral
boundary beyond which one cannot safely go, for Fuller,
there is no line: his land is shark-infested and his sea is
man-infested.

Of all the brilliantly shot underwater sequences, the
last is perhaps the best. As Caine and Professor Mallare
(Barry Sullivan) load gold into metal baskets and send it up
to their ship, someone above sends down bloody chunks of
fish to excite the sharks which then attack and kill Mallare.
In a single shot, as the last basket of gold makes its way
from the bottom of the frame to the top, the bits of fish
tails float down with a graceful flutter from the top of the
frame: the equation of the predatory (the bait) with the
mercenary (the gold) hammers home the unique moral code
of the film and sets up the final sequence of reversals on
board ship which climaxes as each character turns against
the other.

Not only the shark attacks but all the fight sequences
stand out as the most interesting sequences in the film.
When Caine discovers that Mallare and Anna are holding out
on him, he forces them to make him their partner.   Fuller
begins the scene with emphatic, intense close-ups of each
character and, as the fight begins, cuts to a high-angle
shot which frames the action within the four walls of the
room and puts the whole fight within the confinement of a
single cell.   When Anna enters the fight, Caine knocks her
down and proceeds to demolish the room and Mallare along
with it.   This single-take high-angle action sequence ends
with Caine's victorious lines: "from now on we'll do everything together.   Just one big, happy family--father (he helps
up Mallare), daughter (he puts his arm around Anna), and
son-of-a-bitch (he points to himself)."   Although the remainder of the film doesn't always stay consistent with it,
this scene, in which all three major characters struggle
with each other within the context of futility (the four en-
closing walls and the high-angle), crystallizes Fuller's approach to his characters and to his story.

If the physical climax of the film occurs during the
fight sequence, the emotional climax occurs immediately
afterwards in an operation sequence.   Caine has another,
adopted partner, a cigar-smoking orphan whom he calls
Runt (Charles Berriochoa) and to whom Caine teaches the

fine art of thievery.   During one of the last fight sequences,
Runt is pushed down a stairway and knocked unconscious.
The town drunk (Arthur Kennedy), a doctor with the d.t.'s,
is fetched by Caine and liquored-up so that he can perform
a delicate brain operation.   Fuller's frames during this
scene are fantastically composed with lines of depth and
tension.   Bottles of liquor in the foreground and bare light
bulbs in the background frame the medium shots of the
vertical but bent figure of the doctor and the horizontal
body of the boy stretched out on the hotel bar.   A high-
angle shot, with a ceiling fan slowly rotating in the foreground, sets up the full scene, with the operation and those
watching it in the same frame.   Then, when Caine threatens
to kill Mallare if the boy dies, Fuller cuts to a lateral
track, in close-up, of the faces of the onlookers--those indirectly and directly responsible for the attack on the boy.
Fuller's powerfully oppressive use of close-ups and the different quantities of emotion in onlooking faces--all tied together by one continuous camera movement--dramatically
heightens the emotional intensity of the scene.   Only when
the shaky surgeon successfully completes the operation does
Fuller relax his use of close-ups and tensely-framed compositions.

*   *   *

Samuel Fuller has always made low-budget films so that he
could maintain control over his work (interference on a low-
budget film costs money and time, which is the equivalent
of money).   Most of his films have been written and directed by him and whatever film he made, you could be
sure it was all or almost all his.   Eventually, in 1956,
Fuller founded his own production company, Globe Enter-
prises, in order to preserve even greater personal control
over his films.   The history of Shark!, unfortunate in more
ways than one since a Mexican stuntman, José Marco, was
killed by a renegade white shark which broke through a protective net during the filming of the picture, is a sad one.
Not only was the project taken out of the director's hands,
withheld from release for several years (despite a four-page
spread in Life on June 7, 1968, at the time of the stuntman's death) and finally schlepped out for a quiet, almost
anonymous six-day run on the bottom half of a Forty Second
Street motorcycle bill, but the finished product is a distortion of its director's original film.   If the industry allows sharkish producers to mangle good movies, what has
happened to one of its most brilliant and creative directors,

Samuel Fuller, will happen to many other good directors and there will be no end to the degradation of the cinema's most talented craftsmen.

NOTE

1. Eric Sherman and Martin Rubin, The Director's Event, (New York: Atheneum, 1970), pp. 179-180.

c.   Ironic Distance in Douglas Sirk's The First Legion

Douglas Sirk's The First Legion (1951) has the reputation of
being one of the director's best American films.   Its plot,
taken from a 1934 play written by Emmet Lavery (who also
wrote the screenplay), concerns the effect of a religious
miracle on a group of Jesuit priests and on the community
that surrounds their mission.   The story, in itself, is not
particularly Sirkian, though it does present a group of characters blindly groping for something to hold on to, for faith,
power, or physical well-being.   Rather it is Sirk's treatment of the story that makes the film great.

        Sirk does not merely film Lavery's play, he analyzes
it, using its situation and characters to expose the falsity of
the values of his characters and the society around them.
Sirk's analysis consists in looking at characters, events,
and objects from a variety of different angles, almost as if
he were a cubist painter.   His camera does not accept the
world at its face value but rather questions it; the reality
of his world, as a result, is not absolute but relativistic.
The meaning of events gradually becomes more and more
obscure, dependent upon each character's imperfect perception of them.

        The film's central events--the two "miracles"--illus-
trate this.   The first miracle, Father Sierra's recovery
from a supposedly incurable paralysis, seems initially to be
genuine.   As a visitor to the Jesuit mission, Father Quar-
terman, tells the fathers, narrating a film that he has made
of his travels in the Far East about the mysteries of the
Indians' faith in God, Fr. Sierra miraculously rises from
his bed, speaks with Blessed Joseph (a religious statue) and
descends the stairs from his room, looking for Fr. Fulton
whose wavering faith has prompted Fr. Sierra's action.
The reactions to the event are varied.   The rector (Leo G.
Carroll) views it as justification for having Blessed Joseph,
the first Jesuit Bishop, declared a saint.   Fr. Keene cal-
culatingly tries to exploit it to advance his own power within

the order.   Fr. Arnoux (Charles Boyer) characteristically
questions what has happened and, like the criminal lawyer
he once was, tries to cross-examine those involved, the
patient Fr. Sierra, and the attending physician Dr. Peter
Morrell (Lyle Bettger).   To the outside world it is something else.   The sick, the crippled, and the blind flock to
the mission in hope of miraculous cures for themselves.
Newspapers blow it up into sensational headlines.   Profit-
eers sell Blessed Joseph dolls to the curious outside the
mission's gates, lending the event a carnivalistic quality.

Later, in a confession scene that anticipates the one
in Hitchcock's I Confess (1952), the agnostic doctor who at-
tended Fr. Sierra tells Fr. Arnoux that the whole thing was
a hoax, that he had given the crippled priest a drug that
enabled him to walk.   This revelation, naturally, destroys
our initial understanding of the event.   And yet, even this
"true" understanding of the miracle is proven to be false
or incomplete by the subsequent action.

The second miracle, which concludes the film, appears definitely genuine.   The crippled girl who mysteriously walks was, as the doctor who engineered the earlier hoax
tells us, incurable.   The certainty of this miracle forces
us suddenly to question the apparent falsity of the first one.
Was the doctor totally responsible for Fr. Sierra's cure?
Or was Fr. Sierra's concern for Fr. Fulton, like the girl
Terry's for the doctor, the divine agent of the recovery?
Sirk gives no clear answers; he merely celebrates the pure
ambiguity of experience, shattering events into tiny fragments and thereby thwarting any perfect comprehension of
them.   From an ironic distance, the spectator contemplates
the inability of Sirk's characters to know the world around
them.

Sirk's visual style tends to reinforce this analytical
fragmentation of characters, objects and events.   His visual-
ization of space emphasizes its shallowness and disjointedness rather than its depth and continuousness.   Unlike
Raoul Walsh whose fluid pans and tracks follow his characters as they explore their environment, Sirk sets his
characters within static frames, trapping them in the clut-
ter of objects or obscuring them in slabs of blackness.
Walsh's depth of field enables his characters to react with
the world around them and gives the relationship between
his characters and their environment an immediacy that is
missing in Sirk.   Walsh's dynamic visual style gives power

and freedom to his characters. Sirk's frozen compositions
make his characters subject to the things around them;
powerless, they struggle in vain to achieve a rapport with
one another and their world.

The First Legion, like Sirk's later black and white
films (There's Always Tomorrow, 1956, and Tarnished Angels, 1958), has a distinct look. His camera views the action from a slight angle, predominantly from a low one.
Most of his interior scenes are backlit or lit from deep
within the frame, creating a sheet of blackness in the foreground. His characters are, thus, constantly in danger of
being swallowed up by this darkness whenever they move
into the foreground. This dramatic use of lighting reflects
the larger lack of clarity in the characters' world: one
feels that Sirk's characters are constantly stumbling around
in the dark, seeking illumination. A character in a Hawks
or a Walsh film will always know where he is in relation
to the things around him; he is at home in his cinematic
space. But Sirk's characters, unable to really see the
world around them, become just one more isolated piece
in a larger pattern of fragmentation. Sirk's world has no
center; it is held together only by the overriding presence
of his camera.

d. Prisoners of Paranoia

Edgar G. Ulmer, one of the least known, seen, and appreciated of American film directors, remains, along with Joseph H. Lewis, one of the greatest filmmakers to emerge from the shadowy lower depths of Hollywood's "B" feature production in the Forties. One of the era's bleakest artists and one of film noir's blackest visionaries, Ulmer remains all but forgotten--except for a handful of admirers (myself included) and a score of detractors.

Ulmer, to many, is a totally unknown or at most obscure, murky figure in film history. Since his career and the conditions under which he worked are somewhat unusual, a few facts about his life--though they will not necessarily shed any light on particular films or on the ideas contained within them--will, I hope, draw him from obscurity into sharper focus.

Ulmer, like von Stroheim, Sternberg, Lang, Wilder, and Preminger, was born in Vienna at the turn of the century (on September 17, 1904). After studying architecture at the Academy of Arts and Sciences, he became, at the age of 16 or 17, a set designer for the legendary stage director, Max Reinhardt, at his Josefstadt Theater. There he met F. W. Murnau. In 1923, Ulmer came to the United States with Reinhardt's play, The Miracle, and did some work for Universal as a set designer. Also in 1923, he became one of Murnau's assistants, assisting him on The Last Laugh (1924) and Faust (1926), and worked with Murnau on most of his American productions as assistant director and set designer, uncredited except for his work on Sunrise (1927), until Murnau left the country in 1929 to film Tabu. After this long apprenticeship with Murnau, during which he also reportedly worked with DeMille, Ulmer returned to Berlin to make his first feature, the documentary-like Menschen am Sonntag (1929), which he co-directed with Robert Siodmak. In 1930, Ulmer moved back to the U. S. where he worked, until 1933, both as an art director at

Metro-Goldwyn-Mayer and as a stage designer for the Philadelphia Grand Opera.

Because Ulmer wanted to direct his own films and to maintain control over their production, he worked for small-budget, independent production outfits. His anonymity enabled him to work without producer interference on a variety of projects and gave him a control over production (interference or delay on small-budget films made production costs prohibitive and was therefore discouraged) and an independence that only a handful of Hollywood's greatest directors enjoyed.

Ulmer directed his first American film, Damaged Lives, in 1933, with independent financing. And, after making The Black Cat in 1934 for Universal, he worked in the New York city area, making independently financed films for Jewish, Ukranian, Armenian, Black, and other minority groups. At the same time, he was hired by the Roosevelt administration to make a number of foreign-language films, mostly public-health documentaries, for Mexican-Americans, Orientals, and American Indians. In 1942, Ulmer returned to Hollywood with PRC (Producers' Releasing Corp.), a small, independent company, where, under producer Leon Fromkess, he wrote and directed--at amazingly little cost and at an amazingly rapid rate--some of his best work, films such as Bluebeard (1944), Strange Illusion (1945), and Detour (1946).

After PRC went out of business in 1946, Ulmer founded his own short-lived company, Mid Century, and then went back to work for other small outfits. In the late Forties and early Fifties, Ulmer made films in Italy, Germany, Spain, and the United States. In 1961, replacing Frank Borzage who became ill early in production, Ulmer directed L'Atlantide. His last film, The Cavern, was made in Italy and released in 1965. All in all, Ulmer has, by his own count, directed 128 films (though most filmographies list only about thirty-five).

The speed with which Ulmer worked, often completing a film in a week, and the cheapness of his productions, some costing as little as $20,000, makes the quality of his work all the more amazing. Though not all his films are first-rate, a surprising number of them are. The Black Cat (1934), Bluebeard (1944), Strange Illusion (1945), Detour (1946), Ruthless (1948), The Naked Dawn (1954), and The

Cavern (1965) comprise a fantastically consistent oeuvre and reflect the great depth of Ulmer's genius.

Little has been written about Ulmer. Luc Moullet, his champion (along with Truffaut) at Cahiers du Cinéma in the Fifties, parenthetically suggests some of the themes present in his work: "the great loneliness of man without God; the spiritual progression which leads from a yielding to Sin to the salvation of the soul, from the emptiness of existence to happiness, etc."[1] But Moullet does not elaborate or give examples.

For me, what is most important and interesting about Ulmer's characters is not their loneliness, though it is a factor, nor their spiritual progression (if, in fact, there is any) but the nightmarish world they inhabit. Ulmer's world, somewhat like that of Murnau's in its sensitivity to and assertion of abstract, mystical forces which haunt his characters, is an irrational one, governed by the logic of nightmare more than by any coldly mechanical sense of fate. Ulmer's characters do not struggle against an externally imposed chain of events but rather are powerless prisoners of an irrational series of experiences which they can neither understand nor control. They are deliberately inconsistent; they act chaotically. They repeatedly surrender themselves to their intuitive but irrational impulses. Consequently, they lose control over their actions and their environment. Ultimately, they exist only as passive reactors to what happens to them.

The central character of Detour, Al Roberts (Tom Neal), accidentally involved in a man's death, becomes burdened with guilt and then senselessly follows a course which leads to his own demise. By perceiving and reacting to his experiences fatalistically, Roberts helps to make the film's action fatalistic. His hard-boiled cynicism authors such lines as, "That's Life! Whichever way you turn, Fate sticks out its foot to trip you!" and creates a strange sympathy between himself and the nightmarish world around him that binds him to its logic, not that of the normal world. Yet, since this logic remains incomprehensible and mysterious to him, he seems to become its prisoner, caught up helplessly in its flow like a man in a dream.

The world around Ulmer's characters has no fixity; it is ultimately unknowable. His universe, like Poelzig's (Karloff) house in The Black Cat, is built upon a battlefield

that has become a graveyard and is undermined with so
much dynamite that, as one character points out, "the slightest mistake by any one of us could cause the destruction of
all." Ulmer's characters, living on the brink of sanity,
constantly run the risk of making that one mistake and of
unleashing fantastically chaotic forces which will haunt them
to their own destruction and which, to paraphrase Poelzig's
comments on the cat's nine lives, are "as deathless as Evil
itself. "

In Bluebeard, puppeteer and painter Gaston Morel
(John Carradine) experiences a moment of artistic insanity
when he kills a model who disillusioned him. The scene,
which Ulmer shoots on expressionistic sets and with tilted
camera angles (it is presented as a flashback in the film),
seems to be the origin of the insane forces which control
Morel. Ulmer's use of a puppet performance of Faust provides a metaphor to suggest that his central character is
controlled, like Faust was, by abstract forces.

Like Gaston Morel in Bluebeard, Ulmer's characters
resemble marionettes: they seem to be manipulated by
some mysterious, invisible presence. In the Hamletesque
Strange Illusion, Ulmer creates, through an oracular nightmare, a supernatural bond between the dead Judge Cartwright and his puppet-like son, Paul (James Lydon). After
he wakes up from a traumatic nightmare in which he fore-
sees the intrusion as "father" of an "unscrupulous imposter"
in his family, Paul seems possessed by his father's spirit.
His paranoid suspicion of his mother's fiancé, Brett Curtis
(Warren William) and his eventual identification of Curtis as
Claude Barrington, one of the men responsible for his father's death, are treated by Ulmer as inspired by the dead
judge from beyond the grave.

When Paul, suspicious of Curtis, reads about Barrington in his father's files, Ulmer slowly pans from Paul,
at his father's desk, past several objects in his father's
study, to a portrait of his father hanging on the wall. It
is as if the camera, aware of the mysterious psychological
link between Paul and his father, were tracing to its origin
the invisible lines of force that unite son and father.

Ulmer's mise-en-scène roots itself not in logic, as
Rohmer's does, nor in the physical world, as Hawks' does,
but in the abstract, supernatural elements that control the
minds of his characters. Again and again, Ulmer's camera

movements reveal a sympathetic sensitivity to the irrational
forces that surround his characters. At the beginning of
Strange Illusion, a tracking shot through the woods to the
edge of a lake, a shot which obliquely refers to the famous
tracking shot in Sunrise, diverges from, then meets Mac,
the game warden, who is bringing a letter to Paul, written
by his dead father (which the father has left in trust for his
son) and bearing a warning that strangely coincides with
Paul's earlier nightmare. Ulmer's camera, in tune with
these larger, inexplicable powers, seems to follow an invisible path through the woods to its destination. It remains in strange awareness of the mystical levels of experience which elude the understanding of Ulmer's characters.

It is pointless to question the motivation of his characters. Roberts' decision to run away from Haskell's mur-
der/death, then from Vera's has its source only in the obscure nature of guilt itself. Vendig's (Zachery Scott) treachery in Ruthless, though at first explicable as a means of
bettering himself, of acquiring more money and power,
seems finally--because of his dissatisfaction with what he
gets--a totally irrational impulse. Similarly, Jenny's (Hedy
Lamarr) self-centered actions in The Strange Woman which
destroy the men who love her have no logical motivation
beyond her profound attraction to what she cannot have.

Ulmer's women are also, as a rule, mysteriously
motivated and they act irrationally. At times, they seem
drawn by nothing but the force of Evil itself. Fascinated
and hypnotized, like Alison's wife Joan (Jacqueline Wells)
in The Black Cat, they almost become its victims. Maria's
(Betta St. John) attraction to the outlaw Santiago (Arthur
Kennedy) in The Naked Dawn, the young girl's interest in
Vendig in Ruthless, the love of Paul's sister and mother for
Curtis in Strange Illusion, the modiste's amour fou for her
puppeteer in Bluebeard reflect the paradoxical affinity in
Ulmer's world between good and evil that threatens to de-
stroy his characters.

Once Ulmer's characters recognize the existence of
inexplicable and uncontrollable impulses in the world, these
impulses gradually become reinforced and magnified by the
environment until the characters actually become prisoners
of them. Paul in Strange Illusion is eventually a prisoner
in Professor Muhlbach's Mabusean asylum. In The Cavern,
the characters' original sense of entrapment in the cave increases with each failure to find a way out of it until the

cavern itself begins to represent the physical embodiment
of the characters' inner turbulence, fear, paranoia, and
insanity.   All their logical and orderly attempts to escape
fail.   In a final, pathetic act of insanity, one of the characters sets off an explosion which frees the others and
breaks the decor's mysterious grip on them.

The inability of Ulmer's characters to control their
environment, mirrored in their failure to control their own
actions for any purpose other than their self-destruction or
self-punishment, gives a distinctly pessimistic tone to his
work.   The deaths of Vendig and Buck (Sidney Greenstreet)
who fighting, drown one another at the end of Ruthless, represent this pessimism at its extreme.   Yet, his characters'
search (for escape from the cave in The Cavern, for a lost
love in Ruthless, for happiness in The Strange Woman, for
artistic inspiration in Bluebeard) for some positive value or
absolute truth in their worlds makes them tremendously ap-
pealing.   Ulmer's direction reveals sensitivity and sympathy
for his characters' feelings.   When Paul and his mother
discuss her marriage and she refers to her loneliness after
the death of Paul's father in Strange Illusion, their feeling
for one another almost breaks the grip of the forces which
control them (i. e. , the judge and Brett Curtis, respective-
ly).   In Bluebeard, Morel's affection for the modiste briefly
purges him of the demonic presence that haunts him.   Vera's
consumptive coughs and obvious loneliness in Detour get a
sympathetic, human response from Roberts--yet neither
character can break away from the course of action they
are committed to.

Though the world's bleakness often overwhelms its
brightness, the existence of both, almost simultaneously,
in his films reveals Ulmer's deep-seated concern for moral
conflict and sheds light on his interest in the abstract struggle between Good and Evil.   The fact that characters, like
those in The Strange Woman, give in to the evil forces, destroying not only themselves but others is less important for
Ulmer than the struggle itself.

In The Black Cat, Ulmer concentrates on Alison
(David Manners) as an intruder on the Poelzig-Verdegast
relationship, complicating their insane struggle with an un-
comprehending audience.   He focusses not on particular characters in The Black Cat but rather on a pattern of reactions
to events. 2   He pulls focus from the Alisons kissing to Poelzig, reflexively grasping the arm of a bronze nude in the

foreground, watching them. What emerges is an intricately constructed series of moral-psychological encounters too mysterious for the Alisons ever to understand. They remain helpless spectators of a great, yet inscrutable, drama.

Ulmer's irrational universe drives characters like Al Roberts in Detour to the point of a nervous breakdown. Yet he, finally initiated into the mysteries of his world, realizes his own mortal weakness and accepts whatever Fate has in store for him. Ulmer's characters remain quite weak. His plots often contain great gaps in narrative continuity. Yet his visual style, as Jean Domarchi and Andrew Sarris point out, never falters. Cognizant of a level of experience that is mystical, Ulmer seems to understand, with a certainty and sureness that is unique in the cinema, the invisible forces which make his characters' world the nightmare that it is.

NOTES

1. Luc Moullet, "Ulmer," Cahiers du Cinéma, No. 58, April 1956.

2. Mike Prokosch, in "Program Notes for The Black Cat" written for The Orson Welles Cinema, n. d. (probably 1968 or 1969), sets forth this idea of events portrayed in terms of reactions to them. He writes that "Ulmer is interested in showing how the event is to them, not in showing the drama of the event itself."

e.   Edgar G. Ulmer: A Reassessment

Luc Moullet has branded Edgar G. Ulmer "le plus maudit des cinéastes" and the label has stuck.   Andrew Sarris echoes Moullet, judging Ulmer "un cinéaste maudit" and, until recently, the director's reputation was indeed "wretched" and his films considered to be beneath critical consideration.   Ulmer's martyrization by the masses has led to his canonization by the few, myself included.   As Moullet explains, Ulmer's malediction ironically presupposes a genius: to be "maudit" is to be unjustly accursed and the word implies the opposite of what it actually means. Instead of a term of opprobrium, "maudit" has become a term of praise.

Yet Ulmer's work is hardly "blessed," if "blessed" is the opposite of "cursed"; it reflects the vagaries, inconsistencies and incoherencies inherent in rapidly-made, low-budget productions.   Beyond the Time Barrier and The Amazing Transparent Man, for example, were made simultaneously, in only eleven days.   The Black Cat was made in fifteen days, Bluebeard in 8 days, The Man From Planet X and The Daughter of Dr. Jekyll in 6 days each.   Club Havana cost $20,000 to make and Isle of Forgotten Sins, made in 6 days, cost $23,000.   At one period in his career when making ethnic-minority pictures in the Thirties, Ulmer shot between sixty and eighty set-ups a day.   Even though he maintains "that stories of such intensity (such as horror and science fiction films) are, strangely enough, much easier to make on a very short shooting schedule," the final product, though blessed with intuitive intensity, is cursed with an absence of production value.

Thus Ulmer's work is, at times, flawed, clumsy, and laughable--yet his greatest work, in spite of flaws, remains deeply moving.   It is impossible to take seriously films with titles like Girls in Chains, Isle of Forgotten Sins, Jive Junction and St. Benny the Dip and the films themselves fail to transcend their ridiculous titles.   His ethnic films of

146

the Thirties--at least the two Yiddish films I've seen--seem
mired in the dramatic conventions of the Yiddish theater
and similarly fail to transcend genre. But then there are
The Black Cat, Bluebeard, Strange Illusion, Detour, Ruthless, The Strange Woman, The Naked Dawn and The Cavern
which, despite low budgets, improbable scripts, and frequently only adequate acting, reveal a stylistic genius un-
rivaled in the history of the "B" film.

Ulmer's career has yet to be evaluated objectively:
he has either been dismissed out of hand, made "Camp,"
or so enthusiastically praised that he seems another Murnau.
Ulmer clearly is an auteur: his films all bear the stamp
of a single and consistent narrative personality, but the raw
material with which he works--scripts and performers espe-
cially--varies tremendously in quality from film to film.
His set design, lighting, editing, and camera technique frequently transcend the banality of his scripts and the weakness of his actors' performances and on the few occasions
when he succeeded in escaping the limitations of the "B"
film, in "A" films like The Black Cat with Boris Karloff
and Bela Lugosi, Ruthless with Zachary Scott, Sydney Greenstreet, Louis Hayward, and Diana Lynn, or when he has
competent actors with whom to work, like John Carradine
in Bluebeard, Hedy Lamarr, George Sanders and Gene Lockhart in The Strange Woman or the marvelous Arthur Kennedy in Naked Dawn, he proved himself a director of remarkable talent. In fact, after seeing The Black Cat, only his
fourth film, it is hard to understand the direction Ulmer's
career took afterwards. Perhaps the same hiatus in the
production of horror films in the mid-thirties which hurt
Lugosi's career also blighted Ulmer's. More likely, Ulmer
was just not that interested in capitalizing on his own success. Immediately after finishing The Black Cat, under the
pseudonym of John Warner, he made Thunder Over Texas,
a cheapie western for Beacon Productions, which he followed
with a string of mediocre ethnic films. None of this makes
sense from a career standpoint.

If the adjective "maudit" applies to Ulmer's reputation and career, it also describes his most compelling central characters whose lives are cursed either by fate or by
their own irrational behavior. All of Ulmer's character
relationships center on power struggles. Poelzig (Karloff)
and Verdegast (Lugosi) in The Black Cat engage in a battle
of wits and wills, symbolized in their chess game; the fate
of the Alisons, weak, rather foolish pawns in the contest,

hinges on the outcome.   It is a struggle to survive in an
Ulmer film--a struggle that few of his weak characters are
up to.   It is not physical strength that they need, however;
their survival depends on strength of will and strength of
mind.   In Strange Illusion, Paul Cartwright's (James Lydon)
fixation on Brett Curtis (Warren William) seems initially
motivated by a mental failing--paranoia perhaps--but turns
out an intuitively accurate mental judgment of character.
His pursuit of his goal, discovering his father's murderer,
takes psychological stamina.   His prophetic nightmare and
his fainting spells when his dreams begin to come true test
his strength and determination and reveal the toll that his
battle of wills with Curtis has taken on his own sanity.   Yet
his ultimate self-assuredness transforms seemingly subjective paranoia into objective fact.   Similarly, Al Roberts
(Tom Neal) matches his will against that of Vera (Ann Savage), ultimately losing the battle to her.   In The Strange
Woman, Jenny Hager (Hedy Lamarr) uses her beauty to en-
snare, then destroy men.   Ruthless, like Strange Woman,
deals with a character, Vendig (Zachary Scott), whose quest
for power and pursuit of idealized, unattainable goals destroys those around him and ends with a literal battle for
survival between Vendig and Buck Mansfield (Sydney Greenstreet), a man he had ruined and whose wife he had taken,
which results in both of their deaths.   The creature in The
Man From Planet X, sent to scout the Earth for possible
colonization, employs hypnosis to gain power over the inhabitants of a small island off the coast of Scotland.   The
Naked Dawn, in which power is less an objective than freedom of choice, culminates in a three-way face-off between
an abused peasant wife, Maria (Betta St. John), her greedy
husband, Manuel (Eugene Iglesias), and a philosophic thief,
Santiago (Arthur Kennedy).   The titles of Hannibal and The
Amazing Transparent Man are self-evident: conquest, in-
vincibility and power are their subjects.   Beyond the Time
Barrier involves a power play on the part of several scientists to overthrow the benign administration of "The Supreme" (Vladimir Sokoloff) with the aid of mutants.   The
Cavern begins with men at war, Axis vs. Allied powers,
then, trapping these political enemies together in a cave,
exchanges the man against man conflict for a larger one,
that of man against nature, and of man against his own inner weaknesses.

        Most frequently, the central conflict in Ulmer's films
becomes a psychomachia, a moral-psychological battle between good and evil, between virtues and vices for control

of the soul. His innocent characters are tempted by or
drawn to more worldly, quasi-evil characters and vice-
versa. In Ruthless, Vic (Louis Hayward) introduces his
fiancée, Mallory (Diana Lynn), to Vendig who, struck by
her resemblance to his childhood sweetheart, Martha (Lynn),
lures her away from Vic, pursuing her as obsessively as
he has pursued all his other goals. Mallory, in awe of
Vendig's wealth and power, seems to fall under his spell
from which only his death releases her.

     In Naked Dawn, the naïve peasant farmer and his
wife, Maria, are drawn to and corrupted by the outlaw Santiago who, like Verdegast in The Black Cat, ultimately sacrifices himself to restore them to one another. Naked Dawn,
in part, is a reworking of Sunrise--Santiago, with the lure
of money for the husband and tales of the exotic Vera Cruz
for the wife, taking the part of Murnau's "Woman From the
City." Yet for Ulmer, Santiago is no flat abstraction in a
rural-urban dialectic. The abstractness of the Murnauesque
situation is humanized by the idiosyncratic nature of Santiago's behavior; besides, Santiago is equally drawn to Manuel
and Maria and becomes a parental figure, complicating what
would otherwise have become allegorical simplification. In
Maria he sees the ideal woman, admiring her wifely skill in
making tortillas. In Manuel he sees himself before the disillusionment he experienced in the Mexican Revolution.

     Jenny in The Strange Woman is both innocently child-
like and calculatedly evil. By initially presenting her as a
child (played by Ulmer's daughter), he fixes this image of
her in our minds, effectively coloring her actions as an
adult with this initial image of childishness. Jenny is repeatedly torn between good and evil, between virtue and vice.
She donates money to the local church, helps house the poor
and homeless and prepares charity baskets for the impoverished sick. Yet she tortures and destroys. She uses her
father's death and Isaiah Poster's (Gene Lockhart) lust to
become the wealthy Mrs. Poster. She encourages Isaiah's
son, Ephraim (Louis Hayward), to kill his father. This
parricide leads to the son's suicide, which she discovers
and we see her staring with fascination at Ephraim's hanging corpse. And she steals another woman's fiancé. A
revivalist preacher delivers a sermon, looking at her, entitled "The Strange Woman." "The lips of the strange woman drip honey," he says, "and her mouth is smoother than
oil. But her end is bitter as wormwood, sharp as a two-
edged sword." She is strangely disturbed by the sermon,

lighting as many candles and lanterns as she can when she returns home and later confessing her wickedness to her husband.

Fascinated by her own beauty (the film's chief time transition occurs when Jenny, as a child, stares at her reflection in a river and dissolves to her, as an adult, in the same position) and the power it exercises over men, Jenny becomes corrupted by that power; in using it she becomes its victim. Staring at her reflection in the water, Jenny appears to enter a trance; it is as if she were no longer acting of her own accord but rather hypnotized by some greater will, perhaps by the forces of Evil. Here and elsewhere, Ulmer deals with the interplay between free will and fate. His characters seem to exercise free will, making crucial decisions on their own, but, in fact, they are often the victims of the forces they seem to control and their actions are predetermined.

In Ulmer's worst films, the acting is merely wooden. In his best films, it is intentionally trance-like. In The Black Cat, Karloff's Poelzig seems somnambulistic. When his servant announces the arrival of guests over an intercom, Karloff rises from his bed slowly, deliberately, yet mechanically, like a corpse rising from a coffin or like Cesare (Conrad Veidt) rising from his cabinet in The Cabinet of Dr. Caligari. In fact, Veidt's slow, balletic movements, in contrast to the jerky gestures of Werner Krauss's Caligari, seem to have influenced Karloff's acting style here.

At moments, a number of Ulmer's characters seem possessed or seem caught in some hypnotic trance. In The Black Cat, Joan Alison (Jacqueline Wells), under the influence of Dr. Verdegast's powerful narcotics, sleepwalks and later, when Poelzig puts out his cat (which is mysteriously brought back to life after Verdegast has killed it in the sleepwalking scene), he walks, as if in a trance, through his cellar, passing through his gallery of dead, glass-encased women, a zombie among corpses.

Similar in style but not in quality to Karloff's performance for Ulmer is Tom Neal's Al Roberts in Detour. We first see him walking down a desert highway in the dark, his movements spiritless and mechanical. He enters a truck stop, sits at the counter and stares blankly into space, rethinking the chain of improbable events which have robbed him of his identity and made him a fugitive. Neal looks as if he is reliving a bad nightmare, and he is.

Both John Carradine in Bluebeard and Hedy Lamarr
in The Strange Woman appear similarly possessed at crucial
points in their lives, Carradine when he kills and Lamarr
when she fixes her desires on an object (the first mate's
scarf) or a man (Lockhart, Hayward, or Sanders). Even
Strange Illusion, which features some of the least convincing
acting in an Ulmer picture, opens quite effectively with
back-lit figures seemingly sleepwalking through space. The
opening is the hero's dream which, upon his awakening,
starts to become real, like that in Mosjoukine's Le Brasier
Ardent. This introductory image, which the film reprises
at its conclusion, establishes the tone of the film. Its
characters move as if in a dream. They are powerless to
control events around them. When the hero awakens, he
behaves as if he were unwillingly acting a part in a recurrent dream. It is an opening that almost, but not quite,
makes one forget the inadequacies of the performances which
follow in the film's non-dream sequences. Even so, the
film deserves careful consideration. Strange Illusion begins
in the middle of a nightmare. Only clouds and a shadowy
silhouette can be made out in the darkness and fog. Er-
dody's brilliant score and the lifeless voice of the narrator
create a ghostly atmosphere, evoking the opening scene of
Hamlet, whose plot and atmosphere has influenced Ulmer's
film. We see additional obscurely-lit shapes emerge from
the fog. A dark figure appears between the forms of Paul
and his mother. She accepts this figure as her husband and
as Paul's father. Paul's sister also materializes in the
dream, wearing a bracelet given to her by the strange shade.
Vainly protesting that this man is not his father, Paul sees
a car crash into a train, a reenactment of his father's
death. Paul suddenly wakens, shaken out of his nightmare
by his friend and professor, Dr. Vincent (Regis Toomey).
Later that day, Paul gets a letter, left in trust for him by
his father before the latter's mysterious death, which re-
quests Paul to guard his mother and sister from those who
would unscrupulously take advantage of them. Returning
home, Paul finds that his mother is about to marry a
stranger, Brett Curtis, and slowly realizes, through several uncanny coincidences, that his dream is starting to
come true. Paul's strange, almost neurotic behavior seems
unfounded until we discover, through Ulmer's disclosure,
that Curtis is really Claude Barrington, his father's arch-
enemy, and that Curtis is seeking some sort of vengeance
on the Cartwright family. Entering Professor Muhlbach's
sanitorium (on the pretext of a need to recover from a
series of breakdowns), Paul discovers that Curtis and the

professor were responsible for his father's death, escapes
from the asylum and, eventually, rescues his sister and
mother.   Knocked unconscious in the process, Paul dreams,
as in the opening sequence.   The clouds drift away; the
dark stranger is no longer there; his friend replaces his
father between him and his mother; Paul walks off with
Lydia, his old girl friend.   Though it is only a dream, order has been restored.

   Ulmer creates a strong, quasi-mediumistic relationship
between Paul and his death father, who speaks through his
son.   Avoiding, for the most part, a simplistic Oedipal interpretation of the relationship, Ulmer suggests, by framing
Paul beneath his father's domineering portrait, that Paul is
possessed by his father's spirit, yet Paul's gentle treatment
of his mother precludes any suggestion of any unnatural desire on his part for her.   Paul's paranoid suspicion of Curtis and his tracking down of Barrington become necessary
steps for him to take in the gradual exorcism of his father's
spirit that he undergoes.

   The nightmare which opens and the dream which
closes Strange Illusion make explicit the film's concern for
the psychological nature of the experience of its central
characters.   Using a melodramatic format, Ulmer works
out his character's nightmare in the "real" world.   Yet a
basic equation between the dream and real levels of experience underlies the narrative.   The fact that both levels are
shown as equally subjective prevents our evaluation of either
level as more real or more true than the other.   The film
sets forth an essential ambiguity: though Paul seeks out the
truth about Curtis and about his father's death, his search,
motivated by paranoia and guided by a telepathic communication between Paul and his father, is far from objective.
Nor does Paul gain any profound understanding of himself
or of his environment.   Unconscious at the end, Paul remains a prisoner of imaginings.

   After Joan Alison's somnambulism in The Black Cat,
Alison, Poelzig, and Verdegast carry her to her room, then
discuss her behavior briefly on the way to their rooms.
Dr. Verdegast's explanations are partly medical, party psychological, and partly mystical.   He tells Alison that his
wife became "mediumistic, a vehicle for all the intangible
forces in operation around her."   Alison cynically replies,
"It sounds like a lot of superstitious baloney."   Verdegast
solemnly answers him with the film's most oft-quoted lines:

"Superstitious, perhaps. Baloney, perhaps not. There are
many things under the sun. "

Ulmer's films reveal that the director does believe
in intangible forces, whether it be externally-imposed fate
(Detour) or internally-generated, uncontrollable passions
(The Strange Woman, Ruthless), which circumscribe the free
will of his characters. They exercise little or no control
over their destinies. Even apparently freely-made choices,
like Maria's decision to run away with Santiago in Naked
Dawn, are reversed by a larger sequence of events. For
this reason, Ulmer's characters appear "mediumistic,"
helplessly entranced by others (losers in a power struggle),
by an environment of things (the puppets in Gaston Morel's
living room in Bluebeard), people, events or places which
they are too weak to master or by the Mephistophelean
forces of Evil.

Ulmer's characters are rarely shown as the initiators
of action; rather, they are most often presented with an object, character, event, or situation to which they react.
His action sequences are awkwardly staged and edited (e. g. ,
the fist fights in The Naked Dawn, the swordfights in The
Wife of Monte Cristo), but his reaction shots are eloquent
and beautiful. The single cut-away in The Black Cat to
Verdegast during the hotel limousine driver's story about
the bloody battle and the number of dead at Marmorös is
perhaps the most beautiful shot in the film: Verdegast
merely closes his eyes, suggesting that he can still see
the carnage and feel the horror which happened so long ago.
Ulmer, like Murnau, shows characters thinking and transforms physical action into mental experience. His camera,
again like Murnau's, becomes an intelligence through whose
mind the action is viewed, and whose movements suggest
the action of a character's thoughts more than his physical
movements. They both photograph thought. Thus, the first
shot of Maria in Naked Dawn is a long shot of her, lost in
thought, singing to herself by a pool of water. We sense
immediately that she is dreaming, dreams which she later
articulates in her conversations with Santiago. Or we see
her watching and judging her husband as he gets a gun out
of a drawer and prepares to murder their guest and cor-
ruptor-benefactor, Santiago. These are the equivalent of
the voiced-over image of Santiago dying or of Al Roberts
at the diner counter in Detour, yet they are considerably
more subtle.

Ulmer studied architecture at the Academy of Arts and Sciences in Vienna and worked in the theater as a set designer.   In the early Thirties he designed stage sets for the Philadelphia Grand Opera and apparently worked in a similar capacity at M-G-M.   He also worked, without credit, on Universal's Little Man, What Now? and, of course, on the design of all his own films.   His interest in set design emerges most dramatically in The Black Cat in which Hjalmar Poelzig, "one of Austria's greatest architects," lives in a modernistic Bauhaus mansion, situated on one of the bloodiest battlefields of the First World War.   The house features sliding doors, chrome strips on the walls, an open staircase which flows with the lines of the interior, cubelike bedrooms, modernistic furniture and an expressionistic chapel in which Poelzig conducts black masses with his cult followers.   The character name "Poelzig" is itself homage to German industrial designer Hans Poelzig who created the sets for Der Golem.

Ulmer's sets play important roles in his films, creating an atmosphere not so much of horror or suspense as of suffocation.   His sets, though not actually claustrophobic, are frequently enclosed.   His rooms often lack windows and a number of his films take place underground, either in part (the torture chambers and gallery of women in The Black Cat, the Parisian sewers in Bluebeard, the underwater sequences in Isle of Forgotten Sins, the cave in The Pirates of Capri, the underground passageways in Babes in Bagdad, the crypt in The Daughter of Dr. Jekyll) or almost entirely (Beyond the Time Barrier, L'Atlantide and The Cavern).   Films like Club Havana and Carnegie Hall take place almost solely in windowless interiors and here the places, characterized through Ulmer's sets, become the major focus of the narrative, unifying the disparate musical numbers and actions of the characters who enter these settings.

Even Ulmer's exteriors suggest atmospheres similar to those of his interiors.   The desert terrain in Tomorrow We Live and Detour and the barren landscape of snow in Murder Is My Beat and of rural Mexico in Naked Dawn suggest a characterless bleakness which tends to thwart the efforts of characters (like the well-digging Manuel in Naked Dawn) to master their environment.

At the same time, the Mexican landscapes of Naked Dawn play a theatrical role, suggesting the roughness of the

lives that are lived within this setting. The dull, coarsely-
textured adobe walls and earthen floors of Manuel's house,
in contrast to the brightly colored, exotically-staged cantina
sequence, suggests the drabness of the characters' lives.
Yet even here there is a primitive kind of beauty. Maria's
gestures as she makes tortillas, though simple, have a
poetic quality. Similarly, her bath, which Ulmer shoots
in carefully composed close-ups (chicken at her feet, a
smooth earthen jar from which she takes water with which
to bathe), becomes a lyrical ritual. Outside, long fluid
tracking shots give the characters' movements through space
a primitive simplicity. The subject matter of the film and
Ulmer's presentation of local customs and his celebration of
everyday gestures and actions is reminiscent of Courbet.
Yet Ulmer's Realism is poetic, dramatically stylizing traditional Realist content.

Ulmer's studio "exteriors" in all of his PRC films,
but most notably in Detour, are the creations of fog machines and smoke pots. In these interior "exteriors" he
surrounds his characters with a vague, undefined space that
is as constricting and terrifying in its own way as is the
cave in The Cavern.

Ulmer's enclosed settings result in an interiorization
of the narrative, reflecting his concern for the psychological
nature of his characters' experiences. The camera's exploration of Poelzig's cellar in The Black Cat and Paul
Cartwright's snooping in Professor Muhlbach's sanitorium
become, like Vera Miles' investigation of the Bates house
in Psycho, probes into the irrational and the subconscious
of Ulmer's villains. We sense in the interiors of Maria
and Manuel's hut in Naked Dawn the desperation of their
lives and Maria's entrapment in a life that bears no relation to her dreams and illusions. The low-ceilinged, darkly-
lit interiors of Jenny Poster's house in The Strange Woman
seem to be haunted by the ghosts of the men she has destroyed. Significantly, she confesses her role in two men's
deaths in the same room in which she induced Ephraim to
kill his father and her husband (Sanders) sees the ghosts
she has created and flees to the woods to think things over.

His interiors frequently become traps or potential
graves (e.g., the underground interiors) which his characters seek to escape. In escaping, characters attain a pur-
gation of sorts, ridding themselves of fear and guilt and
restoring, in part, a superficial order to their lives which

events in the chaotic interiors temporarily disrupted (e. g.,
the Alisons in The Black Cat).   Yet a bitter cynicism underlies the escapes with which Ulmer's films conclude.   His
films are not entirely cathartic (e. g., the Alisons remain as
foolish and naïve as they were when the film began).   The
final escape from the cave in The Cavern, for example, is
made possible by an act of insanity--the general (Brian
Aherne) detonates boxes of explosives, killing himself but
freeing the others.   Preceding this escape was that of the
sympathetic German officer Hans (Hans von Borsody) who
found a natural passageway out, only to be shot by members of the Italian Resistance.   The only ultimate escape
from the nightmare Ulmer's characters live out is death.

     Ironically, "reality" for Ulmer's actors and for him-
self was occasionally not far removed from nightmare.   Tom
Neal, the ill-fated star of Detour, in which film he accidentally kills the driver who gave him a lift and unwittingly
strangles Ann Savage with a telephone cord, made the headlines when, in 1952, he fractured the cheekbone of actor
Franchot Tone in a fight over Barbara Payton, an actress
who appears in Ulmer's Murder Is My Beat and who, in her
decline, became a Hollywood prostitute (according to Andrew
Dowdy) and wrote poetry ("Love is a memory/Time cannot
kill").   Neal subsequently spent six years in prison for
killing his estranged wife, apparently reliving his role in
Detour.

     Much of Ulmer's career itself has been cursed and
he has been locked into a frustrating cycle of "B" pictures.
The last years of his life were marked by illness.   A series
of strokes left him paralyzed, unable to swallow or eat,
talk, or move anything but the forefinger on his right hand
with which he made communication.   As his wife described
it a month before his death, "this time it is truly his own
nightmare that he endures."   I can imagine that Ulmer lay
there, thinking of the last few lines of Detour.   At the end
of the film, after a series of paralyzing events, hitchhiker
Al Roberts (Neal) walks off, alone, into the night.   He
thinks about what has happened to him and wonders what life
would have been like if things had been different.   "But,"
he observes, "there's one thing I don't have to wonder about
--I know.   Someday, a car will stop to pick me up that I
never thumbed.   Yes, Fate, or some mysterious force, can
put the finger on you or me for no good reason at all."

PART TWO: THOSE WHO PUT THEIR FAITH IN REALITY

1. CLASSICAL STYLE, MELODRAMA, AND THE CINEMA OF EXCESS: GRIFFITH AND BORZAGE

Griffith's mastery of editing within the scene and of parallel editing marks the first steps in the evolution of classical style, a style which tends to naturalize the space within which the narrative is set through "invisible" editing, eye-line matches, cutting on action and other devices which mask the illusionary processes of narration. Both Griffith and Borzage, as melo-dramatists, deal with the moral structures which lie beneath superficial appearances, bringing them to the surface by means of a certain stylistic excess. Though less excessive than the heirs to this tradition (Sirk and Minnelli), Griffith and Borzage melodramatize their style, either through an emotional editing (Griffith's cross-cut chases) or camera style (Borzage's God's-eye-view overhead shots in 7th Heaven). Wholly committed to the melodramatic nature of the events under recital, Griffith and Borzage, unlike their generic successors, refuse to soft-pedal melodrama and thus share its naïve vision of the world.

a. True Heart Susie

D. W. Griffith's feature films fall into two categories: the
epic and the lyric. Until recently, the weight of critical
opinion has regarded Griffith's more ambitious, large scale
productions such as The Birth of a Nation, Intolerance and
Orphans of the Storm as more serious works than his less
ambitious, more intimate films like A Romance of Happy
Valley and True Heart Susie. 1 Yet the more Griffith I see,
the harder I find it to distinguish between the epic and lyric
impulses. Intolerance, especially in the Babylonian sequence, achieves its greatest emotional power through the
juxtaposition of history in long shot and melodrama in close-
up. Griffith's work, like John Ford's, succeeds in captur-
ing the momentary beauty of an idiosyncratic gesture against
the eternally impersonal stone face of history.

All of Griffith's epics, constructed on this dramatic
principle, blend history and melodrama into a single narrative fabric. 2 In Orphans of the Storm (1921), he uses the
French Revolution as a chaotic background for his separa-
tion/reunification melodrama. Even in America (1924), history and melodrama are inextricably interwoven. Using the
Montague family as an immediate and personal microcosm
of the American Revolution, America combines national with
personal catastrophe. In one remarkable sequence, young
Charles Montague, who, unknown to his loyalist father, has
gone off to fight on the side of the defiant American cause,
exposes himself to British fire to get much-needed powder
in the battle at Breed's Hill. On his way back to the American trenches, Charles is shot and falls. Griffith cuts a
shot of his sister, Nancy, reading Charles' old letters in an
attempt to comfort their wounded father. Then he cuts back
to Charles who miraculously struggles to his feet, delivers
the gunpowder and collapses, finally dead. Though the cut
to Charles' father is partly ironic--since Justice Montague,
a Tory, is unaware that his son is fighting against the king
--the sequence does illustrate the spirit that lies behind the
son's heroism. The shot of Nancy comforting his father

161

seems to give Charles renewed strength: his own letters
to his father--his devotion to family--mysteriously comfort
him.   Though Griffith conceives of the American Revolution
in family terms--i. e. , the son revolts against his father--
he uses the spirit of the family--the son's love for his
father--to animate and guide his revolt.

In comparison with America, one of Griffith's more
ambitious and didactic pictures, True Heart Susie's (1919)
uncomplicated simplicity and stylistic directness give it a
charming sort of purity.   The absence of an historical background and of the specificity of detail such a background demands creates a freer, more open structure.   Instead of the
usual, multiple-plot narrative, True Heart Susie tells a single story, avoiding a counterplot's symbolic or metaphoric
commentary on the central action.   This simplification of
the action results in a greater formal simplicity.   The film
feels less rigidly structured.   For example, there is practically no cross-cutting between two separate events for
dramatic effect.   And when Griffith does cross-cut, as in
the sequence which compares Susie's (Lillian Gish), Bettina's
(Clarine Seymour) and William's (Robert Harron) actions on
the evening of the fatal rainstorm, he does not so much
oppose these three characters as explore the worlds which
isolate them from one another.   Though Susie's maternal
nursing of her aunt mirrors, inversely, Bettina's naughty,
child-like desertion of William in order to attend a party
in town, their actions are merely different; they are never
diametrically opposed.

Nor does Griffith construct separate, irreconcilable
worlds, each with its own internal order and logic, whose
conflict gives birth to a new world.   For example, in
Broken Blossoms (1919), the two major sets--Battling Bur-
row's (Donald Crisp) cold bare, waterfront shack and the
Yellow Man's (Richard Barthelmess) warm, exotically detailed storetop apartment--delimit the two, polarly different
worlds that exist for Lucy in the film.   Her "home" consists of a stove on which she cooks her father's meals, a
table at which he (but not she) eats, and a bed.   Bare brick
walls--windowless, of course--and floors give the setting a
rough texture which echoes that of Burrows himself.   It is
a place of domestic drudgery, abuse, and unhappiness.   The
Chinaman's becomes a peaceful refuge from that; it is a
setting created to house her.   After the Chinaman gently
places her on an alter-like, elevated bed, he decorates the
room for her with tapestries, dresses her in precious Chi-

nese robes, and surrounds her with Oriental art objects.
It becomes a world of visions and dreams--a world which,
when Battling Burrows enters it to retrieve Lucy, Burrows
smashes to pieces.   After Lucy is cruelly beaten to death
by her father, the Chinaman, though he arrives too late to
save her life, nevertheless "rescues" her from the grim
waterfront setting in which she was killed.   After he shoots
Burrows, the Chinaman carries Lucy back to his own apartment where we see them for the last time.   The heavily
tragic action at the end (her death and his suicide) is
lightened by their minor triumphs: Lucy escapes her world
and the Chinaman escapes his.

        True Heart Susie lacks this Dickensian dialectic of
decor: there are no good or evil settings, nor are there
conflicting worlds.   Rather, Griffith creates a single universe, flawed only by its fragmented separation of one character from another. [3]   The opening shot of the film, a high-
angle shot of two farmhouses separated by a dirt road that
runs between them, presents a single community or world,
unified in time and space.   The subsequent editing which
reveals William's father working outside one house with his
hoe and Susie's aunt sitting inside the other house sewing,
does not oppose worlds as much as characterize separate
parts--i. e., male/female, exterior/interior--of a single
world.

        The subsequent introduction of Susie and William at
the country schoolhouse, like the opening shot, sets up a
physical unity whose forthcoming violation and restoration
will have its roots in the fragmented nature of the composition itself, a fragmentation that is more internal (i. e.,
perceptual) than external (i. e., physical).   Griffith shows
William and Susie, standing next to one another in a spelling
bee, in a single frame.   William misspells "anonymous."
Susie, for whom the word has much more meaning, spells
it correctly and exchanges places with him in line.   In
another, more formal Griffith film, such a switch in position would, because of the moral rigidity of spatial positioning in his melodramatic, tableau-like compositions, indicate
a dramatic reversal or turning point.   The ease with which
it is made here reflects the looseness of Susie's and William's relationship.   But although William and Susie stand
together, there are differences which separate them.
Though the difference--Susie spells better--seems, at first,
rather slight, it foreshadows the greater gulf in awareness
that eventually isolates one from the other, a gulf dramatized

in Susie's "anonymous" sacrifices (sending William to college, lying for Bettina).

It is hard to analyze the lovers' separation beyond its physical fact. In most such melodramas, the characters' separation arises out of an externally imposed design. Their differences in class (Orphans) or race (Broken Blossoms) prevent their union. Or the action itself, like the war in The Birth of a Nation, Henriette's loss of the abducted Louise in Orphans or the storm and ice floe that separate David from Anna at the end of Way Down East, keeps the characters apart from one another. In True Heart Susie, the separation seems to grow out of characters themselves, out of their blindness (William) and shyness (Susie), out of their own inertia and inability to change the way things are at the start of the film. The repeated motif of the frustrated kiss dramatizes this inertia and introduces an element of stasis into the relationship which becomes the subject of the film. True Heart Susie thus deals with the notion of fidelity, i. e., lack of change, in both its positive and negative aspects.

The absence of an externally imposed formal structure shifts the dramatic balance between form and content in True Heart Susie. Griffith's direction reveals a greater concern for characterization than narrative development. It is through the characters, not the plot, that he expresses and defines the nature of the characters' separation.

The power of the film lies in the tremendous performances Griffith gets out of Lillian Gish and Bobby Harron. Their scenes together evoke a sense of emotional disjointedness. Though both are physically alive to one another, the self-containedness of their gestures reveals a deep isolation that neither can easily escape. The way William strokes and twirls his new moustache upon his return from college suggests a narcissism that blinds him to Susie's merits. Earlier in the film, on their way home from school, William and Susie stop by a tree. They look at one another; they start to kiss, then draw apart without touching one another. Instead of kissing her, William carves Susie's initials, along with his own, into the tree. The frustrated kiss which recurs throughout the film emphasizes not only the physical space but also the emotional gap between them. It finds visual resonances in the physical barriers which come between the lovers: the fence outside Susie's house, the garden hedge and the window in the last scene.

The film's settings, both the exterior, rural landscape and the interior, orderly domesticity of Susie's house,
set off, frequently in a humorous way, the idiosyncratic actions of the characters. The physical presence of the world
of nature works as a foil for the unnatural gestures that appear within it. When William rehearses his first sermon,
Susie's rapture in his wild, fire-and-brimstone gesticulation
works ironically with the beautiful but oblivious grove of
trees within which the scene is set to underscore the unnaturalness of William's action. In a way, their unnaturalness within nature serves to characterize the stasis of their
relationship as itself "unnatural." Earlier, as Susie and
William walk down a country road in long shot, Susie's
right foot kicks out. A characteristic trait, the spasmodic
foot betrays externally the inner self-restraint--violation of
natural impulses--which prevents Susie from fully expressing her love for William. Inside her own home this restraint vanishes and Susie explodes like a firecracker. She
jumps around, dances, and physically delights in her excitement over a non-committal letter she receives from William
away at college. The static quality of this interior space
makes her frenetic actions appear all the more chaotic.
Her aunt's Dickensian request that Susie "deport" herself--
the aunt repeatedly represses Susie's natural desires which
serves to "explain," in part, Susie's repressed behavior
toward William--makes Susie's violation of the order of her
setting all the more outrageous.

At the end of the film, after Bettina's death, William
learns of Susie's sacrifices for him and, with a new maturity, goes to tell her of his love for her. He approaches
her at her window as she waters flowers with a huge watering can. When he tells her that he loves her, she (inside
the house) hides shyly behind the watering can. Finally,
William leans through the window and kisses her. Though
the ending unites William and Susie, their unification is
made only with difficulty. The presence of the window and
the watering can between them gives the scene and their
actions an awkwardness reminiscent of their earlier scenes
together. Yet the composition, combining male and female
and exterior and interior, resolves the separations introduced in the film's opening shots and reflects a new stability
and balance in Susie's and William's relationship.

Though the window scene unifies the couple, it also
preserves their separateness: William and Susie remain on
different sides of the window wall. The final image of the

film, a postscript of sorts for their relationship, presents
them not as they are, but as they were.   We see them as
childhood companions, walking down a country lane together.
Though no longer separated by the architecture of the set
design or the fragmented landscape, the characters achieve
an idyllic happiness only by regressing into the past. [4]

The narrative action of Griffith's previous features,
from The Avenging Conscience (1914) to The Hearts of the
World (1918), moves forward in time, often finding resolution in a utopian vision of the future.   Henry Walthall's
poet, in Avenging Conscience, shares his success as a writer with Annabel (Blanche Sweet) in a setting near a river
bank.   Surrounded by satyrs, child-like nymphs and tame
animals, the lovers inhabit a fairytale world of fantasy
purged of nightmare, murderous thoughts and carniverous
animal life.   The Birth (1915) ends with a visionary sequence of "a golden day when the bestial War shall rule no
more."   Hostilities cease on the battlefield; we see, through
superimpositions, Christ's Second Coming and a vision of a
celestial city.   Intolerance similarly depicts the advent of
the Millenium; peace comes to the world's battlefields.   A
title tells that "instead of prison walls bloom flowery fields,"
and we see a prison transform itself into a field of flowers.
Vegetation has overgrown cannons and children now play in
former battlefields.   A cross of light appears in the sky.
Though less utopian than its predecessors, even Hearts of
the World looks forward in its final image to the dawn of a
new era, haloing its hero and heroine with a Murnauesque
sunrise which appears above their heads.

True Heart Susie, concluding with an appeal that the
viewer try to imagine William and Susie as they once were,
retreats into the world of memory and, as such, prefigures
the sort of reactionary escape from the problems which be-
set the modern world that occurs in Broken Blossoms.   The
lovers in True Heart Susie are denied, by the very nature
of the separated unities around which the narrative is built,
a future.   In remaining faithful to former images of themselves, William and Susie look back to a pagan Golden Age
rather than forward to a Christian Utopia.

The lack of stylistic sophistication in True Heart
Susie makes it one of Griffith's purest and most immediate
films.   There is nothing that distances us from the characters.   In a film built around chaotic adolescent behavior,
there is a remarkable simplicity of characterization: Grif-

fith, like Ford, creates characters with an economy of gesture. The physical presence of the natural countryside
throughout the film lyricizes the central relationship--it has
none of the pressing inner necessity of Griffith's more constricting interior films. In comparison with his other work,
True Heart Susie seems unique in its lyrical directness.
There is no great story or idea that moves it, but rather a
series of awkward, idiosyncratic gestures and a feeling, on
Griffith's part, for the beauty of his characters' love.

NOTES

1. Lewis Jacobs, in The Rise of the American Film (New
   York: Teachers College Press, 1968), views Griffith's post-Intolerance work as inferior. Tom Gunning's Museum of Modern Art program notes on
   True Heart Susie represents an attempt to redress
   Jacob's slighting of the film.
2. In retrospect, Intolerance appears less unified in its
   blending of history and melodrama than Griffith's
   subsequent epics, especially Orphans of the Storm.
   Intolerance seems the product of two opposing theatrical traditions, that of nineteenth century melodrama (narrative in orientation) and that of turn-of-
   the-century spectacle (presentational or non-narrative
   in orientation). The tradition of spectacle is best
   represented by the shows mounted on the enormous
   stages of the Hippodrome Theater in New York.
   Characterized by tracking shots, cranes, and a variety of camera movements, the style of spectacle
   presents rather than narrates action. As such, it
   signals a reversion to the panoramas of pre-Griffith
   cinema like Scenes From Luna Park (Biograph,
   1907). In Intolerance, the narrative flow virtually
   stops for spectacular panoramas of the Babylonian
   set and the aesthetic integrity of the work suffers
   for it. The epic impulse, associated here in part
   with the impulse toward spectacle, thus separates
   itself from the lyric impulse.
3. This idea derives, in part, from Harvard Film Studies
   program notes written by Mike Prokosch on November 2, 1969.
4. Tom Gunning discusses the equivocality of this temporal
   reversal in his MOMA program notes, dated May
   1975.

b. The Art of the Melodramatic Style: D.W. Griffith and
    Orphans of the Storm

One of the truly great tragedies in the short history of film
and the even shorter history of film scholarship has been
the institutionalization of D.W. Griffith as the "Father of
American Cinema." Griffith's films have, in the process,
suffered tremendously, becoming antique visual textbooks;
his techniques have been lumped together into a sort of
stylistic primer to illustrate the evolution of a bogus "film
syntax." His style, once fresh and powerful, has been
slowly ossified into archaic paradigms, declaimed into
meaninglessness by generations of inferior imitators. In
short, Griffith has been terribly misunderstood--especially
by those who remember only the historical significance and
the epic scope of The Birth of a Nation (1915) and Intolerance (1916) and forget the charm and beauty of Broken Blossoms, True Heart Susie, Way Down East and Isn't Life
Wonderful?

It is about time that someone attempt to "rediscover"
Griffith, to look at his films not as educational museum
pieces but as works of art. It is important for us to see
that Griffith is not only great but also good--that there is a
beauty in his films that goes beyond mere technical innovation. It is important for us to see that his films work, not
as illustrative definitions of a cinematic vocabulary, but as
highly emotional experiences which, at their best, seem to
defy description and analysis. Unfortunately, or rather fortunately, it is easier to see Griffith's greatness than to write
about it, but it is my hope that, by writing about the beauties
of his style, I can encourage some people to look again at
his films and, perhaps, to see how good they really are.

Orphans of the Storm

Griffith's films stand, along with the plays of Chekhov and
Ibsen, at the end of nineteenth-century melodramatic tradi-

tion. His films' emotional power has its roots in this tradition and, in order to understand the beauty of Griffith's treatment of his stories, it is necessary to accept these stories and the melodramatic conventions that they contain for what they are.

Griffith made Orphans of the Storm in 1921, after Way Down East. Set in Paris in the time before and during the French Revolution, Orphans, on first glance, resembles the historical epics of The Birth of a Nation and Intolerance more than the elegiac melodramas of Broken Blossoms, True Heart Susie, and Romance of Happy Valley. Yet beneath Orphans' surface lie the elements of pure melodrama. If this surface is stripped away, it becomes clear that Orphans is not really about the politics of the French Revolution but about the relationships of characters and families projected by Griffith upon an historical event. The way he treats the characters who made the French Revolution will illustrate what I mean. Throughout Orphans, Griffith develops historical figures like Danton and Robespierre not as political but as melodramatic characters. For Griffith, their historical significance becomes much less important than their moral relationship to the film's central characters. Robespierre, for example, as a result of his melodramatic function, is less of a power-hungry politician than a prude. Thus, when he quotes Robespierre's remark that "France must be purged of all vice," Griffith characterizes Robespierre's political acts (e. g. , his persecution of Henriette) in purely moral terms. Similarly, Danton, though he functions doubly as Henriette's and France's savior, draws more of his power in the film from the sad beauty of his frustrated love relationship with Henriette than his success as a leader of the revolution. Because of the way Griffith treats it, the French Revolution becomes a melodramatic event. It develops naturally out of Griffith's characters and their situation. But, in order to see exactly how the revolution functions as melodrama, we must first examine the nature of the melodrama Griffith uses in Orphans.

Griffith repeats a single melodramatic situation over and over again in Orphans: the destruction of the family unit. With each repetition, the act becomes more powerful, more involving, and more emotionally devastating. The film's opening scene begins this pattern, sets the mood and determines, in part, the nature of what follows. In a sense, the whole film grows out of an initial melodramatic act: the

slaying of the Marquise's commoner husband by aristocrats
and the taking away of her baby, Louise. This destruction
of the family unit creates an imbalance, a sense of a dis-
ruption of a natural order, and implies, true to the conventions of a traditional "separation" melodrama, the ultimate
restitution of that unit--which is the subject of the remainder
of the film.   At the close of the first scene, the baby is
left on the foundling steps of Notre Dame.   A destitute
father, hoping to leave his own baby for some richer family to adopt, brings her to the same steps and finds Louise.
Returning home with both babies, the father creates a new
family structure.   In the first few scenes, Griffith leads us
from one family structure to another, beginning the long
process of recreating a new family unit out of an old--not
necessarily one based on blood ties but more on a common
moral and spiritual bond.   This new family structure, seen
in the tableau at the end of the film, represents a new order, containing the best elements of the old--Pierre Frochard, the Chevalier, the two orphans, and Louise's mother.
It is towards this final tableau that the whole film builds.

The Master Shot and the Moral/Emotional Universe

It is difficult to appreciate the beauty of the final tableau in
Orphans and to understand that, stylistically, it works as
the visual climax of the film without first seeing how Griffith uses the tableau or master shot elsewhere in the film.
He tends to use it to define, in an almost theatrical way,
the spatial limits of the action of a scene, the edges of the
frame representing, as it were, the proscenium of a stage.
Griffith usually (he frequently breaks this pattern for special
effect) begins and ends each scene with a master shot which
shows the full range of the scene's action and includes all
its constituent parts.   As the scene progresses, he regularly cuts within this tableau to accentuate one or more of its
parts.   Griffith's first shot of the de Vaudrys, for example,
shows the count at his desk in one half of the frame and
the countess (seen initially in the first scene) sitting on a
chair in the other half.   Cutting in to a close-up of the
countess (remembering her lost child, Louise) and then the
count (not understanding her look), he breaks his master
shot into two parts, each with a different sentiment or feeling to it equivalent to our different feelings about each character.   When the de Vaudrys' impoverished tenant, Jacques
Forget-Not, enters, Griffith cuts back to the original master
shot and then, as Jacques stands between the count and the

countess, cuts in to a close-up of him and his basket of
fruit.   When Jacques remembers his father's torture (an
inset flashback) at the de Vaudrys' hands, Griffith establishes a specific mood for his part of the tableau also.
The result becomes quite complex: each part of the frame
(i. e. , each character and the space around him) has a different emotional tone or texture to it.   When Griffith cuts
back to a master shot--uniting these three parts into a single frame, he also unites these three sentiments or moods
into a single emotional world.   That is, he shows a variety
of feelings inside the borders of a single shot but keeps
these feelings distinct.   The different parts of Griffith's
frame don't fuse together into a single, emotional effect--
much as his characters remain static in the frame, so their
emotions remain distinct.   Whereas someone like Eisenstein,
by cutting outside of the frame and juxtaposing two or more
different spatial and emotional worlds on separate pieces of
film, creates an emotional synthesis, i. e. , a single emotional level; Griffith, cutting within a single spatial world,
creates a complex spectrum of emotions.   Griffith, then,
establishes a scene with a master shot and analyzes its
parts with close-ups (often using a simple abba shot structure).   Since he never shows a world outside of the master
shot (except through parallel editing which I'll discuss later),
his master shots come to represent self-contained worlds,
each somewhat separate from the other.   In Orphans, each
world (master shot) is defined by a family unit or social
class--the de Vaudrys, the Frochards, the orphans, the
aristocrats, the common people.   Yet as the film progresses
and as Griffith's repetition of master shots, like his repetition of the film's initial melodramatic act of separation,
reinforce the distinct moral qualities of these worlds, each
shot becomes more and more powerful, involving, and emotionally complex than the one that precedes it.

     In the first half of the film, each world remains
somewhat distinct from the other.   But by the middle of the
film, characters start appearing outside of their respective
master shots, outside of their worlds, as they become more
and more lost or separated from their original family.   In
a sense, the breaking up of each family parallels the breaking up (rearranging of parts) of the master shot.   As a result, the final tableau at the conclusion of Orphans--a master
shot which we have never seen before--visually represents
Griffith's creation of a new world for his new family to inhabit.

Parallel Editing/The Cross-Cut

The structural backbone of Orphans of the Storm is the
cross-cut.   It literally ties all the film's stories together.
Once having established several different family units with
his master shots, Griffith cuts back and forth from family
to family, from situation to situation suggesting, through
editing, similarities and differences between two or more
separate actions.   It is this parallel editing which makes
these separate actions seem to be one single, larger action
and which foreshadows the actual unification of stories in
the film's last few shots.

     It's difficult to describe exactly how Griffith's paral-
lel editing works.   To treat it only as a schematic organi-
zational device is a bit unfair because, in his hands, the
cross-cut becomes a highly emotional thing.   It almost has
a supernatural redemptive force (e. g. , the end of Intolerance).   In the first half of Orphans, Griffith uses this force
to separate his characters as well as to pull their stories
together--and in so doing, reverses the cross-cut's normal
function of unification.   For instance, Griffith accomplishes
the central act of separation, that of Henriette from Louise,
through parallel editing.   Before the orphans set out for
Paris, Griffith introduces the city and several of its inhabitants to us.   He cuts from the Frochards--hard-working
Pierre, his scheming mother, and his no-good brother,
Jacques--back to the orphans, shifting from one family unit
to a totally different one.   Midway in their journey, the orphans encounter a despicable aristocrat who plots the ab-
duction of Henriette.   As the orphans continue, Griffith begins to cross-cut to the aristocrat's henchmen setting their
trap for Henriette.   When the orphans arrive in Paris, he
cross-cuts from them awaiting a family friend to the aristocrats' orgy.   Henriette is finally abducted and taken to the
orgy.   Louise, left alone in the streets, is found by Pierre
Forchard who is powerless to prevent her kidnapping by his
own mother.   The whole sequence is set up rather powerfully.   It's as if Griffith, by cross-cutting away from the
orphans to the aristocrats' orgy or to the Frochards, were
pulling Henriette and Louise apart--each one being drawn by
a different social class.   (Henriette, the real commoner,
when taken by the aristocrats, leaves her natural class and
Louise, the child of an aristocrat, is taken even further
from where she belongs in society.)   Griffith, making their
separation a metaphor for the separation of society as a
whole with its rigid social stratification, projects his characters' melodrama upon the world they live in.

This separation is made all the more final and total
by the subsequent cross-cutting between the two sisters--
each with her own lover-rescuer (the Chevalier, Pierre) is
separated socially and spatially from the other (and also
from their respective lovers by class distinctions). Cross-
cutting between Louise's descent (socially and spatially) into
La Frochard's sewer-home and Henriette's rise to the second floor of a house where the Chevalier installs her, Griffith seems not only to accentuate the physical separation of
the two orphans but also to foreshadow their first re-en-
counter. For later, as Henriette sits in her room with
Louise's mother, Louise sings in the streets below, accompanied by her false "mother," La Frochard. Cutting back
and forth between the two imbalanced "family" units, he
works up to a shot which includes Henriette and Louise in
the same frame but separated by their positions (i. e. eleva-
tions) in space. Griffith, frustrating their reunion, shows
each girl again abducted by the representatives of a family
unit (Frochard) or social group (gendarmes of the aristocrats) and, thereby, lays the emotional groundwork for our
belief in the necessity of the destruction of "false" families
and societies before the orphans can be reunited.

The outbreak of the revolution melodramatically
marks the turning point in the film inasmuch as it represents the temporary destruction of certain boundaries separating characters (e. g. , the "prisons" which contain both
Louise and Henriette). As the revolution breaks out, Griffith cross-cuts between it and Pierre's own personal revolt
against his family when he saves Louise from Jacques. In
another part of the city, Henriette is released from jail.
Yet the destruction of boundaries is only temporary. For
when the people, celebrating their overthrow of the old order, begin dancing the snakelike Carmagnole, Henriette gets
caught up in it and is unable to find her sister.

Visually, the outbreak of the revolution and the dancing after its success represent a break with the sort of
images which precede them. Up to this point, Griffith's
frames, generalized in his master shots, remain orderly
and the characters in them, static. The revolution, with
all its movement and chaotic action, works to free-up the
master shot, to displace the characters in it, and to destroy this old visual order. The revolution frees Griffith's
characters from their separate and separating backgrounds.
It supplies the dramatic impetus needed to reverse the separating process that controlled the first half of the film. It

is with the outbreak of the revolution that Griffith's parallel editing begins to pull characters together again.

After the Carmagnole, Griffith's frames become orderly and static, reflecting the new but equally inflexible world of post-revolution Paris. Though the sisters still remain separated, the barriers dividing them are now set by the revolution. But within this new social order, counterbalancing the Jacques Forget-Nots and the Robespierres who continue to separate the orphans, stands Danton. Danton's near-divine intervention at the end--again built up through parallel editing into a spectacular chase-rescue scene--saves Henriette and the Chevalier from the guillotine. Danton himself performs the melodramatic function of reuniting the lost sisters. Though his feelings for Henriette are quite clear from the way he carries her down from the scaffold, Danton, repressing his affection for her, draws the Chevalier into the group and, with a gesture, creates the basis of the film's final tableau. (Danton's physical presence but spiritual exclusion from this scaffold tableau poignantly heightens the emotional effect of the reunification. He is a man without family.)

It is important to restate here that neither Griffith nor his characters are revolutionaries. If anything, they are political reactionaries trying to reestablish something they lost in the past (family). But it is wrong to give political labels to Griffith's characters or his film. To do so is to misinterpret his melodramatic view of the world for a political one; it is to misunderstand his films, to fail to see that their beauty lies in the strength and purity of the emotions they evoke.

Griffith's melodrama works in Orphans because of the directness with which it is told. Griffith does not transcend his material so much as he animates it and brings it alive: he makes us feel the full impact of each melodramatic situation in a direct way (in contrast to the equally great indirectness of Sirk's and Mulligan's melodramas). In large part, this is due to the vitality of the performances he gets from his actors--especially that of Lillian Gish. But it is also due to the emotional power of Griffith's visual style. The directness and simplicity of his cutting in the first scene of Orphans will give an idea of what I mean. Griffith begins his film in medias res; we enter the story at its emotional peak and in the middle of an action we are powerless to stop or, if we accept the melodramatic con-

vention Griffith uses, question. The scene concludes quickly and seems to be more the ending of another story than
the beginning of this one. Yet the narrative almost pulls
us along with it. Within a matter of seconds, a man is
killed and a baby is taken from its mother; we have seen
the destruction of a family unit. Yet though the scene, for
which Griffith gives us no preparation, seems irrelevant to
the sequences which follow, it does have the effect of transferring a great deal of emotional power from the end of the
former story to the beginning of the present one. Griffith
does this by centering our concerns on the baby. He concentrates the emotional power of the whole scene on the
baby rather simply and directly by means of his cuts from
medium shot--a tableau of mother, dead father, his slayers
--to a close-up of the baby, then a close-up of a note ("Her
name is Louise. Save her."), and finally a close-up of a
locket, which contains the note and which is strung around
the baby's neck. He then cuts back to the original tableau
shot as the men remove the baby and we switch our emotional focus, aided by this powerful close-up editing, to the
perils of the child being carried out of the room.

The power of the scene lies in its simplicity. It is
the emotional directness of scenes like this which makes
Griffith's melodrama work. It is the romantic optimism
of Griffith's treatment of his stories and the mysteriously
vital energy of his central characters that make his happy-
ending both believable and moving. The beauty of his melodrama and his visual style lies in their sublime purity.

c. Souls Made Great by Love and Adversity

One of the reasons that melodrama--and great filmmakers
like D. W. Griffith and Frank Borzage who work within its
conventions--remains in critical disrepute is that, as a
form, it tends to externalize, to transform a character's
inner conflicts into external events. [1] Nineteenth-century
melodramatic literature traditionally presents two-dimensional characters caught up in a melodramatic situation,
often at the mercy of a hostile environment or an extension
of that environment, that is, at the mercy of a villain or
some system that is evil. Though the genre's lack of complexity has a primitive sort of purity to it, it becomes, if
handled poorly, its chief drawback and its greatest limita-
tion.

        The best melodramatic literature--that of Dickens,
Ibsen, Chekhov--makes use of the form but avoids its flaws.
By adding depth to characterization through descriptive detail, it steers clear of simplistic externalizations of conflict. [2] Griffith and Borzage, like their literary and dramatic predecessors, use and believe in the melodrama as a
way of seeing the world but also, by shifting their focus
from the melodramatic situation itself to the characters
caught up in that situation, give the form depth and beauty;
Griffith's and Borzage's whole-hearted commitment to a
melodramatic world view, apparent in the intensity of feeling behind each shot in their films, invests their work with
an emotional level that gives profound meaning to the melodramatic situation and integrity to the characters who are
involved in that situation.

        What distinguishes Borzage's melodramas from Grif-
fith's is their spirituality. [3] Where Griffith concerns himself primarily, like Dickens, with the restitution of the family unit or the creation of a new, family-like unit, Borzage's
interests lie chiefly in the salvation of his characters--not
with external but with internal order. Where Griffith's
characters possess irrepressible physical vitality--a vitality

which makes his films immediate and direct, Borzage's characters radiate from within a unique, spiritual energy that makes them seem luminescently unreal. Yet Borzage's characters also project an utterly captivating but wholly innocent sensuality; they possess a strange, fascinating mixture of spiritual purity and physical attractiveness. Where Griffith tends to evoke either madonna-like innocence (Gish) or wholesome physicality (Dempster) in his characters, Borzage inextricably combines both these qualities in his (Farrell, Gaynor). But the sensuality of Borzage's characters is rooted in their edenic innocence, reflects a total ignorance of the state of sin, and denies an awareness of physical corporeality. Their pre-lapsarian sensuality affirms their spirituality. Borzage's films concern themselves more with the exploration of the essences behind physical reality: unlike Griffith, Borzage attempts to deal purely with the souls of his characters.

Borzage himself explains that "in every face I see I find a story. It doesn't seem hard. The story is right there lying on top, easily visible. You can take it and make something real, vital out of it.... By face I don't mean face literally.... I mean the characters in my story."[4] Borzage's inarticulateness is only verbal. The first few shots of Street Angel (1928), perhaps the director's greatest silent film, describe this spirituality--the stories behind faces--far better than words ever could. The first title of the film sets the mood: "Everywhere ... in every town ... in every street ... we pass, unknowing, human souls made great by love and adversity." After this remarkably explicit title, Borzage's camera wanders through the crowded streets of Naples, observing policemen making their rounds in the market place, lovers walking arm in arm, a lone, beggar girl sitting desolately at the foot of some stairs, circus gypsies arguing with a sausage vendor. Finally, Borzage cuts into an apartment in which a doctor is telling a girl (Angela) that she must buy some medicine in order to save her sick mother.

Each character we encounter in the opening shots of the film (similar to a later scene in which Gino looks for Angela in the crowded streets) has some sort of story behind him and each wears that story on his face. By shooting the sequence and directing the actors as he does, Borzage captures the essence of their stories--he penetrates beneath the physical surface of every action, every gesture, and every face. Though all the stories occur independently

of one another, Borzage ties them all together into a single
spiritual event by use of connective camera movement and
editing.   This sort of thing makes no sense logically, as
it would in Griffith, but it does work intuitively to define
the limits of the spiritual system that exists in the film.
Yet the spirituality in this and most other Borzage films
is much less rigid and limited than the term "spiritual
system" implies.   In fact, the beauty of this opening sequence in Street Angel rests in the intense complexity of
characterization which prevents an inflexible schematization
of spirituality in the film.

        Borzage's love relationships in Street Angel and other
films reveal a highly visual romanticism that has its roots
in the spirituality, not the physicality (as in Hawks), of his
characters.   Angela, escaping from the police when arrested
for theft while soliciting, runs away with the circus gypsies
and eventually meets Gino, an itinerant artist.   When they
fall in love, Gino paints her portrait.   His painting, a
metaphor for the film itself, captures her not as she is,
but as he sees her (her soul).   In order to eat, they sell
the painting to an art dealer.   Yet even though it has been
sold, the painting and the absence of it exert a powerful influence on the lovers.   When Borzage cuts to shots of the
bare wall where the painting was hung, the emptiness there
conveys even more complexly the painting's metaphysical
significance.   Meanwhile, the art dealer, hoping to make a
great deal of money on Gino's painting, hires another artist
to retouch it and to forge out of it an "Old Master."   Several times during the film Borzage cuts back to the painting
of Angela: as she herself becomes more and more transformed by her love for Gino, the painting, as it is slowly
forged into a madonna, also undergoes a transformation.
When Angela, without Gino's knowledge, is taken back to
jail after spending her last hour with him, Borzage cuts to
a shot of the forger painting a halo over her head.

        Borzage's editing of love sequences, in its total dis-
regard for physical space, goes beyond the surfaces of specific places or actions directly to the spiritual origins of
his lovers' relationships.   In his first sound film, Song O'
My Heart (1930), his lovers, Sean and Mary, are separated,
first by a forced marriage of her to another and, then, by
sheer, physical distance.   When Sean sings "The Rose of
Tralee" just before he leaves Ireland for a concert tour in
the U.S., Mary, hearing their old love song, is drawn
across the village to him and stands in his doorway, listen-

ing to him sing.   Later, as Sean sings the same song in a
New York concert, Borzage cuts back to (the dying) Mary
in Ireland looking out her window at falling leaves and,
seemingly, listening to a song that is sung thousands of
miles away.   Similarly, in I've Always Loved You (1946)
former lovers Myra Hassman and Leopold Goronoff, her
piano teacher, play the same piece of music on the piano
at the same moment, though miles apart.   By cutting back
and forth between the lovers in both films, Borzage creates
a strong, spiritual bond between them.

The spiritual quality of Borzage's love relationships
is made all the more powerful by the narrative backgrounds
against which they are set: the hostile environments of war
or depression or both seem to threaten their happiness.
7th Heaven (1927), Farewell to Arms (1932), A Man's Castle
(1933), Little Man, What Now? (1934), Three Comrades
(1938), The Mortal Storm (1940), and Till We Meet Again
(1944) all contain hostile backgrounds which Borzage's central characters ultimately transcend.   Yet the often-chaotic
worlds which surround these characters are no more "real"
in a physical sense than the characters themselves are.
In other words, the backgrounds do not impose real or
physical danger on the central characters; the chaos of the
backgrounds is not a physical but a spiritual one.   In Farewell to Arms when Lieut. Frederick Henry, deserting the
Italian army (including his cynical friend, Major Rinaldi,
and what Rinaldi represents), goes back to search for Catherine Barkley, Borzage surrounds him with death, destruction, explosions, and horrible human misery in the ranks of
the wounded and retreating soldiers.   Henry's search for
Catherine, set in the midst of all this spiritual bleakness,
becomes a metaphorical journey and, because of the strength
and explicitness of its images, the sequence emerges as
one of the most powerfully direct thematic statements in the
film.

The background of Little Man, What Now?, set in
the post-war depression of Twenties Germany, is filled with
voices crying out in the streets--voices like that of the
speaker in the park who preaches equality in the film's
rain-drenched opening sequence, or cynics like the communist who blames "them" for the death of his wife, or
spiritually twisted characters like the grotesque Kleinholz
family or the crazy relationship between Mia Pinneberg
and her dog.   It is the spiritual message of these voices
that threatens Hans Pinneberg, not the physical fact of eco-

nomic depression. Only the innocence and purity of his relationship with Lammchen--symbolized in part by the birth
of their child at the end of the film--enables Hans to escape
the spiritual depression that surrounds him. Man's Castle
is played against the background of the American depression
--yet Borzage sees that depression in terms of its spiritual,
not economic, chaos. As a result, Bill's spiritual aimless-
ness, represented by his attraction to the sound of the train
whistle, and his cynical assurance in his seeming self-sufficiency and independence--an aspect of his character reflected in the self-centered grotesqueness of his promotional
costumes (he becomes a walking neon sign, a clown on
stilts)--endanger the spiritual purity of his relationship with
Trina.

        Even the grim background of war in The Mortal
Storm or Till We Meet Again is less materially hostile than
spiritually suffocating to Borzage's characters. In The
Mortal Storm, set in pre-Nazi Germany, fascism becomes
an insane social-political backdrop for Borzage's family
melodrama: a family fights against an externalized system
of evil which threatens to destroy its cohesiveness. [5] On
one level, the film works as allegory--Borzage treats the
disintegration of the Roth family as a microcosm for the
greater collapse of the state and the world. Yet his handling of the narrative material is less political than moral
and spiritual. [6] When Professor Roth's stepsons, Otto and
Erich, and his best student, Fritz (also his daughter's fiancé and, as such, a would-be member of the family), reveal their conversion to fascism at the professor's birthday
party, their betrayal emerges as a betrayal of a system of
general , spiritual values more than of a specific political
or religious belief. [7] Borzage's editing here, first isolating,
then grouping various characters together according to their
beliefs, transforms the family from one based originally on
ties of blood to one based on a more abstract, yet stronger
bond of mutuality and affinity of spirit.

        Though the family seems to crumble around the pro-
fessor, what emerges is a new alliance of souls: Freya,
becoming more and more disillusioned with Fritz's gradual
nazification, grows closer to Martin, another of her father's
students. Borzage's alignment of characters according to
spiritual affinity creates two distinct spiritual outlooks in
the film. Though one seems to overwhelm the other--the
professor dies in a concentration camp, Mrs. Roth and her
youngest son go to Switzerland, Freya tries to escape from

Germany with Martin but is shot by Fritz and dies in Martin's arms on the Swiss border--the grotesque brutality and spiritual barbarism of that outlook take their toll on those who try to adhere to it.   In the last few shots of the film, Borzage beautifully reaffirms the transcendency of the professor's vision.   Otto and Erich visit their now-deserted home.   Fritz enters and tells them of Freya's death.   After Fritz goes, they argue about what has happened to their family and Erich, the more dogmatic Nazi, also leaves. Otto, transformed by what he sees and what he has learned, walks about the empty house; Borzage's tracking camera shows us what he sees and suggests what he remembers. Then, when Otto also departs, the camera, after a moment or two, follows him outside and tracks down the Roth's walk to their gate, focusing on his footprints in the snow as they slowly fill in with new-fallen snow before our eyes.

The power and beauty of this ending, like that of Farewell To Arms in which Lt. Henry holds his dead "wife" in his arms as peace is announced, lies in the complexity of feelings it evokes.   The disillusionment of Otto with the rigid Nazi dogma that has destroyed his family suggests his conversion to a more transcendent philosophy.   Yet the cost at which this conversion comes, the loss of all that once had meaning for him, qualifies the triumph of his transformation.   Borzage's treatment of this last sequence--especially Otto's partial recognition of his past blindness--leaves us with a sense of the transcendence of the spirit over moral degeneration and cynicism, and the power of spiritual concerns over material ones.

In Till We Meet Again, Sister Clothilde's fear of the outside world, brilliantly visualized in her attempts to shut out--through prayer--the gunshots she hears in the film's first sequence, define that world in terms of its spiritual threat to her.   Though Clothilde tries melodramatically to externalize the forces of evil and to locate them solely in the outside world, Borzage, going beyond the limited vision of any one of his characters, undercuts the authority of the novice's self-confidence and untested surety in her faith by using that world to make trial of her spirituality.   The aviator, a member of the outside world, becomes Clothilde's spiritual mentor and guide to that world and leads her to the realization of a greater spirituality.   For Borzage, Clothilde's cloistered saintliness gives her spirituality no meaning because she has only escaped not transcended the outside world.   Her contact with that world, with the aviator

and his system of values in particular, deepens her faith
and leads her to a more profound understanding of what religion really is.   Clothilde's crucifixion at the end of the
film, representing her conversion to a more complex idea
of spirituality, marks her transcendence of both the outside
world and the cloister.   In Till We Meet Again, as in other
films, Borzage's spirituality is rarely specific.   If the film
contains a conversion to a spiritual system, that system is
defined more by its flexibility than by its rigidity.   His
characters' transcendence, as a result, is all the more
moving because they attain a state that is not restricted,
defined, or limited by dogmatic ideas or rigid beliefs.

        For Borzage, the material world has no material
reality; it only represents a spiritual state.   In Mannequin
(1937), the tangible reality of a flickering light bulb on
Jessie's (Borzage's central character) tenement stairway
is less important than the intangible flickering light it
emits.   Though the source of the light is shown and Borzage's character can temporarily correct its malfunctioning,
the light becomes, like the sound of the train whistle in
Man's Castle, an intangible force that can not be dealt with
physically: later that night the light flickers again and finally goes out, trapping Jessie in the darkness of the stairway.   Though the flickering light is part of a physical environment (Hester St.) that Borzage's character is trying to
escape, he treats it as a visual metaphor of that character's
spiritual state and of the spiritual atmosphere which surrounds her.

        In a way, Borzage's visual style reflects his belief
in the immateriality of objects and characters.   His images
have little to do with real things; rather, like Plato's ideal
forms, they refer to an absolute and eternal reality that
exists on a purely abstract level.   In other words, Borzage's
images often function as spiritual metaphors, revealing the
director's concern for larger, transcendent issues.   In
Strange Cargo (1940), Cambreau, who exerts a strange
spiritual influence in the film, draws a map of an escape
route from the island's prison in a Bible and leaves it behind for Vern to use when he escapes and follows Cambreau
and the other prisoners.   Though Borzage only cuts to the
Bible-map once or twice, the image becomes one of the
most powerful ones in the film, representing, as it does,
the symbolic aspects of the prisoners' escape/journey.   The
explicitness of this brief and brilliant image, consistent with
the explicitness of the film as a whole, illustrates the depth

of Borzage's commitment, on a visual level, to the metaphorical aspects of his story.   In his silent films, even
more than in his sound films, Borzage's images work as
icons of the various spiritual systems present in his films.
And within his frames, each detail or object seems in tune
with each other detail and object and the whole frame comes
to stand for the various states of Borzage's characters on
their way to salvation.   In Street Angel, after Angela leaves
Gino (she is taken back to prison), Borzage shows him sitting slumped in his chair.   On the table in front of him lie
the remnants of his former happiness (last night's dinner
in celebration of his engagement to Angela).   Every element
in the frame reinforces Gino's sadness, seems in tune with
his despair.

Later in the same film, when Angela returns after a
year's absence, looking for Gino, Borzage shows her trapped
outside of Gino's apartment separated from her former happiness by panes of dusty glass and time.   When she looks
through the window, Borzage cuts to point-of-view shots of
Gino's cobweb-covered chair and the bare place on the wall
where his portrait of her once stood.   As in the earlier
sequence, Borzage's images here attempt to articulate the
state of Angela's psyche and to portray her helpless isolation from all that gave meaning to her life.

In The River (1928), Borzage presents Rosalee, waiting for the return of her convict-lover Marsdon, sitting dis-
consolately on the river's edge with the crow that Marsdon
left her.   He intercuts shots of flotsam and debris, caught
in the river's current, which disappears into a whirlpool.
Reflecting her mood and state of mind, the river and its
contents become a metaphor for Rosalee's despair.   The
appearance of Allen John among the drifting wreckage,
since it initially suggests an identification of him with her
gloom, ties the two together into a single spiritual state
that, through Allen John's purity and his subsequent efforts
to evoke emotion in Rosalee, gradually evolves into a positive, therapeutic relationship that redeems Rosalee from
her despondency.

In visual terms, Borzage's backgrounds, like his
tonal environments, have a spiritual rather than material
quality.   In most of his films, Borzage uses studio sets
and, as a result, his backgrounds have an unreal, fairytale quality.   His sets and characters often seem to glow
with an other-worldly luminescence.   Part of this has to do

with the way Borzage lights them--the tones of his backgrounds, often as light as or lighter than his characters'
faces, give his frames a weightless quality.   His lighting,
like Griffith's, is even throughout the frame--i. e. , each
part of the frame seems equally and evenly lit.   Yet Borzage's lighting is softer than Griffith's and his frames lack
Griffith's precision and tremendous resolution in depth.

What is important about Borzage's lighting is that it
creates an evenness of tone within the frame: though the
background and foreground are weightless, they are equally
weightless.   As a result of this evenness of tone and weight,
specific objects or backgrounds never exert specific physical
force on Borzage's characters.   The stove in Man's Castle
and the mirror-dresser in Little Man, What Now? exert a
spiritual force on Borzage's characters.   The relationship
of his characters to objects or to their backgrounds, because of this evenness of tone, does not work out in spatial
terms (e. g. , conflict between foreground and background or
between characters and their environment).   The flatness of
Borzage's backgrounds and their tendency to fall out of focus
in medium shot and close-up do not, as they do in Cukor's
films, separate characters from their backgrounds by dividing the frame into two planes of depth.   Instead, Borzage's
lighting unifies his frames into a single level of depth and
into a single tonal unity of foreground and background.   In
other words, characters do not derive their spirituality from
specific objects or from specific parts of the frame (as in
Griffith) but from the tonal quality of the whole frame and
the succession of frames around it (i. e. , from the editing).

Unlike Hawks, Borzage is not a visual materialist.
At the beginning of Three Comrades, after the transcendent
toast to the "comrades living and dead of all men, " Borzage
introduces his central characters.   When one of them, Otto
Koster, learns that, because of the armistice, his plane is
to be dismantled, he leaves the group and goes outside.
Outside, Borzage tracks in on Koster as he approaches his
plane.   He cuts to an insert shot of a medallion with "Baby"
written on it, cuts back to the original set-up as Koster
takes the pin out of a grenade, drops it into the plane's
cockpit and walks away.   Then Borzage cuts back to a shot
which tracks away from the plane and from Koster.   The
camera tracks back until the grenade explodes; then it tracks
back in on the burning plane.

What makes the scene so emphatic is its simplicity
and economy.   Though the editing is important, the force

that the scene has hinges on the tracking camera which pulls away from the plane.   For me, the tracking shot seems to deny the plane's physical reality, to turn it into an image reflecting that reality (just as the track-in later on Pat's x-ray calls attention to its function as something metaphorically representative of material reality but also something which, in itself, seems flat and unreal).   In terms of Borzage's visual style, material objects have no material reality; they are only representative of a material reality. Though Koster destroys his airplane, it's clear that whatever "Baby" is will live on after the demise of its physical reality.   In fact, we later see an insert shot of the same medallion on Koster's car which he also sacrifices to achieve a spiritual goal--to pay for Pat's operation.   The scene, for me, epitomizes the whole film: characters give objects and one another, through friendship and love, some sort of life of their own which transcends material existence.   Both the objects and Borzage's characters attain an "eternal" reality--something impervious to time and space, to death or physical separation.

There's a sequence in Man's Castle in which Bill, afraid of becoming trapped by Trina's love, leaves her. The scene begins with a two-shot close-up of them together. Bill slowly draws out of the frame, leaving Trina alone on the bed.   A train whistle is heard on the soundtrack.   After a few moments, Borzage cuts to Bill hopping a freight. Then he begins to cross-cut--back to Trina, then to Bill. The shots of Trina are tremendously powerful--partly because of her angled position in the frame.   As if her image were drawing him back through space, Bill first looks back and then jumps off the train to return to her.   Borzage's cross-cuts here, somewhat like Griffith's in Intolerance or Way Down East, go beyond the mere mechanics of suspense: implying an ultimate rescue, they have the force of salvation and exert a mysterious power.

In Borzage's films, as suggested above, the space between characters--even in a single frame--has no deterministic reality.   Where Welles, in the famous breakfast table time montage in Citizen Kane or the stairway sequences in The Magnificent Ambersons, shows the separation of his characters in geographically physical terms--in fact, the space between characters becomes a character itself.   Borzage has an altogether non-physical conception of time and space.   The split-screen phone conversations in Three Comrades reflect this: one character in one spatial matrix can

communicate with another in another spatial matrix. The
use of the split-screen foreshadows a sort of relationship,
like that in Man's Castle or I've Always Loved You, that
can transcend space. For this reason, the physical separation of the lovers throughout Three Comrades is immensely
important to the development of the spirituality of their relationship. Like Koster's plane, it can be seen as another
physical reality that Borzage's visual style destroys and
transcends. As a result, the form dissolve from Pat and
the Christmas tree in the mountain sanitarium to Erich and
the Christmas tree in Alphons' cafe, like that from Mrs.
Dexter's radio to Dean Harcourt's church in Green Light,
transcends the physical reality of space by suggesting a far
greater, spiritual reality that overshadows and encompasses
every action in Borzage's universe.

The shooting of Three Comrades, like that of his
other Thirties work, has a strange, almost mysterious quality to it, as if Borzage were trying to capture in his images
the intangible forces that surround his characters and help
define their spirituality. One sequence in particular--the
time montage that announces the changing of the seasons--
illustrates the totality of Borzage's "romanticized" view of
the universe. Midway through the film, he cuts to shots of
the wind blowing through the trees and through the city
streets when winter comes. He transforms an intangible
thing like time into an almost mystical force that floats his
cork-like characters along, much as the unseen wind does
the newspaper in the streets.

At times, Borzage's shooting seems to epitomize the
emotional state of his characters at specific moments in
time. On Erich's and Pat's honeymoon, his long, high-
angle shot of Erich carrying Pat along the shore back to
their hotel after her sudden collapse seems to transform his
characters, to bring out their inward state and feelings and
project them upon the landscape.

At the end of Three Comrades, almost every shot
seems to capture the spiritual essence of Borzage's characters. The breathtakingly beautiful crane shot as Pat gets
up out of bed after her operation and goes to her balcony
to see Erich and Koster for the last time suggests, as does
the overhead shooting at the end of 7th Heaven and Till We
Meet Again, a supernatural presence which oversees Pat's
ultimate transcendence of the final physical barrier which
separates her from Erich: her body.

Borzage's ending of Three Comrades, which differs
from F. Scott Fitzgerald's (his screenwriter), takes place
in a cemetery outside of the city and shows the three comrades and Pat reunited--a realization of the film's first
lines that toasted "the comrades living and dead of all men."
In the last shot, Erich and Koster (surrounded by the ethe-
realized images of Pat and Gottfried) leave the cemetery
and talk of going to South America. [8] Like the characters
at the end of Man's Castle escaping on the train together or
of Little Man, What Now? with the prospect of a better life
in Holland, Borzage's characters in Three Comrades do not
run away from their chaotic, troubled backgrounds as much
as they grow out of them spiritually. He so totally transforms them that it becomes impossible for them to go back,
as Fitzgerald wanted. Erich and Koster, like Pat and Gottfried, are ultimately liberated from the weight of their own
bodies and chaotic backgrounds that threaten to entrap them.

In conclusion, what makes Borzage's melodramas
unique is the director's avoidance of extreme conflicts:
neither his characters nor their environment struggle mor-
tally with one another. Rather than externalizing his plots
into moral contests between good and evil in which characters defeat or are defeated by the evil that engulfs them,
Borzage, diffusing the conventional melodramatic moral
polarity, permits the co-existence of several moral and
spiritual systems in his films. He merely makes trial of
one by juxtaposing it with another, providing the catalyst
for his characters' growth out of one system and emergence
into another, more transcendent one. The tolerant presence
of inferior spiritual systems in his films only heightens the
beauty and integrity of the superior one. For Borzage, it
is only through love and adversity that souls are made
great.

NOTES

1. This is the approach taken by Robert W. Corrigan in
    his introduction to Laurel British Drama: The Nine-
    teenth Century (New York: Dell, 1967), pp. 7-8.
2. It is necessary to distinguish between "melodrama,"
    which is a purely theatrical genre, and "the melo-
    dramatic," that aspect of the melodrama which sur-
    vives in other forms such as the novel and the film.
    The melodramatic in the cinema becomes, by virtue
    of the nature of the medium, wedded to an essential

realism, which automatically specifies details and
adds depth to characterization.

3. My use of the term "spirituality" needs some clarifica-
tion. It presupposes the quasi-Christian belief in the
existence in man of a soul (as distinct from the
body). Though Borzage's spiritualism lacks the
psychological dimension of that of the Expressionists
(e. g. , Weine, Murnau), his films, like theirs, concern the soul's temptation by the world, its death-
like passage through a narcissistic stage of cynicism
and its rebirth, wherein it regains the innocence
which characterizes it, before Original Sin, in the
Garden of Eden.

4. Peter Milne, "Some Words from Frank Borzage" in
Motion Picture Directing (New York: Falk Publish-
ing Co. , 1922).

5. The insanity of the Nazis is suggested most vividly in
their secret meetings and in the book-burning sequence at the university.

6. The film's success upon its release in 1940 rests largely on its political importance as one of the first
anti-Nazi Hollywood films. Most contemporary re-
views discuss it primarily in those terms. In fact,
the author of the book on which the film was based
wrote a political analysis of the film for The New
York Times, which was printed on June 16, 1940.

7. Indeed, Borzage makes very little of Roth's Jewishness.
Though the suppression of the character's Jewishness
remains consistent with Hollywood practice (see Drey-
fus in Warner Bros. ' The Life of Emile Zola, 1937),
Borzage is clearly less interested in Roth's racial
background than in his overall spiritual and moral
profile.   ´

8. Aaron Latham, in Crazy Sundays, (New York: Viking,
1970), pp. 144-145, discusses F. Scott Fitzgerald's
contribution to the film. Apparently, Fitzgerald
considered the film's present ending to be escapist.
The idea with which Fitzgerald wanted to end the film
was that of "the march of four people living and
dead, heroic and inconquerable, side by side back
into the fight. "

d. Borzage's I've Always Loved You: The Spiritualization
of Decor and Editing

Frank Borzage is best known for the unashamed commitment
to romanticism that animates his Twenties and Thirties
films, seen especially in the luminescently triumphant and
gloriously transcendent lovers he creates in 7th Heaven,
Street Angel, A Man's Castle, and Little Man, What Now?
In each of these films Borzage's lovers conquer, through
the purity of their love, the hostile forces of cynicism and
despair that surround them. External circumstance such as
war or economic depression becomes a foil for the private,
inner life their love gives them--the lovers' vitality of spirit
becomes all the greater set against the deadness in the
world around them. The marvelous power of Borzage's
lovers to escape the weight of the world that threatens to
engulf them has strong religious overtones: their initial
physical attraction, especially in Street Angel and Man's
Castle, grows into a purer sort of spiritual affinity. The
reunion of Chico and Diane at the end of 7th Heaven, in
defiance of Chico's earlier, on-screen death, marks a miraculous rebirth that has its origins in Christian religious
belief--the immortality of the lovers' spirits in 7th Heaven
prefigures the profound religious mysticism that lies at the
heart of all Borzage's later work. In films like Green
Light, Disputed Passage and Strange Cargo, the happiness
of Borzage's lovers grows out of their spiritual rejuvenation, their conversion to a new, more religious outlook
that liberates them from an earlier skepticism. What is
most interesting about Borzage's post-war work is that his
characters' happiness is thwarted less by the hostility of
their environment than by forces within themselves. The
source of their bitterness resides neither in war nor depression but rather in some traumatic event or flaw in
themselves. At the same time, their spiritual transformation grows more out of themselves than out of the presence
of an external agent such as a lover or a religious figure.
The emotional power of I've Always Loved You (1946), perhaps Borzage's most moving post-war film, stems from its

189

deep commitment to the redemptive power of the mystical
forces within his characters that enable them to conquer
their own fears, despair, or cynicism and to work out their
own salvation.

I've Always Loved You tells the story of Myra Hassman (Catherine McLeod), daughter of a once-famous pianist,
who studies and falls in love with maestro Leopold Goronoff
(Philip Dorn), a cynical, self-centered concert pianist.
When Goronoff blindly ignores her love and grows jealous
of her talent, he sends Myra away. She returns home and
marries George (William Carter), her childhood sweetheart,
who farms her father's estate. Though separated from him,
she never quite forgets Goronoff.

The love triangle here, like that in The Shining Hour
(1938), locks Myra, caught between her love for music
(Goronoff) and that for the farm (George), into a sort of
romantic paralysis. Like Olivia in The Shining Hour, Myra
must come to terms with the divergent forces within herself
before she can free herself from this paralysis and choose
between her two loves.

The first two sequences of the film--the one set in
the concert hall/drawing room of a Philadelphia mansion,
the other in the country at the Hassman's farm--present the
two, vastly different worlds Myra inhabits and between which
she is repeatedly asked to choose.

The film opens in a coldly formal world of statues
and polished marble. Within the high-ceilinged, hollow-
spaced foyer of a mansion, the camera pans from a close-
up of an ornament on a wall to a medium shot of the hall-
way, revealing in the background an interior room where a
group is formally gathered around a piano. As the camera
moves, objects--chandeliers, heads of statues--whip into the
foreground, emphasizing the impersonal, surfacy nature of
the room's decor, as if the camera were floating aimlessly,
looking for something to latch onto. As the butler announces
Goronoff's arrival, Borzage cuts to the famous pianist and
tracks backwards with him as he enters the foyer, then the
inner room. Surrounded by open space, Goronoff seems to
glide over and through the room's smooth, cultured surfaces.

The formality of this introduction, coupled with the
camera's disengagement with anything specific in the environment, establishes a world of superficialities where feelings

are more often counterfeit than real. Characters seem out
of tune with what they do: a young man plays Bach as if
it were Debussy. The atmosphere prevents any depth of
feeling; none of the students seem at one with their music
until Myra starts to play. Then, Borzage's reaction shot
cutting shows everyone in the room enraptured by Myra's
performance, revealing the film's first triumph of feeling
over environment.

     The next scene opens in a pastoral setting with a
long shot of the Hassman's farm. Piano music accompanies
this first image. The long shot, exterior introduction establishes the integration of Myra with her music that we
felt in the earlier, recital hall scene, yet the lack of camera movement and the simple directness of the cutting to
the interior of the farmhouse suggests a greater harmony
of feeling and environment. The warm, informal interiors
of the farmhouse and Goronoff's unannounced, unceremonious
entry through an open window differentiate this world's graceful ease from the earlier one's still artificiality.

     Goronoff's theatricality, mirrored in the settings he
inhabits like the South American villa where he sets a stage
for the seduction of one of his many women, is heightened
by Myra's naturalness and naïve simplicity. Though they
have common ground in their music, the two different worlds
they come from separate them: Goronoff's artistic ego and
self-centeredness blind him to Myra's love; Myra, possessed
by an amour fou, refuses to see Goronoff's faults and seals
herself into a one-way, romantic relationship with him.

     During Myra's first concert in Carnegie Hall, Goron-
off sees that Myra's performance is stealing the show from
him. He fights with her musically, drowning her out with
the orchestra, and proves to her that he is her musical
master. Though Myra leaves Goronoff and returns home,
she doesn't recover from the trauma of her first concert/
fight with Goronoff. In one sequence, Myra begins to play
a piece by Chopin just at the moment that Goronoff starts
to play the same piece in Carnegie Hall, miles away. The
camera tracks in on Myra through a window, then cuts inside to a close shot of her as she starts to play. Borzage
dissolves to a long-shot of Goronoff playing the same piece
in concert. Echoing the camera movement that closed in
on Myra, Borzage tracks in, along the aisle, on Goronoff.
As the concert continues, Borzage cuts back and forth from
one to the other--the cutting and the continuous music knit-

ting the two together. As they play, Madame Goronoff
(Maria Ouspenskaya), Goronoff's mother, arrives at the
farm, sees George and, outside Myra's window, explains
to him that through music Myra communicates with Goronoff. "She talks with him. She says to him, 'I play, as
you play, the thing you play. The piano is her voice and
he will hear her. What difference if they are a hundred,
a thousand miles apart. Walls cannot stop that voice, distance, time, nothing."

        Fighting for Myra's love, George goes into the house
and stops her. Borzage cuts to Goronoff who, at the same
moment, suddenly stops playing. As Myra stands up and
walks away from the piano, Goronoff also rises and walks
off stage, his movements and gestures mysteriously tied to
hers. Both characters, caught in the grip of unseen forces
that rob them of their individual will, move mechanically.
Like somnambulists, they appear possessed by some mysterious presence within themselves that they cannot understand or control. Their sudden paralysis, seen in Goronoff's loss of the will to continue playing and Myra's half-
hearted marriage to George, represents a capitulation to
the self-destructive elements inside them. They lose the
vital energy that earlier animated them, walling themselves
off from those around them in a tomb of lonely isolation and
passively acquiescent despondency.

        It is only through a ritualistic re-enactment of an
earlier, crippling incident that Borzage's characters can
free themselves from the strange spirits that haunt them
and recall themselves to life. In That's My Man (1947),
Joe Grange's relationship with his wife, Ronnie, gradually
disintegrates as he is repeatedly drawn away from her by
his desire to gamble. Ronnie can win back and redeem
Joe only by bringing Gallant Man--the symbol of their union
--out of retirement to race again. Gallant Man's come-
from-behind victory, near-miraculous for a horse of his
age, marks not only his but the lovers' rejuvenation. In
Moonrise (1948), Danny Hawkins, haunted by his father's
shadow, withdraws from the real world into one of his own
filled with guilt, fear, and hate. His journey through the
swamp into the hills to visit his grandmother and to look
at his parents' graves takes him back into the past to the
source of his fears. At the end, as he lays down his rifle
on his father's tombstone, he exorcises the self-destructive
spirits that have possessed him throughout the film. In
I've Always Loved You, Myra can only free herself from

Goronoff's mysterious grip by returning to Carnegie Hall, the scene of her original defeat by Goronoff, and playing her concerto with him as she did years ago.

The final concert, shot much like the first one, transports Myra and Goronoff back into the past, suggesting that, in spite of external changes in time and circumstance, Myra and Goronoff inwardly remain the same, that time has stood still for all the intervening years between the two concerts. Yet this return to the past enables Myra to free herself from it, to start a new life, to develop a new awareness of the world around her.

Though Myra works out her own salvation, facing Goronoff and proving her independence from him, Borzage's editing in the final concert sequence creates an atmosphere in which Myra's regeneration becomes inevitable. Midway through the concert, Borzage cuts away from Carnegie Hall to Nicholas, the maestro's manager, listening to the concert on a radio in Goronoff's apartment. When he realizes that Myra and Goronoff are playing together again, he stands up and looks at a picture of Madame Goronoff, now dead, on the mantle. Borzage dollies-in to a close-up of the picture and then dissolves from it to a close-up of Myra at the concert, integrating the dead woman's transcendent presence into the regenerative atmosphere of the concert and linking Myra's transcendence to hers.

The cutting at the concert from Goronoff to Myra to George and Porgy (Myra's daughter) reveals the presence of a larger external force at work, overseeing their spiritual liberation and re-awakening. Unlike Hawks whose cutting rhythms grow out of whatever action he is filming, Borzage creates a rhythm that exists apart from the action, situation, or characters. It has a life of its own, an outgrowth more of a primitive religious mysticism than of any mundane logic or dramatic convention. Unlike Hawks' cutting which grows out of the content of the frame, Borzage's seem externally imposed, drawing his characters into an abstract, invisible, spiritual state that exists outside the borders of the frame. As a result, Myra's discovery that she has always loved George is partly her own and partly one Borzage's editing thrusts upon her. Finally, Borzage's cutting rhythms instill a vitality and energy into his characters that they had earlier lost, making their spirits triumphant and immortal.

The film concludes with a final victory of feeling over environment.   Before the end of her concert, Myra, in an absurdly triumphant gesture, rises from the piano and, as the still-conducting Goronoff looks on in amazement, walks off-stage into the arms of George and Porgy.   Finally released from the forces of the past that had imprisoned her, Myra finds, through the concert, a spiritual regeneration--visually echoed in her delirious movement towards her family--that awakens her to the world around her, to the love of her husband and daughter that has always been there but to which, until this moment, she had been blind.

2. THE COLD VOICE OF CLASSICAL STYLE: LEWIS, PREMINGER, AND SIEGEL

Lewis, Preminger, and Siegel share a noir vision and a predeliction for cool, hardboiled narration. Sharp, hard lines dominate their compositions and they surround their characters with a spatial environment that remains oblivious to their existence.

a. The Spatial Disorientation of Gun Crazy

Gun Crazy (1949), more than any other Joseph H. Lewis film I have seen, reflects, in a clear and forceful way, the director's purest and most total mixture of visual style, theme, and characterization. The reason that Lewis cultists consider Gun Crazy a masterpiece depends, I suspect, on the film's overall integrity: the shooting is a part of its characters and their story. Gun Crazy works, as his equally beautiful, color, swashbuckler The Swordsman (1947) does not, precisely because its characters and story more deeply interest and more directly involve Lewis. I think that most film critics will agree that Lewis has a consistent visual style that marks each of his films with his own authorial personality. One look at any of his films discloses a consistent visual style based on deep focus compositions, tight framing, prominently foregrounded objects and hard lines. Yet even though every frame of a film like The Swordsman reflects Lewis' personality as auteur through its plastics, the film remains incomplete because its story (love settles a dispute between feuding eighteenth-century Scottish clans) is irrelevant to its visual style. The May Day celebration at the Glowans' is a visual tour de force; the subsequent chase and ambush with its close-ups of horses' heads shown in a single, high-angle shot is brilliantly photographed and edited, but this beauty is meaningless because the style lacks a narrative correlative. Gun Crazy works because its visual style rigorously develops and articulates its story and characters; what Lewis expresses becomes one with the way he expresses it. Though this sort of artistic consistency does not necessarily constitute a flawless or irrefutable critical criterion, it does provide us with an approach to a discussion of the peculiarly cold beauty which lies beneath the film and which informs the meaning of every shot in it.

The story of Gun Crazy, like that of Nicholas Ray's similarly noir but outrageously more romantic and symbolic They Live by Night (1949), appears to be nothing more than a somewhat turgid melodrama based on the lives of occa-

197

sionally neurotic bank robbers. Lewis' film deals with a
gun-obsessed youth who falls in love with a sideshow marks-
woman, who convinces him to join her act.   They quit the
carnival, marry and, when their money runs out, hold up
stores, banks and factories. Gun Crazy, like Lang's You
Only Live Once (1937), They Live by Night, Penn's Bonnie
and Clyde (1967), Malick's Badlands (1973) and Altman's
Thieves Like Us (1974), belongs to a sub-genre of the gangster cycle known as the "outlaw couple" film.

What distinguishes Lewis' film from the others is the
aggressive, openly neurotic nature of his heroine who virtually dominates the hero, the icy sexuality which de-roman-
ticizes their relationship and the nature of their deaths.   In
You Only Live Once, the hero and heroine are killed by
American police (costumed like Nazi stormtroopers) as they
attempt to cross the border into Canada.   What gives Gun
Crazy its particularly noir identity is that the couple is
less the victim of society's unrelenting otherness than of
their own chaotic passions: as in Selznick's Duel in the Sun
(1946), the lovers in Gun Crazy kill one another.   Or, more
precisely, the hero kills the heroine to keep her from killing
others and is then killed by those he has just saved.

Superficially, Gun Crazy appears to be a clinical case
study of the abnormal sexuality and the disturbed violence of
gun lovers.   On a deeper level, however, the film concerns
the "lostness" of its characters, their physical isolation from
the world which surrounds them and from one another.   This
"deeper" story level arises, in large part, from the development of Lewis' visual style.   Lewis' use of deep-focus cine-
matography gives his images a cold precision: every object
and character in his frames is seen in sharp focus and, as
a result, spatial relationships are clearly defined within the
frame.   Yet, paradoxically, the "lostness" of Lewis' characters has its roots in this visual precision of spatial relationships.   During the courtroom sequence, for example,
young Bart (Russ Tamblyn), the film's central character,
sits alone near a window in the background while his friends
and relatives talk about him in the foreground to the judge.
Lewis' deep focus here actually accentuates the distance between Bart and the other characters.   This effect is in no
way accidental; nor is it totally attributable to the style of
cinematographer Russell Harlan's photography, for Harlan
also works with Hawks (Red River, The Big Sky, Rio Bravo,
Hatari!, Man's Favorite Sport?) and the result is completely
different.   Where Hawks's moderately deep focus tends to

pull characters together, through compositional grouping, into a single spatial continuum, Lewis' depth of field seems
to isolate his characters from one another in separate di-
mensional planes. This courtroom scene is not a unique
instance. Lewis treats the initial introduction of Bart (John
Dall) and Laurie (Peggy Cummins) in a similar way, isolating them from one another in deep space as they shoot at
each other in a carnival show. Naturally, Lewis' two-shot
framing here and throughout the film implies a relationship
between the elements (e. g. , Bart and Laurie) in his frames.
In fact, Lewis could avoid this sort of implicit relationship
only by using one-shots, which, as it turns out, appear
quite infrequently in the film. Obviously, the relationship
which the deep-focus two-shot implies is important to Lewis,
but equally important is the physical isolation in space within the two-shot.

        Lewis' clarity within the frame in Gun Crazy isolates;
his editing, which works against this spatial precision, dramatically destroys, at climactic moments, any sense of
spatial continuity outside of specific frames. After Bart
steals a gun from the hardware store, he runs away, falls
down in the street and drops the gun. Lewis cuts to the
gun, skittering across the wet pavement, and follows it in
close-up until it comes to rest at a man's feet. Then he
cuts to a close-up of the man's face as he looks at Bart.
Throughout the sequence, we remain unaware of where the
man is standing in relation to Bart. After the spatial precision of the film's first shots during which Bart breaks a
store window and grabs a gun in it, Lewis' editing thrusts
us into spatial chaos--a chaos all the more disturbing because of the order which precedes it. Lewis' frames,
clearly, are not self-contained, like Hawks's. He does not,
like Hawks, establish a master shot then cut to closer shots
within the borders of its frame but, more like Hitchcock,
offsets one frame with another by cutting to something outside the frame. Again and again, Lewis treats the world
outside his frames as something intrusive or threatening;
it becomes a force which repeatedly destroys not only his
characters' stability but also any possibility they might have
to find happiness. At moments, Lewis' frames seem almost
unbalanced in anticipation of this sort of intrusion and, as a
result, the presence of this sort of intrusion is replaced by
the anticipation of it. A gesture repeated by the film's central characters reinforces this tension: from time to time,
Laurie and/or Bart turn around to face the camera over their
shoulders, looking behind them to see if they are being fol-

lowed (e. g. , after their last two robberies and just before
they enter the swamp at the end). This gesture, incorporating the complex tenseness of Lewis' visual style into the
acting style, conveys quite simply yet bleakly the unbalanced
nature of Lewis' characters' relationship to the hostile world
which surrounds them.

Yet this world is not actively hostile; it is the characters themselves who make it that way. The Armour Meat
Plant robbery provides a clear example of what I mean by
this. The environment here is coldly impersonal: hanging
carcasses of meat; long, empty corridors; desks and offices
filled with anonymous workers. Yet the way Lewis uses
this environment deprives his characters of any sense of
power over it. The slabs of meat destroy the potentially
romantic nature of their action. When Bart and Laurie run
through the corridors, they seem confused. They fall, drop
the stolen money, bang into doors. They do not seem to
know where they are going. Though the environment is not
actively hostile, they are clearly at its mercy. It deprives
them of stability, making them seem awkward, confused, and
weak.

Lewis rarely fakes his backgrounds in Gun Crazy.
On one level, the film is the visual documentation of a case
history and the use of studio sets would belie the film's
seeming authenticity. For the most part, Lewis shoots on
location. He even shoots an entire bank robbery, in a single take, from the back seat of Bart's and Laurie's car
without the use of back projection. Yet this whole sequence,
like the Armour payroll heist, transforms naturalistic backgrounds into surrealistic ones.

Hollywood cinema traditionally validates space as real
through invisible cutting, which analyzes that space and, by
moving through it, establishes its depth and solidity. The
way Lewis shoots the bank robbery refuses to guarantee the
reality of the space in which it occurs. Juxtaposing a constant foreground (the backs of Bart and Laurie) against a
constantly changing background (the world which appears to
whip by them beyond their windshield), Lewis, by separating
both ground, calls into question the space's integrity and
thus de-naturalizes it. The result is to estrange his characters from their world.

At one point in the film, Bart describes his participation in the robberies as a "nightmare" and claims that Laurie

is the only real thing in his life. In fact, the robberies do
seem unreal. In the single-take bank hold-up, for example,
Bart and Laurie put on their carnival costumes. The hold-
up becomes an ironic parody of a conventional western--the
"outlaws" dressed as cowboy and cowgirl arrive and escape
in an automobile--and becomes, through this bit of play-
acting, theatricalized and unreal. As a technical device,
the single take reinforces the scene's unreality; it makes
the world seem two-dimensional. As Bart drives the car
through small town streets, the environment, seen through
the front window, whirls around before them, appearing
surfacy and flat. The car's rapid motion and constant change
of direction tend to blur the backgrounds. Again, we have
no sense of where the characters are going. What they
have just done--in fact, the life they are leading--seems
directionless and meaningless.

Lewis' use of landscape becomes devastatingly clear:
it places characters' actions in the realm of fantasy and
nightmare; it overwhelms, with an engulfing anonymity,
their attempts to assert themselves; it reduces their love,
which Lewis shows largely through robberies and acts of
violence, to a blindly futile gesture in a coldly impersonal
world; it robs their every action and emotion of sense and
value, foreshadowing their ultimate self-destruction.

The coldness of Lewis' visual style finds its perfect
counterpart in the frustrating, almost fatalistic isolation of
his characters in space. Yet Gun Crazy does contain brief
moments of emotion and warmth--e. g. , the kiss which finally ties Bart to Laurie and which launches them on their
criminal career together. Lewis slowly shortens his focal
length: as the lovers kiss, they fall out of focus. But the
effect of this seemingly romantic focal change, in the context of the film's overall depth and visual precision, is to
make Bart and Laurie seem even more lost. In short, they
lose even the spatial fixity they formerly had within the shot.
The editing--a quick cut after the kiss to an exploding gum-
ball machine which heralds their first robbery together--
totally destroys the intimate and delicate emotion of the
previous scene. The cold, precise photography returns and
brings with it an explosion of their brief moment of happiness. Time and time again, Lewis uses a change in focal
length to suggest his characters' "lostness": when young
Bart is about to break the window of the hardware store in
the first scene, his face momentarily falls out of focus.
This brief fuzziness of the image suggests the craziness of

his action and prepares us for the futile senselessness of
the action which follows.

One of my favorite scenes and one which uses fuzzy
focus most successfully occurs later in Laurie's carnival
wagon.   Lewis begins with a shot of Laurie's face reflected
in a mirror.   He pulls the focus back, her face in the mirror goes out of focus but the back of her head, as she looks
into the mirror, comes into focus.   Lewis shoots almost the
entire scene with reflections of characters in the mirror but
he never pulls the focus back.   Thus the images in the mirror remain slightly out of focus.   Bart comes in, interrupt-
ing Laurie and Packett (her manager and former lover), and
his entry is seen only in the mirror.   The scene concludes
with Bart shooting the mirror and a shot of Packett's reflected face, fragmented and out of focus in the broken glass
of the mirror.   Packett loses control over Laurie.   Bart
and Laurie express, through the violence of the breaking
of the mirror, their feeling for one another and decide to
run away together (after Packett fires Bart).   The out-of-
focus mirror, in which all of this is seen, dramatically reinforces our sense of the characters' confusingly entangled
relationships and looks forward to the soft-focus images
which will accompany their deaths.

I have written of the characters' "lostness" and described a few scenes in which I find this aspect most clearly expressed in the composition, framing, depth of field, and
editing.   My arguments, up to now, probably seem a bit
forced or contrived.   What I have described in Lewis' visual
style need not necessarily be termed "lostness."   Yet the
final sequence of the film, a scene towards which everything
I have described points, is clearly the most persuasive example of the predicament of Lewis' characters in the entire
film.   As Bart and Laurie run through the woods, the camera tracks with them in tight, medium shot, separated from
them by a partially obstructing procession of bushes and
trees.   The tightness of the framing prevents us from seeing exactly where they are.   Their movement, because it is
matched by that of the tracking camera, seems to carry
them nowhere.   When they stop to rest, Lewis tracks in
even tighter to a close-up of their faces as they hear the
sounds of the posse's dogs pursuing them from somewhere
off-screen.   Finally, they enter a swamp and wander through
it until they fall down, exhausted.   Bart tells Laurie, "we
can find our way out in the morning."   Morning comes.   The
swamp and the screen are filled with a thick grey fog in

which the characters are totally obscured. The visual clarity of the earlier part of the film gives way, here, to
vagueness and confusion. A similar visual progression occurs in The Big Combo (1955) which begins with a fragmented, spatially disorienting chase in the corridors of
Madison Square Garden during a boxing match, the sequence
shot in low key light but with a sharp and deep focus, and
ends with a shoot-out in a fog-enshrouded airport in which
the barely visible figures in the image virtually dissolve
into the darkness and the mist. As this progression in the
two films illustrates, deep focus and soft focus, for Lewis,
have no fixed value; they function contextually. Both are
capable of conveying the spatial confusion which is the subject of the director's work.

     In Gun Crazy, the fog prevents us from seeing where
the characters are in the frame. Lewis slowly tracks in
and, as he does, the vague shapes of Bart and Laurie become a bit clearer and a bit closer. The camera tracks
in to an extremely tight close-up of the pair, a framing
which estranges them from the surrounding space. Again,
Bart and Laurie hear the sounds of the posse. Surrounded
by the fog of the swamp and the voices of their pursuers,
they become entrapped in their lostness. They never leave
the swamp. The last shot of the film cranes upward from
the clump of swamp grass in which Bart and Laurie lie
dead. Obscured by the grass and the fog, they cannot be
seen. As the crane draws up and away from them, they
become more and more a part of their environment. Although the shot gives a strong impression of the futility of
their actions, it does provide a final punctuation for these
actions that magnifies the characters' predicament into a
universal situation, involving not only the posse (including
old friends of Bart's, Clyde, and Dave) and the swamp which
surrounds them but also the audience.

     The swamp in Gun Crazy, like the swamp/bayou
through which Warden Tunner (Barry Sullivan) pursues escaped convict Jory (Vittorio Gassman) in Cry of the Hunted
(1953), stands as a metaphor for the world which envelopes
Lewis' characters and becomes the site of their ordeal to
survive within it. It is an uncharted landscape--an impenetrable and mysterious wilderness--which threatens to absorb
all who enter it. It is the true home of the homeless, the
promised land that belongs to the lost.

     From My Name Is Julia Ross (1946), in which the
heroine loses her identity, to So Dark the Night (1947), in

which the unwittingly amnesiac detective hero discovers that
he himself is the killer he seeks, to the relentless manhunt
of Cry of the Hunted and to the rogue cop investigations of
The Big Combo, Lewis' work has concerned itself with
searches amidst confusion for clarity.   The visual style of
Gun Crazy, combining the exacting precision of deep focus
photography with the disruptive imprecision of disorienting
framing and editing, echoes the thematic motifs which unify
the film.   The confused clarity of its space makes Gun
Crazy one of its director's most explicit works.

[Thanks to Fred Camper and David Grosz for their help in
the preparation of this article.]

b.   The Broken-Field Running of Otto Preminger

The beauty of Otto Preminger's work is, for many, difficult
to see.   In contrast to visually exotic stylists like Hitchcock, Welles, or Ford, whose images dramatically reflect
unique and distinctive visions of the world, Preminger's
less obvious, almost impenetrable visual style makes him
seem less great, less of an artist than he actually is.   The
cool, detached delicacy of Preminger's cinematic style leads
critics unfamiliar with it or unable to see it to argue mistakenly for (at worst) its non-existence or for (at best) the
superficiality, emptiness, and emotionlessness of his vision.

For most, Preminger is a producer of projects, a
director of trashy but popular potboilers like Forever Amber, Exodus or Advise and Consent, a dull exploiter of controversial material (The Moon Is Blue and The Man with the
Golden Arm) or a hammy character actor who played Nazis
in other directors' films.   But, in fact, his sprawling plots
and controversial themes are mere window-dressing; the
heart of his work lies in the subtlety of his visual style,
in his almost unendurably long takes, his fluid camera
movements, his use of CinemaScope, his concept of space.
Preminger's camera discovers tremendous emotional depth
in apparently hollow characters and situations seemingly
void of real feeling.   The grace and sensitivity of his direction, more than his script or an actor's performance, transform his films into profound emotional odysseys; the unobtrusive, orderly but effortless elegance of his compositions
reflects a complex sensibility in tune both with the refined,
restrained passions of his characters and with a larger
sphere of emotional experience that goes beyond articulation.

Each character in a Preminger film serves as a fragment of an overall design.   Much like separate, straight
lines that run endlessly through space without touching one
another, his characters exist independently of each other,
self-contained and self-sufficient.   Occasionally these lines
intersect, but the points of intersection last only a moment;

205

soon the lines diverge again, and the characters regain their
separateness.   Preminger's compositions, whether crowded
with characters or empty, convey a sense of separateness,
of each character's self-preoccupation, which fragments the
mood of his scenes.   The space in Preminger's frames is
both continuous and fragmented. Characters exist within a
single, spatial continuum but remain emotionally independent
of one another: brothers and sisters (Bunny Lake Is Missing), husbands and wives (Advise and Consent, Man with the
Golden Arm) and fathers and daughters (Bonjour Tristesse)
conceal secrets from one another and, though they share
the same space, live in separate worlds.   Each character,
in his infinite separateness, becomes an island in the frame.
What interests Preminger most about his characters' separateness is the random nature of the pattern of interaction--
of intersection and divergence--between and among these
isolated emotional worlds.   A more analytical director
might concern himself primarily with specific dramatic conflict, i.e., with the points of intersection.   However,
Preminger's more distanced and detached approach to his
material enables him to see a larger pattern, a more universal interaction of parts, and to celebrate the intricate
interrelatedness of disparate characters and events.

The Moon Is Blue (1953)

The Moon Is Blue, produced by Preminger and playwright
F. Hugh Herbert, created a sensation on its release by
United Artists in 1953.   Condemned by the Legion of Decency and released without an MPAA Production Code Seal
of Approval, the film broke box office records and, with
them, the stranglehold of the Hays Office on motion picture
production.

Employing such previously forbidden words as "preg-
nant," "seduction," "virgin," and "mistress," Preminger
and Herbert revitalized the vocabulary of the film sex comedy, restoring a naughtiness to the genre that had died with
Lubitsch.   As Time noted, the film's "amorous skirmishes
are verbal rather than real."   It is a bedroom farce set in
the living room.   A Fifties version of the zany Thirties
screwball heroine, Maggie McNamara's Patty O'Neill talks
frankly about sex but extracts from architect William Hold-
en, who picks her up on the observation deck of the Empire
State Building and lures her back to his bachelor's apartment, a promise of "affection but no passion."   Described

by her rival as a "professional virgin," Patty repeatedly advertises her virginity, and the implication is that it is for sale, though all she loses during the course of the film is a needle.

David Niven steals the show as David Slater, part alcoholic playboy and part reluctant father, threatening to "horsewhip" Holden for not sleeping with his daughter (Dawn Addams). Niven's story about his ex-wife's popovers, his exclamation of joy and surprise when his daughter goes to her room when he tells her to ("She went!!") is rivalled only by Preminger's inspired satire of a TV beer commercial in which a lilliputian McNamara pops out of a beer stein and sings a duet with a brobdingnagian Henry the Eighth. Preminger's direction, combining Lubitsch's sexual sophistication and Wilder's bittersweet bite, explores characteristically American preoccupations with sex, money, commercialism, and success with a bemusedly objective smile.

Man with the Golden Arm (1955)

Preminger's battle for control over the production of his own films extended beyond the demise of the studio system. As an independent producer-director, he took on the Production Code Administration, single-handedly forcing them to revise their restrictions about language with The Moon Is Blue in 1953 and about subject matter with The Man with the Golden Arm in 1955 (the Code prohibited the presentation of drug addiction and the illegal traffic in drugs on the screen).

Nelson Algren's novel deals with the return of junkie Frankie Machine, played by Frank Sinatra whose street-wise performance gives credibility and depth to Algren's quasi-allegorical story, from a drug clinic to his old neighborhood, where his nagging wife, Zosch (Eleanor Parker), the local pusher, Louis (Darren McGavin), and the neighborhood gambling kingpin, Schwiefka (Robert Strauss), drive him back to the needle.

Preminger's claustrophobic studio sets, long takes in medium shot, constrictive camera movements and occasional short dolly shots into an extreme close-up create an oppressive atmosphere of victimization in which Frankie becomes everybody's pawn. All the surrounding characters seek to manipulate him for their own ends: his wife, whom he married out of guilt after crippling her in a car accident, pretends to be crippled in order to keep him.   Schwiefka, for whom golden-armed Frankie used to deal cards, has him arrested when he threatens to quit and thwarts his attempts to get a job as a drummer.   The pusher, in collusion with Schwiefka, tempts Frankie and succeeds in hooking him again.   In a film full of physical and emotional cripples, nightclub cashier Molly (Kim Novak) becomes Frankie's crutch, helping him to go "cold turkey" in a series of unendurably claustrophobic, high-angle, long-take scenes shot in her bare, small one-room apartment.

Preminger's methodic direction transforms every moment and encounter in the film into a trial in which his character, pressured from within and without by a complex array of demands and needs, must make a choice or exercise an option.   Frankie, in deciding to go clean and to leave Zosch, regains control over his own destiny.   The process of his reaching this decision and the decision itself become the subjects of the film.

Bonjour Tristesse (1958)

Preminger calls Bonjour Tristesse one of his favorite films, a rare admission on his part.   The story line, presented in flashbacks, involves the interruption of a father's and daughter's carefree, decadent existence at a summer villa in the south of France by the visit of the girl's serious, somewhat prudish godmother, Anne (Deborah Kerr), with whom the father, Raymond (David Niven), falls in love.   The daughter, Cécile (Jean Seberg), plots with her boyfriend and her father's former mistress to break up the romance.   With Seberg watching her plot working from behind a bush in the background, Kerr discovers Niven and his former mistress together and runs away, driving her car over a cliff.   The close father-daughter relationship and some aspects of the story resemble Preminger's Angel Face (1952) in which the daughter attempts to kill her stepmother but accidentally kills her father also.   Seberg's attempt to manipulate Niven and Kerr and her conflict of wills with Kerr make the film a struggle for dominance which Seberg ultimately wins, but her victory proves hollow.

Preminger films the present scenes of Seberg and Niven on the town in Paris in black and white and the past sequences involving his unusual love triangle at a waterside

villa in glorious Technicolor, opposing the drab, meaningless present to the bright color-saturated past and the sterile
cityscape to the rich French countryside. Seberg's memories
haunt her and her indirect responsibility for Kerr's death
erects an unspoken barrier between herself and her father.
Her face, to which she mechanically applies cold cream in
the film's last shot, becomes an emotionless mask. Concealing all feeling, she becomes a lifeless prisoner of her
memories, forever wondering whether her father knows the
part she played in destroying Kerr. Jean-Luc Godard mod-
els his similarly destructive Seberg character in Breathless
(1959) on Preminger's Cécile, saying that his use of Seberg
was a continuation of her role in Bonjour Tristesse: "I
could have taken the last shot of Preminger's film," he explains, "and started after dissolving to a title, "Three
Years Later...."

Anatomy of a Murder (1959)

Preminger holds a degree in law and questions of objective
fact, deliberation, and justice surface again and again in
his films. The narrative of Anatomy of a Murder, which
centers on a murder trial, concerns the legal process,
courtroom dramatics, and reaching decisions and reveals
itself to be Preminger's most thematically explicit work.
In the film, James Stewart's mid-western, small town lawyer defends an itinerant army lieutenant (Ben Gazzara) who
has killed a local bartender for allegedly raping his wife
(Lee Remick), successfully claiming that the defendant was
temporarily insane and that he acted in the grip of "an ir-
resistible impulse."

      The film has its thematic roots in Preminger polici-
ers of the Forties and Fifties like Laura, Fallen Angel,
Where the Sidewalk Ends and Angel Face. These films
noirs take the form of investigations, using the murder
mystery format as a metaphor for the moral, emotional,
or psychological journey of its characters toward some
truth about themselves, others, or the world. Here Stewart, in actions thematically analogous to Duke Ellington's
fragmented jazz score, pieces together, after the fact, the
events which led up to the bartender's murder, interviewing
a variety of witnesses, each with his own secret to conceal
and each working at cross purposes to the other, and sifts
through a mass of contradictory testimony and evidence in
an attempt to distinguish truth from lies. The courtroom,

presided over by Joseph N. Welch, famous former army
counsel in the McCarthy hearings, becomes a battleground
of conflicting ambitions and goals, the truth becoming lost
in the process.

Advise and Consent (1962)

Advise and Consent, based on Allen Drury's best-selling
novel, centers on no one character or issue, though it is
nominally "about" the attempts of a dying President (Franchot Tone) to ramrod his controversial nominee for Secretary
of State through the Senate.   The film begins with the announcement of the nomination in newspaper headlines and
explores the reactions on the Hill to the news.   Preminger's
fluid, "invisible" editing in the first part of the film links
various characters together in a chain of reactions to the
President's action, moving from the headline to Senator
Stanley Danta (Paul Ford) who first sees it in front of the
Capitol, from there with the loyal party man Danta to Senate
majority leader Bob Munson (Walter Pidgeon) at his hotel.
Munson calls the President, then he and Danta pay a visit
to ally Senator Smith (Peter Lawford) and from his room
telephone Senator Brig Anderson (Don Murray), who will
later head the subcommittee holding hearings over the ap-
pointment.   We also meet the conservative southern Senator
Cooley (Charles Laughton) who holds a personal grudge
against the candidate and vows to do everything in his power
to block the nomination and meet the ruthlessly ambitious
Senator van Ackerman (George Grizzard) who offers his
total support to Munson, both representing extremist reactions to the President's announcement.   Before he introduces
the candidate himself, Preminger sets the political machinery
in motion, showing the workings of the Senate behind the
scenes in hotel rooms and over the telephone and revealing
the subtle checks and balances in operation among the individual factions and contrasting personalities within the President's own party.

Invisible forces are at work in the background.
Candidate Leffingwell's (Henry Fonda) testimony is chal-
lenged by treasury clerk Herbert Gelman (Burgess Meredith)
who claims that Leffingwell was once a member of a communist cell, and this testimony is supported by treasury
official Hardiman Fletcher (Paul McGrath), both men working, it turns out, as pawns of Sen. Cooley.   At the same
time, subcommittee chairman Anderson receives anonymous

threatening phone calls, a victim of blackmailer van Ackerman who seeks to pressure Anderson into suppressing evidence of Leffingwell's communist affiliations by threatening
to expose documents concerning a homosexual relationship
Anderson once had with a fellow soldier in the army.
Preminger cuts from Leffingwell explaining to his son that
he was once associated with communists to Anderson refusing to tell his wife about his past, juxtaposing different responses to similar problems.   Preminger observes this
kind of strategy throughout the film, countering character
with character, thesis with antithesis.   Predictably, the
final outcome is a deadlock in the Senate, all the film's
various forces frozen in their attempts to realize conflicting goals.

The Cardinal (1963)

Preminger's fascination with alternate viewpoints and disparate perceptions of events informs his entire career.
From Exodus, the creation of Israel and Jewish post-war
history he turns to The Cardinal and the history of the
world between two wars as seen by a Catholic eye.   The
dramatic shift from Judaism to Catholicism is less surpris-
ing in the light of Preminger's own biography than it may
initially seem.   A Jew raised in Catholic Austria, he grew
up within two cultures and the film, whose Austrian sequences have an immediacy that the Boston and Roman sequences lack, emerges as a work as personal to Preminger,
who like his central character left part of himself in Austria, as Exodus.

The Cardinal consists of a series of flashbacks on
the part of American Bishop Steven Fermoyle (Tom Tryon)
on the eve of the ceremony in which he becomes a cardinal.
Recalling his youth as a curate in Boston, he expounds on
the miracle of a madonna with a bleeding heart to a cynical
Jew, Benny (John Saxon), who wishes to marry his sister
and whose faith he must convert.   He explains that a broken
steam pipe has made the heart of the virgin bleed and when
Benny asks how he will explain the truth to the believers in
this miracle, Steven asks him what the truth is.   The leak-
ing steam pipe, he explains, is only a fact.   And facts are
only small parts of a larger truth: God made the steam
pipe leak, argues Steven.

The apparently random events in the cardinal's life--
his apprenticeship with Father Halley (Burgess Meredith)

and Archbishop Glennon (John Huston), the death of his sister Mona (Carol Lynley) because he refuses, as a priest, to allow the doctors to kill her unborn, illegitimate child, his anti-segregation efforts in Georgia with Father Gillis (Ossie Davis), his anti-fascist diplomatic mission to Vienna on the eve of Hitler's takeover--emerge as the small parts of Fermoyle's larger truth, his faith. Preminger does leave Fermoyle's faith unquestioned but shows him, on a year's leave of absence in Vienna, coming to the decision that he is a priest, first staring at, then donning, his cassock and appearing in it before Annemarie (Romy Schneider), the Viennese language student who loves him.   The flashback structure turns the film into a reconstruction of how Fermoyle's faith was tested and proven.   Like Preminger's other work, The Cardinal becomes a film about reaching decisions.

Bunny Lake Is Missing (1964)

Preminger's penchant for films involving investigations has led him back again and again to the mystery genre.   His suspense thriller, Bunny Lake Is Missing, thus resembles Laura (1944) more than it does In Harm's Way (1965), a film made at about the same time as Bunny Lake but in a different genre.

Carol Lynley's Ann Lake leaves her four-year-old, illegitimate daughter Bunny at a nursery school, helps her brother Stephen (Kier Dullea) with whom she lives move to a new flat in London and returns to find Bunny missing-- and to discover that no one has seen her.   The police investigation which follows calls into question the very existence of the child, whom Inspector Newhouse (Laurence Olivier) is led to believe is an imaginary creation of Lynley's, modeled after her "pretend" friend as a child.

The undermining of Lynley's assertions that her daughter exists again involves Preminger in the exploration of the objectivity of truth, as in Anatomy of a Murder. The audience, along with Olivier, doubt the child's existence, all evidence of which has been carefully removed.   Preminger's narrative is maddeningly objective, especially considering the subjective nature of the story: he tells us nothing about the characters, forcing us to analyze and evaluate for ourselves the minutest bits of information, forcing us here, as in so many of his other films, to recon-

struct or piece together the truth. The truth, the existence
of the child, ultimately hinges on an apparently insignificant
toy shop repair ticket for a broken doll.

The suspenseful conclusion of the film becomes a
battle of wills and wits between mother and kidnapper, each
working at cross purposes in a characteristically Preminger-
ian fashion. Bunny Lake, though it lacks the sprawling
scope of Preminger's epic treatment of justice (Anatomy of
a Murder), religion (Exodus, The Cardinal) and politics
(Exodus, Advise and Consent), deals with the same basic
struggle for power, identity and survival itself.

Such Good Friends (1971)

The plot of Such Good Friends seems, at first glance melodramatic (in the word's worst sense), meaningless, and
emotionally vacuous: a man (Laurence Luckinbill) enters
the hospital for the simple removal of a mole and, because
of a series of medical blunders, sinks into a coma and
dies. At the same time, his wife (Dyan Cannon), from
whose point of view the narrative is told, learns that he
has been sleeping with her best friends. For the most
part, the melodramatic plot seems governed by the worldly-
wise tone of the screenplay. The film's funny, sophisticated,
cynical script, written by Elaine May (under a pseudonym to
preserve May's status in the Director's Guild), turns even
the most dramatic moments into jokes, even the most grue-
some medical complications and most wrenching marital
discoveries into wisecracks. Yet, because of Preminger's
mise-en-scène, the film is a tremendously moving experience beneath its surface wit and apparently lifeless sophistication.

Juxtaposing two separate yet tangentially related narrative threads, Preminger uses a medical melodrama not so
much as a metaphor for, as a catalyst to, an emotional
chamber play. Centering on the feelings of Julie Messinger
(the wife), the film works as an investigation of sorts, tra-
velling from the dark interior of a bedroom closet to the
bright outdoors of Central Park. As Julie discovers,
through a series of crippling revelations, more about her
husband's infidelity, her growing estrangement enables her
to look at herself, to probe into her own emotions. As she
does this, the world around her gradually grows more superficial, empty, and pointless--a progression paralleled in the

screenplay as her jokes and the morbid humor of those
around her become less funny, grimmer, and more desperate. Yet her experiencing of the world becomes, at the
same time, deeper and more complex. After she learns
from Cal (Ken Howard) of her husband's affair with another
woman, Julie seems to fall apart, to lose control of her
emotions. In one of the film's most moving scenes, she
goes to her stylish, sophisticated mother (whose thighs are
being waxed at a beauty parlor) for comfort but can only
semi-articulately utter, "Mother ... I feel so bad...." and
"Mother ... what should I do to feel better?"

Her verbal breakdown mirrors an inner turbulence:
it represents the evocation of an emotion so immediate that
she does not know how to express it. Preminger's relentless attack on her mask of sophistication, seen in the gradual impoverishment of Julie's vocabulary, reduces her to
speechlessness, a process ultimately crystallized in the
moment of her husband's death, when she is left totally
mute. Yet her silence symbolizes, at this point, not an
emotional paralysis but her transcendence of catastrophe
through pure, direct, unfiltered feeling. The film, in effect, revitalizes formerly dead emotion, creating out of a
seemingly passionless wasteland deeply felt and experienced
sentiments.

The depth of feeling in Such Good Friends grows out
of Preminger's visual style which subtly shapes the way his
audience understands the film's characters. What interests
Preminger is the separateness of the characters and the
apparently random pattern of the intersection and diver-
gence. Characters go to one another for help, as in the
lunch sequence between Cal and Julie. But their separateness soon surfaces: Julie's seductions of Cal and Timmy
(James Coco) serve as grotesquely clumsy encounters with
her husband's friends, encounters which leave her more
isolated from the world around her than she was before.

Preminger's compositions, though crowded with characters grouped semi-formally into an iconographic, tableau-
like unit, are filled with a sense of separateness, of each
character's self-preoccupation, which fragments the mood
of almost every scene. At Cal's party, Marion Spector
(the doctor's wife) stands, detached from the others by virtue of her own self-centeredness, pouring and drinking wine
while looking off-screen. Later, Dr. Mahler, seemingly in
a world of his own, "operates" on his baked apple in the

hospital cafeteria while Dr. Bleiweiss explains to Julie the damage that has been done to her husband's liver.

The ultimate tragedy of Such Good Friends, as in Preminger's recent, more explicit The Human Factor (1979) which equates characters to lines in a Mondrian painting, lies in its vision of characters in perpetual isolation, unable to break out of the tiny, box-like cells into which their lives have led them. Julie's final "liberation," when she leaves behind the friends who await her in her apartment and flees to the open spaces of the park, is truly a liberation circumscribed by her larger isolation within the city and among its anonymous passersby. She has broken out of her cell but remains a prisoner.

Rosebud (1975)

Orson Welles' Citizen Kane is a film about an investigation, a search for the meaning of Kane's dying words, "Rosebud." Preminger's Rosebud, which deals with an investigation into a terrorist hijacking of a ship named "Rosebud" and into the kidnapping of its teenage passengers, pays homage to Welles' film both in its title and in its labyrinthine quest for the meaning of the event--the hijack--which links all the film's characters.

The film opens with a series of pans and tracks that follow the course of Hacam (Josef Shiloa), a Black Septembrist, through the Corsican countryside, one of the first of many visual links established between Preminger's terrorists and the natural landscape. (We later discover their leader Sloat, Richard Attenborough, secreted in a cathedral-like cave in southern Lebanon.) Preminger is characteristically objective in his portrayal of the groups, factions, and individuals who vie with one another for power in the film. His terrorists, though clearly the villains and led by madman Sloat, include the intensely dedicated Hacam in their ranks. The rightist fathers of the kidnapped girls, though sympathetic as parents, come across as hypocrites. One girl's grandfather Fargeau (Claude Dauphin), the target of the terrorists, emerges as a Wellesian Arkadin figure, having concealed his Jewish birth by destroying all records of it and being unmasked first by his own detective, then by the Black Septembrists. Preminger's hero, Larry Martin (Peter O'Toole), a Newsweek reporter and CIA agent who tracks down the terrorists and rescues the girls, is a foppish mis-

anthrope who jealously guards his slouch hat from aggressive butlers and takes great delight in his own cleverness.
Interestingly enough, the good-guy raid led by Martin which
rescues the girls differs not at all in craft or kind from
the bloody bad-guy attack on the "Rosebud" in which the
girls are originally taken.   Preminger seems more interested in processes and the multi-faceted nature of events
than in moral issues of right and wrong.

The kidnapping sets in motion a variety of forces and
special interests--Israeli, British, American, French, German and Palestinian agents all pursue conflicting goals,
leaving the kidnap victims caught in the middle.   The Is-
raelis, for example, pressure the American President to
refuse a terrorist demand, openly endangering the life of
one of the hostages.   Though the hostages are ultimately
rescued and the terrorists captured, the film ends with an
act of terrorism: another Black Septembrist hijacks a
plane, answering Martin's rescue raid with a demand for
the release of his comrades.   For Preminger, international
politics, like the domestic politics of Advise and Consent,
consist of a series of checks and balances,   each action
countered by another and resulting in a perpetual stalemate.

c. Don Siegel: The Last of the Independents

A study of Don Siegel's career reveals a paradox: Siegel styles himself as a rebellious outsider, as "the last of the independents," but, in fact, he relies heavily on others. Although Siegel, since The Killers in 1964, makes films which bear the stamp of his personality, the quality of his films varies with the talents of his collaborators. Siegel's prominence as a director coincides with his association with Clint Eastwood and with writers Dean Reisner and Howard Rodman. Madigan (1968), written by Rodman and Abraham Polonsky, marks a major turning point in the director's career. With it, his scripts become richer, giving greater attention to minor characters and employing them as foils for his major characters. Eastwood's presence in Siegel's next picture Coogan's Bluff (1969), written by Herman Miller, Reisner, and Rodman, catapults Siegel to the status of "Major Director," but Eastwood's performance would have been undefined, dimensionless, and perhaps even as allegorical as it is in the Sergio Leone westerns without the presence of Lee J. Cobb, Susan Clark, Don Stroud, and Betty Field. The flat, Dickensian quality of these minor characters gives dimension to Eastwood who, through his reactions to them, reveals qualities in himself that belie his silence and the implacable intransigence of his surface appearance. Leone's "Man with No Name" would never reveal his humanity as Coogan does in his last gesture, offering a cigarette to his prisoner. Siegel's success with Eastwood and Walter Matthau (Charley Varrick) and his failure with Michael Caine (The Black Windmill) and John Wayne (The Shootist) can be traced, in part, to the quality of his scripts. Albert Maltz, over the objections of Budd Boetticher, re-wrote Two Mules for Sister Sara and The Beguiled (with John B. Sherry); H. J. and R. M. Fink and Reisner worked on Dirty Harry and Reisner and Rodman collaborated on Charley Varrick, Siegel's best work of the Seventies. The Black Windmill, a disappointing film which fails in spite of Michael Caine, was scripted by Leigh Vance and The Shootist, a flawed film rescued by John Wayne's performance, was written by Scott Hale, a friend of Siegel.

Siegel's earlier work is similarly mercurial, rising and falling in direct relation to the abilities of those who worked with him. Count the Hours (1953), though full of characteristically Siegelian treacheries and betrayals, is remarkable solely for John Alton's lighting and camera work. Riot in Cell Block 11 (1954) and Invasion of the Body Snatchers (1956) were both produced by Walter Wanger, one of Hollywood's most independent and daring producers. Wanger's earlier work with Fritz Lang (You Only Live Once, Scarlet Street, Secret Beyond the Door) and his recent stretch in jail (he had shot his wife's agent, Jennings Lang) surely contributed first-hand experience to the realistically nightmarish quality of both films. By contrast, none of Siegel's earlier work is as intensely felt as are these two Wanger pictures. Siegel's screenwriter on Body Snatchers was Daniel Mainwaring, whose screenplays for Siegel and others reveal a concern for characters in similar situations, for the individual struggling against the impossible odds of a larger, impersonal organization. For Siegel, Mainwaring, a staff writer for RKO, also wrote The Big Steal (1949), An Annapolis Story (Allied Artists, 1955), Baby Face Nelson (UA, 1957) and The Gun Runners (UA, 1958). More characteristic of Mainwaring's concerns, however, are his screenplays for Jacques Tourneur, Out of the Past, and Phil Karlson, Phenix City Story. Mainwaring's pessimistic, paranoid vision of post-war America provides Siegel with a psychological background for his largely physical foreground of chases and action sequences. The stakes involved in Siegel's chases are no longer material riches (the stolen loot in The Big Steal) but the preservation of his central character's emotional identity.

I do not suggest that Siegel's contribution to Riot in Cell Block 11, Invasion of the Body Snatchers and Baby Face Nelson was any less than that of his collaborators, but a look at his other films of the period--Duel at Silver Creek (1952), China Venture (1953), Private Hell 36 (1954) and Crime in the Streets (1956)--reveals a director of only minor talent. With the notable exception of The Line-Up (1958)-- and even here Siegel leans heavily on a strong screenplay by Sterling Silliphant and the format of an existing TV series--Siegel failed to prove himself during the Fifties.

The visual style of Siegel's best films of the Fifties is lean and economical, eschewing the expressive interplay of light and shadow that characterizes the films noirs of the period. His decor, unlike that of Minnelli or Welles, is

neutral and tends to depersonalize those within it. This
neutrality becomes a major stylistic factor in a film like
Invasion: the drab houses with blank walls seem to literally drain the protagonists' humanity out of them, much as
the pod in the foreground on Jack's pool table slowly soaks
up his distinctive features. Siegel's characters must struggle against the drabness of their settings in order to stay
human. Siegel's lighting, Alton's Count the Hours to the
contrary, tends to be flat. Similarly, his camera lacks
expressive movement, panning only on motion or to connect
one motion or character with another and his camera angle,
though rarely eye-level, avoids extremes. In effect, Siegel's
camera does not interpret action, but rather records it in
short, prosaic, simple statements, making him an ideal director, stylistically, of Hemingway material, an author to
whom he turns twice in his career (The Gun Runners, The
Killers).

Though Siegel's camera is unobtrusive, its placement
in Riot, Invasion, and Nelson is hardly haphazard. Siegel
positions his camera to emphasize the moments of encounter
between characters and between a character and the world
around him. By that I mean that there is a restive uneasiness to the lines of each frame's composition; there is no
place for his characters to relax in his sets nor is there
time for them to become human; nor can they domesticate
their space, as characters in Hawks and Walsh films do.
Siegel's sets and camera positions are designed to keep his
characters on the move and the camera, which is rarely
static, is prepared to follow them to their next encounter
with other characters or places. There is a deadness to
Siegel's backgrounds which the positioning of his camera
poses as a threat to his characters: the moving characters
encounter this deadness, lose some of their energy to it
and are forced to continue moving to stay alive. This is
in marked contrast to the relationship between character and
setting in Hawks films in which a constant exchange of energies takes place. In a larger sense, Siegel's dynamic
characters passionately fear stasis and fear entrapment
either in claustrophobic settings or in relationships with
other characters which involve serious commitment.

Siegel's interest in energy, vitality, and movement
naturally draws him to the action genre and, though some
of his films exist outside of this genre, his best work draws
on the conventions of the male-oriented action picture. His
police films, westerns, and crime dramas focus on physical

action and character relationships are largely expressed in
physical terms, i. e. , violence. His characters display few,
if any, domestic qualities: they have neither homes nor
families.   Charley Varrick, whose wife is killed in Charley
Varrick's opening sequence and who lives in a trailer, is
the exception that proves the rule.   Most Siegel heroes wander from hotel to hotel; the bare, nondescript decor of their
rooms tells us nothing about them.   Siegel defines his characters partially through the absence of certain relationships:
his heroes lack parents, wives, and children.   Even in The
Black Windmill (1974), British spy Tarrant (Michael Caine),
though married and a father, is estranged from his wife and
loses his child to a kidnapper.   He rescues the boy only by
functioning as a professional spy not as a vengeful parent.

Siegel's women emerge as threats to his men in action because they seek to remove their men from the world
of action.   In Dirty Harry (1971), Chico's wife persuades
him to leave Harry and the police force after he is seriously wounded by the "Scorpio" killer.   Both Tarrant's and
Madigan's wives dislike their husbands' professions.   Though
Hawks's women initially disapprove of the dangerous professions of their men in films like Only Angels Have Wings and
Red Line 7000 and remain outside of the world of action,
they come to admire and respect the professional identity
of their men, finally participating in this world of action as
spectators.   Siegel's women--and his men--lack the flexibility of Hawks's characters; his films are unable to bridge
the gap between the worlds of melodrama and action.   The
vulnerability of Siegel's action figures in melodramatic situations is no better illustrated than in The Beguiled (1971).
A wounded Union soldier named McBurney (Clint Eastwood)
hides from Confederate soldiers in a Southern girls' school,
intrigues with the school's headmistress, her assistant, students, and the Negro cook, loses his leg and, finally, is
poisoned.   McBurney brings about his own death in daring
to compete with women in the more feminine sphere of
domestic interiors and love triangles.   If the involvement
of Siegel's heroes with women results in treachery and betrayal (Becky in Invasion, Sheila Farr in The Killers), then
the only alternative for them is to go it alone.

All of Siegel's heroes involve themselves in the quest
for certain goals which they can only attain on their own.
The dramatic action in his films is the drama of conflicting
goals.   Clustered around the major conflict between the hero
and his antagonist are an assortment of minor characters:

they all struggle, independent of one another, to achieve disparate, often conflicting goals.   Each character in Coogan's
Bluff, for example, becomes a foil for and an obstacle to
Coogan in his pursuit of Ringerman (Don Stroud).   The social worker, Julie (Susan Clark), wants to rehabilitate Ringerman's girl and prevents Coogan from seeing her.   Mrs.
Ringerman (Betty Field) shields her son from Coogan.   And
the bureaucratic New York police chief, McElroy (Lee J.
Cobb), has too many other problems to worry about Coogan
and his.   Similarly, the goals and procedures of the mayor
(John Vernon) and the police chief in Dirty Harry conflict
with Harry's: their bureaucratic caution makes it more
difficult for him to do his job.   The bleakness of Siegel's
later works is the result of his characters' inflexibility in
pursuit of their goals.   Though their tenacity--e. g. , Lee
Marvin's Charlie in The Killers--is seen as a strength, their
refusal to compromise, to reconsider their goals, leads to
their further alienation from society or to their death.   As
American policemen thinking of Harry's pension have pointed
out, Harry need not have thrown his badge away after killing
"Scorpio" at the end of Dirty Harry; he could have stuck it
out until he was eligible for his pension (which Magnum
Force and The Enforcer lead us to believe he did).   But,
for Siegel, Harry was incapable of adapting to the codes
and goals of society.   Harry, like many other Siegel heroes,
is the victim of his own inflexibility.   He himself refuses
to change and he cannot change the world around him.   The
result is less a stalemate than a defeat.   He has attained
his goal but become in the process as much an outlaw as
"Scorpio. "

    All of Siegel's best films focus on conflicts between
the individual and the hostile society around him, ending,
quite often, with that individual's defeat.   Siegel often involves his characters in situations in which they must literally struggle to stay alive; his films are essays on survival.
Films like Invasion and The Beguiled treat this issue quite
directly, incorporating it into the plot, but the mood, spirit
and atmosphere surrounding actual life-and-death struggles
pervade all of his films, even Dirty Harry in which Harry's
own life is never in question.

    Siegel clearly establishes but varies the terms of his
characters' struggle for survival in his films.   He often
surrounds his central characters with hostile minor characters.   In Invasion, the entire town becomes an impersonal
unit which seeks to transform the hero into an emotionless

pod. (The film, though definitely anti-fascist, is ultimately
ambiguous in terms of American political history. Are the
pods Communists or are they McCarthyites?) Similarly, the
western towns in Stranger on the Run and Death of a Gun-
fighter turn against Siegel's main characters; the police pursue his outlaws in Baby Face Nelson and The Line-Up and
both the police and the Mafia track Charley after he robs a
bank which contains Mafia money in Charley Varrick. The
environment of hostile characters which surrounds Siegel's
heroes is paralleled in the architecture and setting of his
films: the physical environment becomes hostile and alien.
New York City in Madigan and Coogan's Bluff becomes his
policemen's chief antagonist and cities in other Siegel films
--San Francisco in The Line-Up and Dirty Harry, London
and Paris in The Black Windmill--range in character from
deadeningly impersonal to cruelly threatening. Even his
western landscape is full of dangers. The credit sequence
of Two Mules for Sister Sara (1970) establishes the wildness
of the setting through which Hogan (Eastwood) rides. Siegel
pans from close-ups of wild animals in the foreground to
long shots of Hogan in the background, setting up a rhythmic
sequence that climaxes in a shot of a snake that is suddenly
crushed by the hoof of Hogan's horse and setting up the
terms of violence and physical pain that are to dominate the
film.

     The hostility of the world around them frequently
produces paranoia in Siegel's characters. In Invasion, in
which children fear their parents and Dr. Bennell ends up
in a police station raving like a madman about "pods," the
paranoia is justified. The pods are really out to get Siegel's
characters; less extreme forms of a similar paranoia
emerge in all of his films. His heroes distrust the people
around them; they can go to no one for help because, as in
The Black Windmill, their apparent allies are often, in fact,
their enemies. Their actions are automatically self-protec-
tive. When Charley Varrick breaks into the dentist's office
to remove his dead wife's x-rays (so that the police cannot
trace or identify her remains), he switches his own x-rays
with those of Harman (Andy Robinson), an action which later
enables him to substitute Harman's body for his own and to
escape both the police and the Mafia. Charley does not
plan Harman's death, but he does not pass up an opportunity
to safeguard his own life by using it.

     Varrick is Siegel's cagiest character. He engages
in a battle of wits with the police and with the Mafia's Molly

(Joe Don Baker), surviving only by forcing them to make mistakes and by making none himself. Siegel's other heroes are less perfect: they are vulnerable and make mistakes. In Siegel's first feature, The Verdict (1946), Scotland Yard inspector Grodman (Sidney Greenstreet) errs and the wrong man is convicted of a crime and executed. Forced into retirement by the scandal, Grodman acts independently to bring the real murderer to a kind of justice: he kills the man himself, making it look like an unsolvable, perfect crime. He watches his successor at the yard make the same sort of mistake he himself made when he convicted the wrong man on circumstantial evidence. Grodman is a prototype for Siegel's Madigan and Harry, cops who take the law into their own hands. In the first scene of Madigan (1968), Dan Madigan (Richard Widmark) makes a mistake: he takes his eyes off his suspect for an instant, the suspect takes his gun and escapes. Madigan spends the remainder of the film in pursuit of the suspect, occasionally employing questionable tactics to track his man down. Harry violates the rights of the "Scorpio" killer when he arrests him, torturing him to discover the whereabouts of a kidnapped girl. Harry's lawlessness forces the D. A. to drop the case against the killer, and Harry embarks on a personal crusade to get the killer behind bars, watching and waiting for him to commit another crime. Harry takes his job personally, transforming his pursuit of "Scorpio" into a battle of wills. The challenges he presents to a bank robber in the first scene and to "Scorpio" in the last underscore this aspect of Harry's battle with his opponents. After a gun battle, Harry addresses his antagonist:

> "I know what you're thinking," he says. "'Did he fire six shots or only five?' Well, to tell you the truth in all this excitement I've kinda lost track myself. But seein' this is a 44-Magnum, the most powerful hand gun in the world, and would blow your head clean off, you've got to ask yourself one question--'Do I feel lucky?' Well, do ya, punk?"

"Scorpio," unlike the bank robber, accepts the challenge; his will is as strong as Harry's but, in accepting the challenge, he makes a mistake and pays for it with his life.

The conflict between Siegel's heroes and his villains, as Jon Landau points out in a Rolling Stone review of Charley Varrick, is one of ego versus alter ego. If "Scorpio"

is Harry's nemesis, he is also his alter ego: Scorpio is
pure violence and lawlessness. In Varrick, Molly (Baker)
is Charley's opposite. A member of the organization, he
wears business suits and smokes a pipe; Charley, who is
"the last of the independents," wears work clothes and chews
gum. Landau explains that

> In the end, every element of the film is directed
> toward defining the gulf between Charley's and
> Molly's worlds. Thus the former's antiquated
> plane and the latter's souped-up car become per-
> fect extensions of their characters. And when,
> at one point, Charley tries to start an auto that
> won't ignite, he stares at it with his patented look
> of disgust for all things modern. . . . That moment
> lasts for all of five seconds, but seen in context,
> is a small piece of poetry, dwarfed only by the
> much larger moment when Charley and Molly face
> each other on the battlefield--an automobile grave-
> yard--in a fight between the plane and the car.

Charley wins his battle for survival but at the cost of his
identity. Though he outwits the organization and, as an individual, triumphs over modern anonymity, he himself is
forced to become nameless. He fakes his own death and
the film ends with the image of his crop-duster uniform,
with his name on it, going up in flames.

Dirty Harry and Charley Varrick are unquestionably
Siegel's best films; brilliantly structured in terms of character and action and stylistically unpretentious, they are
disturbing portrayals of loss in gain, of defeat in triumph,
a bleak reversal of John Ford's more positive vision of gain
in loss and triumph in defeat. Siegel's less successful
films present similar thematic concerns but are flawed by
obtrusive stylistic excesses. In these films, Siegel's own
ego comes between the action and the audience; he forces
his signature upon the content of the film with his camera.
The Beguiled, which Siegel considers his most personal
work, plays with color and camera angle in ways that seem
irrelevant to the action. The sepia opening evokes the atmosphere of gothic horror, but lasts only for the credit sequence, changing there to full Technicolor. What is the
point? At the same time, Siegel exaggerates camera angle,
especially in close up and medium shot, calling attention to
his own presence behind the camera. (The director has even
named these camera set-ups "Siegelinis.")

In a similar way, he overstates his symbolism: the
crow with the broken wing that is tethered outside McBurney's room symbolizes the wounded soldier's predicament.
Siegel has rarely practiced restraint in such matters, even
in his best films.   The Killers (1964), a film obsessed with
sight and time, begins with a shot of Charlie (Lee Marvin)
reflected in the sunglasses of his partner (Clu Gulager);
they enter a school for the blind, where all the students
wear dark glasses, and kill a man.   Close-ups of a glass
of carrot juice ("It's good for the eyes."), of braille watches
and of stop watches, coupled with Charlie's, "Lady, I haven't
got the time," hammers home the blindness and haste which
plague the film's characters, first Johnny North (John Cas-
savetes) and then Charlie.   As Charlie and his partner approach the school for the blind in the first scene, they pass
two blind children who are playing cops and robbers on the
lawn; one child shoots the other, who feigns death.   The
film's last scene brings its hero (Marvin) full circle.   Shot
by Browning (Ronald Reagan), Charlie staggers down the
walk outside Browning's house (in the first scene he goes
up a walk).   He falls.   With tortured effort, he vainly tries
to shoot at an approaching patrol car summoned by his earlier gunshots.   But he does not realize that he has lost his
gun and shoots, in a reflex action, with his fingers--his
gesture recalling that of the blind children in the first scene.
Siegel's narrative neatness and use of symbols is almost,
but not quite, slick, rescued only by the intensity of Marvin's gut-physical performance.

Even Dirty Harry suffers from a heavy-handed use
of symbolism, Siegel transforming Harry into half-gladiator
(the Keezar Stadium sequence) and half-Christ figure (the
cross in the park on which "Scorpio" crucifies him).   Yet
Siegel refuses to indulge these moments; the momentum of
his action narrative pulls us from these over-directed scenes
into other, less obtrusive ones.   The Shootist (1976) sets up
an overly-obvious parallel between the passing of an era
with the death of Queen Victoria, headlined in the newspaper
J. B. Books (John Wayne) buys when he enters town, and
that of Books himself, the last of the Old West's legendary
gunfighters.   But Books's repeated references to Victoria's
death ("Queen Victoria went out in style") overstate the
parallel.

The Shootist, as a collaborative effort, has too much
Siegel and too little Wayne.   Siegel makes his presence felt
in elaborate crane shots, low-angle wagon wheel shots, shots

taken through glass doors, mirror shots, whisky glass shots, sunbursts, and hand-held camera.   The director's transitions are occasionally pointlessly slick: he slowly zooms in on the face of Mrs. Rogers (Lauren Bacall) watching Books going off to his last gunfight through her window, then cuts abruptly to a close up of a pair of handcuffs being taken off one of the men who will shoot it out with Books, zooming out from close-up to medium shot in a reversal of the earlier movement.   Only the most forced of interpretations--that is, that "all of Siegel's characters are confined in one way or another"--can justify the editing together of the two, quite different images.

Like Buffalo Bill and the Indians (1976), which Dino di Laurentiis also produced, The Shootist reexamines the myths of the American West.   Siegel surveys the Wayne persona with clips from Hawks, Ford, and Farrow pictures, before the action of his own story begins.   His emphasis on Wayne's potential for violence in the clips reflects a narrow approach to the actor's persona: most of Wayne's performances are built less around action than reaction. At the same time, Siegel ignores Wayne's gregarious sociability.   Though Wayne is often simultaneously apart from and a part of the communities around him in his films, he always reveals in his performances a sense of the value of that community.   Eastwood is an ideal actor for Siegel in that he is laconic, self-contained, and a loner; he is cynically independent, willing to take on the whole world but unwilling to ask anyone for help.   Wayne, especially since True Grit, has become somewhat garrulous, his gestures more open and he more frequently seeks the company of others.   Siegel's mistake is to frustrate this side of Wayne, shooting his conversations in one-shots rather than in two-shots thereby aborting Wayne's scenes with James Stewart and Bacall.

Siegel reduces Wayne, at times, to cliché, playing upon the actor's own bout with cancer by afflicting him with it here and by setting up his final shoot-out with TV cowboys (Richard Boone and Hugh O'Brien), confronting a figure of Western myth with his decidedly less mythic successors.

He surrounds Wayne's J. B. Books with unbelievably hostile characters, making, by contrast, even the pods of Invasion look friendly.   Even before he gets to town, a highwayman tries to hold Books up.   The local milkman insults him.   Once his presence is known, Mrs. Rogers (Bacall) tries to evict him from her boarding house, calling in Marshall Thibido, who rejoices to learn that Books is dying and vows to dance on his grave. Siegel gathers vultures around him: a newspaper reporter wants to syndicate Books's life story, capitalizing on his death. A former girlfriend turns up, willing to become Mrs. J. B. Books and hoping to cash in on his name by authorizing a biography of him after his death.

Books, one of Siegel's heroes forced to yield to the present, lives by an outmoded code, but one with which Siegel surely sympathizes. Books tells young Gillum Rogers (Ron Howard): "I won't be wronged. I won't be insulted. I won't be laid a hand on. I don't do these things to other people and I expect the same from them." But Books, even if he did not have a cancer, could not survive in the modern world: everyone wrongs, insults, and lays hands on him. Books decides to go out in style (like Queen Victoria). He stages a shoot-out in the Metropole cafe with three local gunmen. What is fascinating about this shoot-out is that even though it is suicidal for Books, he struggles to survive it. Even having made the decision to die, he fights to stay alive; killing the three gunmen, Books, in turn, is shot in the back by the Metropole barman. Siegel's world proves too treacherous for heroes of the Old West.

The impact of the film's final scene, the shoot-out, is dissipated by subsequent action. Gillum avenges Books, killing the barman, and he and Books exchange ambiguous glances before the former discards his bloody gun and the latter dies. The film ends with a series of highly angled shots and hand-held shots of Gillum returning home, Siegel making a final directorial intrusion upon the action only to obscure the significance of Gillum's gesture and of the final exchange of looks.

Siegel's career remains one of promise. He has elicited performances from Eastwood that no other director, save Eastwood himself, has been able to equal. Siegel's masterpieces, Dirty Harry and Charley Varrick, are clearly two of the ten best American films made in the Seventies. Like the characters in his films, he has struggled to survive in a hostile industry, but, unlike his heroes, he cannot make it alone. His directorial tag should read, "The Last of the Dependent Independents."

3. THE CINEMA OF SELF-EFFACEMENT: HAWKS AND RENOIR

Bazin praises a style which effaces itself before reality, which puts itself at the service of its subject matter. Hawks positions his camera so as to enable the action to unfold naturally before it. Events determine the style in which they are shot, not vice versa. Like Hawks, Renoir respects the integrity of events. As Bazin points out, Renoir "uncovered the secret of a film form that would permit everything to be said without chopping the world up into little fragments, that would reveal the hidden meaning in people and things without disturbing the unity natural to them." Though by no means "style-less"--self-effacement is a kind of style--Hawks and Renoir pare down their narrative rhetoric to a minimum. They are, as Bazin suggests of the invisible man "who must wear pajamas and smoke a cigarette," visibly invisible.

a.   Hawks & Co.

Howard Hawks's characterization is rooted in the physical.
As Jacques Rivette has observed

> It is actions that he films, meditating on the pow-
> er of appearances alone.   We are not concerned
> with John Wayne's thoughts as he walks toward
> Montgomery Clift at the end of Red River, or of
> Bogart's thoughts as he beats somebody up: our
> attention is directed solely to the precision of
> each step--the exact rhythm of the walk--of each
> blow--and to the gradual collapse of the battered
> body. [1]

Hawks's characterizations work primarily on a physical, not
a psychological level.   Where a director like Ford idealizes
his characters (through fanciful lighting) or one like Borzage
etherealizes them (through light, almost weightless backgrounds), Hawks "materializes" them--he makes them seem
real by relating them in a very physical way to their environment.

     The believability of Katharine Hepburn's characteriza-
tion of Susan in Bringing Up Baby, for instance, hinges, in
part, on her ability to manipulate her environment and to
turn fortuitous events into tools which help her to trap David.
She uses the jail set at the end of the film to become
"Swinging-Door Susie"--her voice changes, her mannerisms
change: she relates in a very physical way to her setting
in order to control it.   Similarly, Vince Barnett's (Angelo,
Fishbone) inability to physically control his environment in
Scarface (the telephone gags) and Tiger Shark (his clumsiness in imitating Pipes' tricks) defines his character.
Clearly, actors in Hawks's films act with their bodies; we
come to understand them on a physical level--by watching
their mannerisms, gestures, eyes, body movements, and
voice intonations.

But Hawks's actors, unlike Hitchcock's, act with
their whole bodies. To return to the Red River scene
which Rivette describes, it is the total physical movement
of Dunson (Wayne) that conveys the meaning of this scene.
Although it's often tempting to focus on a single hand gesture, look, body movement, or voice intonation in a Hawks
film, these isolated gestures and movements only stand out
within the context of each character's total physical presence. For example, Rinaldo (George Raft) in Scarface is
characterized by his coin-flipping. This mannerism draws
our attention but does so against a stiff and static "background"--it derives its meaning partly from Rinaldo's overall stiffness, his lack of mannerism and movement. If
Hawks were to cut into a close-up of Rinaldo's coin-flipping
(as Hitchcock might do), he would isolate the gesture from
the character's physical totality. Even in Tiger Shark,
when Hawks begins a wedding sequence with a close-up of
the ring (on Mike's hand/hook), he tracks back to show the
totality of the scene; he connects a specific part of Mike's
body to the whole. [2] Hitchcock, by contrast, tends to see
his characters in parts, not as physical wholes. The introduction of Hannay (Robert Donat) at the beginning of The 39
Steps is done in parts: close-ups of his feet, his hands at
the ticket window, etc. Hitchcock characterizes Bruno
(Robert Walker) and Guy (Farley Granger) in the first few
shots of Strangers on a Train with close-ups of their feet
before he ever shows us their faces or their whole bodies.
Hitchcock, unlike Hawks, also tends to break up movement
or action into tiny pieces--witness the montage of Forio
and Marnie jumping the stone fence in Marnie, or the highly-
cut shower murder in Psycho. Hitchcock's use of Kuleshov's "bowl-of-soup" montage and insert shots in Rear Window, coupled with reaction shots of Jeffries' (James Stewart)
face or eyes, though it breaks up the physical continuity of
Stewart's acting, reinforces his performance in a supra-
physical way by suggesting what's going on in his mind.
Though Hawks sometimes shows a character thinking--e. g.,
Susan before she bangs the telephone against the fireplace
grating to scare David into thinking that she has been attacked by Baby in Bringing Up Baby, or Walter Burns (Cary
Grant) in His Girl Friday with his similarly "planned" the-
atrics--Hawks never shows what's going on within his characters' minds. We can only guess at that by interpreting
their physical gestures--e. g., Burns's darting eyes and nervous hand movements just before he tries another routine to
win back Hildy. Lang's actors, by contrast, lack gesture
and mannerisms; they wear expressionless, mask-like faces
which conceal rather than reveal their real feelings.

Where Hitchcock isolates gestures--he shows part of an action to give a sense of the whole--Hawks co-ordinates an isolated gesture with a character's whole physical presence to emphasize the physical continuity of gesture and movement. Where Hitchcock's actors--especially Stewart in Rear Window--have no independent existence in the frame because they are constantly seen in isolated parts or shown reacting to objects, events, and characters outside their own frame, Hawks's characters seem whole and tremendously self-sufficient--partly because their actions are shown in totality and partly because they react physically to whatever enters their frame (e. g. , the single, uncut shot of the shark eating Mike's hand in Tiger Shark). In other words, Hitchcock's use of cutting and montage makes his films and actors function on an abstract, psychological level; Hawks's self-contained frames establish extremely physical relationships by showing the actual space between his characters and the environment (objects and things) which surrounds them.

Professionalism and Acting Style

The relationship of Hawks's characters to their environment has an almost deterministic force on their acting style. Not only do Hawks's actors relate directly to their physical environment, but this environment also defines them. By "environment" I mean both the literal background of each frame and the space which surrounds his characters, and also whatever physical activity Hawks's characters are engaged in. In the adventure films, his male characters are defined by what they do for a living; they are fliers, race car drivers, gangsters, fishermen, hunters, etc. In a sense, their profession is part of their environment. Their ability to control that environment determines just how "good" they are at their profession. It becomes almost impossible to divorce profession from personality. Camonte's doomed struggle to control his environment in Scarface ("The World Is Yours") and Mike's boasting in Tiger Shark ("I the best fisherman in the whole Pacific ocean") become, like the former's scar and the latter's hook, more than professional trademarks: they become integral (here also physical) parts of their personality. Or, in the comedies, Susan's and Walter Burns's rubbery adaptability and their deft manipulation of fortuitous events--in other words, their relationship to their "environment"--reflect the qualities necessary for survival in their world.

Though Hawks primarily defines his characters in

terms of what they do for a living, within this context of
professionalism there exists a wide range of individual idiosyncracies and distinct personalities. In Hawks's early adventure films--especially in Tiger Shark (1932) and Dawn
Patrol (1930)--the director's visual style and the structure
of his films are based almost directly on the relationship
between his characters and what they do--both in the general
sense of their profession and in the specific sense of their
gestures, mannerisms and movements within the frame. In
Tiger Shark when Mike (Edward G. Robinson) scratches
Pipes' (Richard Arlen) back--the gesture is repeated throughout the film--the action defines the paternalistic nature of
their relationship. It's also clear from the gesture that the
tie between the two men is a strong one and one based on
physical contact. Unlike Mike's relationship with Quita
(Zita Johann) which for the most part lacks actual physical
contact, the Mike-Pipes relationship has a strength and
permanence that never comes into question; we know that
Pipes could never be disloyal to Mike, even for Quita.
Their lasting bond of friendship resurfaces at the very end
of the film--Mike dies scratching Pipes' back and falls into
his arms, not Quita's. Though he loves them both, Mike's
relationship with Quita does not involve physical contact; it
would be inconsistent for Mike to die in her arms--the
tenuousness of their relationship would not permit it.

     Mike's whole relationship with Quita is revealed
through their gestures toward one another. When we first
see Quita, she is sitting with her hands limp and her head
thrown back in a rocking chair--her whole form is an image
of resignation and defeat. Mike's demonstrative gestures
seem to bring her to life; she, like Pipes, seems to draw
strength from Mike. It is almost as if their restrained gestures robbed Mike's broad, unrestrained gestures of their
power and efficacy. Later, when Quita tells Mike that she
does not love him, she puts her hand on his arm, restrain-
ing him. The gesture, though involving contact, is both a
linking and an endistancing one. It represents the honesty
of her response to him, an honesty which is the real basis
of their relationship; but the gesture also means that she
does not love Mike. And still later, just before she and
Mike go off to be married, Quita, in a gesture which epitomizes her relationship with Mike, reaches out toward him
to fix his hair but never seems to quite touch him. It is a
tentative, sympathetic gesture--one which suggests the emotionally restrained nature of her commitment to him. Yet
it is also this sort of gesture which isolates and destroys
him.

The film contains other characters defined by their physical idiosyncracies. Pipes, for example, plays the guitar and possesses a deftness of movement which Mike's sweeping, open gestures lack (similarly, Pipes is more adept at getting girls). He rolls coins over his knuckles, performs cigarette tricks and can flip plates. Fishbone, though he has no trouble finding girls, is more clumsy. In fact, Fishbone is defined through his clumsiness by the very gestures which also define Pipes. When Pipes shows him how to flip plates, Fishbone fumbles and breaks the plate. When Pipes shows him a cigarette trick, Mike enters, slaps Fishbone on the back and makes him swallow the cigarette. Both characters, of course, are foils for Mike. Just as Angelo's clumsiness and fondness for new clothing (his hat and new suit) and Little Boy's deftness and success with girls comment indirectly on the Camonte character in Scarface, so Fishbone's fumbling and Pipes' coordination bracket Mike's exaggerated but ineffectual gestures.

Hawks's use of the physical idiosyncracies of his actors in Tiger Shark relates quite directly to the structure of the film as a whole. Throughout the film Hawks alternates sequences of tension between characters with scenes which lack character tensions. This roughly corresponds to the alternation between interiors (tense) and exteriors (not as tense), studio sets and real locations, story footage (love triangle, character vs. character) and documentary footage (man vs. nature, fish). The interior sequences present characters as highly idiosyncratic; the frames are cluttered with detail; the lighting is complex, several textures operating within each frame. The semi-documentary fishing sequences, on the other hand, tend to dissolve inter-character tensions and to set up, instead, tensions between man and nature[3]: the frames are less cluttered and more open, the textures are simpler (two shades of gray), the background (sea and sky) is devoid of tensions and the characters' idiosyncracies seem to disappear in the action. The characters become almost impersonal; they lose their personality in their work.

Although it is not an action or documentary sequence, the scene which best illustrates this loss of personality is the shipboard burial of Manuel Silva. It is here that the overwhelming presence of Nature (the wind and the sea) makes itself felt most strongly. The sequence begins with a long shot of Mike's boat, small and surrounded by sea

and sky. It is a shot that puts everything in its place. It
suggests an order outside that of the boat--an order which
is, most simply, cosmic. When Hawks cuts in to the funeral service, the backlighting and lack of frontlighting depersonalize all the men but Mike (whom we can barely make
out and then only because he is in close-up.) The rest of
the men seem to blend with the shadows in the foreground,
to become part of the boat, to lose their identity in it as
they are overwhelmed by Nature.

A similar phenomenon occurs in the dawn sequence
before the start of the cattle drive in Red River. The backlighting puts the men in shadow, deprives them of their individuality and blends them with the landscape. The subsequent editing (the rapid succession of close-ups as they yell
to start the cattle drive) though shot in full light, makes the
men into impersonal figures because the quickness of the
cuts does not give them enough time to establish their individuality (there's a similar sequence in His Girl Friday
when the newspapermen get ready to report the capture of
Earl Williams in the Court House press room). The action
sequences in Red River, e. g. , the stampede, which is also
shot with backlighting, or the crossing of the Red River,
also tend toward the impersonal--shots of wagons, riders,
and cattle which seem to bear little relation to the film's
central plot situation. In these shots, the action or event
itself takes on a meaning and existence of its own, devoid
of the tensions between characters which exist in the remainder of the film. The conflict between Dunson and Matt
is relaxed by changing the tensions from interpersonal (man
vs. man) to impersonal (man vs. nature): men cast aside
their idiosyncracies in order to control the herd. They
subordinate their own individuality to a larger identity to
achieve their goals. This process, which occurs in one
form or another in almost all of Hawks's films, reflects a
tendency toward the integration of his characters with their
environment. In Air Force this process is at its clearest:
Hawks alternates close-ups of the individual crew members
in the plane with long shots of the Mary Ann in flight. The
men in a sense, become the plane; their own idiosyncrasies
and goals, seen most dramatically in the integration of Winocki or in Sgt. White's suppression of his own grief over
his dead son, become secondary to a larger goal--that of
keeping the Mary Ann in the air.

The clearest example of action as a release or outlet
for tensions occurs in the last 20-minute, exterior sequence

in Rio Bravo. The greater part of the film is shot in interiors (the jail, the hotel, bars). The entrapment of characters in these interiors and the growing tensions between the central characters (or the tensions within Dude) seem to dissolve when they step outside. It's almost an explosion: the single cut from Chance, internal-framed in the doorway of a grain barn, to Chance, without that internal frame, suddenly places Chance in the open and seemingly free, but vulnerable as he finally confronts Burdett. (This cut occurs just before Chance calls out, "Burdett ... Burdett ... Nathan Burdett!") The openness of the scene (even the tops of the walls and adobe ruins are broken and without ceiling), and the teamwork involved in exploding the dynamite work out the tensions which had developed in the interiors.

A very similar phenomenon takes place in Hawks's first sound film, Dawn Patrol; what he develops throughout the film is the pattern of inevitability. Characters remain trapped by the professional roles they must perform. This can be felt most dramatically in the acting style, especially in the mixture of rage and emotional resignation in the characters' repetition of the reply, "Right!" to orders they would rather not obey. The static nature of the film as a whole and the tenseness of many of its scenes result, in part, from characters playing against themselves, from the conflict between their personality and their profession. The restrained, self-contained gestures, like Courtney's hands on his face, the lack of physical contact in the film make the acting style of Dawn Patrol peculiarly isometric. By "isometric" I mean actual stress against one's self, strained and restrained gestures. Each character becomes trapped between the inevitability of his situation or profession and his own personal feelings. After Brand's departure, we see Courtney in the same position, performing similar actions (answering the telephone and carrying out its impersonal orders) and using similar gestures. Courtney is trapped into becoming Brand by performing Brand's role, just as Scott becomes somewhat like the earlier Courtney. The friendship between the two becomes strained by their roles, and this tension reinforces the film's overall structure which consists of alternation between movement and static set ups, between the freedom of personal idiosyncracy/individuality and the stasis of professional necessity, between mobility and immobility, between an organic exercise of free will and a schematic pattern of inevitability.

Although the action sequences in Dawn Patrol seem
to free characters from the stasis of responsibility and give
them a sort of freedom, they are anything but hedonistic
exercises of individuality.   In fact, characters here, as in
Air Force, lose their individuality in the action sequences;
they become one with their planes.   Though Hawks cuts to
close-ups of the pilots, actual action is seen primarily in
long shot and distinct personality is not a visual factor; all
we see is the plane.   When Courtney takes off on his final
flight, the take-off is shot without cuts (except one which
shows the face of his mechanic after take-off) and without
camera movement.   As the plane moves further and further
away from the camera, we become less and less aware of
Courtney's personality and more and more aware of the
plane.   Courtney becomes one with the plane.   So, in one
sphere of action (the flight commander's office), professionalism is static and in another (the air), it is fluid and mobile; but in both it tends to rob characters of their uniqueness, to make them impersonal parts of machines.   In one
sphere, characters resist this, and the result is tension; in
the other, they give themselves willingly over to their mission and resolve their tensions through cathartic action.

The action sequences in Tiger Shark also work as an
impersonal release from the plot's tensions, as Fieschi has
suggested.   Though the men in the film are defined by what
they do, they paradoxically also lose their individuality in
their work.   They become part of the boat; like the men in
Red River, they become part of team.   Here the loss of individuality is necessary for the maintenance of sanity and
stability.   When idiosyncracies interfere with the work
(e. g. , when Mike shoots sharks for no reason), there is a
sense of the perversion of that work.   Nature is being
abused; Mike seems insane.   When a character's personality conflicts with the achievement of the goals of his profession, as Dunson's ultimately does in Red River, the character is seen to have lost sight of his place in the cosmos;
he seems to go insane.   The perversion of action, profession, or work for personal, idiosyncratic ends becomes insanity; this appears quite clearly in Red Line 7000 when
Mike Marsh tries to run Dan McCall off the track.

The flying sequences in Dawn Patrol, Only Angels
Have Wings and Air Force, the battle sequences in Today
We Live, the action sequences in Scarface, Sergeant York,
Red River, The Big Sky, Land of the Pharoahs, and Hatari!,
the fishing sequences in Tiger Shark, the exterior action se-

quences in Rio Bravo all have essentially cathartic functions:
they serve to relax the character vs. character tensions of
the film's interiors by means of exterior action. Nevertheless, the sense of two worlds--one of intercharacter tensions, one of impersonal action--and their ultimate separateness remains strong in Hawks. The resolutions of his films
demand resolutions in each world; Rio Bravo does not end
when Chance, Dude, and Stumpy blow up the Burdetts in
the film's climactic action sequence, but ends with the dis-
solution of tensions between the central characters, e. g.,
Chance's acceptance and acknowledgement of his relationship
with Feathers. Red River, similarly, does not end with the
completion of the cattle drive: Matt still has to face Dunson.

Hawks, clearly, does not use action or plot to avoid
treatment of character. In fact, what is so pure about the
conclusion of Red River is that Hawks totally disregards
plot expectations (Dunson and Matt killing each other at the
end) in order to remain true to his characters. Matt could
never kill Dunson (witness the scene when Matt takes the
herd), and Dunson could never kill Matt (this is shown indirectly in the scene with Tess when he gives her gun back
and asks her if she wants to use it). The bond between the
two would not permit it.

Character Consistency

The most essential ingredient of Hawks's characterization
and acting style is consistency. The consistency of a Hawksian character exists, for the most part, in the consistency
of his behavior, physical gesture, tone of voice, dialogue
and even costume. There's a minor character (Capt. Rey-
nard's tall, thin, silent bodyguard) in To Have and Have Not
who says nothing. At one point in the film Morgan turns to
him and says, "Don't you ever ask any questions? Don't
you ever say anything?" The man does not answer. What's
interesting about the treatment of this character is that Morgan later takes advantage of the consistency of the bodyguard's
behavior: at the climax of the film, Morgan asks him for
a cigarette, knowing that he will not answer. Morgan then
teams up with Slim, gets a gun from a desk instead of
matches, shoots the bodyguard and takes control of the situation. A similar phenomenon occurs in Rio Bravo when
Dude sends Chance back to the jail with Burdett's men,
knowing what Stumpy will do. Dude is aware of and relies

on the consistency of Stumpy's behavior (Stumpy once even
shot at Dude when he tried to enter the jail). This predict-
ability of behavior gives a certain stability to Hawks's characters. The consistency of their behavior becomes their
greatest strength. As a result, his characters never seem
to undergo dramatic changes--even at the end of films.
Geoff Carter in Only Angels Have Wings doesn't "ask" Bonnie Lee to stay; he flips a coin that he knows has two heads
and says, "Heads you stay, tails you go." Chance doesn't
tell Feathers that he loves her; he just says, "I'll arrest
you if you go downstairs in those things [her tights]."

Since Hawks characterizes on a purely physical level,
physical appearance in his films can be tremendously important. Even the clothes his characters wear become part
of their personality. Sgt. White in Air Force for example,
wears a Chicago Cubs cap, and his dialogue is full of base-
ball metaphors. Characteristically, Hawks frequently uses
different types of clothing--especially hats--to distinguish
minor characters from one another. Even in Red River no
two cowboys look alike--there's one who even wears a derby. This hat business culminates in El Dorado, in which
Mississippi's hat becomes an integral part of his identity.
Character consistency in Hawks's adventure films depends,
in part, on consistency of costume. In Rio Bravo when
Chance changes from a red to a blue shirt, it is a major
event. It also happens to coincide with a greater flexibility
in his character--he first appears in blue, smiling broadly
after spending the night with Feathers. Then in a remark-
able scene with Stumpy, Chance kisses him on the forehead.
For the most part, Hawks's characters in the early adventure films don't seem to go through many costume changes.
What's so striking about the comedies is the flexibility of
Hawks's characters. In a film like Bringing Up Baby,
change of costume brings on a change in personality. When
David puts on a negligee, he goes "gay all of a sudden."
The same thing happens to Rochard at the end of I Was a
Male War Bride and in Bringing Up Baby David's initial inflexibility breaks down from costume to costume (lab coat
to riding outfit). Physical changes in Hawks--even the taking of a bath in Rio Bravo or El Dorado--suggest personality
changes (Dude and Harrah get better); even in the adventure
films, these changes have comic overtones.

Gestures and Characterization in Only Angels Have Wings

Geoff Carter, like Chance in Rio Bravo, is always without
matches; he constantly borrows them from others. As Carter himself explains it, he "never lays in a supply of anything." Though Carter is the most independent and powerful
figure in the film, his gestures reveal a dependence on those
around him: Carter derives his power from using people.
When Carter first appears (in a doorway), he's giving flight
instructions to Joe Souther. While doing this, he starts to
light a cigarette and strikes a match against the doorway.
The match breaks. He walks to the middle of the bar,
looks around for a second or two, sees Bonnie's cigarette
and takes it to light his own. All this is done quite naturally and without dramatic effect; the focus of the scene, after all, is on the orders and the characters' reaction to
those orders. But at the same time, Hawks immediately
establishes a physical relationship between Geoff and Bonnie
before they are actually introduced. Grant continues talking
to Joe and, as he is about to return Bonnie's cigarette,
starts gesturing with his hand. Bonnie tries to get her
cigarette back but Geoff's gesture pulls it away from her.
Bonnie finally grabs her cigarette out of Geoff's hand and
gives him a dirty look. This simple piece of business sets
up and informs Geoff and Bonnie's whole relationship.

As a counterpoint to the earlier scenes with Bonnie
Lee, the Geoff-Judy scene reveals, through gestures, their
former intimacy. In a remarkable synchronization of gesture, Judy automatically and without thought or hesitation
strikes a match for Geoff. This gesture is even more revealing than their almost spontaneous kiss, which opens the
scene.

Thematically, Only Angels Have Wings is about integration: the integration of Bonnie Lee into the group is one
of the film's central concerns. But the film is also about
the integration of Bat and, though it may not appear obvious
at first, of Geoff. Gestures in the film reflect this process
of integration. Bat's gestures are highly self-contained (perhaps Hawks is exploiting Barthelmess' acting style; see
Dawn Patrol) and physically isolate him from the rest of the
group. Bat does not touch other characters or reach out,
willingly, to them. His handshake is reluctant when he's
first introduced to the other fliers. In Geoff's office, his
gestures are similarly self-contained: he fidgets with his
hat band and spins the propeller blade of a model plane on

Geoff's desk.[4]   The final scene with Bat in the bar--his two
hands burned and bandaged--is both consistent and moving.
The fliers make an attempt to integrate Bat into the group:
the dead Kid "buys" him a drink, Les puts the drink into his
bandaged hands, Pancho gives him a cigarette and Geoff
holds Bat's cigarette while he drinks.   Though Bat's gestures are still essentially self-contained (because his hands
are burned, he can't use them), the other characters, some
like Les and Geoff wounded themselves, draw Bat into their
group.

Part of Bat's integration is accomplished through gesture.   It is also reinforced by Hawks's composition, which
physically defines the group by setting the fliers off from
the characters who surround them.   Thus Gent who stands
at the bar in the background and who has become an outsider
because he was not good enough--he was afraid to fly the
nitro--becomes a defining force within the frame: his health
emphasizes the fliers' injuries which they got doing their
job.   It is partially the presence of Gent, who was not good
enough, that integrates Bat into the group of fliers who are
good enough and who have the injuries to prove it.

Throughout Only Angels Have Wings Hawks uses background characters as defining forces on foreground action.
But he does this in such an unobtrusive way that one rarely
consciously articulates this process.   The initial antagonism
between Bat and the fliers, especially since it is worked into
the script, is fairly obvious.   As a result, Bat's physical
presence in the frame changes the nature of the composition
--usually Hawks isolates Bat from the group and, by making
his presence felt, heightens the tensions in the frame between this isolated figure and the group.   However, what
Hawks does with Bonnie Lee, a somewhat similarly intrusive
figure, is much more subtle.   Like Gent, Bonnie is also
seen--in the middle of the film--in the background of the
frame.   The best instance of this occurs when Bat and the
two girls, Felicia and Elena, arrive on the mail boat.
When Geoff enters the bar to meet Bat, he passes Bonnie
and leaves her standing in the back of the frame.   When he
says hello to the two girls who, like Bonnie, have come in
on the boat and whom Geoff has known in the past, it's possible to see Bonnie in the background.   Though the emphasis
of the scene remains on the identification of Bat, on seeing
through the confusion of names and faces, Bonnie's presence
in the background adds another dimension to the action.
Perhaps, she sees here, as she does later when she spies

on Judy and Geoff, her future. She could become another
Felicia. Or another Judy. As Kid says, when it rains,
"every third drop" falls on a girl who's been in love with
Geoff. Her presence in the background not only shows her
exclusion from the group, it also helps clarify her relationship with Geoff.

Any director who puts two people or a group of people in a single frame naturally implies a relationship. Even
if one character is ignorant of the other's presence, the
frame creates a relationship. Still, Hawks uses the frame
in a way that is peculiarly his own. Hawks's framing and
treatment of space helps his actors act; his visual style, as
I've suggested above, functions as a defining force. Groups
in Hawks, clearly, are not only welded together on a narrative level by a common danger or goal but also on a compositional level by those who stand on the fringe of their
group who do not share those dangers or goals. Major
Brand in Dawn Patrol, for instance, operates as a defining
figure: his exclusion from the group of pilots defines that
group. Similarly, in the opening sequence of Tiger Shark,
the exclusion of one man in the dinghy defines the strength
of the relationship between Mike and Pipes, the other two.

Hawks's use of composition to set up conflicts within
the frame and to define the relationships among his characters reflects, on a visual level, his interest in the integration of his characters with one another and with their environment. When they are totally integrated into a group or
environment, i. e. , when they have subordinated their own
desires, idiosyncrasies, and needs to the larger needs of
the group, Hawks tends to show them (though this is completely unschematic and intuitive on his part) in two-dimensional space. When his characters' conflict with their environment or one another is unresolved, Hawks suggests this
visually in more or less three-dimensional space. In Air
Force, for instance, he alternates two-dimensional shots of
the plane in the air (in which the men become the plane) with
three-dimensional shots of the plane landing or taking off
amidst smoke, damaged hangars, trees, etc. (conflict between the plane and its environment). All of Hawks's films,
by alternating three-dimensional, personal, idiosyncratic
footage with two-dimensional, impersonal action footage,
work toward a goal of total integration in two-dimensionality.
As his characters continually interact with and are defined
by their backgrounds, they gradually, through an explosive
release of tension in action, surrender their egos to their

environment--both losing themselves in it and, at the same
time, maintaining themselves through it.   They and their
environment become one.

Hawks's visual style is, then, not schematic; it is
intuitive and organic, growing naturally out of his characters
and their situation.   What continually amazes me about
Hawks's work is its coherence and integrity--his acting
style, his script and his visual style are all one.   Though
each element seems to have an equal weight in relation to
the others, they are all ultimately inseparable. [5]

NOTES

1. Rivette, Jacques, "Rivette on Hawks," Movie, No. 5
    (December 1962), 19.
2. This is a standard visual device that Hawks uses to es-
    tablish relationships in a physical way.   The song se-
    quence in Rio Bravo, for example, begins with a
    close-up of Dude's face and subsequently cuts back
    to show Dude's spatial relationship to the group, to
    men or things outside of himself.   It has the effect
    of stabilizing Dude's recovery of sobriety and self-
    respect by showing him reacting to things outside of
    himself.
3. J. A. Fieschi originally noted Hawks's alternation of
    scenes with character tensions and scenes of action
    in a short note on Tiger Shark in Cahiers du Cinéma,
    No. 139 (January 1963).
4. What links Bat and Judy, in a subconscious way in our
    minds, is this latter gesture.   When Judy enters
    Geoff's office, she also plays with the plane's pro-
    peller.   No other characters do this.
5. The author would like to express his indebtedness to the
    unpublished writings of Fred Camper, Mike Prokosch,
    and William Paul on Hawks.

b. The Expressive Stylistics of Scarface

Scarface (1932), universally acknowledged as one of the greatest gangster films ever made, has achieved a notoreity that few other American films have. Unseen commercially in this country for over thirty years, Scarface, like its enigmatic owner-producer Howard Hughes, has become something of an underground phenomenon, surfacing from time to time in poor-quality, 16mm dupe prints at film society screenings and in university film courses. [1]

The History of the Film

The film was originally released in the spring of 1932 billed as "the gangster film to end all gangster films." And in many ways it was. Its release not only marks the high point of the gangster cycle but also introduces the element of censorship into the genre, indirectly resulting in the rise of The Legion of Decency and helping to put new teeth in the Production Code. Like the earlier Hughes project of Hell's Angels (1930), Scarface was a super-production, employing 1500 extras in one scene, using 62 different sets in three separate studios and smashing up countless automobiles during the filming of chase sequences. Hughes liked Hawks's action scenes, especially the car crashes. (After seeing one day's rushes, he told Hawks, "That car smash is marvelous. Do some more." "I made nineteen more car wrecks," Hawks relates. "I had to--Hughes kept egging me on.")

The extravagance of the production and the controversy surrounding the film's release are part of the Hughes trademark. Hughes' battle with the censors won him and his picture so much publicity that by the time it opened in New York crowds of people stood in long lines to see it. The release of the film was delayed for over a year and a half because of censorship problems. Shooting of the film was completed by the middle of 1931, but the Hays office

245

demanded that Hughes make certain changes before they
would approve the film.   Most of the censors' objections
came in response not to the openness of the film's sexual
relationships nor to its violence (though the latter did dis-
turb the Hays Office), but to the film's sympathy toward and
favorable depiction of Tony Camonte (Paul Muni), its gangster hero.

The characters and events in the film came out of
contemporary newspaper headlines--the killing of Big Jim
Colisimo on 22nd Street in Chicago, the St. Valentine's Day
Massacre, the besieging and capture of the notorious "Two
Gun" Crowley and, of course, the exploits of then current
public enemy Al Capone.

The film's opening scene is patterned after Colisimo's
own death. [2]   Likewise, Crowley had recently barricaded
himself in his apartment fortress and held off the police for
hours before he was finally subdued.   And Capone, as every
newspaper reader in the country knew was "Scarface."   The
immediacy of the film's subject matter, in the face of recent events, proved to be too much for the censorship lobby.
As Lewis Jacobs reports in The Rise of the American Film

> The spectacular gang killing on February 7, 1932,
> of Vincent Coll, "baby killer," by machine-gun fire
> in a drug store in New York City; the kidnapping
> of the Lindbergh baby on March 1, 1932 ... out-
> raged the public.   Advocates of censorship attacked
> crime pictures as incitements to lawlessness, en-
> couraging brutality, violence, glorification of the
> criminal, the lust for easy money and luxury of
> the gangster's life.   The agitation finally culmi-
> nated in the formation of the Legion of Decency
> (p. 523).

Scarface, which opened in Los Angeles in March and
in New York in May of 1932, became an obvious target.
The censors, appalled by Ben Hecht's script, wanted Hughes
to take a stronger stance against gangsters by transforming
his film into an appeal for public condemnation of men like
Capone.   On the other hand, William Wellman's Public Enemy, which opened in May of 1931, escaped the moral in-
dignation heaped upon Hughes' picture, even though its ending, in which Cagney's brother opens the door and his bandaged corpse falls through it, is more violent.   Scarface
seems to have been singled out by the industry censors.

The pre-Code Hays Office was, in fact, little more than a mouthpiece for the studio front offices; it was primarily an agency for the control of their stars' morality. At any rate, Warner Bros., producers of Public Enemy, obviously had more clout with the Hays Office than did Hughes and United Artists, his distributor. Hostility within the pre-Code industry toward independent producers in general and Hughes in particular was undoubtedly as much a factor in the attempt to censor Scarface as the film's unfortunate timeliness.

The Hays Office suggested that the title be changed to Scarface: The Shame of a Nation; they forced the inclusion of a moralizing written preface, numerous cuts and a new ending in which Camonte is tried and hanged, not shot down in the street. Hughes, at first, agreed to these demands but, after screening his censored film, decided to release it as it was originally shot. Compromising with the Hays Office on the title: Scarface: The Shame of a Nation, and by including a moralizing scene in a newspaper publisher's office, Hughes eventually obtained an MPPA seal of approval. And he was also able to get a lot of mileage out of his battle with the censors. His publicity on the film made full use of its controversial production history. It was advertised as "The picture that powerful interests have tried to suppress--in its uncut, unaltered, original version."

For the censored version, Hawks had shot a new ending. Muni, who played Camonte, had by this time returned to the New York stage and was unavailable. Using a double for his star, Hawks shot the required courtroom and execution scenes obliquely, with shots of Camonte's back and feet. In the original, Camonte dashes out into the street, driven out of his fortified apartment by tear gas. As cameraman Lee Garmes describes it, "we showed the police riddling him with bullets and he fell into a big pile of horse manure, where he belonged. The censors didn't like that; they wanted something different, so we did it over again."[3] Society and the legal establishment in the original are given no opportunity to moralize over the gangster. His execution occurs at the hands of the police, whom Hawks treats as an integral part of the gangster's world and, thus, his professional colleagues.

After Hawks left the picture, a scene in a publisher's office was added. In it, citizens' groups express their outrage and denounce gangsterism. Both this scene and the

courtroom ending are dramatically alien to the original concept of the film in that they violate the integrity of the world
which Hawks's gangsters inhabit. This world is a closed
society, including only other gangsters, police, and crime
reporters. It naturally excludes those such as publishers,
civic groups, judges, and juries who normally have no direct contact with the underworld.

Hughes satisfied the Hays Office with his compromises
but, when he opened the film in New York, the state censors
refused to approve the picture. Hughes apparently exhibited
the censored version he had made (and later junked) for the
Hays Office in New York while he fought the state censors,
eventually winning the right to exhibit his picture, without
censorship, in New York.

Meanwhile, the film's censorship problems were so
well publicized that New York critics and audiences began to
speculate on what had been cut. Reviewers in the Daily
News, World Telegram, and Herald Tribune reported to
their readers that cuts had been made but gave no details.
In an article in the Sunday News, in May, columnist Sidney
Skolsky wrote a detailed description of more than a half-
dozen scenes that had reportedly been cut from the New
York print. Skolsky discusses, among others, an auction
sequence, scenes between Camonte and his mother, scenes
with his grandparents, and he details various bits of dialogue that had been excised. Many of the dialogue cuts are
authenticated by other critics, but some of Skolsky's excised
sequences, according to Hawks, were never shot. 4

The Style of the Film

Ben Hecht's cynical, tough story, somewhat like his screenplay for Sternberg's Underworld (1927), deals with the rise
to the top of the underworld of a naïve, flamboyant, ambitious, ruthless, yet vulnerable gangster. Like many of
Hecht's other hard-boiled characters, his Tony Camonte
maintains the illusion of independence: after getting paid
off for killing his former boss, Camonte recites his motto
to his friend, Little Boy (George Raft). He advises, "Do
it first. Do it yourself. And keep on doing it." But
Hecht's character finally discovers that he is dependent upon
others and confesses his need for them, revealing a romanticism, sentimentality, and emotional vulnerability that soften
our initial conception of the character.

Camonte's strength lies in his sureness of self and in the professional directness with which he pursues what he wants, winning both control of the gang and his boss's girl. His weakness is less professional than personal, stemming from his quasi-incestuous relationship with his sister Cesca (Ann Dvorak). His jealousy prompts him to kill Little Boy, who has secretly married her. This irrational killing, differing from the earlier killings which were impersonal, professional, and expedient, enables the police to charge him with murder, resulting in a final shoot-out in which Camonte and his sister die.

For Hawks, Scarface is something of an unusual film. Though it reflects the concerns of his earlier and later films, especially in its treatment of the conflict created between contradictory personal and professional goals, it doesn't look much like his other work. Visually, it is almost Expressionistic, full of dark shadows, Murnauesque camera movements, and symbolism. The film's first image is of a street lamp going out, a symbolic preface to the murder which follows. At the same time, Hawks's camera is surprisingly detached from the action, reflecting a narrative presence exceedingly rare in his other work. For example, in the first shot the camera tracks from the image of the street light into a large meeting hall, past a janitor sweeping up after a party, to a group of men seated at a table. This group breaks up and the camera follows one of its members to a telephone booth where he places a call. It then pans to the right to pick up the shadow of a figure with a gun (Camonte) who has entered from the back of the hall. The camera watches as the shadowy figure murders the man in the phone booth, shows the janitor discovering the crime, and follows him as he starts to run away.

The camera, as if it were a third person viewing the scene, links one character to another, imposing its will upon the action and the characters involved in it. The choreography of different characters' movements and the killing itself seem determined by the camera. The obtrusiveness of Hawks's camera here establishes an atmosphere in which the obsessive behavior of his characters becomes unobtrusive. As a result, Little Boy's compulsive coin-flipping and Camonte's ritualistic whistling of an aria before he kills appear to be natural gestures rather than heavy-handed expressionist devices (compare Peter Lorre's whistling of a theme from Grieg's Peer Gynt in Fritz Lang's M).

Also, Hawks's characters establish their own symbols, as Camonte does with the neighboring "The World Is Yours" neon sign; its use is less intrusive because it becomes an integral part of the character's world; it is not extraneous to the place or the action.   When Hawks pans up in the film's last shot from the dead Camonte lying in the gutter to the "The World Is Yours" sign, his camera is making an ironic statement; yet Camonte's two earlier references to the sign have carefully prepared us for it.   As a result, the shot does not seem forced or contrived.

The only blatant expressionistic device in Scarface is the use of "x"es to denote murders.   Yet even this intrusive device is integrated as much as possible into the action.   Thus when Camonte kills the North Side's gang leader (Boris Karloff), Hawks films the scene in a bowling alley.   A close-up of the score card shows that Karloff's last ball was a strike (x).   As Karloff rolls his next ball, he is machine-gunned.   Hawks's camera follows the path of the ball down the lane and observes it knock down all the pins save one which spins for a while then falls.   This action, showing another strike, takes the place of entering a final "x" on Karloff's score card and, at the same time, symbolizes (in the falling pin) Karloff's off-screen death. This kind of symbolism, using objects naturally at hand to represent an action, is characteristically Hawksian.   For a director who rarely employs symbols (I can only think of a few other instances in which he's used them--e. g. , the last shot of I Was a Male War Bride viewing the Statue of Liberty through a porthole), Hawks uses them remarkably well, making them integral parts of his action.   His symbolism, unlike that of more abstract directors like Hitchcock and Lang, is rooted in the physical reality of objects or things.   His symbols, like the neon sign and bowling pin in Scarface, function primarily as the things themselves not as symbols.   It is only secondarily that they stand for other objects or things.

Scarface, like Hawks's other work of the period, reflects the director's interest in experimenting with verbal and visual styles.   Hawks's innovative use of dialogue in Dawn Patrol (1930) and The Criminal Code (1931) has its visual equivalent in Scarface with its expressionistic look and rapid pacing of action.   The uniqueness of Scarface in Hawks's oeuvre makes it all the more interesting in that it reveals a different facet of the director's attitude towards visual style, although he subsequently rejects the style he experimented with here.

The reason for Hawks's use of expressionistic techniques in the film is unclear. It may have been due to the influence of his cameraman Lee Garmes. It may have been a reaction to the realistic, documentary style of William Wellman's Public Enemy (released a month before Hawks began shooting Scarface) which treats gangsterism as a sociological phenomenon. Obviously more influenced by the elaborate Sternbergian stylistics of Underworld, Hawks views the milieu of the gangster as a dark, subterranean world of fantasy. The dreamlike impermanence of its inhabitants demands a stylized, expressionistic treatment. Whatever his reasons, Hawks achieves a striking look in Scarface that makes the film one of his most visually dramatic works.

NOTES

1. Subsequent to Hughes's death in 1976, Scarface has been rereleased by Universal 16. It was screened at the New York Film Festival in 1979.
2. The film's opening shot of a street light/street sign establishes the setting as 22nd Street, the scene of Colisimo's death.
3. Hollywood Cameramen, ed. Charles Higham (Bloomington: Indiana University Press, 1970), p. 43. Prints of the film currently available end with the gutter death scene originally shot by Garmes.
4. Letter from Hawks to the author dated June 5, 1974. Gerald Mast, in a letter dated July 24, 1981, explains that the excised scenes were in Hecht's original screenplay but were probably never shot.

c. Hawks, Warner Bros., and the War

Howard Hawks's association with Warner Bros. dates back
to Dawn Patrol (1930), his first sound film and culminates
with Rio Bravo (1959), an association spanning several dec-
ades and generating ten feature films. Hawks's lean, jour-
nalistically direct visual style mirrors that of the studio as
a whole. Warners directors, with the exception of expressive stylists like Michael Curtiz, shot simply, quickly, and
economically. "Wild Bill" Wellman, the quickest on the lot,
is said to have rarely shot more than one take of a scene
and is even reported to have shot and printed camera rehearsals. Even Curtiz, who took time to light his sets carefully, managed to direct at least four films a year for the
studio. Rooting its style in the aesthetics of the action
genres upon which it thrived, Warners let the nature of the
events to be filmed determine camera set-up, lighting styles,
and editing patterns. Hawks, undoubtedly a director who
helped Warners evolve this kind of visual style, developed
a "look" which perfectly suited that of the studio.

Hawks's approach to characterization in terms of professional identity neatly meshed with the studio's interest in
stories about the working class. But he studiously avoided
the didactic social consciousness that characterized the Warners product in the Thirties. Thus The Crowd Roars (1932)
and Tiger Shark (1932) may look like Wellman pictures of
the period such as Heroes for Sale (1933) or Wild Boys of
the Road (1933), but they lack the latter's polemical pointed-
ness. Hawks's films were wholeheartedly Warners movies
in style but not in terms of content.

In the Forties, Warners' social consciousness gives
way to patriotism: the subject matter of their films shifts
from the individual's economic or social estrangement from
society, as in I Am a Fugitive from a Chain Gang (1932), to
that individual's necessary commitment to the war effort, as
in Casablanca (1943). All of Hawks's war films for Warners
in the Forties deal with this issue of commitment, but each

does so in a different way. Sergeant York (1941), made before Pearl Harbor, wrestles with the moral issues of American involvement in a European war, isolationism, pacifism,
and an individual's membership in and responsibility to the
world around him. In many ways a conventional Warners
historical biography resembling films like Yankee Doodle
Dandy (1942) or Gentleman Jim (1942), York looks backward
to a more innocent era, treating complex issues with a simplicity that is altogether absent in Air Force (1943), made
at the height of the war. Where York (Gary Cooper) an-
guishes over his decision to fight, the men in Air Force respond spontaneously to the changing events around them without doubt or deliberation. Embarking on a routine training
mission on December 6, 1941, they literally fly into the
war and have no alternative but to fight their way through
the Pacific. To Have and Have Not (1944), surprisingly
critical of patriotism, presents a commitment to people not
to causes or ideas and functions as a critique of the typical
Warners war film.

All three Hawks films deal in tangible terms with
commitment to the war, eschewing the appeals to sentiment,
sacrifice, and idealism made by many of the studio's other
films (see Captains of the Clouds, Yankee Doodle Dandy,
Casablanca, Watch on the Rhine, Passage to Marseille and
Uncertain Glory). York, the least successful of Hawks's
war films, tries to deal with abstract ideas through concrete actions but succeeds only in undercutting the sincerity
of York's hillside conversion to the American cause by di-
vorcing it from any meaningful action that might convey the
depth of his patriotic commitment. York's answer just
comes to him as he sits on the hill. His commitment is
presented as the result of a rustic kind of contract (much
like that earlier contract whereby he hoped to acquire a
piece of bottom land). The motivation behind his commitment seems, for this reason, questionable. York decides
to "render unto Caesar the things that are Caesar's and unto
God the things that are God's." Although York's decision
appears patriotic, it is, as its context in the film and the
above language imply, a kind of debt that he is forced to
pay. His act of heroism is presented as nothing more than
an attempt to save the lives of the men in his platoon. It
is largely a response to the physical situation in which he
is placed by the war and is not motivated by patriotic ideals.

York's pacifism and martial heroism appear to be
contradictory qualities that are left unresolved, confusing

moral issues in the film.   York apparently betrays his religious ideals when he chooses to stay in the army and later
kills the enemy.   Hawks, less concerned with morality than
with character, explains the real Alvin York's behavior--a
"given" for the purposes of this biographical tribute--in
terms that are consistent with Hawks's treatment of character in his other, non-biographical, fiction films.   York responds to his setting--whether it be rural America or war-
torn France, he acknowledges his commitment to others.
At first detached from the backwoods community around him
(i. e. , we see a drunken York shooting up Pastor Pile's
church), York eventually integrates himself into that community.   The film's crucial scenes depict this awareness
of a need for and responsibility to others: York, stunned
by lightning outside the church, staggers into Pastor Pile's
(Walter Brennan) revivalist meeting, and is accepted into
this religious community.   The singing of the congregation
and Hawks's rhythmic cutting from York to the congregation
merge York's individuality with that of the larger group.
The action physically celebrates York's conversion from
violence to pacifism and marks his recognition of his need
for others.   Much as Pastor Pile, in another scene, observes how the tree around which York is plowing derives
its strength from the earth and has roots in something outside of itself, so York realizes that he cannot isolate himself from the world around him.

The battle sequence in France marks, for York, a
similar realization and acceptance of his responsibility to
the men around him.   Seeing his comrades cut down by enemy fire, York uses his skill as a marksman--a skill Hawks
has carefully established in the turkey shoot--to save them.
A Hawksian man, York adapts himself to his wartime environment, changing as it changes yet retaining his personal
integrity in the process.   Hawks's characters live in the
present, not in the past, and react spontaneously to its demands.   Their acceptance of and reaction to the world
around them is what makes them so alive.   The real Sgt.
York was undoubtedly a jumble of contradictions.   Hawks
fashions out of these contradictions an underlying integrity--
he sees in them the man's commitment to the demands of
the world around him.

Air Force, unlike York, has no central character
whose conversion becomes the focus of the film.   John Gar-
field's cynical loner, Winocki, is just one of many charac-
ters--e. g. , James Brown's pursuit pilot Lt. Rader; Ed

Brophy's idiosyncratic marine sergeant--who pool their efforts to keep a B-17 aloft and in action.   Hawks introduces
each of his characters separately and isolates them within
separate spaces of the plane.   But through their relation to
the plane, the characters lose their separateness and become
a unit, even crossing over the barriers which separate one
branch of the armed forces from another.   Each character
performs a necessary job: the crew's dependence on the
navigator in the first half of the film to get them from the
States to Pearl Harbor to Wake and to Manila serves as a
preliminary example of the total interdependence that is
achieved later in the film when the crew rebuilds the damaged plane and, with the aid of the marines, gets it into
the air moments before the Japanese capture the airstrip.
The climax of the film--the battle sequence that occupies
most of the last reel--can be seen in the coordinated cooperation between the pilot and the mid-section and tail gunners as the former--almost rhythmically--maneuvers the
plane to enable his gunners to get the enemy planes within
the sightlines of their machine guns.

    Hawks views the crew's commitment to the war ef-
fort in terms of their loyalty to one another and to their
airplane, in terms of tangibles.   Even though the film was
made at the suggestion and with the cooperation of the Air
Force, it contains little flag waving.   The crew's patriotism
surfaces less in speeches than in action.   Like To Have and
Have Not, the film begins with the frustration of action and
builds tensely towards a decisive outburst of retaliatory violence.   The plane flies across the Pacific unarmed and,
though eager to strike back at the Japanese for their attack
on Pearl Harbor, is forced to avoid combat.   The final air-
sea battle signals a release of formerly suppressed feeling
(i. e. , the deaths of Capt. Quincannon and Sgt. White's son).
Like Harry Morgan at the end of To Have, the crew finally
gets a chance to strike back and the result is certainly the
most satisfying combat sequence ever filmed.

    The motivation and commitment of the men in Air
Force is tested but never questioned by Hawks.   The film
observes the men as they grow into a fighting unit but avoids
sentimentalizing their actions or drenching them in patriotic
spirit.   Yet the film's dedication to the war effort--its
propagandistic drive--is total.

    To Have and Have Not (1944) deals more cynically
with the war and with characters' commitment to it.   As

reviewers at the time pointed out, To Have bears a certain
resemblance to Casablanca (1943) in its anti-isolationist
message. Both films star Humphrey Bogart (not to mention
Marcel Dalio and Dan Seymour), are set in bars in exotic
corners of the world, deal with the corruption of the Vichy
government, feature piano players as secondary characters
and conclude with the conversion of an initially self-serving,
individualistic Humphrey Bogart to the Free French cause.
But To Have and Have Not is, in many ways, a reaction
against the sentimentality of Casablanca, much as Rio Bravo
is a reaction against High Noon. Hawks portrays the Free
French as ineffectual and amateurish idealists who fail in
their missions. And he views his hero's conversion less as
a commitment to a cause than to a select group of people.
When Frenchy (Dalio) asks Morgan why he has joined the
Free French cause, Morgan answers, "Maybe because I like
you and maybe because I don't like them (the Gestapo)." In
Casablanca, Rick, after seeking and winning back Ilsa (Ingrid Bergman), romantically sacrifices his love for her, as
she earlier did hers for him. In the Hawks film, Morgan
initially rejects--or at least parries--Slim's (Lauren Bacall)
advances but eventually accepts her. The Hawks film ends
with a sense of gain rather than of loss.

    To Have and Have Not is very loosely based on Er-
nest Hemingway's novel. "Hemingway had a wonderfully
strong character in the rum runner out to battle the world
alone. That's what I bought, the character and, of course,
the title," says Hawks. But while Hemingway's hero dies
cursing that "a man alone ain't got no bloody, fuckin'
chance," bewailing his isolation, Hawks's hero survives, in
part, through a recognition of his need for others. Morgan's (Bogart) toughness and self-sufficiency, mirrored in
Slim (Bacall) who also takes on the world alone, become the
subject of the film. His insolence is matched by hers.
Bacall is a female Bogart and Hawks uses each as a foil
for the other. Both are independent, rejecting offers of
help from others. Slim refuses to let "Steve" (her pet name
for Morgan) help her to get passage money back to the
States and he will not take money from her. Morgan's independence, however, is only superficial. In a gloriously
visual realization of his independence, Morgan asks Slim to
walk around him. She slowly understands the significance
of his request as she circles him and acknowledges that
"there are no strings tied to you, Steve." Moments later,
Morgan discovers that his friend Eddie (Walter Brennan) is
being questioned by the Gestapo and, as Morgan dashes out

to help him, Slim playfully cautions him to "look out for
those strings ... You're liable to trip and break your neck."
Morgan, in spite of his protestations to the contrary, is
tied to the characters around him. As their dependence on
his strength and skill grows, so does his sense of responsibility to them. Morgan's circle of dependents gradually
increases to include not only Eddie, Slim, and Frenchy but
also the de Bursacs, the agents sent by the Free French on
a mission to Martinique, an expansion of dependents which
echoes his growing awareness of the world--and of the war
--around him. Though he remains hard-boiled, Morgan's
cynicism softens a bit and his independence changes to interdependence. The climax of the film's conflict between Vichy
and Free French occurs when Morgan teams up with Slim,
grabs a gun in his desk drawer and commits himself, through
decisive action, to the rescue of his friends.

Just as Hawks breaks down Morgan's self-imposed
isolation from the world around him, so he integrates Slim
into the group. Her first appearance, slinkily and sulkily
leaning against Morgan's door frame, identifies her as an
icy, cold, self-sufficient loner. Her tone and her gestures
bristle with insolence. Hawks views her growing awareness
of her need for others as a sexual phenomenon. At first,
Slim cynically uses her sexiness to get things--whether it
be a match from Morgan, a wallet from Johnson, or a bottle
of wine from a French officer. Morgan refuses to let her
"use" him and he exposes a vulnerability beneath her hard-
boiled exterior. His antagonistic manner serves as a catalyst for her transformation: their initial sparring mellows
into a mutual respect. Slim's earlier sexual hypocrisy disappears. She becomes sexually honest--her body no longer
lies but tells the truth, echoing her emotions. Slim's song
and hip-wiggle at the end of the film reflect her feelings;
she is happy and communicates that happiness through her
movements.

Hawks links Slim's sense of who she is to her new
awareness of her body; he draws a parallel between her discovery and Morgan's realization of his own responsibilities
and needs. Morgan and Slim come alive through each other.
Being alive, for Hawks, involves moral responsibility: characters exist only in terms of the people and events around
them. They are defined by their relationships with others,
retaining their vitality only through an exchange of energies
with the world around them. Morgan and Slim discover
strength not in independence but in inter-dependence and,

unlike the egotistic characters who nobly but secretly sacrifice themselves for each other in Casablanca, Morgan and
Slim share their discoveries with one another.

Sergeant York, Air Force and To Have and Have Not
all deal with the commitment of characters to the world
around them--a theme that belongs both to Warner Bros.
and to Howard Hawks.   But Hawks, unlike Curtiz in Casablanca, treats that commitment in a physical way.   His
films contain no idealistic sacrifices or emotionally-charged
patriotic gestures, such as Casablanca's inspired singing of
the Marseillaise.   Hawks's characters commit themselves to
one another, not to causes.   They respond to real events,
not to abstract issues.   Though he remains faithful to the
Warners themes of the Forties, through his treatment of
those themes he constructs a subtle critique of them.
Hawks's war films for Warners show that he is both a part
of and apart from the studio, using it to further elaborate
on concerns developed in his other, non-Warners films.

d. Ball of Fire and A Song Is Born

Hawks has been labeled an anti-intellectual, largely on the basis of a handful of comedies which depict scientists as absent-minded idiots (Bringing Up Baby, Monkey Business) and scholars as an assortment of naïve, squirrelly cherubs and doddering old fools (Ball of Fire, A Song Is Born) and on the strength of his sole venture into science fiction, The Thing, which, like all other films of the genre, conveys a distrust of reason and a criticism of dispassionate scientists.

Actually Hawks, along with Buster Keaton, is the cinema's greatest logician, revealing in his scripts a relentless chain of causes and effects and celebrating the inventively pragmatic intelligences of his heroes and heroines. Characteristically, Hawks's biblical epic, Land of the Pharoahs, focuses on the architects who designed and built the pyramids as much as on the pharoahs for whom they were built.

The intelligence of Hawks's encyclopedia researchers in Ball of Fire and A Song Is Born is knowledge in a void, serving no real function until it begins to intersect with the outside world. In Ball of Fire, the outside world first intrudes on the professors' ivory tower in the form of two garbage men (window washers in Song) seeking answers to a radio quiz; then Professor Potts (Gary Cooper), suddenly realizing that the material for his entry on "slang" is outdated, embarks on a field trip to gather new data. Finally, the professors use Archimedes, Tate's Oriental Philosophy and Greek myth (the sword of Damocles) to turn the tables on the gangsters who threaten them and use ancient Chinese torture techniques and a knowledge of local geography to locate Pott's abducted sweetheart, Sugarpuss O'Shea (Barbara Stanwyck).

Gregg Toland's deep focus photography of the interior of the Totten Foundation where Hawks's eight professors live and work creates an enclosed, fairy tale atmosphere,

259

isolated in its own space from real experience; and Billy
Wilder's witty script amplifies this idea by making parallels
in plotting and characterization with Walt Disney's Snow
White and the Seven Dwarfs.   Stanwyck, introduced in a sexy
night club number with drummer Gene Krupa, functions as
an erotic, worldly Snow White who liberates a group of intellectual giants/emotional dwarfs, bringing sex and sunlight
into the monastic lives of Hawks's professors.

        Cooper, in a comic variation on his Academy Award
winning role in Sergeant York to which Hawks refers when
a gangster wets his gun sight, breaks out of a self-imposed
isolation and discovers something that's "a heap bigger than
I be": the world around him outside of the Totten Foundation.

        Hawks remade Ball of Fire several years later with
A Song Is Born, filmed in Technicolor with Danny Kaye and
Virginia Mayo on the same set, with the same script and
cameraman, occasionally even repeating sequences from the
earlier film shot for shot.

        The changes Hawks makes in the script are all for
the better.   His scholars become historians working on an
encyclopedia of music.   Benny Goodman plays a professor
and the film features guest cameos for Tommy Dorsey,
Louis Armstrong, Lionel Hampton, Charlie Barnett, Mel
Powell and Buck and Bubbles, all of whom collaborate on
a performance of the title number which is a history of jazz
from African drum beats to American down beats.   Like
"knowledge" in the earlier film, "music" is instrumental in
defeating the gangsters who hold Professor Frisbee (Kaye)
and his colleagues prisoners, dislodging a drum on a shelf
which knocks a gunman unconscious.   The film's best sequence consists of Frisbee's rendition, for his staid patron-
ess Miss Totten (Mary Field), of a Polynesian mating song.
Encouraged to join in the song, Miss Totten responds to
Frisbee's chants with sensual grunts, momentarily escaping
her civilized repression and giving vent to primitive sexual
urges.   Both films deal with the liberating discovery of
sexuality and, though intelligence plays a positive role in
each film, Hawks clearly celebrates the physicality of his
characters.   Hawks's films, rooted in his characters' basic
material needs, turn away from abstract issues such as pure
knowledge and explore the very tangible world of physical
experience.

e. The Narrative Structure of I Was a Male War Bride

I Was a Male War Bride (1949), though one of Howard
Hawks's funniest films, is also one of his bleakest, blackest, and most serious works. This deeply unsettling paradox underlies almost every scene--even, for instance, the
film's tenderest, gentlest, and perhaps most intimate sequence in which Henri Rochard (Cary Grant) rubs liniment
on the sore back of Lt. Catherine Gates (Ann Sheridan).
Rochard's consideration and concern for her throughout this
scene reflects itself in the warmth and deliberation of his
gestures, e. g. , as he screws the bottle cap back on, and
in the sympathetic kindness of his actions (he opens the
window, puts out the overhead light and adjusts the bedside
lampshade so that it will not glare in her eyes). The sound
of the rain outside throughout the scene reinforces our sense
of the intimacy that exists between the two central characters. But the whole effect of the scene's intimacy depends
upon the rather cold premise that Gates only allows Rochard
to touch her when he is ministering to her. Our further
realization is that this intimacy is possible only because she
is asleep, and the conclusion of the scene, when the innkeeper's wife pushes Rochard out of Gates's window, completely obliterates the sense of harmony, privacy, and mutual understanding with which the scene began. (Aspects of
this scene are very similar to those in a later scene when
Rochard, alone on a driverless motorcycle, tells Gates that
he likes her. Hawks works the scene for comedy, but we
also realize that her presence would probably destroy the
intimacy of what Rochard says.) It is this overall seriousness in Male War Bride that brings it closer in mood and
theme to a film like Red River than one like Gentlemen
Prefer Blondes or Man's Favorite Sport? and which justifies
my more or less serious approach to the film and to its ideas.

Film as Journey

Like the cattle drive in Red River (1948), the journey from

Heidelberg to the Statue of Liberty in Male War Bride becomes a sort of trial or test of the film's central characters.   The greater part of Male War Bride consists of tra-
velogue, journeys from one place to another: Rochard's
taxi ride in the credit sequence, the motorcycle trip to
Baden-Auheim, the voyage to the United States.   Hawks
fills his frames with characters in transit, like the people
in the foreground and background of the credit sequence
walking or riding bicycles, like the war brides and their
children on their way to the U. S. A. in the background of
the second half of the film, and with various modes of
transportation--cars, motorcycles, trains, rowboats, planes,
buses, horses, and ships.   Yet, at the same time, the film
contains a confused sense of destination: its characters,
quite unlike those in Red River, never seem to know, either
literally or figuratively, where they are going; they have no
clearly-defined, ultimate destination.

        In the credit sequence, for example, Rochard asks
directions for Heidelberg; later, Lt. Gates gets them lost,
in spite of her maps, on their way to Baden-Auheim.   Both
scenes introduce a theme which culminates in Rochard's
wandering search for a bed and a night's rest in Bremer-
haven.   As Rochard goes from one place to another, each
character he meets (the unfriendly, pipe-smoking sergeant
with a bed--and a wife in it, the private from Brooklyn, the
MP from Yonkers, the knitting desk clerk in the "female"
building--all men without women and women without men,
like all the film's characters except for the innkeeper and
his wife who never appear together) presents a different attitude towards him and towards his predicament.   All these
brilliant minor figures, because of the great variety of their
characterizations, turn Rochard's sleepless night into an
odyssey of moods and attitudes towards male-female rela-
tionships--each character becoming a further test of his en-
durance and flexibility.

        Hawks, clearly, treats the Gates-Rochard relationship
as a journey, but what's most interesting about this treatment of it is its to-and-fro motion, its seeming lack of
destination.   Their first scene together in the corridors of
Army HQ captures this perfectly: the tracking camera follows them, first down one corridor, then another.   They
seem to be moving in a maze, and their occasional exchange
of positions in the frame heightens this sense of geographic
confusion.   (This scene recalls Rochard's similar to-and-fro
movements moments earlier when he goes from door to door

in the corridor, reading bureaucratic abbreviations and trying to guess what they stand for, while in search of Gates's office.) Later, the montage sequence depicting the to-and-fro bureaucratic shuffling of their application requesting permission to get married becomes a visual equivalent to this earlier, corridor/maze scene; the application now takes their place. It goes from office to office, back and forth across hallways, gets roughly stamped (as do they in a figurative sense) on its journey through bureaucracy, and finally gets lost somewhere in someone's desk. On the surface, Hawks's red-tape montage sequence appears quite conventional, something that can be seen in dozens of dull, uninspired films. What makes the Hawks sequence different --and better--is that he varies the convention: he interrupts the flow of the montage for a pair of scenes that reveal how the application got "lost." By breaking up the continuity of the montage sequence, Hawks neatly foreshadows the difficulty the couple has with army red tape which separates them in the last half of the film. While satirizing the convention of the Hollywood montage sequence, he also uses it to satisfy his thematic needs.

The action of this sequence is, of course, comic and the mood optimistic. The final stamp of approval sanctions their wedding and looks ahead to the direction, i. e., the happy ending, the film finally takes. The trip from Heidelberg to the Statue of Liberty, then, reflects the progression of their relationship both geographically and emotionally but Hawks, strangely enough, shows this progression towards the relationship's realization in terms of the restrictions placed upon the couple.

Entrapment

The movement of Rochard's car at the beginning of the film, shown by means of pans, tracks, and fluid dissolves, gives him a sense of freedom in terms of his ability to move through space; his ability to get directions to Heidelberg demonstrates his power over and control of his movements. As the film continues, however, Rochard loses more and more of his ability to move, his freedom, his power. Hawks conveys the progressive confinement which parallels Rochard's increasing commitment to Gates in several ways. 1) Framing. In the credit sequence, when his car stops for directions, Rochard is shown in the center-background of the frame, sandwiched between his driver and a traffic cop in

the foreground.   The framing gives a sense of his powerlessness and corresponds to the narrative content of the scene:
his driver has lost his way.   But when Rochard gets sought-
after directions from an American soldier, Hawks cuts to a
different, less constrictive two-shot set up and frees Rochard from his boxed-in position in the frame.   At critical
moments throughout the film, Hawks suggests Rochard's entrapment and powerlessness by framing him in three-shot
between two other characters, one of whom is quite often
Lt. Gates.   We see this framing in Prendergast's office
when Rochard gets his new assignment to work again with
Gates, in Rumsey's office, at the motor pool, and at the
hotel when Billings interrupts him and Gates on their wedding night.   In almost all of these scenes, Gates stands on
one side and the army, or its representatives, stand on the
other.   2) Sets.   The dark, narrow hallways within Army
HQ, the claustrophobic sidecar of the motorcycle, the jail
in Baden-Auheim, the small cabin on the ship to America
at the end, all reflect the way in which spaces gradually
imprison Rochard during the course of the film.   3) Gags.
Even the baldest comedy routines--when the train's signal
gate lifts Rochard high into the air, the business with the
door handle in the inn, Rochard's discomfort in Gates's
wooden chair and bathtub, his arrest at the black market in
Baden-Auheim--become funny, in part, because of Rochard's
isolation and, in part, because of his awkward confinement.
Behind the comic gags, with all the restrictions they place
upon Rochard's movement, lies a more serious notion: the
view of Rochard's relationship with Gates as a form of entrapment.

        In this light, the motorcycle-and-sidecar which the
couple requisition becomes a perfect visual metaphor for
their initial relationship: it binds them together physically,
but places Rochard in a position of inferiority in the sidecar.   At the same time, the first gag using this prop, in
which the sidecar gets left behind by the motorcycle, is
more than a gag: it visualizes their initial love-hate antagonism and symbolizes their apparent inability to work
together as a couple.

        Although Robin Wood's article on Male War Bride in
his book on Hawks suggests that many of the film's episodes are
"loosely strung together," I find that they are, on the contrary, tightly interwoven not only narratively but thematically.   The door gag, for example, in which Rochard locks
himself into Gates's hotel room in Baden-Auheim, comments

rather directly on the confining nature of their relationship.
Even within this scene, the chair gag--a beautifully funny
bit of business in itself--further strengthens the sense of
confinement, but does so with unusual subtlety. Although
the chair itself does not imprison Rochard, as the bathtub
does later on in the film, his use of it as a bed sets up an
awkwardly comic disparity between the shape of the contain-
er and that of the thing contained--a device Hawks uses later
with almost as much success when Rochard puts on the short
innkeeper's too-small clothes or when he dresses up as
"Florence" in a nurse's uniform. What's interesting about
the scene is that Rochard restricts himself spatially in his
attempt to fit himself into the chair. Rochard's fantastic
flexibility within a constricting environment is, in a sense,
his greatest characteristic. It is this flexibility which prevents his loss of identity and masculinity in the second half
of the film. The trouble he has with his hands in this sequence betrays his actual helplessness and, in a larger
sense, reflects the temporary awkwardness in his relationship with Gates. Yet his ultimate flexibility (he finally falls
asleep, albeit gracelessly, in the chair) underscores the optimism with which we must finally regard their relationship.
There is a freedom in confinement: what Rochard does
within the limited space he is given defines the unique form
of freedom that his love relationship with Gates grants him.

Structurally, I Was a Male War Bride falls into two
parts. In the first half of the film, Hawks traps Rochard
and Gates together, starting with the motorcycle sequences
and culminating in the inn sequence; in the second half, he
reverses this process and traps them apart from one another: a two shot sequence shows us Gates sleeping with Kitty,
then Rochard sleeping in the bathtub. At the same time, it
becomes clear that the restrictions on their relationship in
the first half are self-imposed (as seen in the chair gag);
they come from within, from her prudishness, from his reluctance to commit himself to her. In the second half, as
the bathtub sequence illustrates, the restrictions are imposed
by society--in this case the Army; they are separated by
external factors.

Paradoxically, their entrapment together in the first
part, at least until the mission is completed, seems to bring
out their antagonism--an antagonism based upon their unwillingness to admit that they really want each other. Yet
the film's second half, which separates them, also unites
them together against society, red tape, and the Army. The

final image of them in their small cabin on the boat locking
the world out and, simultaneously, locking themselves in
defines the paradoxical nature of their relationship beautifully.   In order to achieve this freedom in confinement, their
love must first be tested.   Only then will they be permitted
to consummate it.   Their "confessions" that they love one
another in the first half's haystack sequence are not enough;
their love demands a test and the second half of the film
provides that test.

Sexual Reversals

The first half of the film concludes with the haystack scene.
In a sense, this scene is parallel to the film's last scene
in the ship's cabin.   In both, Rochard and Gates are enclosed together and, ironically, their love seems free and
without restrictions.   Although one assumes from the jokes
later in the film that they do not have intercourse in the
haystack, the scene itself, like the last scene, is shot as
if there could have been a sexual consummation.   What's
important about the haystack sequence is that it is a culmination of the first stage of their relationship and, at the
same time, the final test of Gates's womanhood.   For if
the last half of Male War Bride is a testing of Rochard's
masculinity, culminating in his final disguise as "Florence,"
then the first half of the film tests the femininity of Lt.
Gates.   Her masculine traits, her domination of Rochard
throughout the first half of the film, although more or less
objectively motivated by the action and situations of the narrative, nevertheless rob her of her femininity.   For example, the action of the film dictates that she must wear pants
to drive the motorcycle and that her uniform be somewhat
masculine, but when she puts on her helmet over her al-
ready-short hair, she loses the last visual indication of her
femininity.   In the very first scene, when Rochard returns
her laundry, itemizing--in public--her various undergar-
ments, Gates seems outraged not only by his gesture's suggestion of sexual intimacy but also, apparently, by the arti-
cles which represent her own feminine nature.   Her attempts
at being a woman are weak and awkward.   When she stops
at a railroad crossing to let a train pass and tries to put
on some makeup, she drops her lipstick; Rochard, in his
attempt to retrieve it for her, ends up the victim of another
harrowing, emasculating experience.   Although she wants
Rochard and, seemingly, puts on makeup to attract him
(whatever her purpose, the action remains one of her few

feminine gestures), she bungles it. Even when she gets out
of her uniform, she puts on masculine pajamas--a stark
contrast to the frilly, feminine nightgown she wears on her
wedding night.

If Lt. Gates is a failure at being a woman in the
first half of the film, she's also not quite a success at being a man. Even though she does complete the mission,
she botches up parts of it, nearly sending their small row-
boat over a waterfall in the process. After the mission is
completed, however, she does become a little more woman-
ly. In a romantically-lit, high-key outdoor scene, Hawks
shows her, without helmet, chewing on a blade of grass and
looking dreamily off into the countryside--at the same time
she considerately allows Rochard to sleep. The following
scene in the haystack, then, with its dialogue about Frenchmen and kissing, tests both her femininity (Rochard com-
plains, "If I only had a French girl here") and his masculinity (she evaluates the kiss with, "That was no good. Is
that all there is to it?"). The subsequent kiss which closes
the sequence reestablishes, for the moment, her femininity
and his masculinity, just as the last scene of the film on
the boat, after another series of tests, reaffirms their basic
sexuality and consummates their relationship.

The testing of Rochard's masculinity in the second
half of the film concludes with him in a nurse's uniform--an
ironic travesty of Gates's militantly masculine femininity.
The final few shots show Rochard locked in a ship's cabin.
He rolls down his pants leg, throws away his phony wig,
confronts and triumphs over the ship's captain and chaplain
who want to "forget the whole thing" and bunk him in with
some of the ship's officers. These actions restore Rochard's masculinity and his power; although entrapped, he
maintains control over his trap.

At the end of his fine essay on Male War Bride,
Wood, discussing the confinement theme, writes that, "the
irony of the concluding shot of the Statue of Liberty (as
seen from Henri's cabin-cell) is the film's final masterstroke
and perhaps the nearest thing in Hawks to overt comment on
modern society."[1] The final shot, to which Wood rightly
draws attention, pulls all the thematic threads of the film
together into a single image. It is, above all else, an extremely blatant image of sexual union--it depicts a phallic
object, the statue, as seen through a round porthole. At
the same time, the internal frame of the porthole is,

as Wood suggests, confining; but the object confined is
the Statue of Liberty.   It is, as Wood says, "ironic," yet
it conveys the thematic notion of freedom in confinement
more succinctly than any other image in the film.   Finally,
this last shot comments directly on the relationship-as-
journey motif.   A geographical landmark, the statue stands
at the terminus of their journey and symbolizes the realization of their relationship.   The last shot of the film conveys
the consummation of this relationship and, at the same time,
its paradoxical nature: i. e. , Rochard and Gates realize a
uniquely Hawksian freedom in their commitment to one
another.

NOTE

1.   Robin Wood, Howard Hawks (New York: Doubleday,
      1968), p. 88.

f. The Organic Narrative Style of Monkey Business

Robin Wood calls Monkey Business (1952) Howard Hawks's greatest comedy. "Here the disturbing elements that characterize the comedies are assimilated into an entirely coherent, perfectly proportioned whole."[1] According to Wood, Monkey Business is Hawks's greatest comedy because it is "the most organic." What makes the film so is that "once the principle has been grasped, every detail of the film falls into place."[2] One might object that all classical narratives are, in some way, "organic," i. e., they develop linearly and logically. Even non-classical, self-reflexively formalist narratives, such as Eisenstein's Potemkin (1925) are constructed organically.[3]

Like Eisenstein, Hawks is also an engineer (though less visibly so), building his narratives brick by brick, much like the architect-builders in his own The Land of the Pharoahs (1955). Hawks's narratives are organic in that they consist of a series of actions which grow logically out of one another and whose sequence cannot be altered. His narratives set in motion a chain of events which sweep his characters along in their flow. Events in a Hawks film observe a logic of their own and characters, if they wish to survive or control the environment of events, must give themselves over to them. Hawks begins Rio Lobo (1970) with an event: a Union gold shipment is hijacked by a band of Confederates who cleverly tap telegraph wires, grease rails on a steep grade, chase Union guards away with a hornets' nest and "catch" the runaway traincar containing the gold with a succession of ropes. He presents this event in great detail--each detail presented as a step or stage of a larger process. He shows actions and their consequences. John Wayne's Union officer chases the Rebels to the cave stronghold, is captured and, in turn, captures his captors. The story would seem to be over: we have seen an action's beginning, middle, and end. But the film's opening action was itself set in motion by an earlier event: someone in Wayne's outfit sold information about the gold shipment to

269

the enemy. The remainder of the film deals with Wayne's attempts to catch this traitor, to trace the gold heist back to its origin, to its "prime mover." What is organic about the narrative is that Hawks follows the major characters involved in the film's initial event through all the consequences of that event. It is actions and their consequences that structure the narratives of Hawks's films.

The narrative of Monkey Business is similarly organic, evolving like a tree which grows out of an acorn. When the scientists confuse one monkey, Esther, with another, Rudolph, in an early scene, Hawks sets us up for a subsequent scene in which a baby is mistaken for the hero, Barnaby Fulton (Cary Grant). Similarly, the intercutting, in intense close-up, between Barnaby experimenting with chemicals and Esther watching him and mimicking his facial gestures leads us quite naturally into the monkey's inspired imitation of the scientist's actions in the next scene. The line of Hawks's ruthlessly organic narrative pushes almost every gesture, every action in the film to its logical extension and, then, beyond logic to the borders of a comic insanity.

Wood's use of the word "organic" is particularly appropriate. Not only do the scenes grow out of one another and the characters develop naturally from one scene to another, but the shooting style of the film also seems to suggest some sort of progression. For example, Hawks's use of crosscutting in the latter part of the film between the baby and Barnaby not only prepares us visually for Edwina's (Ginger Rogers) confusion of the two, but also builds the action toward their eventual encounter at the end of the film. Edwina no longer treats Barnaby as the infant she thinks he is in the first scene (e.g., when she undresses him or, in a later scene, when she puts her coat on him as they leave the Pickwick Arms), but recognizes and accepts him as an adult.

Furthermore, Hawks's use of diagonals in his compositions reflects a progression from the first scene to the last. In Monkey Business, Hawks composes almost all his interiors with sharp angles in the background, i.e., two planes (walls) usually intersect at some point (corner) in the background. In Rio Bravo, Hawks characters drift into corners and the corners seem to entrap them. [4] In Monkey Business, although characters do not drift into corners, the intersecting diagonals in the background do set limits to the characters' actions (Grant's greatest insanity, for instance, occurs outdoors). More importantly, however, the sharp angles in the background add a great deal of tension to Hawks's compositions, and by extension, to the subjects (characters, relationships) within his frames. His treatment of diagonals in his compositions reflects a progression. When Hawks begins an interior scene, such as the first lab scene, his first few shots contain strong diagonal lines: the backward tracking shot of Barnaby's entry into the lab reveals a diagonal line (the lab bench) in the foreground and several others (benches at angles to it) in the near background. The subsequent cutting to closer shots tends to exclude one or more diagonal lines and, as a result, reduce the level of tension in the compositions. Not only do individual scenes develop this way, but the film as a whole moves towards a resolution of compositional tensions. Consequently, the last shot of Monkey Business, although preceded by highly angular, spatially disorienting one-shots, contains far less tension than the first. Whereas the doorway scene has several planes of action and intersecting diagonals which suggest conflict, the last scene in the Fultons' bedroom eliminates compositional tensions in the background. In fact, Hawks seems to almost collapse the background into the foreground, to flatten his frame into one single plane.

Moreover, the textures of Hawks's frames, if one compares the first and last scenes, like the tensions between foreground and background, progress towards a single level. In the first scene, for example, the lighting sets off different textural levels (sharp black vs. sharp white) in the frame. But, in the last scene, the soft lighting which surrounds the couple seems to blend the various parts of the frame into a single texture that unifies the elements of the composition into a whole and serves to enhance their final reconciliation.

The first scene of Monkey Business contains the thematic seeds out of which the subsequent scenes grow. During the title sequence, Cary Grant opens a door and comes out of his house. A voice off-screen says, "Not yet, Cary," and Grant, remaining in character (Barnaby Fulton), re-enters the house. Repeatedly, throughout the first scene, Barnaby opens and closes the door, walks in and out of the doorway, goes first one way and then another, absentmindedly turns lights off and on. When his wife Edwina (Ginger Rogers) comes to the door, she, like the voice in the titles, attempts to impose some sort of order upon Barnaby's actions. She gives him a set of instructions to follow (first turn on the porch light, then turn off the hall light, and then lock the door). Barnaby confuses her directions and ends up locking himself in. He does what she says, but not in the proper order. The blocking-out of the action (Grant's directionless movements in the doorway) and the lighting (his random switching on and off of lights in different parts of the house) visually represent his inward (mental) and outward (physical) confusion and suggest a sort of insanity (the first one of many levels of irrational behavior that occur in the film). This first scene presents a chaotic absence of order and clearly foreshadows the topsy-turvy reversals of natural order that inform the action of the rest of the film. Barnaby's confused actions reflect a dissonance with his environment and the disparity of the couple's actions reveals a comic discordance in their relationship. To underscore that lack of harmony, Hawks frames them in one-shots and closes doors between them. In the next scene, although he frames them together, Hawks actually increases the physical distance between the couple (one at either end of the frame or at different levels of it) as Edwina follows Barnaby around, turning on lights one by one. The tensions increase in the scene with Hank (her backless dress, the hot soup, three-shot, two-shot, and one-shot framing to alienate Hank) and remain unresolved when Hawks closes the scene by tracking in on a ringing telephone (their refusal to answer it is actually an attempt to go back to an event in the past--the night they didn't go to the Winstons' party--rather than confront the present).

But more important in this first scene is what Hawks does with time. Barnaby's actions are chaotic primarily because they lack temporal sense--they have no logical order in time. The off-screen voice warns him, "Not yet, Cary"; Edwina tells him to do first one thing and then another. Barnaby complies with her directions, but not in the proper sequence. His insanity distorts the normal sequence of events in time. One of the central themes of Monkey Business concerns the recognition and acceptance of this sequence, the discovery that one thing naturally grows out of another--in short, the coming to terms with one's environment, with time, old age, and mortality.

On a simple plot level, Barnaby's experiments with B-4 are an attempt to reverse the natural aging process, to reverse the normal sequence of youth, then old age. The

insanity which ensues reflects the chaos which Barnaby's experiments create.   Nearly all the characters in Monkey
Business participate in this insanity.   Even those who do
not take Esther's formula, like Hank, Edwina's mother, Miss
Laurel, and, until the last scene, Mr. Oxly, represent one
or another stage of aborted natural development: Hank still
loves Edwina, his childhood sweetheart, and tries to reject
the fact of her marriage to Barnaby; Edwina's mother still
prefers Hank to Barnaby as a husband for her daughter, and
she still treats Edwina like a little girl; Miss Laurel, as
Barnaby himself remarks, is still "half-infant" and perhaps
the most disturbing case of arrested development; Mr. Oxly
wants to regain his youth and sexual potency and, consequently, is the most vocal and most romantic ("the phoenix
rising out of the ashes of age") supporter of B-4.   The only
characters in the film who do not participate in this insanity
are, strangely enough, Esther, the children, and the baby.
They seem to have both a self-awareness which the other
characters lack and a knowledge of the proper sequence of
events.   When Esther breaks out of her cage and begins
mixing the formula, there is a great naturalness in her actions.   Although she in no way knows the significance of
what she is doing (as, for example, Barnaby does when he's
experimenting), she does have a great awareness of how to
do it.   It is her sense of sequence that constitutes her sanity and the other characters' lack of that sense that com-
prises their insanity.   One step seems to follow another
smoothly and naturally (like her smooth swing on the cage
door to Barnaby's stool).   Unlike Barnaby who, moments
before, seemed uncertain about what came next, Esther first
mixes one chemical and then another.   And when she has
finished, she tests it by tasting it (an act that makes a
great deal of sense to me) and then goes right to the water
cooler.   Finally, in the last lab scene, when Rudolph and
all the scientists are running around acting like monkeys,
Esther sits on her stool mixing chemicals and acting like a
scientist.   Although the scene primarily illustrates a comic
reversal of roles, it also reinforces Esther's earlier characterization.   Her action is not necessarily a comment upon
knowledge (the formula for youth is locked up in the head of
a monkey) or scientists (e. g. , that scientists are monkeys)
but a brilliant counterpoint to the scientists' insanity.   She
functions, not as a scientist, but as a monkey imitating a
scientist.   Her actions are pure and direct.   She knows how
to act like a scientist, but she also knows how to act like a
monkey when the situation calls for it (with Barnaby at the
board meeting).   What is important is that, at all times,
she functions naturally.

The group of kids playing cowboys and Indians also
have a sense of themselves and a sense of their own limitations which Hawks's insane grown-ups lack.   For example,
when Barnaby asks them to burn Hank at the stake, one kid
wisely replies, "It won't work.   The minute you light a fire,
they come and put it out.   They always do."   Not only are
the children more aware of their limitations than the adults,
they also seem to have a rudimentary sense of cause and
effect (even the scientists who keep drinking from the water
cooler are somewhat weak in this area).   In the same scene,
when Barnaby suggests scalping Hank, the same kid reminds
him, "You can't scalp a man unless you have a war dance
first."   Hawks's kids, like some of Godard's, have a sense
of a proper sequence of events: first you do one thing and
then you can do another.   Their sense of their own limitations and of a natural sequence of events in time is directly
related to their sanity, to their sense of themselves, and
to their harmony with their universe, and, as a result, the
children point out most dramatically Barnaby's lack of self-
awareness and his unnaturalness within his environment.

Finally, the infant, whom Edwina supposes to be
Barnaby, works in the film much as the monkey and the
children do--as counterpoint to the actions of others.   His
actions are simple and direct, but are exaggerated and mis-
interpreted by Edwina and Oxby.   The three-shot of them
in Oxby's office serves as a perfect example of Hawks's use
of the baby as counterpoint: he just sits there quite naturally as the adults apply deep significance to his every move.
From his entrance to his exit, the baby retains his character
and a sense of self (Barnaby, when he talks to the baby in
the next scene, seems to recognize him as an individual).
As a result, just as the humor in I Was a Male War Bride
depends upon Grant retaining his masculinity throughout his
emasculating adventures, so the humor in Monkey Business
arises from characters like Esther, the children, or the
baby (especially in the taxi cab scene) who preserve their
essential identity through all the uncertainty and confusion
of the chaotic action.

In every sense, then, Monkey Business is relentlessly
logical and compulsively consistent.   Shot after shot and
scene after scene deal with the recognition and acceptance
of certain relationships--not only relationships between people, but between things and between events.   Yet Hawks is
not so much interested in the scientific relationship of cause
and effect--for instance, we never know what causes the

monkey to make B-4 or to put it in the water cooler or why the baby crawls into Edwina's bed--as in the unscientific relationships of people to themselves, to one another, and to their environment. What Hawks does in Monkey Business is simply to show what happens when his characters lose their identities in an attempt to reverse normal temporal sequences, endanger the stability of their inter-personal relationships through a reluctance to accept maturely the responsibility for their own actions toward each other, and come into conflict with their environment in an insane pursuit of an ideal world of their own design.

The action of Monkey Business is chaotic and seemingly illogical, i. e., Hawks creates a universe in which his characters attempt to reverse temporal sequences, to upset nature. Yet the structure of the film remains organic: it grows from shot to shot, from scene to scene. It is his ordered structuring of his characters' chaotic experiences that leads them to an understanding of their own actions, to a confrontation with their own insanity, and to a final recognition of nature and accord with the world around them. Barnaby and Edwina's experiences with the formula teach them to accept one another, faults and all. Although Barnaby remains as absent-minded at the end--as seen in the incident with his suspenders--as he was at the beginning, Edwina's approach to his absent-mindedness is no longer condescending or motherly: she treats Barnaby like an adult. Both learn to adapt to the changing world around them.

Paradoxically, Monkey Business functions on two levels--one is organically logical, the other inorganically irrational. The film contains thematic elements that counterpoint other thematic elements and this thematic counterpoint produces a slowly emerging pattern of interwoven ideas--a pattern that rigorously observes its own logic and that gradually develops toward its own, inevitable conclusion. Hawks's direction, with its use of counterpoint and its relentless movement forward reveals a narrative intelligence more common in engineering than in the cinema in that all of its parts, like the parts of a machine or engine, function as a single unit to accomplish the task for which it was designed.

NOTES

1.   Robin Wood, Howard Hawks (New York: Doubleday, 1968), p. 78.

2. Wood, p. 83.
3. See Eisenstein's analysis of the "organic-ness" of Potem-
    kin in his essay "The Structure of the Film" in Film
    Form (New York: Harcourt, Brace & World, 1949),
    pp. 159-174.
4. William Paul, in conversation, made this observation.

g. Narrative Density in Rio Bravo

I have often wondered whether there were any deeper affinities between Howard Hawks and William Faulkner than the simple fact of their friendship, their fondness for flying and for storytelling, and their ability to work together successfully in Hollywood. In terms of the superficial organization of the narratives, the two would appear quite incompatible. Faulkner's stories, unlike Hawks's, are told subjectively, often from one or more points of view, and structured by the strong, intrusive personality of a narrator. The plots resemble jig-saw puzzles: each character, each chapter and each narrative point of view supplies another piece to the puzzle, whose design or subject only becomes clear upon completion. Faulkner's verbal style mirrors his structure: each word, each sentence, and each paragraph interlock; and each piece is shaped against the contours of the subject(s) within the picture. All the pieces eventually form a complete picture. Though, because of his reliance upon limited, first-person narration, the stories never have total clarity; the ends of his stories, like the ends of mystery novels, satisfyingly reveal more of the mystery of what has gone before than they conceal. Even though the reader is struck by the impossibility of any one of Faulkner's characters ever seeing anything clearly or in its entirety, the reader himself can see. Characters fall into place; relationships become more clearly delineated; and there are faint traces of beginnings, middles, and ends to each story. And the novel itself assumes a distinct shape.

Hawks, on the other hand, possesses a narrative clarity and stylistic objectivity that resembles, in its construction, a pyramid more than a puzzle. The closest that he ever really comes to Faulkner's complexity of plotting is The Big Sleep (1946), scripted by Faulkner and others from an already intricate novel by Raymond Chandler; but Hawks's direction turns the script's complexity into a chaotic background of events which foregrounds an elegantly-developed love story (which did not exist in the original novel). Here,

as in his comedies, he surrounds his central characters
with a cast of bizarre characters and with a series of seemingly irrational events that belie the narrative's apparent
resolution of its intrigues.   The Big Sleep is a jig-saw puzzle in which the shape of the pieces, i. e. , the characterization, and the fitting together of one or two of the pieces
(i. e. , the relationships between characters and between characters and their settings) has more interest for Hawks than
the finished puzzle itself.   In fact, he never even attempts
to finish the puzzle.   The Big Sleep remains a whodunit that
never finally reveals whodunwhat.

What makes Hawks Faulknerian is not so much this
jig-saw complexity of plot that suits Douglas Sirk so well in
Tarnished Angels, but the simultaneity of a single, organic
action, revealed in the separate stories of several characters.   By this I mean that Hawks's narratives, especially
in films like Only Angels Have Wings, To Have and Have
Not, and Rio Bravo (all reworkings of a single story), sustain several stories and carry them easily and naturally to
their conclusions in a single, structural matrix of nearly
simultaneous events which feed into and off of one another.
The action of Rio Bravo, for example, takes about four days.
Unlike films such as Sergeant York (1941), Red River (1948),
or The Big Sky (1952), everything in Rio Bravo (1959) is
compressed into a time span of a few days; everything seems
to happen at once.   In Red River, actions and images continually recur throughout the course of the film.   In Rio
Bravo, actions, relationships, and images occur simultaneously; rather than being spaced out in time, they seem to
happen on top of one another.   Red River and The Big Sky
have single-action narratives; by this I mean that the characters in the film are grouped together by virtue of their
common goals or objectives (i. e. , the cattle drive or the
trading expedition).   In both of these films, the men are
tied together because they are participating in the same
events; the characters are defined in terms of their relationship to these events.   The number of different actions,
stories, and relationships in Rio Bravo give it a density,
complexity, and closeness that distinguishes it from Hawks's
other westerns.   Yet its images have a simplicity that almost defies the complexity of the plot and the events which
occur within the film.   Because the backgrounds are so
static, i. e. , devoid of movement, detail, and depth, Rio
Bravo's images appear simple and easy to read.   At the
same time, the characters who stand in front of these static
backgrounds achieve a complexity that goes beyond the seem-

ing simplicity of the film's images. Red River has an exciting, dynamic background, full of movement and action;
Rio Bravo is almost the opposite: its static backgrounds
serve to confine the action which occurs in front of them,
to restrict the movements of characters within them. Rio
Bravo is not an action film nor an epic as are Red River
or The Big Sky; it is a film more obviously about the characters than the events which tie those characters together.

In Rio Bravo, every character and relationship comments simultaneously on every other character and relationship: the relationship between Dude and Chance parallels,
somewhat, that between Feathers and Chance; Chance's relationship with Colorado resembles that which he has with Dude;
and Dude and Colorado serve as foils for one another. Even
Nathan Burdett's attempts to rescue his brother Joe--which
culminates in the trade of Dude for Joe--mirror in a distorted way (because Joe is "no good" and Dude is) Chance's
attempts to restore Dude's self-respect. The difference is
that Chance does not try to give Dude his self-respect back;
instead, he helps Dude earn it.

In discussing Hawks's treatment of the self-respect
motif in Rio Bravo, Robin Wood notes a similarity amongst
the characters in terms of this motif. He writes:

> If the traditional western theme of the defence
> of civilized social values is taken for granted,
> where, then, does Hawks put the emphasis? On
> values deeper than the social level, but on which
> social values, if valid, must necessarily be built:
> man's innate need for self-respect. As a motif,
> it will be easily seen that this pervades the film.
> It is stated through every character, usually on
> his first appearance, like the subject of a fugue,
> and developed contrapuntally thereafter with a fugal
> rigour. Dude (Dean Martin) grovelling for the coin
> in the spittoon; Chance (John Wayne) preventing him;
> Colorado (Ricky Nelson) remarking, when Chance
> questions Pat Wheeler (Ward Bond) about him in
> his presence, "I speak English, sheriff, if you
> wanna, why don't you ask me?" Pat, too old and
> unsteady to be of direct use, risking (and giving)
> his life to get others to help Chance; Stumpy
> (Walter Brennan) asserting his independence by
> disobeying Chance's orders and standing in the jail
> doorway; Feathers (Angie Dickinson) refusing to

stop gambling and wearing feathers as an easy way
of escaping a suspect past; Carlos (Pedro Gonzalez
Gonzalez) insisting with sudden touching dignity on
his right to arrange matters as he pleases in his
own hotel; all these constitute variants on the
theme, each distinct from the others in tone and
moral weight, hence each a variation, not a repetition.... The density of this thematic statement
and development is increased by the element of
parody introduced by the villains. Nathan Burdett
(John Russell) goes to such lengths to get his
brother out of jail not from motives of affection
but from pride in his position: his actions are
dictated, that is to say, by the need not to lose
face, a caricature of the motives for which the
heroes act, rendered further invalid by the fact
that he is defending a morally indefensible action
(Joe Burdett's murder of the man in the saloon). [1]

What also needs to be stressed is that all these similar actions and relationships clustered around the self-respect
motif occur simultaneously.   At the same time, they are
presented with a uniquely Hawksian integrity.   Hawks completes every action/relationship that is begun; but while treating it fully, he also treats--at the same time and in the
same action--every other action/relationship in the film.
What distinguishes Rio Bravo from Hawks's earlier westerns
and what links it to "character" (as opposed to "action")
films like Only Angels Have Wings and To Have and Have
Not is the interdependence of these actions and relationships
and their total integration into the film. [2]   Hawks, for example, does not isolate a single action, such as the moment
when Dude pours the drink back into the whiskey bottle without spilling a drop, or relationship, such as the screwball
one between Chance and Feathers, from the others around it.
In fact, he makes it clear that it was Dude's relationship
with a girl like Feathers in the past which prompted his alcoholism; thus the successful working-out of the Chance-
Feathers relationship is tied to Dude's own recovery (in that
the source of Dude's problem--a bad relationship with a girl
in the past--is erased by the reworking of a similar, but
healthier, relationship in the present).   Hawks's film is not,
as Wood suggests, about a single issue such as self-respect,
a single relationship, or a single character; it is about the
integration of all its elements, relationships, actions, characters, and events into an inseparable, irreducible whole.
This, I think, is what Fred Camper means when he writes

"that in the deepest sense, Rio Bravo, cannot be about any of its characters, but rather about the general idea of relationships, between character and character and between characters and the world. What the film traces is not so much the progress of specific characters as the progress of this idea."[3]

NOTES

1. Robin Wood, "Who the Hell Is Howard Hawks?" in Focus!, No. 2 (1967), p. 11.
2. This is not to discount another factor which links the three films--screenwriter Jules Furthman.
3. Quoted from an unpublished book, written in 1969, on the films of Howard Hawks.

h. The Backstage Musical: 42nd Street and French Cancan

Classification according to type or genre is perhaps the most
ancient form of critical analysis.   Aristotle's Poetics organ-
izes existing prose and poetry into a handful of categories--
tragedy, comedy, epic, pastoral, lyric--and, through "scientific" inquiry, identifies the underlying patterns or principles which works within the same genre share.

If Aristotle's search for categories marks the beginnings of rational, analytical thought, it also reflects the
limitations of conceptual critical method in the face of pre-
conceptual art. [1]   By that I mean not only that Aristotle's
rational classifications have only limited value when applied
to pre-rational works but also that they simplify and reduce
literature to mere formula and convention, ignoring the
uniqueness of individual works.

To this day, critical approaches to film genres re-
tain, to a large extent, the steam-roller mentality of Aristotle, levelling differences and reducing films of similar
type to their lowest common denominator. [2]   Similarity of
plot or setting frequently becomes the sole criterion for
genre grouping and the chief subject of genre analysis.
What is left after the critics have done their job is not an
enriched experience of the film but a set of worn conventions and banal clichés.   Genre directors face a similar
problem: they must give meaning somehow to conventional
forms, animate stock characters and make dramatic familiar
situations.   The films of Howard Hawks and Alfred Hitchcock
differ in every possible way save one: the scripts of both
obsessively avoid cliché and continually seek new ways of
dealing with traditional forms.   If Hawks tends to avoid
cliché largely through character (e. g. , his oft-noted role
reversals), then Hitchcock varies his films through visual
style, constantly experimenting with new narrative techniques.

One way of avoiding the reductionist pitfalls of genre

282

criticism is to seek out differences as well as similarities, to concentrate less on conventions and formulae than on the way in which they are revitalized--if they are revitalized. Though genre provides a context of films and a system of conventions without which certain characters and situations make little sense, it is style which restores value to those conventions, vitality to those characters, and meaning to those situations. Style emerges as the variable factor, the factor that permits freedom within the limits of formula, enabling genre films to achieve a degree of complexity that goes beyond superficial categorization.

Of all genres, the musical is the most dependent on studio-controlled stylization, for it is chiefly through a stylization of reality that it can make believable and natural its basic actions, singing and dancing. Expressive use of lighting, set design, camera angle, and camera movement (in the Busby Berkeley numbers at Warners in the Thirties), color, costume design, and exaggerated emphasis on production value (at M-G-M in the Forties and Fifties) de-emphasize the basic artificiality of the action, permitting shifts from prosaic dramatic sequences to more poetic musical numbers. Stylization subverts realistic dramatic expectations and its sudden infusion into a scene often signals an impending song and dance number, easing both the characters and the audience into another, more nearly ideal world. When Gene Kelly, as a prelude to the "You Were Meant for Me" number in Singin' in the Rain, guides Debbie Reynolds into the sound studio, poses her on a ladder, bathes her and the set in colored lights and activates a wind machine, he acknowledges the genre's need for the atmosphere of illusion that only a studio can provide. In contrast, musicals shot outdoors, like 7 Brides for 7 Brothers and West Side Story, must overcome the weight of their backgrounds, rarely achieving the "lift" or "liberation" which audiences have come to associate with a studio musical.

The motivation of a song or dance number is a major problem for writers of musicals--which is perhaps the reason they turn so frequently to the sub-genre of the backstage musical. From The Broadway Melody (1929) to The Bandwagon (1953), the staging of a Broadway show has justified countless production numbers. In using the backstage situation for their initial cycle of musicals (42nd Street, Gold Diggers of 1933 and Footlight Parade) Warners characteristically explored the genre's realistic aspects. At the other end of the spectrum, stood the Lubitsch-Chevalier operettas

at Paramount: romantically conceived characters in mythi-
cal kingdoms or exotic Old World settings roleplayed their
way through fanciful plots formally structured around elaborate love triangles.

The inter-relationship of studio and genre involves
questions of studio style.   Warner Bros. , like Paramount or
M-G-M, has more than a distinct "look. " The studio conveys, through its genre preferences, its contract personnel
--including actors, actresses, directors, writers, composers, cameramen, and art designers--a personality or image
to the public.   Much as the realistic premise of its backstage musicals distinguishes it from Paramount's highly
polished fairy tale operettas, so its contract performers--
James Cagney, Bebe Daniels, Dick Powell, Ruby Keeler,
Ginger Rogers, Joan Blondell, Guy Kibbee, and Ned Sparks
--project a more proletarian, less romantic, and decidedly
less glamorous image than Paramount's (Maurice Chevalier,
Jeanette MacDonald, Miriam Hopkins, Claudette Colbert).
In contrast to the more operatic musicals at M-G-M with
Nelson Eddy and Jeanette MacDonald or the more sophisticated Cole Porter and Irving Berlin scores in the Fred Astaire and Ginger Rogers RKO films, even the music in
Warners musicals, lowbrow Broadway show tunes written
by Tin Pan Alley composers Al Dubin and Harry Warren
contributes to the studio's popular, working class image.

The look and sound of Warners musicals reflect the
studio's larger, thematic concerns.   Warners genre cycles
of the early Thirties mirror, in subject matter, mood, and
spirit, the political and social reality of Depression America.   Much as their gangster films were Depression-inspired
"success tragedies" (as Robert Warshow points out), their
backstage musicals took the shape of "success comedies. "
This similarity is surely no accident: Darryl Zanuck, who
would later produce the socially conscious The Grapes of
Wrath, How Green Was My Valley, Gentleman's Agreement
and Pinky as head of Fox in the Forties, oversaw production
of both genre cycles, using them as sounding boards for examining contemporary social problems.

If the gangster films celebrate individual initiative in
attaining success, they also emphasize tragic weaknesses--
in the non-Warners Scarface (1932), Camonte realizes--too
late--his need for others, acknowledging that success involves interdependence.   Characters in Warner's early musicals realize that individual success involves dependence on

others. As Mark Roth notes in discussing the political im-
plications of these musicals, "the ideal of individual success
has been transformed into an ideal of success through collective effort under the guidance of a strong director," Roth
viewing the films as metaphors of national recovery, of collective success through individual sacrifice. [3] Lloyd Bacon's
42nd Street (1933) adheres to the success comedy formula of
the backstage musical genre at Warners, but it is distinctly
darker in mood than the other films in the cycle, partly because its "strong director" is not that strong. The director
in Footlight Parade (released June, 1933) is, as Roth points
out, a Rooseveltian, New Deal figure, full of optimism and
energy. But the director in 42nd Street (written in 1932,
released in March, 1933) is a pre-New Deal figure, projecting the pessimism of an earlier era. [4] The difference between the two films is as much that between the screen
personalities of James Cagney (Footlight Parade) and Warner
Baxter (42nd Street) as it is the optimism after and the pessimism before Roosevelt's first hundred days in office.
Cagney's screen character is active and dynamic; his gestures are youthful and exuberant. Baxter's persona is passive and static: his features and mannerisms are older
than the actor's actual years. Cagney, whether gangster
(Tom Powers in Public Enemy, Cody "Top of the World"
Jarrett in White Heat), song and dance man (here and in
Yankee Doodle Dandy), politician (A Lion Is in the Streets)
or business executive (One, Two, Three), is success oriented. Baxter, as the ruined Dr. Mudd in Prisoner of Shark
Island or as the battle-fatigued Capt. Laroche in Road to
Glory, plays worn, weary characters whose spirit is broken
by defeat.

   42nd Street makes use of Baxter's age and his ability
to project nervous exhaustion, introducing him as a once-
great Broadway director, wiped out in the stock market
crash, who desperately seeks one more success before ill
health forces his retirement from show business. Baxter,
as Julian Marsh, belongs, with actress Dorothy Brock (Bebe
Daniels), to an earlier generation, a generation which has
already tasted success and failure. In contrast to these
fading talents are set chorus girl Peggy Sawyer (Ruby Keeler) and juvenile lead Billy Lawler (Dick Powell)--he sings
"Young and Healthy"--whose fortunes rise. (That both Baxter and Daniels were silent stars and Keeler and Powell were
newcomers to pictures gives an added dimension to the contrast.)

The darkness of 42nd Street is amplified by its careful juxtaposition of success and failure. Brock, sidelined by
an accident is replaced by Sawyer and, after wishing her
luck, announces her retirement. Marsh, his job done, sits
alone outside the theater, listening to the audience as it exits belittle his talent as director and extoll that of his new
stars. The editing at the end of the film drives home the
success-failure interconnection. The title number culminates
with a long crane shot, the camera moving up the face of
an enormous cardboard skyscraper to Sawyer and Lawler
who sit perched on its top. Bacon cuts directly from them,
literally at the "height" of their success, to a high-angle,
somewhat dwarfing shot of Marsh, sitting alone at the bottom of a fire escape in a darkly-lit alley outside the theater.
The film concludes with Marsh's exclusion from the triumph
of his "Pretty Lady" show and this image reverberates reflexively back through the film, redetermining the mood of
what has gone before.

Bacon's collaboration with choreographer Busby Berkeley is nowhere more effective than in this final cut from
production number to dramatic story, from "musical" to
"backstage." Bacon's handling of dramatic action throughout
the film has been static, his passive camera drily observing
the conventional histrionics of backstage love triangles.
Berkeley's direction is flamboyantly kinetic: as soon as
characters step on the stage for rehearsals, his camera
begins to move. Lateral tracks and dolly shots knit individual characters together into an interdependent, theatrical
community. Personal melodramatics give way to the larger
needs of the community, Berkeley's mobile camera never
resting long enough on one face to establish its distinctness,
drawing all the characters momentarily into a quasi-demo-
cratic anonymity.

Berkeley's production numbers stress the collaborative
nature of the theatrical community, so much so that, as Ted
Sennett observes, Berkeley frequently (here in the "Shuffle
Off to Buffalo" number) divides up song lyrics among several
members of the chorus. [5] RKO's Astaire-Rogers musicals
tend to have one elaborate production number (e. g., the
"Piccolino" number on the Venetian set in Top Hat), the
scale of the other numbers being smaller and more intimate
in tone. When Astaire and Rogers dance, they also act:
their dancing becomes an extension of their individual characters, marking stages in the evolution of their love relationship. Berkeley's musical sequences, for the most part,

are all large-scale production numbers which function as expressions of communal rather than individual identity. Individual characters become part of a larger design, yet each dancer remains necessary to that design, an integral part of a kaleidoscopic machine. Considering Berkeley's military background, the shape of his numbers recalls the ancient Greek phalanx--in itself an extension of Greek political and social structure--in which the shield of one soldier protects the man next to him. Berkeley's communal dances similarly reflect the ideal of New Deal society in general and the cohesiveness of the theatrical community in particular.

Berkeley's dancers do not always dance. They often merely stand, rigid as statues, on stages which revolve (42nd Street frequently employs three revolving stages). Rather it is his camera which always dances. It tracks through the set or is moved, between shots, from set-up to set-up, discovering geometrical shapes and forms within the dances thereby linking visual patterns to musical rhythms.

42nd Street ends with an unbroken series of production numbers, each more lavish and fantastic than the one before it. The stylistic explosion which Berkeley engineers here marks an expressionistic escape from the bitter realities of the Depression-afflicted world which surrounds the characters earlier in the film. It is as if we had suddenly entered another film, another time, another space. But much as Berkeley's camera and choreography break down the confinement of the theater proscenium, exploring the space behind it and liberating the action from the weight of the real world around it, so Bacon's final image of Marsh in the alley undercuts the escapist lift which Berkeley achieves, returning us to an extremely mortal and vulnerable character who is unable to participate actively (as a performer) or passively (as a member of the audience) in the cathartic release the musical numbers generate.

42nd Street's off-beat ending plays against convention: in effect it frustrates us, excluding us, through the distancing figure of Marsh, from the general euphoria with which a musical ought to end. The last scene forces us to rethink the film and question its generic categorization as an "escapist musical" or as a "success comedy." We may still leave the movie theater whistling "42nd Street," but the tune is likely to be a little less gaudy, bawdy, or sporty than it might have been if the film had ended onstage rather than backstage.

Careful examination of 42nd Street justifies its status
as a motion picture "classic." It is one of the few excep-
tional genre films made without the unifying personality of
an auteur--whether producer, director, screenwriter, or
star--making its excellence all the more noteworthy. It is
remarkable in that it is a genuinely collaborative work--the
product not only of two directors, but of its producer,
studio, and cast.

French Cancan (1956) is also a collaborative enter-
prise, but it bears the stamp of an auteur--Jean Renoir.
Though its cast, set design, and color photography contribute to its emotional impact, it is ultimately the product of
a personal rather than a collective vision, complicating any
superficial analysis of it as merely a genre piece. It participates in the sub-genre of backstage musical and even
bears a remarkably strong resemblance, in terms of plot
and character type, to 42nd Street but is markedly different
in tone and in its attitude toward its subject matter. It is
a film of sharp contrasts--youth and age, experience and in-
experience, success and failure--and, though its emotional
power derives from the juxtaposition of these contrasts, its
inability to bridge these differences and resolve these contrasts frustrates genre expectations, leaving the audience
with a profound sense of disharmony. French Cancan is not
necessarily a better picture because, as the work of a single
author, it is more unified--criteria of aesthetic excellence
are relative and prevent absolute value judgments--but Renoir's presence behind the camera does add another dimension
to the film, making it somehow more than a backstage musical.

Both 42nd Street and French Cancan deal with the
world of the theater: 42nd Street is, as its title implies, a
film about a place and the people in it and provides a pseudo-
documentary history of a Broadway show from the initial
signing of contracts to opening night. French Cancan is also a history--that of the Moulin Rouge, celebrating not only
a place but its incarnation of the spirit of an era (the 1880's),
and takes us from the planning and actual building of the
theater to the first performance in it. Both films build,
through a succession of frustrating, unfinished, or inter-
rupted rehearsal numbers, to spectacularly cathartic finales,
each climaxing in an extended series of musical numbers.
And in each, backstage melodramatics in the form of love
triangles threaten the opening of the show.

The leading characters in both films are similar in type. French Cancan's aging impresario, Danglard (Jean Gabin), like 42nd Street's Marsh, is the genius behind the show, discovering talent, shaping it, then withdrawing him- self once the performance begins. La Belle Abbesse, like Brock, has had her success and sees younger talent take her place (both professionally and romantically). And if anything, French Cancan takes the cyclical rise and fall structure of character fortunes found in 42nd Street two or three turns further; La Belle Abbesse grudgingly gives way to Nini (Françoise Arnoul) who, in turn, yields to Esther Georges (Anna Amendola) and so on.

Though many of the characters in French Cancan, as genre types, resemble those in 42nd Street, the resemblance is only superficial. Fuller comparison reveals important differences which reflect the larger differences in vision be- tween the two films. For example, both Danglard and Marsh, during the final musical sequences, are removed from the show, unable to participate directly in it. But Danglard is irresistibly drawn back into the world of the theater, physically as well as spiritually participating in the ecstatic feeling generated by the cancan. Unlike 42nd Street which ends discordantly, French Cancan unites all its major characters, breaking down all the barriers between them.

The casting of Jean Gabin as Danglard is crucial to the tone of the film. In contrast to the pessimistic Baxter, Gabin is a romantic and a dreamer; though no longer young, he continues to explore and discover, fascinated rather than beaten by the experience of life. His earlier pictures with Renoir (Les Bas Fonds, La Grande Illusion, and La Bête Humaine) and his films with other directors (e.g., Pepe Le Moko, Le Plaisir) develop the romantic side of his screen personality. André Bazin reports that before the war Gabin insisted that his films contain one violent or explosive scene of anger. 6 Renoir gives Gabin such a scene in French Can- can--his backstage pep talk to Nini before the final cancan-- but he motivates Gabin's anger romantically--not out of his love for Nini or for any individual but out of his love for the theater.

Renoir links Gabin's romanticism to a sense of dis- covery: when his enthusiasm flags, it is always rekindled by a discovery of beauty or talent in the world around him. Renoir sees Gabin's passionate interest in life as the sign of a true artist and uses Gabin, in this role as director, to

act out his own notions of art as the recognition of the beauty that exists in the life around the artist. [7]

Gabin is more a part of his world than is Baxter:
Danglard actually falls in love with his discoveries, involving himself in all facets of their lives. He is their lover,
their director, their audience. Through Danglard, the separate worlds of the musical and the backstage melodrama
are brought together. Melodrama and spectacle, life and
theater become inseparable; Renoir's world, unlike that of
42nd Street, is, though full of different characters with different (and often opposing) goals for themselves and others,
one, unified by the artist's vision of it.

French Cancan shares with a number of other major
French post-war films a nostalgic interest in the past--
specifically in the French past. Beginning with Marcel
Carné's Les Enfants du Paradis in 1945 (an obvious influence on French Cancan), there is a backward-looking movement in French film, an attempt, perhaps, to recall and
regenerate the national spirit and character of pre-World War
I France. (e. g. Les Dames du Bois de Boulogne, Casque
D'Or, Madame de ..., Le Rideau Cramoisi and a number
of internationally co-produced color spectacles including Les
Grandes Manoeuvres, Une Vie and Lola Montes). Renoir
himself returns to the period of French Cancan in his next
picture, Elena et les Hommes (1956), which similarly combines melodrama, music, history and spectacle.

Seen in this context, French Cancan is as much a
spectacle in the French tradition as a musical in the American tradition. As spectacle, it develops, as does Lola
Montes, the relationship between audience and actor, gradually dissolving the difference between the two. One of the
ways Renoir does this is by viewing the spectacle or performance from a variety of perspectives, exploring all its
dimensions. For example, French Cancan opens with a shot
of a poster of La Belle Abbesse, dressed in an exotic, revealing costume. From this static image of her, Renoir
cuts to her act which is sensual and dynamic--she is dancing for every man there, his camera viewing her act from
the position of the audience. The cut preserves the illusion
of her performance, yet the presence of the audience reminds us that it is a performance. Renoir then cuts backstage to Danglard who enters the theater and speaks a few
words of encouragement to his latest discovery (the whistling
clown). La Belle Abbesse is visible dancing in the back-

ground. From the stage she makes a flourishing gesture of
greeting to Danglard, then incorporates the gesture into her
act: she dances for all men and for him alone. The cutting establishes two sets of relationships--that between the
actress/dancer and her audience and that between her and
her lover/manager. Rather than separating the two sets of
relationships, the cutting equates and links them. The
backstage view takes us behind the scenes, behind the illusion, but rather than destroy that illusion it shows another
side of it, revealing the integration of personal feeling and
the public display of it. Here and throughout the film,
Renoir intertwines the public world of the theater and the
private worlds of those who perform in the theater, weaving
both worlds into one.

Later, La Belle Abbesse, Danglard, and their theater
friends go slumming to La Reine Blanch, a popular cafe in
Montmartre, where they mix with laundresses, bakers, pick-
pockets, pimps, and whores. Danglard and his company
watch the locals dance the chuchut--once again Renoir transforms natural, everyday action into theater, complete with
performers and audience. Danglard discovers and falls in
love with Nini watching her dance, their relationship beginning and continuing as much that of spectator and performer
as lover and lover. Danglard's subsequent discovery of
Esther Georges carries similar overtones. Having just suffered a setback, Danglard appears depressed and lifeless.
He hears a voice singing off screen and suddenly perks up.
Looking out the window he sees Esther in a window across
the way, framed by the window as if within a theater proscenium. The presentation of the love relationship here, like
that earlier with Nini, suggests its metaphorical function:
it is like the relationship between the artist and his art.
Art, for Danglard (and Renoir), is everywhere--in the cafes,
in the streets, in neighboring apartments, in unconscious
gestures and song; the ability to recognize, develop, and
encourage other artists makes Danglard himself an artist,
Renoir acknowledging, through Danglard, the importance of
his own role as director.

At La Reine Blanche, Danglard and his friends join
in the dance, easily crossing the bridge between audience
and performers. As Danglard dances with Nini, they, in
turn, are watched by La Belle Abbesse and Paulo (Franco
Pastorino), Nini's boyfriend. Jealousy transforms the cafe
into a theater for melodrama, complete with amorous intrigues and love triangles, and changes the people in it into

one-dimensional melodramatic types.   Paulo and La Belle
Abbesse, the jealous lovers, become jealous of Nini and
Danglard.   Baron Walter (Jean-Roger Caussimon) and an
officer, the opportunistic interlopers, note La Belle Abbesse's jealousy and make overtures to her.   Prince Alexandre (Gianni Esposito), the shy suitor, falls hopelessly in
love with Nini, conveying it in a glance when he tenderly
retrieves a hair comb she has dropped.

        Renoir's melodrama constantly threatens to disrupt
the cohesiveness of the theatrical community, a community
symbolized by the Moulin Rouge building.   Each stage in
the actual building of the Moulin Rouge is accompanied by
highly theatrical, melodramatic confrontations between the
members of these two love triangles.   First La Belle Abbesse assaults Nini at the building's official dedication and
Paulo attacks Danglard, knocking him into an open ditch.
Later, when construction (financed by the prince) starts
again, La Belle Abbesse, still jealous, tells him that Nini
is Danglard's mistress.   In another theatrical scene he confronts Nini, she confesses her love for Danglard and the
prince melodramatically shoots himself, again halting construction.   The final resolution of the film's romantic intrigue occurs on opening night.   Nini senses that Danglard
has given her up for his new star, Esther, and refuses to
dance in the cancan.   The intensity of Nini's romantic frustration is most strongly felt on opening night when she
watches Danglard while he, peering through the curtain,
watches Esther sing.   Nini and Danglard stand backstage at
either end of the curtain.   The drama going on here is as
theatrical and moving as the one out front.   The emptiness
of the frame echoes Nini's isolation and emotional distance
from Danglard.   Her movement away from the curtain
matches that of Danglard, yet their separateness in space
and their movement in different directions heightens her
loneliness.   Moments later, she sees Danglard and Esther
kissing; Nini stands in the foreground, Danglard and Esther
in the deep background, emptiness between.   Opposed to
these empty shots are the cluttered frames outside of Nini's
dressing room after she refuses to go on.   The real weight
of the scene lies in the presence of other characters before
and during Danglard's harangue.   The presence of the theater community, which Nini refuses to recognize by denying
her identity as a dancer in favor of her identity as a lover,
exerts a powerful influence on her, forcing her to choose
between membership in a community and lonely alienation,
between the theater and her personal desires.   After Dan-

glard's speech, the theater members slowly exit the frame,
leaving Nini alone. The sudden emptiness of the frame, as
if it were being drained of life and movement, helps her
realize that she has nothing if she does not have a place in
this community. She hurriedly dresses for the cancan number.

   Nini's suitors represent the various choices she can
make, the various identities she can adopt. Paulo offers
her marriage and children, Sundays in the country as in
Partie de Campagne. Prince Alexandre offers her romance
and riches--sheep, tobacco, and roses. Danglard offers her
nothing, not even his love; but he does offer her an identity
as a performer. Like Camilla (Anna Magnani) in The Gold-
en Coach, Nini chooses the theater over her three lovers.
And the theater is epitomized in the cancan.

   The film builds toward the final cancan sequence.
Through numerous rehearsals of the cancan Renoir develops
our expectations (something Godard intentionally frustrates
in his version of One Plus One) and satisfies them--the
dance, like the building of the Moulin Rouge, symbolizes the
culmination of all the film's disparate themes and characters, drawing them, finally, together.

   The cancan spectacularly dissolves the distinction between stage and audience. Waiters move the customers'
tables, putting guests on the stage itself, and clear a place
in the audience section for the cancan. There is a physical
integration of audience and performers (predating that of
modern theater). The dancers emerge out of papered walls,
climbing down ropes, leaping from balconies. Weaving in
and out among the customers at their tables, they seem to
come from everywhere, surrounding the audience. As they
dance, men from the audience join in: they run from their
tables to mingle with the dancers; they lie on the floor,
becoming hurdles for dancers to leap over. They rise and
catch dancers in mid-air, then set them down. Like the
first scene in La Reine Blanche, the spectators take part in
the event, communing with the performers.

   During the cancan, Renoir cuts backstage to Danglard,
exhausted after his angry pep talk to Nini. Danglard, the
catalyst, has set all this in motion, yet remains removed
from it. But even he joins in the dance. He begins to kick
his feet backstage, sitting in a chair, irresistibly drawn into
the rhythm of the dance. The sense of his emotional partici-

pation in the cancan is heightened by his physical isolation
from it.   Ultimately, he is drawn out into the audience,
completing, with his presence, the integrity of the event.
Once in the audience, he discovers a woman singing, reaf-
firming his role as theatrical impresario and driving home
the point that art exists everywhere.

      The cutting of the final sequence is consistent with
the event's communal quality.   Renoir's cutting does not analyze the action or isolate his characters in separate spaces.
What his cutting achieves is a kind of mise-en-scène.   In
Welles' The Magnificent Ambersons, the camera relates the
characters to objects and to one another in a temporal and
spatial continuum (though the foreground and background are
often separated by an empty middleground).   Like Welles'
long takes in Ambersons, Renoir's cutting in French Cancan
relates characters to the setting around them and to one
another.   Unlike Eisenstein's or Hitchcock's analytical editing, which breaks up action and draws it out, Renoir's, like
Pudovkin's, is synthetic; it links shot to shot.   His cutting
on action, like Hawks's, draws characters together and emphasizes the continuity of action.   Both Berkeley and Renoir
break their musical numbers out of the confinement of the
theater proscenium, achieving a spatial freedom crucial to
the cathartic spirit of the musical.   But Berkeley's cutting
imposes its own order and rhythm on the musical number:
Renoir's grows out of the cancan, echoing its rhythm.
Renoir's unobtrusive editing achieves a mise-en-scène outside of the shot.   In other words, his cuts have a cumulative
effect, relating one shot to the shot before and after it, as
if there were no break in the action at all.   The spirit of
the event overrides everything.   The rhythm of the cancan
creates an emotional momentum that soothes Paulo's jealous
anger and unites La Belle Abbesse and Baron Walter.   Renoir's editing of the cancan number draws everyone into its
spirit.   All the characters, though retaining their individual
identities, become part of the musical number, as audience
or as participants, free for a moment from all personal
concerns.   Renoir's cutting and the cancan itself even lure
the film's audience, as it does the Moulin Rouge audience,
into this swirl of movement; the film audience joins the
spectators in the film in the cathartic magic of the moment.
As few other musicals do, French Cancan erases the distinction between audience and performers.   The liberation
of the film's characters through the cancan becomes ours
also.

Narrative cinema, as 42nd Street and French Cancan reveal, consists of a nexus of particular times, places, and people. Each film is a product of specific social, historical, and technological factors which, in part, determine its content and style. Both films reveal the cinema to be a complex of styles: national (American and French) and personal (Bacon/Berkeley and Renoir) styles are tempered by the fixed personae of individual actors and the rigid conventions of specific genres.

Film criticism must reflect the medium's eclectic nature. Genre study, like director study, is in itself reductionist and limiting. It desperately needs to seek out, explore and celebrate that which defies easy categorization. Genre criticism needs to go beyond genre.

NOTES

1. See John Finley's Pindar and Aeschylus, (Cambridge, Mass.: Harvard University Press, 1955), pp. 10-11.
2. See, for example, the reductionist classifications made by Will Wright in Sixguns & Society: A Structural Study of the Western, (Berkeley: University of California Press, 1975), especially his "inventive" reading of Duel in the Sun.
3. Mark Roth, "Some Warners Musicals and the Spirit of the New Deal," The Velvet Light Trap, No. 1 (June 1971), p. 22.
4. Ibid., p. 23.
5. Ted Sennett, Warner Brothers Presents, (New Rochelle, N.Y.: Arlington House, 1971), p. 91.
6. André Bazin, What Is Cinema?, Vol. II. (Berkeley: University of California Press, 1971), pp. 176-177.
7. See Renoir's description of Gabin in My Life and My Films, (New York: Atheneum, 1974), pp. 268-269, which suggests the existence of a strong, unspoken affinity between the two men.

PART THREE: ACTORS AND AUTEURS: CHAPLIN,
                        LLOYD, WRIGHT, STEWART, AND WAYNE

1. ACTORS AND AUTEURS: CHAPLIN, LLOYD, WRIGHT, STEWART, AND WAYNE

Over a period of years and through a variety of roles, actors and actresses develop a persona. Either through their own selection of parts to play or through a producer's, studio's, or director's guidance, they create a screen identity based, in part, on their physical characteristics and, in part, on the nature of the roles they play. Thus Chaplin establishes himself as "the tramp" and Lloyd as the "glass" character (i. e. , the guy who wears glasses). This persona often undergoes transformation: Chaplin's transition to sound leads him to new characters--Adenoid Hynkel, M. Verdoux, Calvero, and Shadov replace the tramp, though the latter, as Bazin suggests, still lurks beneath these subsequent masks. Other actors--Stewart and Wayne--create a persona which they then play against. The following essays attempt to deal with the creation of personae, with questions of acting style and with the director's shaping of actors' performances.

a. The Tramp

Charles Chaplin structures the narratives of his films more around character than around plot; action is less important to Chaplin than reaction. Unlike Keaton whose comedies subordinate character to action, creating a smooth-flowing story line rivaling that of Howard Hawks, Chaplin sacrifices plot to character and develops a very human narrative built on iconographic items of dress, idiosyncratic gesture, facial reaction and bodily movement. The "action" of his films consists of a series of episodic bits and gags unified by character--Chaplin is involved in them all--and unity of character, in turn, creates a thematic consistency.

Though he began films with Mack Sennett, Chaplin was essentially out of place in the King of Comedy's madcap chases and broad slapstick routines. Sennett's frenetic pace and mechanistic manipulation of situation never gave his star any time to establish or develop character. A character actor, Chaplin's birth as a comedian thus comes with his creation of the tramp persona in 1914. Chester Conklin, a colleague of Chaplin's at the Sennett studio, describes the historic moment:

> One time, I was making a picture with Mabel Normand called "Mabel's Strange Predicament." We were in a hotel. We had the hotel set up on the stage, and the diffusers were drawn over the set, to keep the rain off. We weren't working that morning. Charlie came in our dressing room, where Ford Sterling and Roscoe Arbuckle and myself were sitting playing pinocle, and put on my cutaway coat and Roscoe's hat and Ford's big shoes, and picked up a piece of hair off the make-up bench and held it under his upper lip, and he liked it and he stuck it on and he went out, and he started clowning around in this hotel set, doing a drunk ... and Sennett heard all the laughter and came out. He sat back and watched him, and

301

pretty soon he went up to Charlie and said, "You do that in this picture."

In Chaplin's case, clothes make the man. Each item of his wardrobe helps define his character. As George West observes, "the derby, too small, is striving for dignity. The moustache is vanity. The tightly buttoned coat and the stick and his whole manner are a gesture towards gallantry and dash and 'front.' He is trying to meet the world bravely and to put up a bluff." The clothes, though shabby and worn, suggest a certain dignity, or rather, pretension to dignity, which reflects an Old World sensibility to class distinctions. Chaplin asserts his dignity only to have it violated in gag after gag. In The Immigrant, Charlie treats a girl to a meal in a restaurant with a new-found coin only to discover, to his embarrassment, that he has lost the coin through a hole in his pocket. In The Adventurer, Charlie, at a posh party, drops a scoop of ice cream down his pants. And in The Gold Rush, Charlie struggles to keep his falling trousers up first with his cane then with a rope, at the other end of which is tied a dog. An aristocrat at heart, if not quite in dress, Chaplin behaves towards women, children, and the weak with the gallantry and courtesy of a gentleman but towards cops, bullies, and figures of authority with the malicious contempt of a mannerless tramp.

Chaplin's sympathies remain with the lower class, the downtrodden, the social outcast. A defender of the individual's rights, Chaplin distrusts the attempts of reformers to change the beliefs of others. The Salvation Army "reforms" Charlie in Easy Street: he changes his tramp clothes for the uniform of a cop and brings order to one of the city's toughest slum streets, reforming himself and others to win the love of a mission girl. In The Cure, Chaplin, abandoning his tramp costume, plays a rich alcoholic taking the cure at a sanitarium. Charlie's devious methods of getting liquor and avoiding his cure both draw our admiration and poke fun at the temperance movement.

Though Chaplin's anti-authoritarianism and sympathy for the little fellow--he always emphasizes his short stature by playing opposite big, bruising villains--suggest a leftist political orientation, the tramp character is no revolutionary, socialist, or communist. In fact, the tramp is something of a reactionary, a combined product of nineteenth-century Romanticism (glorification of the individual) and Victorianism (rigidly moral melodramatic outlook). Charlie's tramp finds himself continually at war with the modern world and its impersonal machines--whether in the form of a revolving door (The Cure), an escalator (The Floorwalker) or a folding bed (One A. M.). In Modern Times, Charlie takes on a threatening array of machines battling industrialization and automation and celebrating the individual. At the end of Modern Times as at the ends of most of his films, Charlie rejects this modern society and together with Paulette Goddard walks romantically off into the countryside. Just as Chaplin is more drawn to the pastoral than to the urban society, so he is more attracted to the rich emotional values of the past than to the barren wasteland of the present. Keaton, a product of the twentieth century, adapts himself through action to the world around him, controlling it with a uniquely American ingenuity and inventiveness. Chaplin, with an Old World inflexibility, continually wages war with the modern world and, more often than not, loses to it; yet his spirit remains undaunted and the integrity of his character intact. Chaplin's defeat at the hands of larger, modern forces ennobles the character and the values he represents.

b.   A King in New York: <u>The Survival of Classical Style</u>

Film, unlike many of the other arts, cannot really be discussed in terms of well-defined periods.   Classical, Romantic, and Neo-classical movements in literature and music
have no identifiable counterparts in film, perhaps because
of the shortness of the cinema's history and our lack of distance from it as an art form.   From the vantage point of
the Seventies, film history appears to be more of a continuous phenomenon than a series of discrete periods.   The
cinema's narrative and visual style looks back, in an unbroken line, to the work of D. W. Griffith, the originator of
what most of us call the classical tradition.   Eisenstein,
von Stroheim, Sternberg, Ford, Renoir, Lang, Hitchcock,
Capra, Hawks, Welles and countless others are, in one way
or another, trustees of the Griffith estate.

Only a handful of filmmakers operate outside of this
tradition.   Vertov, Epstein, Man Ray and Buñuel consciously rejected classical narrative, striking out, with varying
degrees of success, on their own (though often, in the case
of the French Avant-Garde artists, working within another
set of conventions, those of surrealism).

It was only during the Fifties that a break of any
major significance from this classical tradition occurred. [1]
Early in that decade young filmmakers, perhaps a part of
a new, post-war consciousness, began a reevaluation of
visual and narrative technique that found added support later
in the decade in the self-critical work of Italian and New
Wave directors.   This break with the classical tradition that
Griffith began launched a new era of filmmaking (which we
are presently experiencing).   Classicism has been joined by
iconoclassicism.

Throughout the Fifties, classical and iconoclassical
films were made side by side.   The crowning work of old
line directors like Renoir, Ophuls, Ford, Hitchcock, Hawks,
Mizoguchi and Ozu shared the screen with the more radical

movies made by Ray, Fuller, Aldrich, Antonioni, Fellini, Godard and others. The work of the best classical directors also changed during this period, in response partially to new, post-war concerns and partially to the more psychological, subjective acting style of the period.

The reasons for this dramatic rupture with classical tradition are obscure. Technical innovations demanding complementary stylistic adjustments may have had something to do with it. Not since the traumatic transition to sound in the late Twenties had the industry undergone such a comprehensive transformation. Color, 3-D, stereo sound, widescreen and CinemaScope made traditional methods of composition and editing obsolete. A more personal and expressive use of the camera--what Andrew Sarris labels a "new surge of stylistic ambitiousness"--accompanied new thematic concerns. [2] Interest in sex (see films of Tashlin/Mansfield, Wilder/Monroe, Hawks/Monroe) and in a psychological treatment of character caused a shift from the more objective narratives of the past and gave a new, albeit neurotic, life to the conventional genres of the musical (see films of Minnelli and Donen) and the western (see films made by Ford, Walsh, Mann, Boetticher and de Toth).

The stylistic and thematic innovations of the Fifties increased rather than diminished the freedom of individual filmmakers. Directors could shoot their films in black and white or in color (or both--Preminger's Bonjour Tristesse [1958]), in a studio or on location, in a standard (1. 33 to 1) or a widescreen (1. 85 to 1) or an anamorphic(scope) aspect ratio. Many classical directors changed with the times. John Ford, for example, showed a greater psychological interest in character in films like The Searchers (1956), Sergeant Rutledge (1960) and Two Rode Together (1961). Others, like Charles Chaplin, remained with their feet firmly planted in the past and watched sadly as the world changed around them.

In this article I would like to discuss the only feature Chaplin directed in the Fifties, A King in New York (1957), in terms of the film's treatment of the Fifties and modern America.

A King in New York deals with the adventures of an impoverished, recently-dethroned monarch, King Shahdov (Charles Chaplin) of Estrovia, in New York City. Forced to make television commercials to support himself, the king brings a graceful, quiet dignity to the raucous and deceitful world of advertising. The old king's idealism--he patiently waits for government officials to read his plans for harnessing atomic energy to build a utopia--clashes with the commercial cynicism of those around him, especially with that of his prime minister who absconds with treasury funds at the start of the film and Ann Kay (Dawn Addams) who lures him into television, but he finds a youthful counterpart in the person of Rupert Macabee (Michael Chaplin--Charles' son), an obnoxious but dedicated and impassioned boy whom the king meets at a progressive school. The relationship between the king and the boy, vaguely reminiscent of that in The Kid (1921), results in the king's subpoenaed appearance before the House Un-American Activities Committee (because the boy's schoolteacher-parents admit to having been communists). After proving to the committee the absurdity of their suspicion that he, a king, is a communist, Shahdov, fed up with the emotionally and spiritually bankrupt country to which he fled at the film's beginning, departs for France and, presumably, a saner society.

The film contains obvious autobiographical elements. King Shahdov's political ouster from Estrovia bears similarities to Chaplin's own forced exile from the United States in 1952. [3] At the same time, the king's voluntary departure from the U. S. at the film's conclusion, reflecting a conscious rejection on Chaplin's/Shahdov's part of this country's values, distorts the facts of autobiography into the fantasies of art. Ultimately, the film's autobiographical aspects give way to larger narrative and thematic demands, invalidating the contemporary, short-sighted analyses of the film as Chaplin's retaliation for his poor treatment by the American press and government.

On its release in London and Paris, A King in New York (Chaplin's first British-made film), was considered anti-American by the world press and the American film industry (which refused to distribute it) because of its attacks on contemporary political institutions like HUAC. Chaplin never intended to release the film in the U. S. , though his reasons were more financial than political. He had lost money on M. Verdoux (1947) and Limelight (1952) and his growing unpopularity in this country made him unsure of the American market. Considering the hostility with which the film was received by those few American reviewers who saw it, Chaplin's decision was a sensible one. The film would not have been understood.

Years later, it is possible both to see A King in New York and to understand it in terms of its relationship to Chaplin's other work, something that was extremely difficult for viewers to do at the time.[4] Clearly, the film is both extremely personal and consistent with Chaplin's earlier work. Chaplin's own disappointment with America becomes King Shahdov's disillusionment with its values. At the same time, this disillusionment makes perfect sense in the light of films like Modern Times (1936) and M. Verdoux. Chaplin has always been distrustful of authority, especially authority personified in government (which may explain why he never took out U. S. citizenship). The Great Dictator (1940) is as much anti-government as it is anti-Fascist: Chaplin's emotional speech at the end, combining the demagoguery of Hinkel, the humanism of the Jewish barber, and the actor/director's own messianic utopianism, calls for the supremacy of the individual over the state.

Chaplin, the artist, is hardly the revolutionary or socialist-communist most Americans consider him to be. In fact, he is actually something of a reactionary. A product of Victorian England and its melodramatic, music hall tradition, Chaplin finds himself continually at war with the modern world. The tramp persona, an extension of this sensibility, struggles with society for the necessities of life --for food, shelter, and work. The emotional weight of this character is enhanced by the simplicity of his wants and, indirectly, comments on the inability of the world to satisfy these basic needs. In Modern Times (1936), Charlie's tramp battles industrialization and automation, the necessary evils of a post-Dickensian, Industrial Revolution. At the end of the film, Charlie rejects this modern society and, together with the gamin (Paulette Goddard), walks romantically off into the countryside. Just as Chaplin is more drawn to the pastoral than to the urban society, so he is more attracted to the rich emotional values of the past than to the barren ones of the present.

With the coming of sound--for Chaplin this innovation was characteristically delayed as long as possible (until 1940)--the tramp persona, whose silence was integral to his emotional simplicity, was discarded in favor of more contemporary guises: though the Jewish barber in The Great Dictator (1940) retains many of the tramp trappings, including mustache and cane, Hinkel, although for obvious reasons sporting a mustache, is a total break with former Chaplin characters. M. Verdoux (1947) and Limelight (1952) mark

further evolutions in the Chaplin screen persona. Both Verdoux and Calvero are unique creations: though products of
the modern world, they remain rooted in the past. Verdoux's existence in an alien world becomes meaningless after
the death of his wife and child. Calvero's tragedy is seen
in his gradual eclipse by a younger star, a relationship that
strangely prefigures that between King Shahdov and Rupert in
A King in New York. By the time of A King, all that is
left of the original tramp persona is his dignity, which Chaplin has refined into an exquisite nobility not only of character
but of gesture.

Modern Times, a Capraesque thesis comedy, deals
with the economics of industrialization. Men are put out of
work by machines. Charlie's human emotions are set against
an impersonal machine age. M. Verdoux, a comic film
noir, is less concerned with the cold, economic reality of automation than with a more pervasive spiritual and emotional
barbarism created by the Depression and the post-war society.

The central concern of M. Verdoux is with the hypocrisy of modern morality, a by-product of the Industrial Revolution. Verdoux's murders violate human laws, yet the morality behind those laws is hypocritical, as Verdoux himself
points out during his trial. Verdoux, in a way, is the last
of the great romantics: his actions are justified sentimental-
ly. He does what he does not for himself but for his crippled wife and son. Though he and the audience ultimately
realize the wickedness of his actions, we also cannot quite
forget the emotional vividness of the values which motivated
them. The idyllic scenes between Verdoux and his family
linger in our memory, especially in contrast to the emotionless scenes between him and his vapid victims. Even Verdoux's contempt for the system that executes him is romantic in origin. Near the end of the film, he surrenders himself to what he calls his "destiny," denying, in a way, the
jurisdiction of his peers. Indeed, his last gesture of accepting a glass of rum because he has never tasted rum before
is the act of an inveterate romantic.

A King in New York, like M. Verdoux, continues the
Chaplinesque dialectic between nineteenth-century Victorian
and twentieth-century modern sensibilities, equating the
struggle between the individual and the state with the struggle between Old World and New World values--"Old World"
in both a geographical and a temporal sense.

The narrative of the film, like that in all of Chaplin's work, is episodic. The action consists of a series of bits and gags loosely strung together but thematically coherent. Unlike Keaton, whose comedies subordinate character to action and thereby create a smooth-flowing story line rivalling that of Hawks, Chaplin sacrifices plot to character and develops a very human narrative built on idiosyncratic gesture, facial reaction, and bodily movement. Keaton, a product of the twentieth century, adapts himself through action to the world around him, controlling it through a uniquely American ingenuity and inventiveness. Chaplin, with an Old World inflexibility, continually wages war with the world and, more often than not, loses to it; yet his spirit remains undaunted and the integrity of his character intact. Chaplin's defeat at the hands of larger, modern forces ennobles the character and the values he represents.

Chaplin presents his conflict with modern American society in A King in New York in a variety of ways. Earlier, I spoke of the technical innovations in filmmaking during the Fifties. Each of Chaplin's artistic decisions as director reflects his unwillingness to bend to these new conventions. Not only is A King a studio picture shot in black and white but it is also filmed in an aspect ratio of 1.33 to 1--a ratio which, since 1955 at least, had been superseded by 1.85 to 1 and CinemaScope. [5] To insure that projectionists would show his film in its proper ratio, Chaplin marked the leaders of each print with projection information (as he does with all his old films in their current re-release). Within the film itself, Chaplin satirizes CinemaScope and, during this bit, aims a few barbs at the content of American films in the Fifties. A trailer for a brutal murder mystery is followed by one for a sexual problem film which, in turn, is followed by one for a shoot 'em up western. Violence, sex, and the Western--the three cornerstones of cinema in the Fifties--become crude, vulgar, and ridiculous in Chaplin's hands. The filmmakers (and audiences) of the Fifties, to Chaplin at least, seem to have gone berserk.

Chaplin's acting style and his gags, like his aspect ratio, look back to silent cinema. A good deal of the film's humor is based on pantomime. King Shahdov, upon his arrival at the airport, poses for press photographers, briefly striking an hilarious Napoleonic posture. Later, at a noisy New York restaurant, the king, seated beneath a jazz drummer, tries to order caviar and turtle soup, pantomiming his order to the waiter. The clarity and economy of his ges-

tures--the king turns a plate over the back of his hand and
walks it across the table with his fingers to convey the idea
of "turtle"--reveals an eloquence of expression that has disappeared from the sound film.

Yet Chaplin's gags are not restricted to the visual.
The restaurant scene, for example, works only because the
deafening noise in the background necessitates a series of
charades.   Often sound works as an ironic counterpoint to
images.   At the airport, the king speaks over the radio to
the American people about their country's freedoms as he is
fingerprinted by immigration authorities.   Action speaks
more clearly than words.   Chaplin remains distrustful of
words because they do not communicate feelings as truly as
eyes and hands do.   During his 1972 visit to the U. S. ,
Chaplin said almost nothing; instead, he talked with his
hands.   He waved; he blew kisses; he signaled to his audience that his heart was theirs.

At his hotel room, King Shahdov, excited by the
prospects of a night on the town, warmly cries out, "New
York! New York!"   Chaplin cuts from this romantic exclamation to the cold, ugly city itself.   Low-angle shots of
glass skyscrapers show them looming menacingly over the
occupants of the city.   On the street, the king is surrounded
by crowds and noise.   Chaplin's heart has always yearned
for the road and the pastoral setting as opposed to the city
and the evils of its civilization.   His view of New York confirms his Romantic roots.

The people who inhabit this city share the degeneracy
of its spirit.   The king, lured to a dinner party by a pretty
television advertising expert, Ann Kay, entertains his boor-
ish hostess and her guests with a soliloquy from Hamlet.
Without his knowledge, his antics are being broadcast over
TV.   The hypocritical insanity of this Madison Avenue society is personified in Ann Kay who periodically interrupts her
conversation with the king to read commercials for anti-
perspirants (the king takes a carnation from his buttonhole
and discreetly puts it under his arm) and tooth-paste.   Shahdov's relationship with her, after he later agrees to do commercials to support himself, is moving yet pathetic.   She
obviously has nothing to offer him but her body and remains
insensitive to what he offers her--beauty, feeling, and sentiment.   The body and the spirit were never so tragically
alienated as they are here.

At one point, Ann Kay convinces the king to get a
face lift in order to enhance his appearance for a hormone
commercial. The face lift is an obvious metaphor for the
superficial nature of the values of her society. At the same
time, it also reflects the public's dissatisfaction with Chaplin's image. His new face, however, is rigid and mask-
like: he cannot even smile or laugh with it. A slapstick
comedy routine in a night club fortunately destroys this
emotionless mask. The king's attempts to suppress his
laughs during the routine capture the repressive quality of
the persona society has thrust upon him. His laughter destroys his plastic face and gives a cathartic release to the
human feelings within him.

At the end of the film, the king bids Ann Kay an
emotional farewell while she, career woman to the end,
thinks only of getting back to the station in time for her
television program.

On a visit to a progressive school (another target of
Chaplin's anti-progressive shafts), the king meets Rupert,
a child genius, who harangues him with political philosophy.
Later, the king sees the boy standing in the cold outside
his hotel and takes him in. The king's gesture is sentimental, not political. In fact, he finds the boy rude and
obnoxious. He gives Rupert shelter in spite of his dislike
for the boy; his humanity overrides the personal and political antipathy he feels. As their relationship continues, a
bond grows between the two. Both are lonely outsiders.
The American mainstream of citizens, newsmen, and HUAC
congressmen who persecute people for their political ideas
has no place in it for aging kings or youthful communists.
Their mutual attraction grows out of their recognition of a
shared isolation as a result of their idealism.

At the end, in the film's most moving scene, the king
says good-bye to Rupert at the boy's school. Shahdov's
utopian dreams remain unfulfilled yet uncompromised. He
is leaving the country victorious, though in defeat. Rupert's
spirit, however, has been broken by the state. To save his
parents, Rupert has betrayed their friends, handing their
names over to HUAC. Hope for the future of America,
symbolized by the boy, has been shattered. Clearly, there
is nothing left in this country for the king; his departure
becomes a spiritual and emotional necessity.

The last few shots of the film show the king, seated

in a plane, returning to Europe. The long, aerial shots of
the plane flying over the New York City skyline epitomize
the feelings developed in the film. Like the tramp at the
end of countless earlier Chaplin films, the king, rejecting
the modern world he has fought against, moves off into the
distance, bound for an older, saner and more humane civilization.

A King in New York was not released in this country
until December, 1973. It is, nonetheless, a seminal film
of the Fifties. It depicts aspects of the era that most of us
wish to forget and that few of us feel nostalgic for. At the
same time, it is a very moving and beautiful film for it reaffirms both the classical tradition of filmmaking that, along
with directors like John Ford, is slowly dying out and a system of values that unfortunately endure only in our memory.

NOTES

1. From the vantage point of 1982, this statement does not
   appear entirely accurate. Bazin, of course, associates the breakdown of certain elements of classical
   style, e. g. , editing, with the films of Orson Welles.
   The aesthetics of film noir, surfacing in the mid-
   Forties, constitute a critique of the classical narrative style of the Thirties. This new tradition becomes consolidated in the Fifties.
2. Film Comment (Spring 1971), 58.
3. After the completion of Limelight, Chaplin sailed to Europe and discovered, in mid-voyage, that the State
   Department had refused to allow him to re-enter the
   country. Rupert, in A King in New York, makes
   reference to this in his tirade against passports and
   restriction of travel.
4. Variety (9/18/57) found the film "unfunny" and suggested
   that the film's critics might describe Chaplin as "nib-
   bling at the hand that has prosperously fed him" (p.
   6). But see Jean Domarchi's intelligent critique of
   the film in Cahiers du cinéma, 77:11-17, December,
   1957.
5. The image on 35mm prints is printed full-frame; there
   is no widescreen masking on the print itself, though
   it can be--and has been--masked in projection to
   create a widescreen image. The film was probably
   composed for both the 1.33 and 1.85 formats. The
   titles and the positions of the cue marks, indicate, to
   me, a 1.33 to 1 ratio to be the preferred ratio.

c. The American Comedy of Harold Lloyd

Harold Lloyd titles his co-authored autobiography An American Comedy. If Lloyd sees himself, until 1928, at least, when the autobiography was published, as "American" and his life as "comic," it is perhaps because he finds aspects of national character in himself and shares the success-oriented goals of the country as a whole. "I was average and typical of the time and place," he writes. "Supposing Atlantic City had been holding Average American Boy contests, with beauty waived, I might have been Master America most any year between 1893 and 1910" (pp. 3-4).

Lloyd, always an actor in search of a "mo," takes pains in his autobiography to create for himself, much as he did on the screen, a narrative persona, a familiar character type from literature with whom his readers might identify. Lloyd portrays himself in terms of classic American types: he sees himself as Tom Sawyer, middle class, ornery but respectable, as opposed to the lower class Huckleberry Finn, "the kid from across the tracks whose lawless life Tom envied" (p. 3).

I begin my discussion of Lloyd as an American character type with his autobiography not because it sheds light on the "real" Harold Lloyd, quite to the contrary, the autobiography carefully avoids any revealing personal details. But his autobiography does present a narrative voice which illuminates Lloyd's screen personality. Lloyd's "glass character" is as American, middle class, and respectable as Mark Twain's Tom Sawyer. Much as Lloyd sees his youth as "typical of the time and place," so Lloyd's screen character seeks to be average. As Harold Lamb, for example, in The Freshman. Lloyd presents himself to his new classmates as "a regular fellow" and, to borrow his own image, desires only to "make the team."

At the same time, Lloyd's screen character embodies uniquely American contradictions. He wants to be average,

yet competitively strives to best those around him: to return to his autobiography, he wants to win the Average
American Boy contest. Lloyd is part Tom Sawyer but he
is also part Tom's alter ego, Huck Finn: he is a vicarious
and a real adventurer; he is quixotic in dreaming of success
yet pragmatic in his attempts to attain it. One suspects
that the civilized Lloyd, like Tom, envies the lawless freedom of Huck. As his dual roles in His Royal Slyness
(salesman and prince) and Grandma's Boy (contemporary
coward and Civil War hero) suggest, Lloyd's character ex-
hibits the potential of becoming its opposite.

      As Richard Hofstadter observes in The Age of Re-
form, the native American of the Teens combines a "nation-
alist belligerence" and a "genuine streak of Christian pacifism" (p. 273). Sgt. Alvin York, conscientious objector and
highly decorated war hero, exemplifies the two-sided nature
of the American coin. York's America, like Lloyd's, was
both isolationist and imperialist. America sends missionaries to China and marines to the Caribbean. Obviously,
Lloyd's glass character, a passive milquetoast transformed
into an active dynamo when provoked, has its origins in pre-
World War I American political figures, in the naïve, idealistic pacifism of Woodrow Wilson and in the materialistic
and pragmatic militarism of Theodore Roosevelt. Turn-of-
the-century American intervention in the Caribbean by Mc-
Kinley (Spanish-American War), T. R. (Panama) and Taft
(Nicaragua) was as much an attempt to maintain order as
to insure American hegemony. This double-edged American
foreign policy finds comic expression in Lloyd's Why Worry?
(1923), a film which reveals a characteristically aggressive
American neutrality toward neighbors to the south. Lloyd
plays Harold Van Pelham, a wealthy clubman and hypochon-
driac. With his nurse and a suitcase full of pills, he sails
to the island republic of Paradiso seeking peace and quiet
but stumbling, instead, upon a violent civil war. Lloyd's
American abroad is less ugly than innocent; all he wants for
himself is tranquility, not economic advantage or power (the
goals of his American counterpart, renegade Jim Blake)
and, true to the American spirit of fair play, he fights back
only after he himself has been attacked. Lloyd takes no
sides in the war but does take steps to restore order. With
the aid of a large, grateful friend (played by giant Johan
Aasen), he subdues the warring factions within the town,
repels an invading army and cures himself of hypochondria.
Lloyd's character reflects the paradoxical nature of American diplomacy abroad: he is both a pacifist and a policeman;
he is part Wilson, part Roosevelt.

The screen characters of Charlie Chaplin and Buster
Keaton, Lloyd's greatest comic contemporaries, observe an
Aristotelian unity: their characters are single, coherent,
and consistent. Lloyd's character, on the other hand, reflects a dual personality; it is a disjunctive combination of
opposite qualities. All of his films contain turning points
at which his character reverses itself: the coward in
Grandma's Boy becomes brave, the weakling in Why Worry?
becomes strong, the idealist in The Cat's Paw becomes a
pragmatist, the failure in Mad Wednesday becomes a success. Of course in Sherlock Jr. Keaton creates an alter
ego for himself, becoming the world's greatest detective in
his dreams. But his alter ego remains a dream. Even
Chaplin, in The Circus, daydreams for a moment, imagining
the defeat of his rival, Rex, King of the Air. Similarly,
in Girl Shy, Lloyd, a girl-shy stutterer, becomes a modern-
day Don Juan. The dream sequence in Girl Shy, however,
is something of an exception for Lloyd. Where Keaton and
Chaplin fantasize their opposites, working out their repressions through dreams, Lloyd generally becomes his opposite
and literally lives out his repressions in the real world.
At the end of Girl Shy, he becomes a confident man of action, races to prevent the marriage of the girl he loves to
another, and actually carries her off.

Most of Lloyd's films, with the notable exception of
The Milky Way, (which suggests that Lloyd has somehow lost
something valuable in his transformation from meek milkman
to flamboyant fighter) treat his change from caterpillar to
butterfly as a positive and necessary evolution in character.
If Lloyd's dual personality reflects the deep contradictions
in the character of the American people, his transformation
from passive to active, from failure to success, mirrors
the only resolution of those contradictions possible in success-oriented American society. Lloyd's inevitable realization of his potential for success dramatizes traditional middle class myths about the nature of the American economic
order and perhaps explains the actor's popularity with the
middle class. As Hofstadter describes it,

> The economic order [is] not quite so much ... a
> system organized for the production and distribu-
> tion of goods as a system intended to stimulate
> and reward certain traits of personal character.
> The public to which Wilson appealed had been
> brought up on the nineteenth-century ideal of op-
> portunity and the notion that success was a reward

for energy, efficiency, frugality, perseverance,
ambition and insight. In their thinking, people
competed--or ought to compete--in the exercise
of these qualities, and success ought properly to
go to those who had the most of them. The metaphor they most often and most significantly used
in describing their economic ideal was that of a
race--"the race of life," as it was commonly
called (pp. 224-225).

Lloyd's attainment of success in his films can be
seen as a reward for praiseworthy character traits; his
success comes as a reward for energy in Sailor-Made Man,
for common sense in Dr. Jack, for ambition in Safety Last,
for spirit in The Freshman and for perseverance in Speedy,
Movie Crazy and Mad Wednesday. Yet his positive traits
exist side by side with negative ones: he is physically weak
(in all his films); he stutters (Girl Shy); he is rich, ne'er-
do-well, and overly confident (A Sailor-Made Man, Why
Worry? and For Heaven's Sake); he is unassertive (Grandma's Boy, Girl Shy and Hot Water); he lacks ambition (Dr.
Jack, Speedy) and has too much of it (Safety Last, The
Freshman, Feet First); he is vain (Movie Crazy, The Milky
Way).

Occasionally Lloyd's success involves competition with
a rival or the defeat of villains. But most frequently he
succeeds by triumphing over his own weaknesses--an inter-
nalization of dramatic conflict rarely, if ever, seen in Chaplin's or Keaton's films. He succeeds in spite of his own
shortcomings; Lloyd's imperfections make him all the more
sympathetic as a middle-class hero.

"The race of life" is an apt phrase for Lloyd's pursuit of success: races and chases provide the climaxes to
many of his films (as they have to many post-Sennett comedies). His chases are uniquely success-oriented; they come
as a trial or test of the character's new-found strengths;
they become events which enable Lloyd to prove himself
worthy of the success which follows. Lloyd rescues the girl
from the Rajah's palace in A Sailor-Made Man; he catches
the tramp in Grandma's Boy and, reversing the film's opening image of him as a child, wheels the criminal back in a
baby carriage; Lloyd even chases himself, pursuing his insane alter ego in Dr. Jack; he races to the goal line and
wins the game for Tate in The Freshman; he dashes to his
own wedding with a streetcar load of drunks in For Heaven's

Sake and in The Kid Brother races back to Hickoryville with
the real criminal, arriving just in time to prevent the lynch-
ing of his father; and Lloyd, the "Speedy" of the title, races
against time and thugs hired to stop him to save a streetcar franchise in Speedy. His scaling of the De Vore Department store in Safety Last is even presented as a race: he
climbs to successively higher and higher floors in an attempt
to catch up and exchange places with a professional stunt
climber who, in turn, is being chased by a policeman.

Safety Last (1923) appears to be the archetypal Lloyd
success story, yet, in a way atypical of his films, it ques-
tions--if only momentarily--the goals which Lloyd's character has set for himself. The picture begins in the train
station of Lloyd's small hometown as he sets out for the
big city, intent on becoming a success. As he bids farewell to his girl, promising to send for and marry her once
he has become a success, we sense that the character has
fallen into a kind of trap. It is not that he would like to be
successful--he must be. The first shot of the film, a familiar gag from Keaton's Cops (1922), frames Lloyd behind
bars, a hangman's noose grimly prominent in the background. What seems to be the condemned man bidding farewell to the world is revealed, in a reverse-angle cut, to
be Harold at the station, departing for the city, fame and
fortune.

The sight gag sets an odd tone for a conventional
scene. In Cops, Keaton's initial gag, which dooms the
hero's subsequent quest for success, returns at the film's
conclusion. After eluding police for the greater part of the
film, Keaton appeals to his girl. She rejects him and
Keaton gives himself up, voluntarily placing himself behind
bars. Lloyd's visual entrapment at the beginning of Safety
Last evolves, later in the film, into a compulsory role
playing: he is trapped into pretense. Really only a clerk,
he pretends to his girl in his letters that he is a success.
When she visits him at the store, he pretends to be the
manager. Lloyd's success drive is a product of his fears.
He fears his girl will discover he is a failure; her presence
forces him to be successful. Earlier in the film he fears
he will be late for work; he pretends to be an accident victim and is rushed to work in an ambulance. In both cases
he is finally successful, but his success has its origins in
fear.

Lloyd's entrapment in the upward spiral toward success finds a brilliant visual metaphor in the final sequence.

He grabs at a chance for a bonus and offers to stage a publicity stunt for his store.   As Frederick Lewis Allen reports
in Only Yesterday, America in the Twenties was obsessed
with fads and stunts--non-stop airplane flights, marathon
dancing, and flagpole sitting (pp. 185-186).   Lloyd, in Never
Weaken and Safety Last (and later in Feet First and Mad
Wednesday) became the Lindbergh of building climbers, Hollywood's Human Fly.   Like the glasses, skyscraper stunts
became part of Lloyd's comic "costume."   If the skyscraper
was peculiarly American, then Lloyd's use of it as his ladder to the top--both for his screen character in his films
and for himself in the film industry--marks an original insight into the relationship between American architecture and
the society's capitalistic goals.

In Safety Last, because his stunt climber is wanted
by the police,   Lloyd is forced to climb the building himself.
He must pay for his ambition and prove his worthiness for
success.   Each floor presents him with a different challenge
or test; he struggles with pigeons, with a net, with a dog,
with a mouse, with a flagpole, with a clock spring and with
a weather vane.   But Lloyd does make it to the top and,
quite significantly, he finds his girl waiting for him there.

Though Lloyd makes it, the suspense and anxiety of
the climb are not easily forgotten.   He surely is not critical
of the goals his character strives to reach, but his choice
of comic metaphors for the means to these goals, the frenetic race or chase, the nerve-racking ascent of the face of a
building, conveys the nightmarish realities behind the middle-
class daydreams of success.

Though Lloyd occasionally plays wealthy, upper class
characters (A Sailor-Made Man, Why Worry? and For Heav-
en's Sake), he is essentially middle class.   His class identification emerges quite distinctly when he is compared with
Chaplin and Keaton.   Chaplin, true to his origins, plays
lower class characters (though his characters often aspire
to nobility).   An immigrant himself, he communicates
through universally understood pantomime to all audiences
but especially to those whose new world experiences and
old world values he shares: the immigrants.   Keaton, born
in a trunk and reared in a largely democratic vaudeville
community, has the classlessness of the adventurous American frontiersman: adaptable, inventive, and self-reliant,
Keaton relies for his sense of self on no larger group and
stands apart from ethnic or class identification, unique in
terms of his needs and goals.

Unlike Keaton's rugged individualist, Chaplin's tramp persona is characterized by basic needs, his need for food, shelter, and a job. The tramp is generally hungry, homeless, and unemployed. Keaton's needs are less physical than metaphysical: he seeks only to be in tune with the world around him.

Lloyd is middle class not merely because he regularly plays salaried, white collar workers (a clerk in Girl Shy, a dry goods salesman in Safety Last, a shoe salesman in Feet First and an office worker in Hot Water and Mad Wednesday), but also because his needs are dictated by his contemporaries. He does not struggle to survive, as Chaplin does; he struggles to succeed, to win the approval of his peers. Lloyd is an example of what David Riesman designates in The Lonely Crowd as "the 'new' middle class," a bureaucrat, a salaried employee in business, a consumer (rather than a producer). In terms of Riesman's categories of typical American character types, Lloyd is an "other-directed" individual. He is guided neither by tradition nor by inner instinct; he does what his peers expect him to do. As Riesman explains, "the goals toward which the other-directed person strives shift with (his) guidance; it is only the process of striving itself and the process of paying close attention to the signals from others that remain unaltered throughout life" (p. 37). Seeking the approval of others, Lloyd strives to be a "regular fellow," to be popular. The process of striving is the greatest constant in his character from film to film.

A tradition-directed individual adopts the goals of his parents or ancestors (e.g., characters in John Ford films); an inner-directed individual sets his own goals (e.g., characters in a Howard Hawks film); Lloyd, as an other-directed individual, shares the goals of his contemporaries. All these character types conform but are motivated to conform by different factors: the tradition directed person conforms out of fear of being shamed; he is controlled by his fear of not reaching traditional goals. The inner-directed conforms out of feelings of guilt; he is controlled by fear of not reaching goals he set for himself. The other-directed conforms out of anxiety; he fears that he will not live up to what society as a whole expects of him.

Lloyd's other-directedness and sense of general anxiety can be clearly seen in his Harold Lamb character in The Freshman. In seeking to be popular at college, he selects as his model collegian first a character in a college

film whose jig-handshake he copies and then Tate College
BMOC, Chet Trask, whom he emulates by going out for the
football team of which Trask is captain, and by sponsoring,
as "Speedy the Spender," the "Fall Frolic," a college dance
sponsored the previous year by Trask. Lloyd tacks Trask's
picture on his wall; the fate of his own picture, first placed
below, then alongside, then above Trask's, marks his changing status in college society. When he discovers that he is
really the "college boob," his picture falls off the wall and
into a nearby wastebasket.

Lloyd's anxiety reaches fever pitch at his "Fall Frolic." Wearing a loosely-basted suit, he is in constant fear
that he will come undone, which he eventually does. Lloyd's
self-confidence is as "loosely-basted" as his suit. His anxiety during the dance derives from a fear of public humiliation; he is obviously uneasy about what others think of him.

Even after he realizes that the whole college has been
laughing at him, he continues to seek the approval of his
classmates. His girl sensibly tells him not to pretend to
be more than he is; she advises him to be himself. Lloyd
responds to this sound counsel by vowing to "show them" in
the big game the next day. Though he does become the college hero he has dreamed of being by winning the game, he
clearly cannot "be himself" because his sense of self is
determined by others. His most joyful exclamation in the
entire film is: "I MADE THE TEAM!"

Lloyd's autobiography ends in 1928. Its innocently
optimistic tone is typical of the time and place, Twenties'
America. The stock market crash in 1929 and the social,
economic, and political upheaval which followed gave Lloyd's
American comedy a bittersweet edge. The characters he
plays in sound films seem older and more experienced, due
in part, no doubt, to the slow deliberation of his screen
voice. Though still on the make, the Lloyd character lacks
the energy he had in the silents. There is a thoughtfulness
in his sound film performances that wasn't there earlier--
perhaps the result of working from fixed scripts instead of
improvising.

In Feet First (1930), Lloyd's shoe clerk seems pa-
thetically desperate in his attempts to reach his goals; he
even takes a correspondence course in "how to become a
success" and boorishly discourses on the history of leather
to a shoe magnate. At the same time, Lloyd's human fly

routine is more nightmarish than ever. His success is
more the product of accident than of his own initiative.
His scaling of the building here, unlike that in Safety Last,
is unrelated to the attainment of his goals. It is seen less
as a test than as a metaphor of the times. Lloyd, a victim
of forces beyond his control, exits the security of a womb-
like mail bag and enters a chaotic world of danger and fear
in which his survival is seen less as a reward for his
strength than as a bit of dumb luck.

        Lloyd's films generally avoid grappling with the cru-
cial social issues of the day. The Red scare of the early
Twenties; the rise of the Ku Klux Klan, anti-Catholicism
and racism; and Fundamentalism rarely, if ever, find their
way into his films. (However, the prints I saw had been
edited for offensive ethnic and racial material.) Even Pro-
hibition, the greatest issue of the Twenties, plays a minor
role in Lloyd's films; perhaps it is more significant in its
absence than in its presence. In Hot Water, his mother-in-
law lectures on temperance at dinner, creating an anxious
moment for Harold, who has just taken a few drinks gener-
ously offered by a neighbor to give him enough courage to
face his mother-in-law, who is identified in the titles as a
"woman with the heart of a traffic cop. " Reformers crop
up again in For Heaven's Sake, set in a Salvation Army-type
mission on Skid Row. Lloyd lures the local toughs into the
mission, but he is clearly more interested in the minister's
daughter than in reform. Later, he struggles with a group
of friendly but drunk converts as he rushes to get to his own
wedding. Lloyd's comedy never takes sides or reaches the
level of social satire: reformers and drunks are indistin-
guishable to him.

        The one great exception to Lloyd's avoidance of poli-
tical issues is The Cat's Paw. Made in 1934 and based on
a story by Saturday Evening Post writer Clarence Buddington
Kelland, The Cat's Paw seems to be a comic reworking of
recent history, of Franklin Roosevelt's first year in office
and of his creation of the National Recovery Administration,
which sponsored drastic reforms in order to stimulate the
nation's recovery. Lloyd plays Ezekiel Cobb, the son of
a missionary reared in China on the philosophic insights of
the legendary Ling Po. Cobb journeys to America, intent
on finding himself a wife and returning to China to perpetuate his father's mission.

        The reform candidate for mayor in the city of Stock-
bridge--a clergyman whose house Lloyd visits--dies on the

eve of the election. Lloyd, a missionary and thus an ideal
reform candidate, is chosen to take the clergyman's place
on the ticket. Lloyd's backers really expect him to lose:
he is the cat's paw of the title, being used by the corrupt
mayor to insure the latter's own reelection. Lloyd, however, upsets his opponent, wins the election and, discovering the corruption of his predecessor, begins a clean-up
campaign. In effect, he becomes a Chinese missionary in
America, applying Ling Po's philosophy in his attempts to
reform a graft-ridden political system. Lloyd is eventually
framed by his enemies and forced to resign, but before he
does, he makes one final effort to clean up the city. He
orders his police chief to arrest all known criminals and to
imprison them in the cellar of his friend, Tien Wang, in
Chinatown. His actions are clearly illegal: he arrests
gangsters without evidence or warrants; he denies them the
right of counsel, phone calls, and bail. All Lloyd offers
the criminals is an opportunity to confess their crimes, and
when they refuse, he begins to execute them one by one,
using the sword of Fu Wong, a legendary Chinese hero who
once beheaded all the outlaws in a small village. Lloyd's
executions, though really only a magic show, work. He
extorts confessions from every one he has arrested and
clears himself. He decides that, rather than returning to
China as his fiancée Pet suggests, he will remain in the
United States, continuing his missionary work.

Lloyd's suspension of the Bill of Rights and his drastic purging of the city of its less desirable elements suggests
that the only way of dealing with outlaws is to go outside the
law. Lloyd's benevolent dictatorship is a dictatorship nonetheless. What difference is there between him and Huey
Long? However, the film asks no such questions, nor does
it linger over the illegality of Lloyd's actions. If anything,
it accepts them as necessary.

Lloyd's last day in office is not remarkably unlike
FDR's first hundred days in the Presidency. Roosevelt had
pushed an Emergency Banking Act through Congress, cut
federal salaries and veterans' benefits, legalized beer, pro-
posed paying farmers to produce less, set up the Civilian
Conservation Corps and the Public Works Administration.
Roosevelt's biggest step, however, was the creation of the
National Recovery Administration, which placed codes of
fair competition on industry and gave to government controls
on industry and business. But in 1935, the NRA was ruled
unconstitutional by the Supreme Court, much as Lloyd's

illegally obtained confessions would surely have been thrown
out of court.

Lloyd's quasi-fascistic character is not unusual in
films of the period. The President (Walter Huston) in
Gregory La Cava's Gabriel Over the White House (1933) assumes dictatorial powers, uses national police to arrest
criminals, arranges for them to be tried and finally for
them to be shot by firing squads. Lloyd's actions are modest compared to those of other New Deal leaders in film.

Lloyd's attempt to provide a model for Cobb's behavior in the figure of Fu Wong suggests that the extremity
of Cobb's actions derives in part from their Oriental origin.
In fact, Lloyd makes use in The Cat's Paw of racial fears
to achieve his objectives. The gangsters--and even Lloyd's
supporters--fear that he, though a white man, is capable of
Chinese barbarism. Lloyd exploits the stereotype of the
"inscrutable" Oriental, using Chinatown as a setting for his
phony executions, recounting exotic legends, using elaborate
far-Eastern ceremony, speaking Chinese in order to make
his bluff more effective.

If The Cat's Paw is Lloyd's essay on FDR's New
Deal, its tone is non-didactic and its politics are noncom-
mittal. Lloyd's Cobb is a cross between Plato's Philosopher King and Nietzsche's Übermensch. Though his dictatorship is benevolent, aimed at the highest possible good, it is
rather undemocratic, motivated by a sense of moral superiority: Lloyd's innocence justifies, as far as he is concerned, his quite necessary ruthlessness.

Lloyd's purge of the local criminal elements is in
part designed to clear his own name, to gather evidence to
prove that he has been framed. But his actions are less
selfish than selfless: he originally intends to sacrifice himself and his political career for the common good of the
city. Ironically, he achieves just the opposite: his unconstitutional methods get results that win the approval of the
press and the populace, further building his reputation as
an incorruptible reformer. Though Lloyd makes his familiar
transformation, here from cat's paw (used by others) to dictator (using others), he makes that transformation not for his
own advancement but for that of others.

The seriousness of The Cat's Paw reflects a change
in Lloyd's concerns. In Hot Water and, to some extent, in

For Heaven's Sake, Lloyd laughs at reformers, at Prohibi-
tionists, and at Skid Row missionaries. The hard economic
realities of the early thirties seem to have awakened Lloyd,
if only momentarily, to the serious need for political reform. Once aware of this need, he tries to satisfy it with
characteristic energy and determination, occasionally step-
ping outside the law to achieve his goals. If the American
comedy, because of hard times, has become a bit less funny, so has Lloyd; but neither has given in to despair.

Preston Sturges, in his film study of Lloyd's screen
character (Mad Wednesday), observes a similar transformation from the Twenties, when Lloyd is a young, optimistic
man-on-the-make, to the Thirties, when he is an older man,
a dull bureaucrat, more serious and less interested in success. Lloyd still participates in the middle class American
success myth, but both Lloyd and the myth have lost their
ideals. No longer are industry, energy, and ingenuity necessarily rewarded. Lloyd and his success myth have fallen
victim to experience. Though not quite as cynical as
Sturges, Lloyd sees that chance also governs success. Just
as Lloyd spends the greater part of Mad Wednesday in an
attempt to discover what happened on the Wednesday he cannot remember, so his later films present him trying to re-
capture, relive--or at least understand--the American dream
that guided him to success in his earlier films.

BIBLIOGRAPHY

Frederick Lewis Allen, Only Yesterday: An Informal His-
        tory of the 1920's, (NY: Harper & Row, 1964).
Andrew Bergman, We're in the Money: Depression America
        and Its Films, (NY: Harper & Row, 1971).
Roger Butterfield, The American Past, (NY: Simon and
        Schuster, 1947).
Richard Hofstadter, The Age of Reform, (NY: Vintage
        Books, 1955).
Harold Lloyd (with Wesley W. Stout), An American Comedy,
        (NY: Dover Publications, 1971).
David Riesman, Nathan Glazer and Reuel Denney, The Lone-
        ly Crowd, (NY: Doubleday Anchor, 1953).
Richard Schickel, Harold Lloyd: The Shape of Laughter,
        (Boston: New York Graphic Society, 1974).

d. Teresa Wright in the Forties

In an era dominated by the wholesome sexuality of the pin-up, Teresa Wright is something of an anomaly. Betty Grable's power at the box office in the Forties reflects the changing values of American audiences which, having over-dosed on the innocent antics of Shirley Temple in the Thir-ties, sought cover girl glamour and middle class, leggy al-lure in the Forties. Unapproachable and enigmatic screen goddesses such as Garbo and Dietrich seem to sense the changes in the air and shed their aristocratic mystique for a more democratic "ordinariness," if such a word can be applied to their image-breaking roles in Ninotchka and Two-Faced Woman (Garbo) and Destry Rides Again (Dietrich).

Grable, Rita Hayworth and Lana Turner give the girl-next-door an untarnished sexuality that suggests neither the perversity of Dietrich or Mae West in the pre-code Thirties nor the supervirginity of Doris Day in the Fifties and Sixties. Teresa Wright combines the adolescent charm of Judy Garland and Deanna Durbin with the intelligence and wit of Katharine Hepburn, providing Forties' audiences with an alternative to the impersonal cheesecake of the pin-up. No cover girl, Wright rarely wears make-up on screen. Her coloring is more suited to the realities of black and white than to the gaudy tonalities of Technicolor. Her face is a face, not a mask. Her concern is with inner charac-ter rather than with superficial appearance.

Wright is the antithesis of Grable, Hayworth, and Turner in that she cannot be viewed as a social phenomenon or as a mass-marketable screen personality. She is, in short, an actress not a movie star. In a period in which every Hollywood starlet wanted to be Veronica Lake, Wright idolized Helen Hayes. An indication of her seriousness as an actress can be seen in her avoidance of the usual kind of publicity designed to sell a "star" to the public. In an attempt to preserve the dignity of her profession as actress, Wright had the following clause written into her contract with Samuel Goldwyn:

The aforementioned Teresa Wright shall not be
required to pose for photographs in a bathing suit
unless she is in the water. Neither may she be
photographed running on the beach with her hair
flying in the wind. Nor may she pose in any of
the following situations: In shorts, playing with
a cocker spaniel; digging in a garden; whipping up
a meal; attired in firecrackers and holding sky-
rockets for the Fourth of July; looking insinuating-
ly at a turkey for Thanksgiving; wearing a bunny
cap with long ears for Easter; twinkling on prop
snow in a skiing outfit while a fan blows her scarf;
assuming an athletic stance while pretending to hit
something with a bow and arrow....

Her interest, clearly, lies in parts not in publicity or pro-
motion. In fact, her tenure with Goldwyn came to an end
over an issue of artistic integrity: arguing she was an actress and not a publicist, Wright refused to do a full-scale
promotional tour for her latest Goldwyn picture, Enchant-
ment (1948). Years later, in another gesture of selfless
devotion to her craft, Wright took a cut in salary from
$100,000 to $20,000 per picture to appear in The Men, an
ambitious Zinnemann project which, like Wyler's The Best
Years of Our Lives, deals with the readjustment of wounded
servicemen to civilian life and which provides Wright with a
demanding role as the sympathetic fiancée of a paraplegic
veteran (played by Marlon Brando).

Her merits as an actress did not escape the notice
of her colleagues in Hollywood who nominated her for Academy Awards as Best Supporting Actress in her first screen
role as Alexandra Giddens in The Little Foxes (1941) and,
the very next year, as Best Actress for her characterization
of Mrs. Lou Gehrig in Pride of the Yankees (1942). Also
nominated in another category that year as Best Supporting
Actress, Wright won an Oscar for her role as Vin Miniver's
aristocratic wife Carol, who is unexpectedly killed in an air
raid, in Wyler's Mrs. Miniver (1942).

Born in New York City in 1918, Wright grew up and
went to school in Maplewood, New Jersey, where a teacher,
impressed by her acting ability, got her a scholarship to
train in summer stock at the Wharf Theatre in Provincetown, Massachusetts. Later, a friend from Provincetown
who was in the cast of Our Town, encouraged Wright to read
for the part of Dorothy McGuire's understudy. She got the

part and toured with the company, eventually taking over the role herself.   After another season in stock, she read for and won the part of Mary Skinner, the ingenue in Life with Father, where she attracted the attention of Lillian Hellman who suggested her to Sam Goldwyn for the role of Alexandra in the film version of The Little Foxes.

Married to writer Niven (Duel in the Sun) Busch in 1942, Wright starred in a number of her husband's pictures after leaving Goldwyn, most notably in Pursued (1947) and The Capture (1950).   Divorced from Busch in 1952, Wright married playwright Robert Anderson in 1959, subsequently playing in Broadway productions of his Tea and Sympathy (1965) and I Never Sang for My Father (1968).   They separated in 1975.

Wright is best known for her roles as ideal daughters (in The Little Foxes, Shadow of a Doubt, The Best Years of Our Lives) or young wives or daughters-in-law (in The Pride of the Yankees, Mrs. Miniver, The Men) whose strength, loyalty, and courage serve as a model for the behavior of other characters.   Wright's stalwart devotion to her sick father (Herbert Marshall) in Little Foxes functions as a foil to display the greed and treachery of her mother, Regina (Bette Davis), and of her other relatives.

Playing opposite emotionally or psychologically disturbed older characters in Little Foxes, Pride of the Yankees (in which Lou Gehrig's mother verges on the neurotic), Shadow of a Doubt (in which her psychotic Uncle Charlie [Joseph Cotten], the "Merry Widow" murderer, almost kills her) and Pursued (in which she helps cure her foster-brother-and-husband of amnesia), Wright's emotional and psychological stability provides a background of moral certainty and strength against which the complex psychodramas of the adult world are played out.

Other actresses who played adolescents in the period lack Wright's strong familial loyalties and self-sacrificial nature.   There is a romantic self-containment and self-contentment to Joan Fontaine in Rebecca, Suspicion and Letter From an Unknown Woman which belies any need for or responsibility to others.   Similarly, David O. Selznick's Jennifer Jones, whether the idealistic novice in Song of Bernadette, the hallucinatory girl who inspires A Portrait of Jenny, the adolescent in Since You Went Away who transfers a crush on her uncle to a lonely soldier (Robert Walk-

er) or the passionate Pearl in Duel in the Sun, demonstrates
more concern with her own feelings than with those of others.

Wright, on the other hand, conveys loyalty, responsibility, and self-sacrifice in her performances. She becomes
the force which holds her family together in Shadow of a
Doubt and The Best Years of Our Lives; she is the girl-
woman who selflessly inspires the sick or disillusioned in
Pride of the Yankees, Best Years and The Men.

Her most interesting performances are built around a
rite of passage from adolescence to adulthood. It is impossible to forget her defiance of her tyrannical mother in Little
Foxes or her triumphant departure which concludes that film.
In Shadow of a Doubt, Hitchcock traces Wright's transformation from a moodily romantic teenager into a guilt-ridden,
disillusioned young woman. Her growth is measured in
terms of innocence lost and knowledge (of evil) gained.
Her Picasso-like face reflects the dilemma of a character
suspended between youthful idealism and middle-aged cynicism, between loyalties to family and to society, between
the illusions of childhood and the realities of adulthood.

William Wyler, who directed Wright in Little Foxes,
Mrs. Miniver and Best Years, sees in her perseverance a
kind of patriotic spirit, unclouded by doubt or hesitation.
In Best Years, Wright, as Peggy Stephenson (Frederic
March's daughter), accommodates March's eccentricities and
Fred's (Dana Andrew's) post-war anxieties, providing them
both with something to fight for. As Wyler himself points
out, the Wright character is

> knowing, aware of the larger world about her, in-
> terested in problems beyond her own. ... It is she
> who understands that the conflict in Fred Derry
> (Andrews) is the conflict between the old way of
> life in America, and a newer, healthier way of
> life born out of the experience and sacrifice of the
> people who fought the war.

Wright's values synthesize those of old and new America,
enabling others to make the transition from the past to the
future.

In Pursued, Wright fluctuates between a loyal, understanding fiancée and a treacherous, embittered wife, turning

in a tremendously complex performance.   The film explores
the psychological make-up of a family in a way that no previous Wright film does.   Director Raoul Walsh and screenwriter Busch acknowledge the guilty consequences of a quasi-
incestuous love between Wright and her step-brother, Jeb
Rand (Robert Mitchum).   Torn between love and hate for
Rand, who has killed her jealous brother in self-defense,
Wright marries him, plots to kill him on their wedding
night, but, realizing the depth of her feeling for him, is
unable to carry out her plans.   Combining the qualities of
both sister and wife, Wright contributes a multi-faceted
characterization in Pursued which reveals the range and
depth of her acting abilities.

Adapting herself to more mature roles, Wright ex-
cels in the part of Jean Simmons' mother in George Cukor's
The Actress, as Annie Sullivan in John Frankenheimer's
memorable TV production of The Miracle Worker and as
the tragic Margaret Bourke-White in the TV drama of the
same name.   More recently appearing on Broadway in a
revival of Paul Osborn's 1939 play, Morning's at Seven,
Teresa Wright embodies the quintessential virtues and faults
of the small town America celebrated by Thornton Wilder in
Our Town, her first professional production.

Teresa Wright's career remains intertwined with
Forties notions of innocence and involvement, with loyalty,
courage, self-sacrifice, and strength.   As Wyler notes
about Peggy in Best Years, Wright symbolizes a certain
transformation in American character from the isolationist
innocence of the Thirties to the involved experience and
commitment of the Forties.   Teresa Wright characterizes
the fascinating contradictions of America's own rite of passage from childhood to adulthood.

e. James Stewart

Though James Stewart's emergence as a popular screen star
in the late Thirties and early Forties reflects what Edgar
Morin refers to as the "embourgeoisement," i. e., the de-
divinization, of the medium and represents a certain tendency towards the naturalization of performance styles which
characterizes classical Hollywood acting styles of the period,
Stewart's screen personality is in no way monolithic; it is
built, instead, around a labyrinth of contradictions. As
David Thompson points out in A Biographical Dictionary of
the Film, Stewart's best roles consistently play against his
popular image as the good-natured, charmingly awkward boy
next door who lives with his mother (often Beulah Bondi) or,
when away from home, writes her regularly, falls in love
with and marries the girl next door (often June Allyson),
has a couple of children and lives happily ever after.

Stewart is not that easy to type. His roles alternate
between idealistic, Jeffersonian, agrarian reformers (Mr.
Smith Goes to Washington, 1939) and bitter, disillusioned
cynics (It's a Wonderful Life, 1946); between a member of
a family (The Man Who Knew Too Much, 1956, and Mr.
Hobbs Takes a Vacation, 1962) or groups (The Stratton
Story, 1949; The Glenn Miller Story, 1954; and Strategic
Air Command, 1955) and lonely outsiders (the Anthony Mann
westerns); between courageous contemporary Americans
(Monty Stratton, Glenn Miller, and Charles Lindbergh) and
neurotic voyeurs (the crippled photographer in Rear Window,
1954, and the dizzy ex-detective in Vertigo, 1958); between
comically corrupt, mercenary marshalls (Two Rode Together, 1961, and Cheyenne Autumn, 1964) and earnest, young
crusading lawyers (The Man Who Shot Liberty Valance,
1962).

Stewart's screen character remains independent of
studio, genre, and director--factors whose personalities tend
to shape the persona of an actor with whom they are associated. Though under contract to M-G-M before the war,

Stewart never really fit the studio's image of him, even in
masterpieces like The Shop Around the Corner (Lubitsch,
1940) and The Mortal Storm (Borzage, 1940). I Uprooted
from the context of American landscape and culture through
which his character defines itself, Stewart is ultimately out
of place in the European settings of these films, though
Lubitsch successfully explores the bourgeois ordinariness
which informs much of the actor's image and though the
character's fervent anti-fascist idealism in the Borzage film
acknowledges an aspect of his persona which Capra earlier
uncovers. As a tabloid reporter in The Philadelphia Story
(Cukor, 1940), a role which won him an Oscar, Stewart reveals a fascination for imaginative experience and an ability
to infuse the jaundiced cynicism of the hard-boiled journalist
with a sappy, starry-eyed romanticism, giving the kind of
dialectical depth to his part that characterizes his greatest
performances. But as a middle-class intruder into playwright Philip Barry's Mainline Philadelphia social circle,
Stewart evokes none of the anguished self-doubt or discomfort that he does, similarly out of place, as a novice junior
Senator in Capra's Mr. Smith.

    Unlike Cagney's or Bogart's, Stewart's persona never
becomes associated with a single studio. It also crosses
genre lines, ranging from romantic melodramas (The Shop-
worn Angel, Made for Each Other) to comedies (the Capra
films, No Time for Comedy, Harvey, Bell, Book and Candle) to biographies (The Stratton Story, The Glenn Miller
Story, The Spirit of St. Louis) to suspense thrillers (the
Hitchcock films) and to westerns (especially the Mann, Ford
and McLaglen films). Even Stewart's westerns--with the
notable exception of the Mann films--mix genres and, like
Destry Rides Again, are as much comedies as westerns.
Ford, especially, exploits Stewart's abilities as a comic
misanthrope in Two Rode Together and Cheyenne Autumn,
indulging Stewart's gift for sarcasm and self-irony in elaborate, long-take set pieces that have an uncharacteristic--for
Ford--improvisational quality. Seated on a river bank
alongside Richard Widmark's cavalry Lt. Jim Gary, Stewart
rambles on about his relationship with the volatile Belle
Aragon and her business-like proposal of marriage in which
she offered to raise his percentage of her saloon's profits
from ten to fifty per cent. And later, his drunken imitation
of Greely Cleg's backwoods pronunciation of "firewood" as
Gary prepares to fight the Clegg brothers over Shirley Jones'
Marty Purcell reveals a similarly remarkable playfulness in
the character Stewart plays in Two Rode Together. Stewart's

comic exchanges with Thelma Ritter (he compares her advice to that found in the Reader's Digest), Grace Kelly (after she calls his description of a diet of fishheads and rice "deliberately repulsive," he replies, "Deliberately repulsive! I'm just trying to make it sound good."), and Wendell Corey ("what do you need before you can get a search warrant-- bloody footsteps leading up to the door?") in Rear Window and with Barbara Bel Geddes in Vertigo figure importantly in his performances for Hitchcock. By the same token, his loss of his sense of humor later in Vertigo, when he is unable to laugh at Midge's self-portrait as Carlotta, functions as an indication of the obsessive nature of his neurotic involvement with Kim Novak's Madeleine.

Just as Stewart cannot easily be typed as a romantic lead, wry comedian, or folksy western hero, so does his persona elude association with the personal vision of any single director (unlike Dietrich's with Sternberg, or Hepburn's with Cukor). Stewart's major work comes in response to four very different directors: Frank Capra, Anthony Mann, Alfred Hitchcock, and John Ford. Each uses Stewart differently, but they all have one thing in common: they recognize that his persona is a complex of paradoxes and contradictions.

Capra's Mr. Smith actually seems to discover Stewart's roundness--to borrow E. M. Forster's description of a character type from Aspects of the Novel--during the course of its narration. Capra introduces Stewart as a flat stereotype. At a banquet celebrating his nomination to the Senate, we see him, deeply placed within the shot, slumped in his chair near the rostrum. He fidgets nervously with his hands and hesitates when he speaks, a hesitation echoed, moments later, by the Boy Ranger who presents Stewart with a briefcase. Yet his stumbling manner guarantees his sincerity-- he speaks from his heart about his father and about his respect for Sen. Paine and the Senate. Stewart is a grown up child--a man who, shortly after his arrival at the nation's capitol, demonstrates bird calls to members of the Washington press, and a wide-eyed idealist duped by boss Jim Taylor's political machine. Then Capra forces this boy to grow up, to become a multi-dimensional character, who first acknowledges and comes to terms with, then battles the corruption in the world around him. After defeat at the hands of Taylor's machine, Stewart's resourceful populist, Jefferson Smith, creates his own mini-machine (using Saunders' political expertise, his Boy Ranger organization and their press) to fight Taylor. Exchanging his former idealism for

a more realistic, though morally questionable, pragmatism,
Jeff even manipulates the Senate's parliamentary procedures,
delaying the passage of an urgently-needed bill through his
filibuster in order to expose the corruption of his enemies,
much as they had earlier used parliamentary procedure and
Senate machinery to discredit him. Jeff's speeches reveal
a similar transformation: his nervous, adolescently cracked-
voice proposal of his National Boys' Camp bill later gives
way to a highly emotional, demagogic filibuster. Initially
ill at ease with words, he learns to manipulate them to
achieve his own goals.

In shaping Stewart into a figure of populist mythology
alongside men like Jefferson (Jefferson Smith's namesake),
Jackson, Lincoln, and Bryan, Capra, unlike his predecessors, exploits Stewart's highly idiosyncratic features--his
twangy, western drawl, his gangling, Abe-Lincolnish frame,
his youth, his boyish innocence and his physical awkwardness. Yet Capra also demythicizes his character, playing
upon Stewart's physical frailty and psychological vulnerability as Mann and Hitchcock will later do. Jeff's initial energy and enthusiasms are soon gone: he begins to lose his
voice (aided by drops of bichloride of mercury which the
actor applied to his vocal chords) near the end of his filibuster and finally collapses from physical exhaustion. Capra's final image shows him lying unconscious on the floor of
the Senate.

Stewart apparently rethought his pre-war screen image
as a small town, boy-next-door, Norman Rockwell caricature
during his years in the Air Force, opting for parts on his
return to pictures after the war that were more mature (Wonderful Life, Rope, Harvey), more obsessively tenacious (Call
Northside 777, Rope, the Mann and Hitchcock pictures of the
Fifties) and more psychologically complex (again the Mann and
Hitchcock pictures). As George Bailey in It's a Wonderful Life,
Stewart's pre-war optimism has soured. His bitterness and disillusionment are such that, as the picture opens, he is pre-
paring to commit suicide. The post-war Wonderful Life presents a nightmarish inversion of Capra's populist mythology
of the Thirties, especially in the sequence in which Bailey
wanders, like the amnesiac somnambulist of so many film
noirs of the period, through Pottersville as it would have become had he never been born and as he searches in vain for
his family and friends.

Stewart's desperation in Mr. Smith--the result of the
unwillingness of Senators to listen to or believe in him--is

magnified in Wonderful Life to the point of paranoia (in the
"Pottersville sequence") and becomes, in subsequent films like
Harvey and Rear Window, an integral part of his screen persona.
Contradictory tendencies within the Stewart persona contribute
to the character's desperation; his feelings toward Mary (Donna
Reed), like those later towards Madeleine/Judy in Vertigo, combine attraction and repulsion. Capra dramatizes these tendencies in George's early scenes with Mary. On their way home
from a high school dance, George and Mary stop outside an old
deserted house (a house they later restore and inhabit). George's
hostility towards home and family, which he views much as a
prisoner views shackles, is reflected in his gesture: throwing
a stone at the house, he makes a wish and breaks a window.
His wish, of course, is for a life of adventure--a life which
would take him away from Mary and Bedford Falls. Mary,
echoing his action, breaks a window and makes a wish of her
own, a wish she never divulges (but which undoubtedly reflects
her desire to marry George, move into that house and raise a
family there with him). George's gesture, which recognizes
the house as both a means of and an obstacle to attaining his
desires, encapsulates the contradictory nature of his feelings.
Later, his mother points him, after his brother's marriage, in
the direction of Mary's house; George starts off in that direction, then turns and walks off in the opposite direction. Eventually ending up at Mary's house, George passionately and
angrily kisses her, attempting to deny his feelings for her
and declaring his refusal to be tied down by marriage.
Capra's tightly claustrophobic yet nonetheless romantic two-
shot close-up of the couple fades out; then, ironically denying George's wish, the film fades back in on their wedding
day. The editing eliminates any sense of the Stewart character's control over his own destiny.

Stewart's momentary self-doubt in Mr. Smith becomes
extended throughout Wonderful Life and intensified into a suicidal
self-hatred. Though Bailey knows what he wants to do--to travel, to build bridges, to have quixotic adventures--his failure
to achieve his goals (which in themselves are extremely egotisti-
cal and anti-social) drives him first to question, then to hate the
very populist qualities in himself (such as self-sufficiency, good
neighborliness, disregard for wealth, love of family and faith in
the plain people) that gave him inner strength in Mr. Smith,
making Wonderful Life into a quasi-Brechtian critique of the
values of the earlier film.

Stewart's physical characteristics, like those of Capra's other populist heroes--Gary Cooper, Walter Brennan,
and Harry Carey--make him an ideal actor for westerns, a

genre to which he repeatedly turns in the Fifties. However, unlike Cooper and Carey whose laconic strength and solid physical presences correspond to the stereotypical image of the invulnerable western hero, Stewart emerges as one of the genre's first vulnerable heroes, revealing himself to be physically, psychologically, and morally fallible. Anthony Mann's psychological westerns explore Stewart's weaknesses, subjecting him to excruciating physical pain in Man from Laramie (1955) in which he is ambushed and his gun hand is stigmatized in a quasi-ritualistic, nightmarish sequence and in The Naked Spur in which while wounded in the leg he is toppled off his horse down a ravine and is later forced to scale the sheer face of a rocky cliff using his spur as a grip.

Mann presents Stewart as a neurotic loner, trauma-tized by some past event--the unnatural murder of a parent by a son in Winchester 73, his loss of a brother (Man from Laramie), or his betrayal by a woman (Naked Spur). In his quest for revenge, Stewart pursues a doppelgänger across the rugged western landscape, confronts his double who is literally his brother (Winchester 73) or a man like himself (Naked Spur, Bend of the River) and either kills him or be-comes indirectly responsible for his death. Though the con-clusions of Mann's westerns are less than cathartic, Stewart does partially purge himself of his obsessive hatred, but he does so at a cost to himself, for in killing his psychological double he destroys part of himself. Mann's westerns match the paranoia, self-hatred, and self-doubt of Wonderful Life and even go beyond that film, making the psychologically unstable Stewart distrustful, mercenary, callous, brutal, quick-tempered, violent, and even masochistic. Driven by furies within himself, Stewart, in films like Naked Spur, stubbornly refuses to reconsider or swerve from his goals, even though he is aware of their morally ambiguous nature. This self-destructive tenacity serves as the cornerstone on which Alfred Hitchcock builds his films with Stewart.

Hitchcock plays off Stewart's tenacious striving for omniscient perfection as an investigator against his physio-logical impairments which reflect latent moral imperfections: he has a limp in Rope, a broken leg in a cast in Rear Win-dow, and acrophobia in Vertigo. Stewart's moral superior-ity to the criminals in Rope and Rear Window--evidenced in Rope by his delight in uncovering the commission of a mur-der which he enthusiastically re-enacts and in Rear Window by his suspicions of murder which he gleefully relates to

anyone who will listen--is compromised by his own guilt.
In Rope, Stewart's Rupert Cadell, as Brandon's and Philip's
teacher, comes to share their guilt. Though he denies that
he ever intended his ideas (namely that superior individuals
are above the law) to be put into practice and tries to distance himself from his students' murder, his reenactment of
the crime, shot from an intellectually distanced high angle,
suggests his unwilling post-facto participation in it. After
struggling with Brandon over a gun--a fight which recalls
the initial murder--and grabbing hold of it, Rupert sits
down, exhausted and dejected, next to the chest containing
the victim's body. As he awaits the arrival of the police,
Stewart appears more victim than victor; his expression and
posture reflect his realization of his own guilt in the matter.

     Stewart's L. B. Jeffries in Rear Window bears a par-
tial resemblance to Capra's George Bailey.   Recuperating
from a broken leg in his small, two-room, Greenwich Village apartment, Jeffries anxiously awaits the day he will
get out of his "plaster cocoon" and resume his adventurous
career as a globe-trotting magazine photographer. And like
Bailey, Jeffries also somewhat selfishly fears marriage,
arguing that his girlfriend Lisa, though perfect, would tie
him down. Again like Bailey, Jeffries feels trapped; the
summer heat, the boredom and the frustration he feels confined to his wheel chair contribute to a sense of claustrophobic desperation. Voyeurism provides Jeffries with a
means of escape, yet his vicarious involvement in his neighbors' lives and his discovery of a murder become less of
an escape than a self-confrontation, a quasi-therapeutic
working out in the "real" world, i. e. , his courtyard, of
his own contradictory feelings towards Lisa. Like Mann,
Hitchcock employs the doppelgänger to deal with the schizo-
phrenic aspects of the Stewart persona, using Thorwald to
act out Jeffries' suppressed desires and then punishing Jeffries for having these desires by forcing him to watch helplessly as Thorwald nearly kills Lisa when he catches her
looking for evidence in his apartment. Again like Mann,
Hitchcock's use of the double forces Stewart to confront and
deal with his own feelings. Thus the final struggle between
Thorwald and Jeffries in the latter's darkened apartment
becomes a self-confrontation. Hitchcock's direction of Stewart in Rear Window draws upon the actor's charm and nasti-
ness, his sense of moral superiority and his physical vulnerability, his confidence and self-doubt, constructing out of
these qualities a morally ambiguous character.

Stewart's idealism, i. e. , his belief in the existence
of ideals in the abstract, manifests itself in a variety of
ways in his postwar pictures, often realizing itself in a benign sort of insanity. In Harvey (1950), Stewart believes in
a great white rabbit and in Bell, Book and Candle (1958),
in which Kim Novak puts a spell upon him, he comes to
believe in witches and warlocks. Reteaming Stewart and
Novak, Bell, Book and Candle is a parodic remake of Vertigo (1958), a film which explores the serious side of Stewart's insanity. In Vertigo, after quitting his job as a San
Francisco detective because of his acrophobia, Stewart falls
victim to an illusion created by a wife-murderer and his
accomplice. That illusion is "Madeleine" (Kim Novak).
Stewart's psychological instability is initially suggested in
his obsessive fascination with Madeleine whom, at the request of a client, he follows through a series of colorfully
romantic settings, but only fully emerges after her death,
for which he feels responsible. His nervous breakdown,
characterized by vertiginous nightmares, is followed by a
catatonic schizophrenia, then by melancholic despondency
which, in turn, gives way to an obsessive, fetishistic reconstruction of "Madeleine," using Judy Barton (Novak) as
his real-life mannequin.

Stewart's descent into a dream world in the film's
first half, a world characterized by Hitchcock's use of sat-
urated colors, settings associated with the past, and hypnot-
ically magnetic point-of-view tracking shots, is answered in
the film's second half by Stewart's neurotic attempt to reconstruct that dream world, to re-enact Madeleine's death
and thus to exorcise the guilt which haunts him. Yet the
last image of the film is far from cathartic: torn between
the contradictory feelings within himself, a retraumatized,
off-balance Stewart stands precariously near the edge of the
ledge of the bell-tower from which Judy has just plunged to
her death. The once "hard-headed Scot" now struggles with
an inner anomie which threatens to destroy his tenuous hold
on reality. Though cured of his acrophobia, Stewart has
been driven, "one step at a time," closer and closer to an
emotional paralysis from which it is unlikely that he will
ever recover.

Stewart's performances for Ford range from low
comedy to high drama and each also reveals a dual personality. Stewart casts off his image as an amusing buffoon
and mercenary opportunist in Two Rode Together (1961) to
angrily denounce the hypocrisy of the ladies and gentlemen

at the fort who treat Elena (Linda Cristal), a recently freed
captive of the Comanches, as a social outcast.   On his return to Tascosa, Stewart's McCabe rejects his earlier identity, which his deputy, Ward, who copies Stewart's former
dress, has in his absence usurped, and sets out with Elena
for California and a new life.   And in The Man Who Shot
Liberty Valance (1962), he plays both the mature, glib, legendary politician, Senator Ransom Stoddard, and the idealistic, young tenderfoot lawyer, Ranse.   And much as Wayne
dubs him "pilgrim," so Stewart is also saddled with an identity as "the man who shot Liberty Valance."

        Stewart's "pilgrim" in Liberty Valance recalls his
role as Jeff Smith in Mr. Smith, though Ford makes Ranse
an Easterner bringing law and order to the untamed West
rather than a Westerner restoring populist values to the
overly-civilized East.   Stewart conveys, in his classroom
evocations of Washington and Lincoln, the same idealism
and, in taking up a gun to fight the outlaw Valance, makes
similar pragmatic concessions in order to achieve his goals.

        Cast opposite Wayne's more traditional western hero,
Stewart appears weak and indecisive: it requires Wayne's
intervention to save him from being killed by Valance and
later to force him to accept his nomination at the territorial
convention.   Stewart, again unlike Wayne, has a remarkable
verbal facility.   His energetic articulation of abstract ideas
or of specific plans for the transformation of the arid countryside into a garden contrast with Wayne's taciturn conceal-
ment of his feelings and give Stewart an important edge in
his relationship with Hallie (Vera Miles).   Yet Stewart's
careful phrasing and rhetorical posing as Senator Stoddard
in the flashback's framing sequences suggest the gap between
language and feeling of a wary politician: his words have
lost much of their meaning.   Wayne's eloquent performance
serves as a foil for Stewart, calling attention to his physical
awkwardness, his naïve idealism, his lack of strength and
self-confidence and his occasional insensitivity to the unspoken feelings of those around him.   When he discovers
that Hallie cannot read, his persistent protestation of dis-
belief becomes as embarrassing to her as his self-righteous
explanation to the fort community in Two Rode Together that
Elena could not kill herself after being captured by the Com-
manche because her religion forbid it was to Elena, who
stands watching, and ill-at-ease in the background, while he
talks.   Stewart's fascination with abstract ideas causes him
to ignore more immediate feelings and concerns, complicating

his sensitivity to historically crucial issues with an insensitivity to more personal questions.

Stewart remains one of the American cinema's most intriguing personalities. As idealist and cynic, representative of the people and social outcast, determined reformer and frustrated cripple, success and failure, and healthy young man and neurotic, he embodies all the contradictions of American culture and its ideals. His gallery of performances for Capra, Mann, Hitchcock and Ford reveal different facets of a persona that is truly complex and that belies the notion that classical Hollywood acting style seeks to mask ruptures in performance continuity and to erase contradictions in characterization.

NOTE

1. Stewart's association with M-G-M begins in 1935. In 1941, he leaves M-G-M to join the armed forces.

f. John Wayne: As Sure as the Turnin' of the Earth

In the last three years since True Grit (1969), John Wayne
has won an Oscar, been on the covers of Time and Life,
and starred in a half-dozen more pictures. Wayne's re-
discovery by the American press--his popularity with the
post-war American movie audience has never been in question[1]--has been half-hearted at best. His Oscar-winning
performance in Henry Hathaway's True Grit, though good,
was not one of his best. Critics responded to Wayne's
Rooster Cogburn for what I consider all the wrong reasons.
Wayne's detractors, like Time, liked the actor's self-parody,
use of disguise and anti-heroic buffoonery because it mocked
Wayne's screen image as the hard, granite-faced monument
of the Old West. All Wayne had to do was put on an eye-
patch and fall off his horse a couple times and he became
an "actor" overnight.

As Andrew Sarris wrote in his review of True Grit

> if Wayne should obtain his long-deferred Oscar, it
> will be due to the same principle of emasculation
> that denied Cagney, Bogart, and Muni awards for
> their more virile, anarchic parts in Public Enemy,
> Casablanca and Scarface. Cagney did get his award
> finally, but only after wrapping himself up inside
> an American flag as George M. Cohan in Yankee
> Doodle Dandy, Bogart only after letting his whiskers
> grow and acting like a monkey in The African
> Queen, and Muni only after growing a beard and
> impersonating Louis Pasteur and Emile Zola. A
> trick accent, a beard, an eye patch, old-age
> makeup--these are the accoutrements of acting to
> many people. And that is why the worst acting
> is often mistaken for the best, particularly on the
> screen, where being is more important than pre-
> tending, and just standing there often more im-
> pressive than doing something. [2]

What's remarkable about Wayne in True Grit is that, though his part is self-conscious and self-parodic, his performance is not. He plays Cogburn straight and without tricks. Like Bogart, Grant, Stewart, and Cooper, Wayne comes out of the classical mold of acting. He always gives a clean performance. Where Brando creates the Godfather with the aid of makeup and mumbling, Wayne portrays Cogburn in spite of the eye patch. Avoiding repetitive tricks and mannerisms, Wayne always finds a single gesture that expresses what he wants with simplicity, surety, and clarity. Actors like Brando, Dean, or Clift seem to struggle with great effort and pain for the right gesture, tone, or look. As a result, their performances appear neurotic; the characters they play appear filled with inner turmoil. For Wayne, each gesture is effortless. Each movement comes purely, naturally, and intuitively, giving his performances a slow, fluid grace. At the end of True Grit, Wayne twirls his rifle--echoing a gesture that introduced him thirty years earlier in Stagecoach--puts his horse's reins between his teeth, and rides off into a final shoot-out, yelling, "all right, you bastards, fill your hands!" His action is both absurdly comic and heroically grand. It works only because Wayne, the actor, is totally committed to what he is doing, totally absorbed in the action itself. Only Wayne can overstate with economy and carry off an otherwise unplayable scene.

In analyzing Wayne's performances, it's important to make a distinction between Wayne, the phenomenon, and Wayne, the actor. For better or worse, Wayne has become part of the American myth of the frontier. As one Wayne admirer puts it, Wayne is "an authentic American legend, a man who ties together strands of dreams and nostalgia for us simply by existing."[3] Directors, trying to exploit Wayne's image, perpetuate Wayne's depersonalization into myth. The dramatic zoom-in which introduces Wayne in Big Jake (1971), though it reflects the dynamic excitement of Wayne's presence in the film, treats Wayne more as a symbol than as an actor. Similarly, Siegel's pre-credit homage to Wayne in The Shootist (1976), constructed of clips from earlier Wayne features, exploits rather than explores Wayne's persona as icon of the west.

To complicate matters, Wayne's movie persona carries over into his private life: his outspoken political views, seen in statements surrounding the release of The Alamo (1960) and The Green Berets (1968), make it all the more

difficult to separate Wayne's public and private personalities.
Audiences, moreover, confuse the character types Wayne
plays on the screen with Wayne himself and conclude that
Wayne's acting merely consists of playing himself.   What
few realize about Wayne is that the "self" he plays has
been, over the years, carefully constructed; it is as much
a mask as those worn by actors on the ancient Greek stage.
A comparison of Wayne's farewell speeches to his leading
ladies in The Big Trail (1930) and Red River (1948) reveals
that in 1930 Wayne is still Marion Morrison but that by 1948
he has become "John Wayne." The inimitable walk, which
Wayne reportedly borrowed from stuntman Yakima Cannutt,
and the unique phrasing of dialogue characterized by mid-
sentence pauses, which Wayne perfected in the Thirties in
an attempt to make the long passages of dialogue in his
Mascot, Monogram, and Republic quickies more interesting,
are, like Wayne's subsequent development of an idiosyncratic system of hand gestures, conscious creations.   Initially unnatural traits, they have, through repetition, become naturalized, transformed into the cornerstones of a
persona that has been built brick by brick.   Like the classical editing style of Hollywood cinema in the late Thirties,
Wayne's acting style is invisible.   It, like the image of
Wayne as American archetype, needs to be deconstructed
in order for it to be seen for what it is, in order for it to
become visible.

In this essay, I would like to characterize Wayne's
"classical" acting style by concentrating, for the most part,
on his performances in Red River and She Wore a Yellow
Ribbon (1949), roles which test his abilities as an actor and
performances which reveal certain aspects of his persona
which will shape the characters he will play for the next
thirty years.

The key to Wayne's acting style lies in his size and
strength.   Wayne has so much physical power that his presence in any scene dominates the action, even if Wayne is
static or silent.   As Howard Hawks remarks, Wayne is "so
strong and good that he dominates" the other actors; his
least action can bowl over anyone else in the frame.   "I
found out very early that you need a strong man with
him. . . .   In Red River only the fact that Montgomery Clift
was so good kept him from complete domination of the
film. "[4]

What makes Wayne great is his ability to control his
tremendous strength on the screen.   Wayne always seems to

be physically aware of everything and everybody else in the
frame. He's constantly measuring himself against his environment, whether it be a saloon or Monument Valley, and
using his strength to control that environment or to create
a balance between it and him. At the end of Red River,
Wayne walks to a showdown with Clift through a herd of
cattle that parts to let him pass. Though Wayne is looking
dead ahead, not at the cattle, the movement of his body
seems to control that of the herd. Nothing can stop him.

The awesomeness of Wayne's walk at the end of Red
River comes from its seemingly uncontrollable momentum.
It reflects the insanity of Wayne's blind, stubborn determination to control the world around him. Wayne is only brought
back into control when he meets resistance--when Clift fights
back and the two crash comically into a wagon full of pots
and pans. Thus, the film ends with a restoration of sanity
and natural order, seen in Wayne's awareness of Clift's
strength and in the establishment of a balance of power between the two.

What makes Red River such an important film for
Wayne is that it unleashes a physical power that had gone
unnoticed in his earlier films. Hawks saw in Wayne a
latent capacity for brutality that Ford either could not or
would not see until The Searchers. Wayne's brutality resurfaces in Rio Bravo (Wayne cracks open the head of a
Burdett man with his rifle in a saloon), in El Dorado (he
shoots to cripple Milt and Pedro to force them out a door
into an ambush meant for him), and in Rio Lobo (he lets
Ketcham burn until he agrees to return stolen property and
water rights). But these outbursts subside quickly and,
though they are violent, never equal the sustained intensity
of those in Red River. Written, as Borden Chase says,
"to give Wayne a part he could play for the next twenty
years," Red River was the first film to realize fully Wayne's
potential as an actor. It not only enabled Wayne to play a
character close to his own age, but also gave him confidence
in his own strength by letting him use it more completely
and more brutally than he ever had before. The result was
one of Wayne's best and most interesting performances.

*   *   *

I think Wayne is a helluva lot better than people give
him credit for being.... It's very hard for Duke to
make a bad scene.... Way back on Red River he asked

my theory about acting and I said, "Duke, you do two
or three good scenes in a picture and don't offend the
audience the rest of the time and you'll be a good actor." So even today he says, "What's coming up?"
and I say, "This is one of the ones that you're liable
to offend them. Get it over with as soon as you can.
Don't do anything."   --Howard Hawks[5]

Wayne is great not only when he's overpowering everyone
else in sight but also when he's not doing anything. Wayne
works well with other actors. He lets them take the initiative in a scene and, then, reacts to them, bouncing back
their emotion with a stronger signal than that with which it
was sent. It's as if his presence controls scenes without
actually taking part in them. The opening sequence of Red
River in which Wayne says farewell to his girl is essentially
one of those potentially "offensive" scenes that Hawks talks
about. It works because Wayne's silent, inflexible presence
cuts the girl's theatrical melodramatics and enables the sincerity of her feeling for him and the depth of his feeling for
her to come through. Later, when Wayne meets Joanne Dru
for the first time, he sits quietly as she paces about and
talks. His responses to her direct questions give the scene
an emotional immediacy that momentarily breaks through
Wayne's rigid resolve to kill Clift. His passive reactions
to her reveal a softening of his character. When he sees
his bracelet (originally belonging to his girl) on her, he
grabs her arm, then slowly and gently releases it. Though
their emotional fencing results in a draw, Wayne's softened
reactions to her foreshadows his ultimate reconciliation with
Clift at the end of the film.

In Rio Bravo, Wayne's solid presence works as a foil
for Dean Martin's rehabilitation. Though Martin gets a lot
of the big scenes, Wayne becomes--through his loyalty, sureness and strength--the emotional center of the film. Martin's recovery of his sobriety and self-respect grows out of
Wayne's silent strength: it's as if Martin's strength comes
from Wayne's own power. Ultimately Martin becomes self-
sufficient and no longer needs Wayne, but it is only through
Wayne that he achieves his independence.

In short, Wayne's static strength enables him to really respond to other actors. Unlike another strong actor,
Clint Eastwood, who seems totally estranged from the characters and the world around him, Wayne's omniscient awareness of and reaction to other actors give his performances

an energy and vitality that Eastwood's lack. Even when he
is "doing nothing," Wayne is fully in character and involved
with what is going on around him.

Wayne himself claims that he does not act but only
reacts. As John Ford writes, "To this day, I would not
call Duke an actor. He is a reactor. Put him in a dramatic situation and he reacts to it as he would in real life.
That kind of performance makes for fine, believable motion
pictures."[6] In Ford's cavalry trilogy, Fort Apache, She
Wore a Yellow Ribbon and Rio Grande, Wayne plays characters whose loyalty to a larger order, e. g., to a superior
officer or to the dictates of duty, frustrates his own desires
and actions. His helplessness in the face of this larger order transforms his actions into reactions. His gestures reflect his powerlessness and, at the same time, deepen his
sense of personal frustration. In She Wore a Yellow Ribbon,
Wayne's last mission before his retirement is a failure.
Hampered by his commanding officer's "female relations,"
he arrives too late to relieve another patrol and finds some
of his men, a stationmaster, and the stationmaster's wife
slain by Indians. He stands next to Joanne Dru, looking at
a burning wagon in the background. He walks over to the
wagon and kicks the wheel out from under it. As it crashes
to the ground, he turns away and says to Dru while patting
her gently on the back, "Well, I guess we missed the stage,
Miss Dandridge."

The burning wagon falls to pieces on the ground, a
symbol of the frustration of Wayne's last mission and of his
sense of failure as an officer. It is as if his whole career
were collapsing. What gives the scene an added dimension
is Dru's presence in the shot and the obliqueness of Wayne's
gesture. He directs his anger not against her (who is, in
large part, responsible for his failure) but against the wagon
and assumes the responsibility for the failure of his mission
himself. Though Wayne says nothing, he communicates his
feelings to Dru yet does so with a controlled indirectness
that remains consistent with the gentleness and affection of
his overall relationship with her. It becomes a double-edged
action that both reflects Wayne's bitterness and disappointment yet preserves the inarticulated sympathy and mutual
understanding that exists between the two (she seems drawn
to Wayne earlier in the graveyard and he to her, perhaps
because she resembles his dead wife).

Ford, through Wayne, collapses all the film's sentiments into a single gesture. The scene conveys Wayne's

feelings of frustration and loss, yet also, in one of Wayne's
rare moments of personal intimacy, lets him share his feelings with another, transforming the negative act of destruction into a more positive realization of a relationship based
on shared loss.   Wayne's gesture and Dru's reaction to it
serve as an eloquent microcosm for the greater gain-in-loss
that they share with the lonely, cavalry outpost community
whose achievements the film's narrator describes as "just
another cold page in our nation's history books. "

Where Hawks realizes Wayne's potential for action,
Ford frustrates it.   Where Wayne's performances for Hawks
tend to be extremely physical and active, those for Ford
seem restrained and passive.   Ford repeatedly puts Wayne
into situations in which he can do nothing and uses his passive helplessness to set up highly emotional sequences.   In
Yellow Ribbon, on Wayne's retirement, his men present him
with a silver watch, inscribed with his name and the motto,
"Lest we forget. "   As his old company rides out under its
new command, Wayne looks on.   As he watches them go,
his hand clasps the hilt of his sabre (attached to the saddle
of his horse).   This self-contained gesture illustrates his
isolation and powerlessness apart from his men and shows
his regret at being left behind.   Wayne's gesture is natural
and unobtrusive, yet intensely moving in its expression of
his loneliness, helpless isolation from his men, and nostalgia for the past.

Ford plays, in Yellow Ribbon, with the notions of
strength and infallibility that constitute Wayne's persona as
archetypal western hero.   Sporting a moustache, Wayne
first appears, in the backstage wings of this historical narrative, wearing red underwear, dressing for the morning
review of his troops.   Before entering the more public stage,
Wayne rubs his knuckles, stiff due to the cold, exhales and
comments on seeing the vapor of his breath, and marches
to the review, his gait gradually increasing in tempo as the
joints of his legs limber up.   An old man who finds it difficult to get warmed up in the morning, Wayne's Nathan Brittles is not only physically but emotionally humanized.   When
he discovers the dead bodies of Ma and Pa Sudrow, he re-
spectfully takes off his hat, then turns and slowly walks
away; he bitterly slaps his holstered, unused gun with his
gloves, announcing that it's "about time I do retire. "   Later,
after telling his commanding officer about his mission's
failure, he nervously fidgets with his hat and audibly sniffles
on his way out of the room.

Less verbal than physical in his approach to acting, Wayne more often establishes character through gesture than through dialogue.   In the opening sequence of The Searchers (1956), which contains only one or two words of dialogue, Wayne, as Ethan, slowly dismounts, walks toward his brother Aaron, stiffly nods at him and formally shakes his hand. Turning towards Martha, his brother's wife and the woman with whom Wayne is in love, Ethan, with a fluid and chivalrous gesture, removes his hat, approaches her and gently places a kiss on her forehead; here and in the subsequent dinner table sequences, Wayne can't keep his eyes off her.

It is through gestures such as these that Wayne charts Ethan's course through the film.   After Martha's death, Ethan's gestures become more and more violent--see his angry rooting in the sandy earth with his Bowie knife after discovering his dead niece.   Violence earlier aimed at the community around him (see the way Wayne tosses guns and canteens at Ward Bond) becomes here turned upon Nature, as it will later upon family (when Ethan tries to kill Debbie [Natalie Wood]).   Wayne even does violence to language, clenching his teeth as he defiantly mutters "That'll be the day!"--a line which, through repetition, comes to symbolize his inflexibility.

The system of gestures Wayne uses in the film comes full circle when, after scalping the Indian who killed Martha and kidnapped Debbie, Ethan roughly grabs Debbie by the shoulders and abruptly lifts her into the air.   The violence of the gesture mirrors the destructive energy which animated his search for vengeance; but the gesture itself, a ritualistic action symbolizing recognition of a child and which dates from Roman times, recalls, as McBride and Wilmington point out, [7] the moment earlier in the film when Ethan picks up Debbie, as a child, for the first time in his arms.   The gesture sums up the character's ambivalence toward notions of family with an economy that is characteristically Fordian.

If Ford explores Wayne's persona in terms of a necessary repression of violence or its displacement onto impersonal objects--i. e. , Wayne's Brittles directs his anger against the burning wagon, Ethan against Nature or language --Hawks views that violence as a necessary consequence of Wayne's strength.   Wayne's violence becomes a means of self-expression, whether in the cathartic fistfight with Clift at the end of Red River, the dynamite-shooting sequence at the end of Rio Bravo (1959), or the playful brawling with

Mitchum in El Dorado (1967). At the same time, Hawks
complements Wayne's physical strength with intelligence,
emphasizing his abilities as a strategist who outwits as well
as outfights his opponents. This aspect of Wayne's persona,
especially as the actor ages, compensates for his failing
powers. In El Dorado, Wayne, a bullet lodged against a
nerve in his spine, experiences crippling pain and long periods of paralysis; he survives more by means of stratagem
than strength. For both Hawks and Ford, Wayne's survival
depends upon a certain tenacity of character. For Hawks,
Wayne possesses, to paraphrase Andrew Sarris, "an inex-
haustible capacity for reinventing the terms of [his] existence,"[8] a doggedness in adapting to, and thus controlling,
the changing world around him. For Ford, especially in
The Searchers, Wayne is tenacious to a fault. Wayne, like
Ethan, remains obsessively faithful to his goals, inflexibly
pursuing them beyond all reason and in defiance of Nature.
Unlike the Comanche who will only chase a thing so far and
who "never learn there's such a thing as a critter that'll
keep on comin'," Wayne vows never to give up, promising
that "we'll find 'em ... just as sure as the turnin' of the
earth."

NOTES

1. Wayne became one of the top ten box office stars in
     1949 and stayed there--except for an off-year in 1958
     when he does not make the list--until 1974, topping
     the list four times.
2. Confessions of a Cultist (New York: Simon and Schus-
     ter, 1970), 455-456.
3. P. F. Kluge, Life (January 28, 1972), 42.
4. From an unpublished interview with Howard Hawks.
5. Ibid.
6. Photoplay (March 1951), 83.
7. Joseph McBride and Michael Wilmington, John Ford
     (New York: Da Capo, 1975), 162.
8. Andrew Sarris, The John Ford Movie Mystery (Bloom-
     ington: Indiana University Press, 1975), 158.

BIBLIOGRAPHY

Ackland, Rodney and Elspeth Grant. "Borstal Days with Hitchcock." In The Celluloid Mistress. London: Allan Wingate, 1954, 24-40.

Allen, Frederick Lewis. Only Yesterday. New York: Harper and Row, 1931.

Barthes, Roland. Image/Music/Text, trans. Stephen Heath. New York: Hill and Wang, 1977.

Bazin, André. Le Cinéma de la Cruauté. Paris: Flammarion, 1975.

_____. Jean Renoir, trans. W. W. Halsey and William Simon. New York: Simon and Schuster, 1973.

_____. Orson Welles: A Critical View, trans. Jonathan Rosenbaum. New York: Harper and Row, 1978.

_____. "La politique des auteurs." In The New Wave, ed. Peter Graham. New York: Doubleday, 1968, 137-155.

_____. What Is Cinema?, vols. one and two, trans. Hugh Gray. Berkeley: University of California Press, 1967, 1971.

Behlmer, Rudy, ed. Memo From: David O. Selznick. New York: Avon, 1973.

349

Booth, Wayne C. The Rhetoric of Fiction. Chicago: University of Chicago Press, 1961.

Burch, Noël. Theory of Film Practice. New York:
   Praeger, 1973.

Camper, Fred. "The Tarnished Angels," Screen 12, No. 2
   (Summer 1971), 68-93.

_____. "Under Capricorn." MIT Film Society Notes
   (March 3, 1969).

Chabrol, Claude. "Hitchcock Confronts Evil," Cahiers du
   Cinéma in English, No. 2 (1966).

Corrigan, Robert W., ed. Laurel British Drama: The
   Nineteenth Century. New York: Dell, 1967.

Danto, Arthur. "Moving Pictures," Quarterly Review of
   Film Studies 4, No. 1 (Winter 1979), 1-21.

Dyer, Richard. Stars. London: British Film Institute,
   1979.

Fieschi, J.-A. "Tiger Shark," Cahiers du cinéma 24, No.
   139 (January 1963).

Finley, John H. Pindar and Aeschylus. Cambridge: Harvard University Press, 1955.

Foucault, Michel. "What Is an Author?" trans. Donald F.
   Bouchard. Screen 20, No. 1 (Spring 1979), 13-29.

Frye, Northrop. Anatomy of Criticism: Four Essays.
   Princeton: Princeton University Press, 1957.

Godard, Jean-Luc. Godard on Godard, trans. Tom Milne.
   New York: Viking, 1972, 36-39.

Grosz, Dave. "The First Legion: Vision and Perception in
   Sirk," Screen 12, No. 2 (Summer 1971), 99-117.

Henderson, Brian. "Two Types of Film Theory," Film
   Quarterly 24, No. 3 (Spring 1971), 33-42.

Hitchcock, Alfred. "Direction." In Film: A Montage of
   Theories, ed. Richard Dyer MacCann. New York:
   Dutton, 1966.

Hochberg, Julian E.   Perception.   Englewood Cliffs, N. J. :
    Prentice-Hall, 1964.

Hofstadter, Richard.   The Age of Reform.   New York:
    Random House, 1955.

Hunter, Tim.   "Alfred Hitchcock: The Mechanics of Clar-
    ity," The Harvard Crimson (June 12, 1968).

Jacobs, Lewis.   The Rise of the American Film.   New
    York: Teachers College Press, 1939.

Joannides, Paul.   "Samuel Fuller: Edited by David Will
    and Peter Wollen," Cinema (UK) 5 (February 1970), 9.

Kuleshov, Lev.   Kuleshov on Film, trans. Ron Levaco.
    Berkeley: University of California Press, 1975.

Lambert, Gavin.   The Dangerous Edge.   New York: Gross-
    man, 1976.

Latham, Aaron.   Crazy Sundays.   New York: Viking, 1970.

Lemon, Lee T. and Marion J. Reis, eds./trans.   Russian
    Formalist Criticism: Four Essays.   Lincoln, Neb. :
    University of Nebraska Press, 1965.

Lloyd, Harold.   An American Comedy.   New York: Dover,
    1971.

McBride, Joseph, ed.   Focus on Howard Hawks.   Englewood
    Cliffs, N. J. :   Prentice-Hall, 1972.

Michelson, Annette.   "Camera Lucida, Camera Obscura,"
    Artforum 11, No. 5 (January 1973), 30-37.

Milne, Peter.   Motion Picture Directing.   New York: Falk
    Publishing, 1922.

Moullet, Luc.   "Edgar G. Ulmer," Cahiers du cinéma 25,
    Nos. 150-151 (December 1963-January 1964).

Perkins, V. F.   Film as Film: Understanding and Judging
    Movies.   Baltimore: Penguin, 1972.

Renoir, Jean.   My Life and My Films, trans. Norman
    Denny.   New York: Atheneum, 1974.

Riesman, David, Nathan Glazer, and Reuel Denny. The
    Lonely Crowd: A Study of the Changing American Char-
    acter.   Garden City, N.Y.: Doubleday, 1953.

Rivette, Jacques. "The Genius of Howard Hawks."   In
    Focus on Howard Hawks, ed. Joseph McBride.   Engle-
    wood Cliffs, N.J.: Prentice-Hall, 1972, 70-77.

Rohmer, Eric and Claude Chabrol. Hitchcock, trans. Stan-
    ley Hochman. New York: Ungar, 1979.

Roth, Mark. "Some Warners Musicals and the Spirit of the
    New Deal, " The Velvet Light Trap, No. 1 (June 1971),
    20-25.

Salt, Barry. "Film Style and Technology in the Forties,"
    Film Quarterly 31, No. 1 (Fall 1977), 46-57.

Sarris, Andrew. The American Cinema. New York: Dut-
    ton, 1968.

_____. Confessions of a Cultist. New York: Simon and
    Schuster, 1970.

Sherman, Eric and Martin Rubin. The Director's Event.
    New York: Atheneum, 1970.

Smith, John M. "Conservative Individualism, " Screen (Au-
    tumn 1972), 51-70.

Taylor, John Russell. Hitch: The Life & Times of Alfred
    Hitchcock. New York: Berkley Books, 1980.

Thompson, David. A Biographical Dictionary of Film.
    New York: Morrow, 1976.

Todorov, Tzvetan. The Fantastic: A Structural Approach
    to a Literary Genre, trans. Richard Howard.   Ithaca:
    Cornell University Press, 1975.

_____. "The Typology of Detective Fiction. " In The
    Poetics of Prose, trans. Richard Howard.   Ithaca:
    Cornell University Press, 1977, 42-52.

Truffaut, François, with Helen Scott. Hitchcock. New
    York: Simon and Schuster, 1966.

Warshow, Robert. The Immediate Experience. New York: Atheneum, 1962.

Wollen, Peter. Signs and Meaning in the Cinema. New York: Viking, 1972.

Wood, Robin. Hitchcock's Films, 3rd ed. New York: A. S. Barnes, 1978.

_____. Howard Hawks. London: British Film Institute, 1981.

_____. "Who the Hell Is Howard Hawks?" Focus! Nos. 1-2 (February-March 1967).

_____ and Michael Walker. Claude Chabrol. New York: Praeger, 1970.

Yoda, Yoshikata. "Remembrances of Mizoguchi," Cahiers du cinéma, Nos. 166-7, 169, 172 and 174 (1965-66).